The Dignity of Commerce

The Dignity of Commerce

Markets and the Moral Foundations of Contract Law

NATHAN B. OMAN

THE UNIVERSITY OF CHICAGO PRESS   CHICAGO AND LONDON

The University of Chicago Press, Chicago 60637
The University of Chicago Press, Ltd., London

Printed in the United States of America

25 24 23 22 21 20 19 18 17 16   1 2 3 4 5

ISBN-13: 978-0-226-41552-9 (cloth)
ISBN-13: 978-0-226-41566-6 (e-book)
DOI: 10.7208/chicago/9780226415666.001.0001

Library of Congress Cataloging-in-Publication Data

Names: Oman, Nathan, author.
Title: The dignity of commerce : markets and the moral foundations of contract law / Nathan B. Oman.
Description: Chicago ; London : The University of Chicago Press, 2016. | Includes bibliographical references and index.
Identifiers: LCCN 2016017327 | ISBN 9780226415529 (cloth : alk. paper) | ISBN 9780226415666 (e-book)
Subjects: LCSH: Contracts—Moral and ethical aspects. | Commerce—Moral and ethical aspects. | Law—Philosophy.
Classification: LCC K840 .O57 2016 | DDC 346.07—dc23 LC record available at https://lccn.loc.gov/2016017327

♾ This paper meets the requirements of ANSI/NISO Z39.48-1992 (Permanence of Paper).

FOR MORRIS SHEPPARD ARNOLD,
SCHOLAR, JURIST, AND SAGE OF HIPPIE ZEN CAPITALISM

Contents

Preface

In a sense, I began this book my first semester in law school. I spent a year and a half before beginning law school working as a Senate staffer while my wife completed her graduate degree. I arrived at law school prepared to dive into the great debates over constitutional structure that I had seen played out in the grinding legislative process on Capitol Hill. To my surprise, however, I found that the mysteries of the common law, especially the common law of contracts, captured my imagination. I wanted to understand where what seemed to be the great buzzing, bubbling mass of contract doctrine had come from and what it could possibly be doing. I realized that "Why does the law enforce contracts?" is a question to which one could offer multiple answers and that the shape of legal doctrine would change depending on which approach one adopted. Fifteen years on, this book offers my considered answer to that question.

When the time came to pursue my research agenda, I turned to the philosophy of contract law. There I discovered what struck me as a deeply unsatisfying division between economic theories of the law and autonomy theories of the law. I found myself persuaded by the normative criticisms of efficiency but dismayed by the dismissal of economic approaches to contract law. It struck me as implausible to assume that the normative justification of contract law was unconnected to the incentives that the law created—incentives that had been studied with such ingeniousness by law and economics scholars. I also felt that economic theorists were fundamentally correct in their focus on market actors and the way in which the law structured market interactions.

My earliest publications explored the division between economic and autonomy theories, seeking possible ways of reconciling them together.[1] I confess that I had a difficult time finding a theoretical approach that I found wholly satisfying.[2] The idea for this book took shape when I was teaching a seminar on private law theory at Hebrew University in Jerusalem. I was struck by two experiences. The first was shopping in the souks of the Old City and the enormous outdoor Mahane Yehuda Market in Jerusalem. The second was talking with Israelis and Palestinians about the massive wall erected by the Israeli government to limit the ability of Palestinians living on the West Bank to enter Israel. I was struck by the way that, in a place perhaps best known for religious and ethnic conflict, Jews and Arabs, Muslims and Christians were constantly bargaining, trading, and serving one another in the markets of Jerusalem. I was also struck by the fact that one of the losses from the Israeli wall was that it made such commercial interactions more difficult and less common. From those inchoate impressions, I eventually produced the law review article setting forth the basic claim defended in this book.[3] *The Dignity of Commerce* deepens the arguments put forth in that article. With the exception of chapter 6, all the material in this book is new.[4]

This is the first book that I have ever written, and finishing it proved more onerous than I'd anticipated. Along the way, I have incurred debts to many. At the risk of forgetting names that ought to be included here, I want to acknowledge those debts. None of those thanked are responsible for the errors that remain. Several of my colleagues at William & Mary provided extensive feedback on early drafts of portions of this book or the arguments presented here, including Pete Alces, Darian Ibrahim, Eric Kades, Alan Meese, Thomas McSweeney, Sarah Stafford, and James Stern. I presented an earlier draft of chapter 1 at the North American Private Law Theory Workshop hosted by McGill University. I am grateful to Stephen Smith for the invitation to participate in that conference and to the participants for their feedback. I also presented that chapter as the annual Blackstone Lecture at William & Mary Law School, where I received useful criticisms in the question-and-answer session after the lecture. I presented an early version of chapter 8 at the William & Mary Private Law Workshop, where I received excellent suggestions from Henry Smith, Andrew Gold, Brian Lee, and Chris Essert. In addition, I have received helpful comments and suggestions from Brian Bix, Russell Arben Fox, Michael Helfand, Chaim Saiman, Rosalynde Welch, Eyal Zamir, Ben Zipursky, and Todd Zywicki. Curtis Bridgman sharpened much of my thinking over curry at a meeting of the Association of American Law Schools. Roy Krietner pushed my arguments in his reply to my original *Iowa Law Review* article.[5]

At William & Mary, Dave Douglas has always been a wonderfully supportive dean, providing me with multiple summer research grants to work on this book. In writing it, I also held in succession the Cabell Research Professorship, the Taylor Research Professorship, and the Elizabeth and Robert Scott Research Professorship. In addition, the Plumeri Award for faculty excellence in research from the College of William & Mary supported my work. I am particularly grateful to the men and women of commerce whose diligence, good fortune, and generosity funded these awards. William & Mary Law School students Colleen Dick, Lauren Ford, Alex Lurie, Henry Aldefer, Derek McMahan, Connor Baer, Bria Cunningham, and Evan Feely have provided excellent research assistance. Felicia Burton, Derek Mathias, Clara Hardy, Gladys Kratsas, Cody Watson, and Nancy Orr, in faculty support at William & Mary, assisted with the preparation of the manuscript. At the University of Chicago Press, I am grateful to Chris Rhodes, who first championed the manuscript before his untimely death in 2015, and Joe Jackson, who has shepherded the book through the process of publication. I also benefited from the comments of the anonymous peer reviewers.

As always, I thank Heather.

CHAPTER ONE

Introduction

Shakespeare and the Predicament of Contract Theory

This book presents a normative argument about contract law and its relationship to markets. Stated as simply as possible, well-functioning markets are morally desirable, and contract law should be organized to support such markets. Contracts are such a ubiquitous part of market exchange that one would think that the moral status of markets would be entwined in contemporary scholarship with the moral status of contract law. Such is not the case. Markets, however, have not always been absent from the moral discussion of contract law. Indeed, they were present at the birth of the common law of contracts. William Shakespeare captures a sense of the moral complexity of markets at that moment of birth and points modern students of contract law toward a richer sense of the moral importance of commerce in justifying that law. A reconsideration of his play is a good place to begin this book's argument.

Shakespeare and the Birth of Contract Law

The Merchant of Venice provides a dramatic window into the world that gave birth to the common law of contracts. As we shall see, its debut corresponded almost exactly with the birth of what became the common law of contracts, and, as a historical document, it provides insight into some of the ideas about contracts and commerce swirling through England at the time. Beyond its historical interest, however, Shakespeare's play frames the basic question of why the law should enforce voluntary agreements.[1] Written at a time when large-scale international trade and commercial society were still a novelty, *The Merchant of Venice* presents the enforcement of contracts not in terms of personal morality but in terms of maintaining a particular kind of social arrangement: the market.

The Merchant of Venice is a play about contracts. The initial driver of the plot is Bassanio, who proposes to earn money the old-fashioned way by marrying Portia, "a widow richly left."[2] It takes money to make money, however, and Bassanio enlists the help of his wealthy friend Antonio. Antonio is a merchant. His wealth doesn't take the form of land or even hoards of gold. Rather, it is in commercial ventures, "argosies with portly sail . . . pageants of the sea."[3] It's an unstable kind of wealth, subject to constant risk, managed through diversification—"my ventures are not in one bottom trusted"[4]—and illiquid. In Antonio's words, "all my fortunes are at sea; neither have I money nor commodity to raise a present sum."[5] Antonio, however, has another asset, one even more ethereal than his "argosies with portly sail": his creditworthiness. "Try what my credit can in Venice do," he tells Bassanio, and the two go to Shylock the Jew to borrow 3,000 ducats for Bassanio's romantic venture. Shylock famously demands that Antonio stand as surety for his friend:

> Go with me to a notary, seal me there
> Your single bond; and, in merry sport,
> If you repay me not on such a day,
> In such a place, such a sum or sums as are
> Expressed in the condition, let the forfeit
> Be nominated for an equal pound
> Of your fair flesh, to be cut off and taken
> In what part of your body pleaseth me.[6]

Much of the rest of the plot of the play revolves around this contract and the ultimate question of its enforcement.

In many ways the play trades on the moral discomfort created by the transition from a medieval worldview to that of an emerging commercial society. Medieval influences on the play can be seen in the sources from which Shakespeare drew in writing it and its anti-Semitic framing of the issue of usury. The evil and wealthy Jew was a stock character in the melodramas of the Middle Ages, a tradition that *The Merchant of Venice* draws on to create the character of Shylock. Shakespeare's play was also clearly influenced by a contemporary work, *The Jew of Malta* by Christopher Marlowe.[7] Marlowe's villain, Barabas, is also a merchant, but we do not see him trading. Rather, having lost his wealth to a Christian prince in the course of the latter's crusade against the Turks, Barabas pursues a course of Machiavellian revenge, murdering those who have taken his wealth and those who seek to expose his crimes. Shakespeare, however, transposes his Jew from the crusader outpost of Malta to the commercial entrepôt of Venice. Shylock's vice is not murder but usury. Thus, *The Merchant of Venice*, unlike *The Jew of Malta*, is not a story of political machinations but of the dangers of commercial contracts.

Shakespeare's story also displays a medieval outlook in how it links Judaism and usury. The relationship between Shylock and the other characters in the play is defined in part by the former's status as a usurer. Antonio proudly insists that he does not "lend nor borrow upon advantage,"[8] and Shylock hates Antonio because the latter complains "in the Rialto" about Shylock's "moneys and . . . usances."[9] Shylock responds with two well-worn defenses of usury.[10] The first is to invoke the biblical story of Jacob,[11] who gained wealth through the increase of his father-in-law's herds. Antonio insists, however, that this was a "venture"—in other words what we would today call an equity investment rather than a loan. "Is your gold and silver ewes and rams?" he contemptuously asks Shylock.[12] Second, Shakespeare is at some pains to emphasize that Shylock regards all Christians as his enemies, an important premise in a medieval Jewish argument over usury. The Torah states, "to a foreigner you may lend upon interest, but to your brother you shall not lend upon interest."[13] Medieval rabbis interpreted this as permitting usury as long as a Jew was lending to a Christian.[14] At the same time, the early canon lawyers relied on the so-called Exception of Saint Ambrose, which held that it was permissible to demand usury of an enemy.[15] So far, so medieval.

Notice that the early framing of usury assumes a basic enmity between the two parties to the contract. The assumed context of the exchange is ultimately war—or at any rate, an uneasy truce between warring enemies. In *The Jew of Malta,* war was literally the context for Barabas's story. Marlowe's is a medieval story of crusaders, heathens, and infidels. In *The Merchant of Venice*, however, war is wholly absent from the plot. Rather, the market looms large. First, there is the ubiquitous image of the Rialto, the great international marketplace of Venice. Antonio's access to wealth comes not from hard assets but from his ability to create relationships on the Rialto, even with Shylock. He is a merchant rather than a duke or some other grandee whose wealth was based on land. The very attraction of Venice as a setting lies in the sense of adventure and glamour wrought by commerce. There are fortunes being made here not through the staid accumulation of land by family but through trade, "the pageant of the seas." At the same time, there is anxiety over the way in which the market structures relationships between individuals. Antonio contrasts his openhearted loaning of money without interest to Bassanio with Shylock's mercenary motives. "If thou wilt lend this money, lend it not as to thy friends, for when did friendship take a breed for barren metal of his friend?"[16] Likewise, Bassanio, for example, describes his friendship with Antonio in the language of commercial debt. "To you, Antonio, I owe the most, in money and in love, and from your love I have a warranty to unburden all my plots and purposes."[17] There is a sense throughout the play that something different and morally complex happens when the Rialto emerges as the structuring context for relationships.

The ideas of market and contract come together in the play's climax. Bassanio is unable to pay Shylock, and Antonio's argosies have all failed. May Shylock now execute his bond on a pound of the merchant's fair flesh? In answering this question, the play offers a particular vision of the normative foundations of a contract—one that links the law decisively to the support of commerce. From the point of view of contract theory, the climax is interesting for what it doesn't do. The dramatic logic of Antonio's tragic moment does not rely on the idea of promissory morality. He is not presented as a man of honor forced into the terrible position of forswearing himself. Absent from Shakespeare's play is the intense concern with fidelity to promises that one sees in a medieval work such as *Sir Gawain and the Green Knight*, for example.[18] One of the central plot elements of that fourteenth-century story is Sir Gawain's struggle against all odds and temptations to keep his solemn promise to an enemy. Nothing in the dramatic logic of *The Merchant of Venice*, however, suggests that Antonio should be understood as facing a similar crisis of personal honor and fidelity to his word. Rather, he is a merchant tragically caught in the demands of the market on which his status depends. The tragedy is not that he will break his word to Shylock but that the logic underlying the law's support for the Rialto cannot relieve him of his contractual obligations. As Antonio acknowledges earlier in the play:

> The Duke cannot deny the course of law;
> For the commodity that strangers have
> With us in Venice, if it be denied,

> Will much impeach the justice of the state,
> Since that the trade and profit of the city
> Consisteth of all nations.[19]

Yet Shakespeare has structured the play so that the audience sees Shylock as in the wrong. The virtue of mercy demands that he not execute on Antonio's bond. The enforcement of the contract is morally questionable. When Shylock calls on the Duke of the city to judge the case, however, the Duke stands ready to regretfully enforce the bond. Like Antonio's earlier statements, Shylock's argument to the Duke also invokes the good of the city's commerce. "If you deny it, let the danger light upon your charter and your city's freedom."[20] Strikingly, when Portia appears disguised as a jurist to decide the case, she maintains the integrity of the contract. Bassanio urges her:

> I beseech you,
> Wrest once the law to your authority.
> To do a great right, do a little wrong.[21]

Her reply again invokes the importance to the city of honoring contracts.

> It must not be. There is no power in Venice
> Can alter a decree established.
> 'Twill be record for a precedent,
> And many an error by the same example
> Will rush into the state. It cannot be.[22]

Rather than presenting contractual obligations as a reflection of promissory morality, the play examines their enforcement in social and communal terms. Shylock can stand on his contract not because Antonio is bound by honor or morality to perform his obligation but because allowing Shylock to demand enforcement makes Venice into a commercial hub. Contracts must be enforced not because of the inherent moral obligations that they create or represent but because their enforcement fosters commerce on the Rialto. Antonio is only saved because Portia insists on the letter of the contract. Shylock may have his pound of flesh, but he may not take any of Antonio's blood. The merchant, the law, and the Rialto are all saved in a neat comic denouement.

The Merchant of Venice was first performed in 1596 or 1597.[23] As it debuted, English judges were hearing the case that would give birth to the common law of contracts. Like the characters in Shakespeare's comedy, they were struggling to adapt medieval habits and practices to a new world of commercial society. During Lent, 1595, a year or two before Shakespeare's play premiered in London, John Slade sued Humphrey Morley before the Devon Assizes. Slade claimed that he and Morley had agreed in May of that year that Morley would purchase his grain crop for £16 at harvest time. Morley failed to pay on the appointed day, and Slade brought an action against him of *indebitatus assumpsit*.[24] From the Devon Assizes, the case was appealed to the court of King's Bench,[25] and from there the final appeal was heard in 1597 by the Exchequer Chamber, where it was debated again in 1598 and 1601 before finally being decided in 1602.[26] Contract was a relatively late arrival to the common law, which lavished the bulk of its medieval attention on the law of real property. Prior to the seventeenth century, actions on agreements to pay a sum of money could be brought using the writ of debt. Later, courts modified the writ of trespass to create the writ of *assumpsit*, which allowed actions based on a theory of deceit where a party had made a promise to do something and subsequently reneged.[27] The protracted litigation over John Slade's unpaid £16 resulted from a judicial disagreement about the relationship between these two writs.

The court of Common Pleas took the position that one could not bring an action in *assumpsit* if an action in debt could also be brought.[28] The court of King's Bench, in contrast, held that an action of *assumpsit* could be brought without first bringing an action in debt.[29] The distinction was important because the action of debt was subject to the defense of wager of law. A defendant could escape liability by simply swearing that he was not liable and bringing oath helpers into court who were willing to swear to the truth—or, at any rate, the trustworthiness—of his oath.[30] Although wager of law seems bizarre by modern standards, in the context of a close-knit medieval economy, it made good sense. As one scholar has observed:

> Within the framework of local markets and regimes of credit discipline, where a trader's good name, personal honor, and reputation for performing his obligations were his principal assets, the risk attendant to false swearing were material as well as spiritual. A tradesman who acquired a reputation for failure to pay debts or for false dealing of any sort would soon find that his credit was naught, or nearly so.[31]

Beyond such practical considerations, however, wager of law traded on the theological power of oaths. To be foresworn was still a sin, a grave moral lapse that could put one's soul in danger of hellfire. As markets expanded in early modern England, however, commercial transactions became increasingly impersonal. Without the immediate fear of reputational sanctions, the temptations to perjury increased and wager of law became an impediment to the enforcement of the informal contracts that increasingly came to dominate commerce.[32]

The judges of Common Pleas also sat in Exchequer Chamber, where they overruled cases brought in *assumpsit* in the court of King's Bench.[33] Rather than bow to the higher court, however, the judges of King's Bench stuck to its position, creating uncertain and conflicting common law rules depending on the court in which one's suit landed. Thus stood the law when John Slade and Humphrey Morley brought their case before the Exchequer Chamber. The details of the litigation are uncertain. Two of the most celebrated lawyers of the time argued the case. Slade retained Sir Edward Coke, while Sir Francis Bacon represented Morley. Through some mechanism that remains unclear, the judges of King's Bench invoked a disused custom and sat with the judges of Common Pleas in the Exchequer Chamber. After nearly five years of debate, the position of King's Bench prevailed. Thereafter, suits could be brought in *assumpsit* even where the action of debt—and, with it, wager of law—was available.[34] Picking origins is always arbitrary, but the 1602 decision in *Slade's Case* has as good a claim as any other moment for marking the birth of what became the common law of contracts. It was the opening up of *assumpsit* that allowed the common law to gradually develop into a fit instrument for the enforcement of contracts in the rising commercial economy of seventeenth- and eighteenth-century England.

The Merchant of Venice offers us a window into the world that gave birth to the common law of contracts. It was a world in which commerce was increasingly important. It is certainly not accidental that *Slade's Case* and the rise of the action of *assumpsit* corresponded with an economic revolution in which trade and market exchange came to rival land as a source of wealth. In the play, the law enforces contracts in order to make commerce on the Rialto possible. It is difficult to divine the precise intentions of the judges of Exchequer Chamber that decided *Slade's Case*, but we do know that during this period commerce was making contract disputes more common and the various common law courts were competing to capture this new judicial business.[35] One of the reasons that King's Bench obdurately stuck to its liberal position on the writ of *assumpsit* in the face of conservative opposition from the appellate courts was surely a desire to create a forum more congenial to the rising tide of commercial litigants.[36] To be sure, the common law developed slowly, and it took time for its law of contracts to become a fit instrument for commerce. A historian could still write that, when Lord Mansfield ascended to King's Bench in 1756, "English lawyers had been so long preoccupied with the problems of real property that they felt themselves strangers to a generation that knew not feudalism."[37] By the eighteenth century, however, contract law was becoming intimately entwined with questions of commerce, as illustrated by Mansfield's dictum in *Pillans v. Van Mierop* that "the law of merchants, and the law of the land is the same."[38]

Nothing as complicated and as historically contingent as the common law of contracts can be said to have a simple origin or represent a single normative concern over the centuries of its history. Nor do contemporary theorists owe a debt of filial piety requiring that they construct their theories in accordance with their field's origins. Nevertheless, *The Merchant of Venice* and the parallel rise of contract law and commercial society testify to the intimate connection between markets and contract law. In the play, the central point of enforcing contracts is to sustain markets and commerce. None of this is surprising. The link between contract law and markets is so palpable, however, that the relative absence of markets and commerce as a topic of moral theorizing in contemporary contract law theory is striking. One would expect that the moral status of markets would be front and center in discussions of the moral status of contract law, yet this is not the case.

Markets and Contemporary Contract Theory

Broadly speaking, two contending families of arguments dominate modern contract law theory. On one hand, there are legal moralists who see in contract law a set of legal obligations that correspond to some roughly analogous set of moral obligations. The best-known contemporary example of such a theory is Charles Fried's claim that contract is a legal instantiation of the moral obligation to keep a promise.[39] Fried, however, is not the only promissory theorist, and promissory theories are not the only approaches to contract law that seek to ground the legal obligations imposed by contract in more primitive but analogous moral or political obligations.[40] The other contending family of theoretical arguments arises from the law and economics movement. These arguments claim that the normative goal of contract law is to create incentives for contracting parties that will lead to the economically efficient allocation of resources. There is substantial disagreement among law and economics scholars on both methodological and normative questions. Methodologically, they are divided between those who adopt an essentially neoclassical economic framework, represented most prominently by Richard Posner, and those who take a more behavioralist approach.[41] Normatively, they are divided between those who believe that normative discussions are exhausted by efficiency concerns and those who believe that efficiency should be paired with other normative goals.[42] Although the ancient enmity between autonomy theorists and efficiency theorists frequently breaks forth into new munity, they share a surprising indifference to the moral status of the market in relation to contract law.

Fried posits a relatively tight relationship between contract law and promissory morality. "Since contracts invoke and are invoked by promises," he writes, "it is not surprising that the law came to impose on the promises it recognized the same incidents as morality demanded."[43] For Fried, the promise principle is a postulate of liberal political morality, a reflection of human freedom and the state's respect for the choices of its citizens. If we do not enforce someone's undertakings, "we infantalize him, as we do quite properly when we release the very young from the consequences of their choices."[44] He is quite explicit, however, in insisting that contract law's normative foundation does not lie in the value of markets. Hence, he rejects the idea that contract law rests on "a distinct collective policy, the furtherance of economic exchange."[45] In other words, on Fried's view, the relationship between contract law and markets is entirely accidental. It may be that market exchange is valuable, but this has nothing to do with contract law. To the extent that contract law facilitates markets, it is a mere by-product of showing a proper legal respect for promising. It may be a happy or an unhappy by-product, but contra the characters in *The Merchant of Venice,* the purpose of enforcing contracts is not to support commerce on the Rialto.

Others applying nonpromissory moral theories to contract law also largely ignore markets in their arguments. Consider so-called transfer theories of contract.[46] According to Andrew Gold, for example, contracts consist of the transfer of property rights.[47] The difference between a contract and the conveyance of a chattel or a piece of real estate is that in the latter case property is acquired in a physical thing; in the case of contract, property is acquired in the promisor's future performance. Furthermore, Gold grounds the requirement of consideration—a *quid pro quo*—as necessary for the just acquisition of a property right in another's performance.[48] Having located contract within the context of exchange, one would think it natural for Gold to link the normative basis for contract with the normative value of the widespread social practice of exchange—namely, markets. This, however, he does not do, insisting that the legal instantiation of exchange is rooted instead in ideas of self-ownership and personal autonomy. His theory "focuses on justice between parties to a contractual dispute, rather than focusing on broader prospective effects of a chosen contract doctrine."[49] Again, the fact that contract law serves to support markets is entirely accidental, a fact about the law that has nothing to do with its normative justification.

To be sure, there are noneconomic theories of contract that have inched toward a greater appreciation for the way in which contractual relationships are ubiquitously embedded in markets. Dori Kimel has offered a painstaking analysis of promissory theories of contract, taking Fried as his archetypal example.[50] Building on the work of Joseph Raz, Kimel notes that the kind of mutual trust engendered by a promise generally depends on some kind of ongoing relationship between the promisor and the promisee.[51] To make an efficacious promise to a stranger, one must convince the stranger that you will treat him or her as though you had some kind of ongoing relationship, even though, by definition, you do not. This is not, however, the case with contracts. Contract, according to Kimel, is more than a legal reflection of promissory morality. Rather, it makes possible a particular form of relationship that is different than the core case of a promissory relationship. He writes, "the practice [of contract] as a whole is designed, first and foremost, to facilitate co-operation or mutual reliance between strangers (so that the invocation of the practice in the context of personal relations can sometimes be utterly inappropriate)."[52] Kimel, however, does not identify the value of such relationships with strangers in terms of supporting commerce and markets as a social practice. Rather, his focus is more individualistic. The value of contracts lies in their ability to facilitate cooperation with someone "without being required to know much or form opinions about the personal attributes of others, without having to allow others to know much and form opinions about oneself. It is, if you like, the value of personal detachment."[53] It is not, however, the value of supporting the Rialto.

The moral theorist who has focused most explicitly on the market and its relationship to contract law is Daniel Markovits.[54] Like Kimel, Markovits focuses on the way in which contract law allows for cooperation without creating thick relationships structured around moral or political solidarity. Contract provides a way for people to engage in a kind of respectful collaboration with one another—a form of human relationship that Markovits takes to be valuable in and of itself. As will become clear in the chapters that follow, I am sympathetic to Markovits's argument. I agree with him that contract supports exchanges whose virtue lies in part in the way that they facilitate cooperation without deep solidarity. My quarrel with Markovits's argument lies in the way that it simplifies the good of market exchange and in particular in the way that it focuses exclusively on the individuals involved in a transaction rather than considering the market as a broader social process. Put another way, the kind of respectful collaboration that Markovits lauds could exist without a widespread practice of economic exchange, as, for example, when neighbors collaborate to spruce up a local playground or engage in some other kind of cooperation that does not clearly involve market activity. What it misses is the way that contract undergirds markets and commerce as collective, ongoing social practices.

Economic theories of contract have paid far more attention to markets than have promissory theories. Generally speaking, economists are celebratory of the power of markets to efficiently coordinate resources, and this positive attitude toward the allocative potential of markets has been hardwired into the economic analysis of law. Most famously, Ronald Coase argued that, in the absence of transaction costs, any initial allocation of resources will result in an efficient final distribution through exchange in the market.[55] Coase's point, of course, is that, in the real world, there are always transaction costs, and therefore the allocation of resources via legal entitlements matters. Building on this insight, Richard Posner originally framed the normative stance of law and economics in terms of ideal markets.[56] Legal rules should be specified, he argued, so that the allocation of resources mimics the allocation that would obtain in a Coasean market of no transaction costs.

Law and economics scholarship has become considerably more sophisticated since Posner's first efforts in the 1970s. It has largely, however, remained focused on the issue of transaction costs. For example, the literature on contract law has employed the idea of a perfectly specified contract.[57] Such a contract would provide guidance to the parties on the proper outcome of the transaction for every possible state of affairs. Of course, a perfectly specified contract is impossible, but it provides a normative guide for contract law. The law should provide the parties to a contract with the terms that they would have chosen had they been able to bargain over the terms. Such rules will, like Posner's market mimicking rules, result in an efficient allocation of resources.

Despite the apparently positive attitude of economic analysis of law to markets, there is an important sense in which efficiency analysis is largely indifferent to commerce. The concepts of efficiency and welfare employed by economists are deeply problematic as a normative guide. They generally define welfare in terms of the satisfaction of preferences and assume that preferences have a stable and transitive structure. Each element of this conception of welfare is mistaken. For normative purposes, we should not treat the satisfaction of preferences per se as a worthy goal. For example, the satisfaction of evil preferences is not morally desirable. The world is not better if a twisted sadist can indulge his desire to watch violent child pornography, even if no children are harmed and the twisted sadist's actions have no other third-party effects. Furthermore, our desires are often conflicting, inconsistent, and changeable. Giving me what I want now is not necessarily good if I also want something utterly inconsistent with what I get and my desires change tomorrow. On these questions I side with Edmund Burke over Alfred Marshall. Burke wrote:

> The nature of man is intricate; the objects of society are of the greatest possible complexity; and, therefore, no simple disposition or direction of power can be suitable either to man's nature or the quality of his affairs. When I hear the simplicity of contrivance aimed at and boasted in any new political constitutions, I am at no loss to decide that the artificers are grossly ignorant of their trade or totally negligent of their duty.[58]

Efficiency as a normative guide strikes me as such an inadequate "simplicity of contrivance." However, there is another problem with efficiency analysis.

Judging the market through the lens of economic efficiency reduces the moral significance of the market to a single issue: the allocation of resources. Although this is surely an extremely important part of what markets do, they do much more than this. Markets are complex social practices, like languages or religions. They allocate resources, but they also instill habits, provide a particular social context for human relationships, and so on. Here Shakespeare gestures toward a more complete vision of the marketplace. Consider the moment in *The Merchant of Venice* when Antonio and Bassanio invite Shylock to dinner.[59] Shylock responds by saying, "I will buy with you, talk with you, walk with you, and so following, but I will not eat with you, drink with you, nor pray with you."[60] Commerce creates the social space where two Christians might invite a Jew to dine, and in his response Shylock sets forth the limits of the interactions that he is willing to allow the market to facilitate. The entire passage illustrates the complex way in which commerce interacts with religious, social, and ethnic differences. Clearly more is going on in this exchange than the allocation of material resources. Shylock insists on maintaining his separateness, but the very fact that his separateness might be threatened within the market is striking. One can read the play as contrasting Belmont, the home of Portia, with Venice.

> In Venice they are held together by combinations of interest; in Belmont by mutual affection. The wealth and power of Venice depend upon the willingness of its courts to hold men to their contracts. The charm of Belmont is to provide its inhabitants with a community in which contracts remain for the most part superfluous. Venice is tolerable because its citizens can flee occasionally to Belmont and appeal from Venetian justice to Belmontine mercy.[61]

The divide presented in this reading of the play, however, is too stark. Shakespeare hints at the possibility that the process of exchange upon the Rialto can break down habits of enmity. But on either reading of the play, the moral significance of markets cannot be reduced to the efficient allocation of resources. Doing so misses this richer set of moral concerns swirling around the process of market exchange.

Restoring Markets to the Center of Contract Theory

The goal of reviewing autonomy and economic theories of contract is not to provide a complete summary of these arguments or offer a refutation of them. Rather, it is to point out a surprising lacuna in current approaches. Contract law is the quintessential legal institution of the marketplace, yet the moral status of markets as an ongoing social practice plays little, if any, role in the normative arguments of most contract law theorists. This has not always been the case. The American Legal Realists, for example, explicitly linked contract law with the moral status of markets.[62] Karl Llewellyn, for example, argued, "Bargain is . . . the social and legal machinery appropriate to arranging affairs in any specialized economy which relies on exchange rather than tradition (the manor) or authority (the army, the U.S.S.R.) for appointment of productive energy and product."[63] George Gardner was more explicit, giving a less poetic version of Shakespeare's argument that contract law exists to support the Rialto:

> "Contracts" are not "enforced" merely because the parties made them, but . . . the law affords only such remedies for breach of promise as seem most likely to promote the orderly and efficient conduct of the community's economic life. It is inevitable, in the nature of organized society, that this should be the fact; and a clear perception of it tends to the highest standards both of commercial ethics and of law. For the honest man is thus confirmed in his instinctive knowledge that the keeping of his word is a private matter which he cannot delegate to lawyers, while the attention of the civil magistrate is directed toward those questions which are his special providence rather than to the attempt to settle questions of morality for people who are perhaps as able to do so as is he.[64]

This Realist insight linking the value of contract law to the value of markets has largely receded from contemporary contract law theory. There are understandable reasons for this.

Most autonomy theories of contract draw in some measure on the revival of liberal political philosophy wrought by John Rawls's 1972 publication of *A Theory of Justice*.[65] As such, they tend to be suspicious of the largely untheorized pragmatism of the Realists.[66] Likewise, legal philosophers schooled in the post-Hartian tradition have little patience with the Realists' theories of law and adjudication.[67] Legal economists are likely to be equally skeptical of the Realists. Writing in the shadow of the Progressive movement and the New Deal, the Realists adopted a view of economic life that is at odds with the neoclassical economic roots of law and economics. Today, we tend to anachronistically see the New Deal in Keynesian terms.[68] The Progressives and the New Dealers, however, were not Keynesians. Rather, they looked to the competence of central administration over cartelized and heavily regulated industries as a solution to the problems of "wasteful competition."[69] To most economists, such commitments seem antediluvian and of limited intellectual interest. For their part, the Realists were far from convinced as to the virtues of markets and tended to accompany their observations on the link between contracts and markets with predictions of the demise of both.[70]

That said, the basic Realist insight that the normative status of contract law rests on the normative status of markets is worthy of reconsideration.

Autonomy theories of contract tend to focus on the "momentary, individualized acts of promising and promise keeping"[71] while largely ignoring both the market context in which most contracts play out and the role of contract law in making that market possible. They tend to be narrowly individualistic in their moral focus by insisting not only that individuals are the ultimate objects of moral concern but that individual action should be the locus of normative analysis. They tend to ignore broader social practices and their moral consequences.[72] Likewise, efficiency theorists, by insisting on methodological individualism in modeling human behavior and its consequences, tend to ignore the complex moral consequences of supporting and expanding market activity through contract law.

This book advances two basic claims. The first is that commerce and markets have a set of morally desirable outcomes that cannot be reduced to the efficient allocation of resources. The second is that the moral status of markets provides the normative foundation for contract law, which serves to strengthen and extend markets, thereby securing the moral goods that they produce. At the outset, it is important to understand the basic structure of the argument. Markets are not somehow valuable in and of themselves, a primary good in the way that one might regard love, happiness, or respect as a primary good. Nor are markets necessarily morally desirable because they are an example of some morally desirable activity. Libertarians, for example, frequently celebrate markets, arguing that they are morally desirable because market exchange represents a kind of autonomous choice and autonomous choice is worthy our moral respect. Alternatively, one might argue, as has Daniel Markovits, that the process of market exchange itself represents a particular form of respectful solidarity that is worthy of moral concern in and of itself. Whatever the merits of these arguments, they are not the ones advanced in this book. Rather, the approach to markets here is consequentialist. Markets are good because as a social practice they produce certain outcomes that we should regard as morally desirable.

Situating the market argument within the common dichotomy between moral and consequentialist theories of contract is difficult. By *moral theories* what we generally mean are deontological theories that see contract law as the legal reflection of a set of prelegal moral obligations. By *consequentialist theories* what we generally mean are economic theories that take the primarily normative goal of the law as the creation of incentives for efficient behavior. The market argument advanced in this book, however, does not fit neatly into either of these camps. It is not a moral theory in the sense of claiming that either contract law or markets are a reflection of some set of more primary moral obligations. It is a consequentialist theory in the sense of finding the moral good of a social practice—market exchange—in a set of consequences that practice has for society. It is not, however, consequentialist in a narrowly material or economic sense. To be sure, material prosperity is one of the goods—a moral good—that markets deliver, but it does not exhaust the beneficent consequences of exchange. Markets also facilitate the liberal goal of peaceful cooperation in a pluralistic society and inculcate certain moral virtues in market participants. These are consequences of markets, but they are moral consequences, consequences that provide moral reasons for fostering market activity.

The normative relationship the market argument posits between markets and contract law is similarly complex. Ultimately, contract law is neither a necessary nor sufficient condition for the existence of markets. As we shall see, markets can exist in the absence of formal legal rules. This does not mean that markets are "natural" or that contract law embodies some prepolitical regime of rights and obligations. Rather, the nonnecessity of contract law flows from the more practical consideration that there are numerous ways of overcoming obstacles to widespread exchange that do not involve formal legal rules. Furthermore, contract is not the sole legal institution that supports healthy, well-functioning markets. Bodies of law such as property also facilitate market exchange, and still other bodies of law seek to limit that exchange when it becomes pathological—as, for example, in the case of criminal prohibitions on the child sex trade.

What, then, is the role of contract law? Markets in the absence of formal contract law tend to be smaller and more fragile than are markets supported by contract law. Contract law serves to strengthen and extend the reach of markets. It is crucially important in facilitating exchange among strangers. In so doing, it extends the scope of the moral goods delivered by commerce. The moral justification of contract law thus operates at a double remove. The moral goods in question are a consequence of markets, and markets are a consequence, in part, of contract law. Hence, in justifying and specifying contract law, we look to support well-functioning markets not because such markets are valuable in themselves but because they have desirable moral consequences.

Focusing on well-functioning markets as the goal of contract law yields concrete suggestions for the structure of legal doctrine. All these will be discussed in greater detail in the chapters that follow. For now, a précis of the arguments will suffice. In the realm of formation, it speaks to the question of which promises the law should enforce. If we take the goal of contract law to be sustaining markets, then we should enforce promises to the extent that doing so will support markets that we find to be morally desirable.[73] Accordingly, the current law should be modified to presumptively enforce all promises made in furtherance of commerce. The market argument also suggests that the law should enforce contracts that are central to market exchange—such as certain contracts of adhesion—even when it is difficult to characterize such contracts as being mutually authored by the parties. For an autonomy theorist, "meaningful" consent is the touchstone of contractual legitimacy. Likewise, economic theories use consent as a proxy for welfare-enhancing transactions and thus assume that contracting parties understand the welfare consequences of their actions. In the case of boilerplate contracts, it is doubtful that the consent of contracting parties can meet the demands placed on it by these theories. In the market argument, however, consent does not play a primary justificatory role. Contract law exists to support the Rialto, not to honor the choices of individuals per se. In the market argument, consent serves only to coordinate privately authored legal obligations. This task requires only the most minimal and pro forma consent. As long as other mechanisms are present that prevent the resulting markets from turning pathological the absence of "truly meaningful" or "fully informed" consent is untroubling for the market argument. The market argument also explains why contract remedies are structured around bilateral damages paid from promisors to promisees and why we empower wronged plaintiffs rather than government regulators to act. Such institutions allow parties in the market to retaliate against one another without escalating conflicts dangerously. The possibility of such retaliation has the ironic effect of increasing the mutual trust on which markets depend.

Finally, focusing on markets allows us to see more clearly what is at stake in doctrines such as unconscionably or contracts made void as violating public policy. Rather than justifying such restrictions with arguments about the limited autonomy of contracting parties or admitting them as unfortunate but perhaps inevitable incursions of collective concerns into the libertarian purity of contract, the market argument sees them as natural extensions of the basis of contract. If contract law exists to support well-functioning, desirable markets, it is entirely natural that we should withhold enforcement from contracts that will create pathological markets. Rather than focusing solely on the agency of the contracting parties, we ask ourselves whether the market that enforcement would support is morally desirable. Likewise, a focus on markets helps to police the boundaries between contract law and other areas of law. For example, we can understand the contractualization of family law—and anxiety about that process—as arising from the injection of markets into the formation and dissolution of families. One's judgment as to the ultimate desirability of these developments will hinge on one's assessment of the moral limits of markets.

Many readers are likely to be skeptical of the claim that markets are morally desirable. Egalitarians will point out that markets can produce vast inequalities of wealth. Others will point to the ability of markets to generate moral evils on a vast scale. For example, the eighteenth century saw the rise of commercial societies in Western Europe and market organization of an ever-increasing share of economic life. Yet the expansion of markets facilitated a massive expansion in the international slave trade as individual entrepreneurs replaced crown monopolies and more efficiently organized the mass kidnapping and degradation of millions of humans.[74] More prosaically, the merchant and the capitalist are not always morally inspiring figures. Although the pages that follow seek to blunt some of these criticisms, in the end one cannot deny that markets can lead to morally monstrous results. Accordingly, the moral limit of the market should mark the limit of contract law. This means, however, that markets are providing the normative foundation for contract law.

The fact that well-functioning markets are morally desirable does not mean that markets standing alone are sufficient to order our social lives. Although much of what follows is celebratory of the moral possibilities of markets, this book is not a libertarian or anarcho-capitalist tract. It does not argue that contract law is the only legal institution that society requires. While I tend to be skeptical of many forms of market regulation, society requires legal institutions beyond those of the market to function properly. Accordingly, to argue that markets cannot do it all is no response to the argument in this book. Rather, the claim here is the more modest one that certain kinds of well-functioning markets are sufficiently desirable to be a fit object of a law's concern. The law of contracts does and should support markets and commerce. To the extent that one is an optimist about the moral possibilities of markets, then one should be enthusiastic about the extension of contract law to govern larger swathes of human interaction. To the extent that one is more subdued in one's assessment of markets' moral value, then one's view of contract law's domain should be similarly limited. Both reactions, however, support the basic claim that contract law should exist to support markets in so far as markets have morally desirable consequences.

This book is divided into two parts. Part 1, consisting of chapters 2, 3, and 4, sets forth the basic theory of contract—what I am calling the market argument—advanced in this book. Part 2, consisting of chapters 5, 6, 7, and 8, shifts from the theoretical focus of part 1 to look at specific issues of contract law, describing how the market argument can be used to structure the specifics of legal doctrine. The shift from the theoretical to the practical is designed to demonstrate that the market argument can not only be justified in the abstract but is useful to lawyers, judges, and others who concern themselves with the concrete application of theory to real legal problems.

The book proceeds as follows: Chapter 2 offers a definition of well-functioning markets as that term is used in the market argument and explains how contract law sustains and strengthens such markets. Chapter 3 sets out the normative heart of the market argument. Well-functioning markets deliver three morally desirable outcomes. First, they generate a set of moral habits—virtues—that support a liberal political order. Second, they respond to the pervasive problem of moral pluralism in modern life, providing a mechanism by which those with sharply differing religious, moral, and political beliefs can peacefully cooperate. Finally, they generate wealth, which has an ameliorative effect on a host of moral evils. Chapter 4 turns to the main theoretical alternatives to the market argument: economic theories of contract and autonomy or deontological theories of contract. While rejecting both approaches as adequate theories of contract law, I argue in chapter 4 that both economic efficiency and deontological morality can be integrated into a single market-sustaining legal order. In brief, my claim is that efficiency and deontological morality should be pursued within contract law as long as doing so supports commerce and well-functioning markets but not otherwise.

The remaining chapters of part 2 turn to the doctrinal implications of the market argument. Chapter 5 looks at issues of contract formation. Chapter 6 examines remedies. Chapter 7 applies the market argument to the problem of boilerplate contracts, focusing particularly on the role of consent in the justification of contractual liability. Finally, chapter 8 discusses the moral limits of markets, explaining how these constraints should mark out the boundaries of contract law.

PART I

The next three chapters present the normative heart of the market argument. The basic claim of this book is that well-functioning markets are morally desirable and that contract law ought to be structured to support such markets. I begin by examining precisely what is meant in this argument by a *well-functioning market.* A well-functioning market, I argue, is not the same thing as the perfectly competitive market of economic theory. Rather, it is a market that is sufficiently open and widespread to deliver certain moral goods. Contract law supports such markets by increasing the trust of market actors, especially among strangers. In the next chapter, I focus on the moral goods delivered by well-functioning markets. Commerce tends to breed moral habits—virtues—that support a liberal society. Well-functioning markets provide a framework for cooperation that does not require deep moral agreement or tribal solidarity; thus, they are especially valuable in a pluralistic society. Finally, markets have proven to be the greatest engines for the creation of wealth in human history. Wealth has an ameliorative effect on a host of social evils, and poverty tends to make virtually all troubling social evils worse. In the final chapter of part 1, I turn to economic and normative defenses of contract law. I offer reasons why both approaches should be rejected as stand-alone defenses of contract law. However, I argue that economically efficient institutions and deontological moral behavior tend to support markets, and thus both approaches can be integrated into arguments about contract law to the extent that they enhance commerce.

CHAPTER TWO

Well-Functioning Markets and Contract Law

The central normative claim of this book is that well-functioning markets are morally desirable and that contract law is justified because it supports such markets. An exploration of the moral consequences of well-functioning markets must wait until chapter 3. There I will argue that they help to inculcate virtues that support a liberal political order; provide a framework for peaceful cooperation among those with sharply differing moral, political, and religious beliefs; and generate social wealth, which can have an ameliorative effect on a host of social evils. Before exploring the moral consequences of well-functioning markets, however, it is first necessary to define what I mean by that term and explain how contract law can support these markets. We can then turn to how the moral consequences of well-functioning markets can justify contract law and guide our thinking about its proper structure.

Well-Functioning Markets

This book argues that a well-functioning market is one that delivers the moral goods of liberal cooperation, wealth, and certain virtues without generating unacceptable pathologies. In more concrete terms, a well-functioning market has five basic characteristics. First, well-functioning markets consist of the exchange of property and services. Second, well-functioning markets are a collective social practice allocating some appreciable portion of society's resources. Third, well-functioning markets are relatively open to all participants. Fourth, well-functioning markets must allow entrance and exit from relations of exchange with particular persons. Finally, well-functioning markets cross boundaries created by the communities that define one's basic identity.

Although markets are often celebrated with the rhetoric of rugged individualism, exchange is actually a response to the absence of human self-sufficiency. Compared to other animals, *Homo sapiens* have an unusually long period in which young are dependent on parents for food and protection. And human dependence does not end with childhood. Most adults depend on others to provide them with such basic necessities as food, clothing, and shelter. Novelists such as Ibn Ṭufail and Daniel Defoe have written stories about individuals cast upon desert islands, utterly dependent on themselves for survival.[1] Much of the interest in the adventures of Hai bin Yaqz 'ān and Robinson Crusoe lies in the fact that they are so removed from everyday life. Most humans simply do not live such independent lives. We require the assistance of others, and exchange is a method of obtaining that assistance.

Markets are certainly not the only response to human dependence. Acknowledging other ways of managing interdependence helps to illustrate what is unique about commerce. For example, many societies maintain strong norms of generosity. One is expected to share out of one's own abundance with others, and in turn one has a legitimate expectation that others will share with you out of their abundance. A classic example of such reciprocal gift giving is the potlatch of Native American tribes in the Pacific Northwest.[2] A person amasses foodstuffs, ceremonial items, furs, and other goods. At a huge, stylized feast, he gives away this wealth. The greater his generosity, the higher his social standing. Sharing as a means of cooperation, however, requires high levels of trust and the ability to keep a mental tally on individuals' generosity so that free riders may be identified and shunned. Not surprisingly, we do not observe gift giving as a central mechanism for allocating goods in complex modern societies.

Adam Smith insisted that mankind has a natural propensity to "truck and barter and exchange one thing for another."[3] He may have been right.[4] Trade, for example, is one of the behaviors that paleoanthropologists associate with evolutionarily "modern" humans.[5] Well-functioning markets, however, are not natural. They are social achievements. Although commerce of some limited kind can be found in every human society, it does not follow that all human societies are commercial. Rather, well-functioning markets require enough widespread exchange that the process of exchange is not an anomaly and allocates some appreciable share of the goods and services in a society. The question of when precisely we can speak of markets existing is of limited interest.[6] The important point is that an exchange cannot be "in a market" without being embedded in a broader practice consisting of many other exchanges. This is important because some of the benefits discussed in the next chapter come simply from the activity of commerce, but others require the broader social context of a market.

Another key feature of well-functioning markets is that access is broadly available. It is not uncommon for societies to develop systems of voluntary exchange that are sharply limited to elites, while others are forced into more abusive forms of economic life. Consider the West Indies during the eighteenth century. In this period, economic life was dominated by sugar production, with a planter elite and a large population of enslaved labor. Among the elite there existed relatively robust markets. Barbados in the seventeenth and eighteenth centuries provides a good example.[7] The first English settlers arrived on the island in 1627. Initially, the society was poor and, compared to what followed later, relatively egalitarian. This pattern shifted in the 1640s with the introduction of sugar cane as a successful cash crop. Landholdings began to concentrate in increasingly larger plantations worked by enslaved African labor. The specialization of the sugar monoculture resulted in much higher levels of market activity as planters used their new wealth to purchase food staples as well as luxury items. Participation in this market, however, was sharply limited to the white aristocracy. The ever-increasing population of black slaves was largely excluded from participation in the market except as chattels.

The African American struggle for civil rights can be seen in part as a struggle for equal access to the market. In the wake of the Civil War, Southern legislatures, beginning with Mississippi, passed "Black Codes" to subordinate the population of newly freed slaves.[8] The Codes systematically excluded African Americans from large portions of the market. Blacks lost the ability to easily own property, carry on certain occupations, and make legally enforceable contracts. In the words of one of the Black Codes:

> All contracts between any persons whatever, whereof one or more of them shall be a person of color . . . shall be void as to all persons whatever, unless the same be put in writing and signed by the vendors or debtors, and witnessed by a white person who can read and write.[9]

Congress responded to these codes with the Civil Rights Act of 1866, passed over President Johnson's veto. Among other things, it stated that "all persons born in the United States . . . shall have the same right, in every State and Territory in the United States, to make and enforce contracts."[10] Along with the Fourteenth Amendment, the Civil Rights Act of 1866 tried unsuccessfully to ensure equal access to the marketplace.[11] The decisive effort to break the legal barriers to full African American participation in the nation's commerce would have to wait for the civil rights movement after World War II, which in part was an effort to build a well-functioning market from which citizens could not be excluded on the basis of race.[12]

Well-functioning markets must also be structured so that participants are not forced into exchanges with particular parties. Although certain exchanges—such as the purchase of food—may be unavoidable, in a well-functioning market, one should not be entirely at the mercy of another market actor. Consider two examples of badly functioning markets. The *repartimeiento de mercancias* system in colonial Latin America consisted of the nominal sale of goods by the Spanish to conquered Incas. In reality, however, it forcibly extracted wealth from the subject population. The Inca purchasers were required by the conquistadors to buy Spanish goods, and the Spanish in turn dictated the price at which the goods were sold. Thus, even though the indigenous population was left with goods at the conclusion of the transaction, in substance it consisted of the expropriation of their wealth through a system of coercion and price fixing.[13] Now consider the different circumstances presented by the case of *Batsakis v. Demotsis*, decided by the Texas Court of Appeals in 1949.[14] The defendant had borrowed money from the plaintiff to purchase food, and the plaintiff brought an action to collect the debt. The difficulty in the case came from the terms of the loan and the circumstances in which it was made. The plaintiff loaned $25 in return for a promise by the defendant to pay $2,000 in the future. The deal was struck in Greece during World War II, when, due to the German invasion, partisan attacks, and Nazi reprisals, much of the population, including the defendant, struggled on the edge of starvation.

What precisely makes these exchanges troubling? It is tempting to differentiate such examples from well-functioning markets by insisting that, in a healthy market, all exchanges must be voluntary. Voluntariness, however, proves to be a slippery concept. First, there is the conceptual difficulty of understanding what is meant by a "voluntary" transaction.[15] At the most abstract level, we must wade into debates about free will and determinism.[16] Supposing that satisfactory answers to these metaphysical conundrums allow us to identify certain forms of agency as voluntary, we still have the problem of behavior that, while volitional, nevertheless seems to be coerced. When a mugger says, "Your money or your life," one is presented with a choice, and there is a sense in which one's act of handing over one's purse is voluntary. The transaction, however, is clearly unfree in some significant way. We might understand the problem in this case as consisting of some mental condition on the part of the victim such that her action is not really voluntary. The exact nature of this mental condition, however, is difficult to define or observe. A more promising approach is to identify voluntariness with the absence of coercion and coercion with particular kinds of threats.[17] What makes the handing over of the purse involuntary is the fact that the mugger threatened the victim with murder. This shifts from the intractable problem of identifying true voluntariness as a characteristic of mental states to the more practical task of defining what sorts of threats are illegitimate.

Even when voluntariness is taken from the ethereal realm of debates over free will to the more humdrum task of defining wrongful threats, problems remain. The Incas victimized by the *repartimeiento de mercancias* were clearly coerced by the Spanish. In cases such as *Batsakis*, however, transactions seem troubling without being coerced. The plaintiff seeking enforcement of the contract in that case had not caused the German occupation and made no threat other than the refusal to lend his money. Was the transaction voluntary? One response would be to stick to one's guns and insist that, unless we can identify something illegitimate in the threat made by the plaintiff, then the transaction was voluntary. Alternatively, noting the necessity and destitution of the defendant, we might insist that the deal was not really voluntary. It seems natural to suppose that, at the time, she felt compelled to enter the transaction. This, however, leads us back to the psychological problem of trying to identify *truly* voluntary acts.

My preferred solution to these dilemmas is to deny that voluntariness per se is an attribute of well-functioning markets. Notice that voluntariness is an attribute of individual actions and transactions. However, markets—both healthy and unhealthy—are social practices. They necessarily consist of many transactions. Regardless of how one thinks about voluntariness, the market in which Batsakis and Demotsis contracted cannot be characterized as well functioning. We do not determine whether a market is well functioning, however, by looking to every transaction, deciding whether it was voluntary, and bestowing a positive judgment on the market if and only if all the transactions meet this criterion. Rather, we look to the structure of the market. Are people able to avoid transacting with particular parties? In the case of the *repartimeiento de mercancias,* the answer was no. The structure of the market ensured that everyone had to contract with the conquistadors. The same was true in the *Batsakis* case. Because of the war, the plaintiff enjoyed what amounted to a de facto monopoly over the defendant's access to food, even if the case did not involve the kind of blatant coercion of the *repartimeiento de mercancias*. What unifies these cases—one involving coercion and one involving monopoly—is not the involuntariness of the transactions. Rather, it is the fact that the quite different structure of these markets denied participants the ability to exchange with anyone other than Batsakis or the conquistadors. As will be discussed below, many of the benefits of markets center on their fluidity. In these two cases, however, poorly functioning markets created static relations of domination.[18] For the market argument, it is this structural feature that is problematic.[19]

It is worth pausing to emphasize this point. Most contract theorists see consent or voluntariness as central to the justification of contract law. For autonomy theorists, contracts merit legal enforcement precisely because they are freely chosen. Efficiency theorists also place significant conceptual demands on the voluntariness of transactions. According to economic arguments, voluntary agreements ought to be enforced because by consenting to a contract the parties make a judgment that doing so enhances their welfare. Legal decision makers should respect this choice because the parties are the best judges of what enhances their welfare. This assumption only holds true, however, if contracting parties understand the consequences of their decision and are free to choose otherwise. If ignorance, coercion, or some other imperfection of consent is present, we can no longer be confident in the welfare-enhancing nature of the transaction. Thus both of the dominant approaches to contract theory look to the idea of voluntary consent to do a great deal of normative work in their arguments. Imperfections in consent represent a fundamental normative challenge to contractual enforcement. In the market argument, however, individual voluntariness is not the sine qua non of legitimate contractual enforcement. To be sure, formal or nominal consent is necessary to avoid a chaos of conflicting contractual obligations. Likewise, "fully informed" or "truly meaningful" consent may be a way of limiting abusive practices in the market, but it is neither a necessary nor a sufficient condition for avoiding pathological markets. Our ultimate normative concern is the character of the markets supported by contract law, not voluntary consent per se. As we will see in chapter 7, this has important implications for how the law should treat boilerplate contracts, an area where commentators have consistently expressed anxiety about the adequacy of contractual consent. The market argument suggests that these concerns are largely misplaced.

Finally, well-functioning markets require that actors be able to exchange with strangers. The concern here overlaps in part with previous discussions. The market for credit in rural India illustrates the problem of markets that exclude strangers.[20] During the colonial period, *kabuliwallah*, itinerant moneylenders, could take as much as 75 percent of a farmer's crop as interest on a loan.[21] Even today, interest on short-term loans can run as high as 8 percent per day, and loans of one year can carry an interest rate of over 40 percent.[22] Furthermore, access to even this level of credit is limited by gender, caste, and family. The borrowers in these markets simply lack the ability to borrow from distant strangers that modern financial institutions afford. The results can be horrific. Muhammed Yunus, the founder of the Grameen Bank, tells the story of a young Bangladeshi woman who manufactured stools. To do so, she had to purchase 22 cents' worth of materials. She lacked the capital to do so and was forced to borrow from a moneylender at a ruinous level of interest or get financing from intermediaries who then sold her stools to the wider market. As a result, she was left with a profit of 2 cents.[23]

> Because Sufiya did not have 22 cents, she was forced into the clutches of the middlemen. The middlemen made her accept a measly pittance of 2 cents for a hard day's labor. Finance would liberate her from the middlemen and enable her to sell directly to customers. But the middlemen would not let her have finance, for they would lose their hold over her. For want of 22 cents, Sufiya's labor was captive.[24]

Sufiya had access to a market, but one that was sharply limited. She had relatively few people with whom she could contract and lacked the ability to make exchanges with those beyond the narrow circle of her village.

There are more subtle and less clearly pathological examples as well. Consider the widespread phenomenon of trade diasporas. Beginning in the third century, for example, famine and political turmoil in China created population pressures in the southeastern provinces of Guangdong and Fujian. Chinese migrants began planting communities along the rim of the South China Sea in what is today Vietnam, Thailand, Laos, Cambodia, Malaysia, Indonesia, and the Philippines. These overseas Chinese were periodically discriminated against and persecuted.[25] As a result, they retained their ethnic and cultural identity. Their descendants have proven economically successful.[26] Without any inherent political power, their success rests on their ability to use the networks of trust and information created by ethnic solidarity as a foundation for successful market interactions.[27] Historically, Jews followed a similar trajectory in the economies of Christian Europe and the Muslim Middle East.[28] For example, in the rough-and-tumble trade of the early modern Atlantic, Jews proved remarkably successful.[29] Likewise, by the eighteenth century, Jewish merchants (along with Greek and Armenian businessmen) dominated the commerce of major cities in the Middle East, and as early as 1000, the so-called Geniza documents, discovered in the storeroom of a Cairo synagogue, show extensive networks of Jewish merchants in the Mediterranean basin and beyond.[30]

As important as such religiously and ethnically based networks are, however, they face inherent limitations. The scope of available trading partners is often limited by the scope of the tribal networks. When patterns of trade rely decisively on the trust and relationships embedded in the tribal network, trading with strangers outside the tribe becomes difficult. Indeed, often the tribal solidarity that allows for successful intratribal trade is simply the reverse side of an alienation from the wider society—an alienation that can often turn ugly, as illustrated by the repeated experience of anti-Chinese violence in Southeast Asia and anti-Semitism in Europe.[31] One of the remarkable characteristics of well-functioning markets is that they do not require bonds of family, ethnicity, or religion. Rather, the market provides a social space in which cooperation and exchange between strangers—often strangers with very different ethnic or religious allegiances—is possible.

It is important to note that in my fivefold definition of well-functioning markets, I have deliberately rejected the economic model of perfect competition as an ideal market. In a formally competitive market, each participant has perfect information and approaches every decision with crisp economic rationality. There are no transaction costs. Entry to and exit from the market is costless. Prices adjust instantaneously, and every agent is a price taker. Perfect competition is a superficially beguiling conception of the market for normative arguments. As was long ago demonstrated, any allocation of resources produced by a perfectly competitive market in equilibrium will be economically efficient.[32] If we take efficiency as a normative goal, then perfect competition provides an ideal definition of a well-functioning market.

There are two reasons for rejecting the model of perfect competition. First, the market argument does not appeal to economic efficiency. I do not believe that markets are valuable because they are economically efficient. In chapter 4, I expand on the role of economic efficiency in the market. For now, it is enough to state that I do not believe that economic efficiency, standing alone is normatively significant. Morally evil market outcomes are consistent with economic efficiency, and the morally desirable consequences of the market I defend in the next chapter do not depend on markets producing formally efficient allocations. Economic efficiency is thus neither a necessary nor a sufficient condition for the moral defense of the market. The markets that I wish to defend need not satisfy the conditions necessary to produce perfectly competitive, and therefore efficient, outcomes.

The second reason is that perfect competition is far too abstract to serve as a defense of any real-world markets. In the real world, market participants never have perfect information.[33] Real markets have ubiquitous transaction costs. Indeed, according to one study, about 40 percent of economic activity in the United States can be characterized as a transaction cost of one kind or another.[34] Real people are often not economically rational, even in their economic decisions.[35] And so on. Whatever can be said in favor of the model of perfect competition, it cannot be said to describe any of the real markets that people have confronted historically or in which they operate today.

A normative argument based on perfect competition would thus have little to offer the defender of actual markets. Indeed, in current policy analysis the construct of perfect competition is offered less as a defense of market activity than as an apology for replacing market processes with some alternative.[36] After all, if markets can be defended only when they are perfectly competitive, it follows that they can almost always be found wanting and in need of regulation to produce outcomes closer to those promised by the frictionless models of economic theory. The arguments in this book are not offered as a defense of unregulated markets. To say that markets provide important moral goods is not to deny that markets can sometimes be bad—an issue that I will discuss at length in the final chapter of this book. My goal is to offer a defense of real markets, the kind of markets that one encounters in the real world as opposed to in an introductory textbook to microeconomics. For that task, the model of perfect competition will not do.

One might object that the enormous variety of market activity suggests the fruitlessness of pursuing any definition of well-functioning markets. One of the appealing characteristics of the model of perfect competition is that it abstracts from particulars and thus offers tools for thinking about the market that are agnostic as to the particular good or service being exchanged. The definition of well-functioning markets offered above shares something of this drive toward abstraction. As Deborah Satz has perceptively observed, however, "For the classical economists the term *market* actually referred to a heterogeneous collection of economic relations. Adam Smith and his followers offered distinct theories of the functioning not only of consumer goods markets, but also of markets in land, labor, and credit."[37] Indeed, once one divorces one's defense of markets from economic efficiency and looks instead to the various other kinds of moral consequences that they have, it seems foolish to frame a defense of markets in the abstract.[38] Rather, it would seem that one must look at every kind of market in its full particularity, judging moral consequences based on the contingent arrangements of different kinds of exchange. In one sense, I agree with this critique. In the next chapter, I will defend the claim that well-functioning markets produce certain morally desirable outcomes. Of necessity, I write in terms of generalities, but that necessity should not be taken to imply a claim that every market exchange produces these moral goods in equal measure. What, then, justifies my appeal to well-functioning markets in the abstract? I have two responses.

First, I invoke the concept of markets for a very specific purpose: to construct an argument about the normative justification of contract law. This of necessity requires that I speak in terms of generalities. One of the things that distinguishes law from the mere exercise of power by government officials is its abstraction. Law purports to provide rules and standards that apply in general rather than specific commands directed toward discrete individuals.[39] It follows that, in order to justify legal rules, it is not enough to justify the outcome in a particular case. Rather, one must offer reasons that speak to the generality of law.[40]

Of course, one could insist on formulating arguments that focus on the features of particular transactions rather than aggregate markets. For example, one could argue in favor of the legal enforcement of promises seriously made rather than enforcing some promises as a means of underwriting a broader social practice of market exchange. The problem is that such an approach fails to appreciate the way in which markets, as aggregate social phenomena, impact our moral universe. Certain consequences of markets can only be understood if we think of them as a social practice rather than as an arbitrary label for a set of individual actions. We must be aware of the dangers inherent in speaking in the abstract of something as pluralistic as markets, but without speaking in this way, I don't think it is possible to appreciate many of their most important consequences.

My second response is that, while I acknowledge the heterogeneity of market activity, there is something conceptually different that separates market activity from other forms of social organization. Furthermore, when markets have certain attributes, they are capable of delivering moral goods on a large scale in a way that they are not capable of delivering when they lack those attributes. Hence, to speak of well-functioning markets is not an attempt to dodge normative objections to certain kinds of markets by sweeping all the difficult questions into the term *well-functioning*.[41] Rather, my argument is that markets are like families. "Happy families are all alike; every unhappy family is unhappy in its own way."[42] Accordingly, I defer the discussion of the heterogeneity of markets to my discussion of market pathology in the final chapter. For now, I turn to the role of contract law in strengthening and extending markets.

The Relationship between Markets and Contract Law

In human history, well-functioning markets have been the exception rather than the rule. Ancient Roman society, for example, had large-scale trade, but most economic activity was organized around decidedly nonmarket activity, such as slave labor on massive latifundia or in mines, tax farming, booty captured by the legions, and the economic dependence of clients on powerful patrons who expropriated the fruits of conquest and distributed them in return for political support. Indeed, the pervasive economic importance of plunder, especially of precious metals, for the Roman economy has led one scholar to label the entire system a "military-coinage-slavery complex."[43] Contrast the Rome of Julius Caesar with a bustling commercial entrepôt such as modern New York or Hong Kong. In these cities, most of the economic activity—although by no means all of it—is organized by widespread exchange between relative strangers. The difference lies in the development of practices and institutions in New York and Hong Kong that make well-functioning markets possible in the way that they were not possible in ancient Rome. Such markets require a set of entrenched social conventions that facilitate exchange and deter predation and opportunism.

The importance of institutions has led some scholars to make rather extravagant claims about the relationship between law and markets. Duncan Kennedy, for example, argued that, "because the government uses force to guarantee respect for private property, and property determines the distribution of income, the 'free'/'private' market is really an artifact of public violence."[44] Even those who do not share Kennedy's radical politics claim that law is a necessary condition for markets. Cass Sunstein, for example, has argued:

> Free markets depend for their existence on law. We cannot have a system of private property without legal rules, telling people who owns what, imposing penalties for trespass, and saying who can do what to whom. Without the law of contract, freedom of contract, as we know and live it would be impossible. . . . Moreover, the law that underlies free markets is coercive in the sense that in addition to facilitating individual transactions, it stops people from doing many things that they would like to do. This is not by any means a critique of free markets. But it suggests that markets should be understood as a legal construct.[45]

This goes too far. Markets can exist without law, and the claims of Kennedy and Sunstein cannot be taken as universal truths about the necessary connection between law and markets. This not because markets are somehow a natural phenomenon rather than a human convention but because other social mechanisms—such as self-help, reputation, or ostracism—can be used to deal with the problems addressed by legal institutions. Law is important not because it is necessary or fundamentally constitutive of markets in some way but because it can at times be a better solution to some problems than the alternatives.

Upon a moment's reflection, the idea that law is a necessary condition for markets is implausible. Markets require respect for property. The basic ideas of meum and tuum, however, do not require a complex set of rules and legal institutions. Any dog with a bone has a rudimentary idea of property, even if, as Adam Smith notes, "nobody ever saw a dog make a fair and deliberate exchange of one bone for another with another dog."[46] Indeed, territoriality among predators in many ways mirrors a property-rights solution to the commons problem, excluding rival claims on a limited pool of resources—in this case, prey animals. This does not mean that any particular configuration of property rights is somehow natural, nor do simple, prelegal intuitions about *mine* and *yours* provide clear guidance in resolving the host of complex disputes that can arise out of property holding. However, it simply is not true that law is necessary for people to develop sufficiently definite ideas and practices around property for exchange to be possible.

Contract law is also not necessary for the development of markets. An example from Herodotus illustrates the issues. He describes how Carthaginian traders first ventured out of the Mediterranean, beyond the Pillars of Hercules (the Straits of Gibraltar) and into the rougher seas of the Atlantic.[47] Crawling down the coast of Africa, they came to a fertile land, and there engaged in a strange ritual. Going ashore, they would lay their cargo of olive oil and bronze tools on the beach. Then they would retreat to their ships, float offshore, and send up smoke signals. A short time later, people would emerge from the forest, examine the goods left by the Carthaginians, and then lay their own piles of gold on the beach. These people would then retreat back into the forest. Once they were gone, the Carthaginians would return to the shore. If they thought the offered ivory and gold constituted a fair trade, they would leave their goods and take the African commodities aboard their ship. If they thought the offer too low, they would return to their ships with nothing. The people would then emerge from the woods and either take back their gold without touching the Carthaginian goods or else would increase the size of their offering until it was accepted by the traders from the sea. The entire process took place without any formal legal mechanisms, even though, in the course of the exchange, each party was vulnerable to the other. The list of other markets that do not rely on formal legal enforcement of contracts could easily be multiplied.

The fact that rudimentary markets can exist without law, however, does not mean that large-scale, well-functioning markets can develop without the assistance of law. In many parts of the world today, people lack access to the basic legal recognition of property and contract. Hernando De Soto, for example, has studied the economic lives of those who live in the vast slums of cities such as Rio de Janeiro. He finds ubiquitous entrepreneurial activity. "The cities of the Third World and the former communist countries are teaming with entrepreneurs. You cannot walk through a Middle Eastern market, hike up to a Latin American village, or climb into a taxicab in Moscow without someone trying to make a deal with you."[48] He also finds, however, that the denizens of such places cannot and do not rely on legal mechanisms to enforce their property rights or their contracts. To be sure, the small-scale markets that one might find in a Brazilian favela can provide some of the benefits of commerce. They facilitate cooperation, for example, but that cooperation is sharply limited. Compared to fully developed markets elsewhere, people in the slums of Rio have a difficult time trading with strangers, especially if the exchange extends over time. As a result, they confine their economic lives to the smaller world of family and neighborhood. The fragility of the markets in which they operate requires that they be constantly on the lookout for fraud, violence, and other predatory behavior. Tellingly, these small-scale markets fail to deliver material prosperity and its attendant benefits.

Contract law strengthens and extends markets when it embodies three basic principles: security of exchange, sanctity of contract, and freedom of contract.[49] Security of exchange can be summed up by the maxim of *pacta sunt servada*, contracts should be performed. One of the central sources of weak markets in the absence of law is the problem of ex post opportunism. In a world of simultaneous exchange, the issues with which contract law grapples generally do not arise. *Quid* is exchanged for *quo*, but neither party must rely on the other's future performance.[50] The entirety of performance is collapsed into the moment of exchange and nothing is left for the future. When exchange is extended over time—as it inevitably must be in all but the simplest of markets—problems arise. Another example from ancient history illustrates this issue. In 73 B.C., Spartacus, a gladiatorial slave, led a revolt against his owner.[51] Other slaves rallied to his cause, and in a short time he commanded an army of several thousand soldiers. For three years, Spartacus's forces marched from one end of the Italian peninsula to the other, defeating the Roman legions sent to suppress the revolt. Finally, Spartacus was cornered at Rhegium, in the toe of the Italian boot. Without a navy, he contracted with Cilician pirates, who promised to ferry the escaped slaves out of Italy in exchange for a share of the vast booty of Spartacus's army. Plutarch records that, "after the pirates had struck a bargain with him, and received his earnest they deceived him and sailed away."[52] Trapped, the Romans captured the Spartacan army, and the consul Marcus Liscinius Crassus lined the length of the Via Appia between Capua and Rome with their crucified bodies.[53]

The fate of the Spartacan army provides a graphic illustration of the dangers of ex post opportunism. In a world where the law provides no recourse in the face of breach, one of three things will happen. First, many trades will not occur. Rather than expose themselves to opportunism by counterparties, people will simply avoid exchanges. Second, the trade that does occur will come to be dominated by simultaneous exchange. As a result, the exchanges that do happen will be relatively simple. The scale and complexity facilitated by exchange over time will be limited. Third, parties will divert resources away from trade and into mechanisms for managing the risk of opportunism. This might take the form of limiting trade to those whom one can trust in the absence of law and investing time and energy in identifying such people. The common phenomenon of trade diasporas and highly commercialized religious minorities can be accounted for in these terms. Common membership in the tribe serves as a proxy for trustworthiness and vulnerability to formal and informal sanctions in the event of breach. Another possibility is self-help. In the ancient Near East, for example, treaties and covenants were often solemnized by hacking up a goat or some other sacrificial animal.[54] The ritual appears in sources from the Bible to *The Iliad*. The dismembered animal was an enacted penalty clause. In effect, a party agreed that, in the event of breach, the disappointed counterparty or his divine helpers could hack up the breacher in the manner that he hacked up the goat. The threats reduced opportunism, but they also raised the constant specter of a violent breakdown in cooperation. Finally, parties will set aside resources to self-insure against the costs of being victimized by others. All three responses will result in significantly constrained markets.

Contract law should also provide for the sanctity of contract. This is closely related to the idea of security of exchange. Sanctity of contract is the principle that once a contract is made, it cannot be unilaterally altered by one of the parties or by a third party. The history of sovereign borrowing provides an illustration of this problem.[55] Kings have often needed money. Lenders faced a problem. A weak king was likely a bad credit risk, because he faced the possibility of military defeat from abroad or a palace coup from within. On the other hand, a powerful king had the ability to unilaterally alter the terms of any loan agreement after it was made. Powerful kings frequently did so.[56] The result was a sharply limited market for sovereign debt. At the end of the seventeenth century, the English crown hit on a solution to this problem through a system of political and financial checks on dramatic unilateral alteration of contract terms. With the rise of parliamentary accountability and the intermediation of the Bank of England, lenders had greater confidence in the security of the initial terms offered by the indebted Exchequer. The result was a massive expansion in willing purchasers of British sovereign debt and the first truly deep and liquid securities market.[57]

Finally, contract law supports markets through freedom of contract. This is the principle that the parties to an exchange should have the discretion to author their obligations in relation to the exchange. Freedom of contract is separate from the idea of security in exchange. Many legal systems have recognized security of contract while containing only the most embryonic ideas of freedom of contract. Under Roman law, for example, most contractual liability was limited to particular transactional forms. *Societas,* for example, specified the rules governing the creation of a partnership as well as the duties each partner would have toward other adventurers.[58] Likewise, contracts of hire, lease, sale, or what common lawyers would call bailment, each came with a set of prepackaged legal obligations.[59] All of these contracts generally required the consent of the parties[60] and gave a disappointed promisee a remedy against the opportunistically breaching promisor. Their terms could not be altered ex post. In short, this law embodied both security of exchange and sanctity of contract. Freedom of contract, however, was limited. Parties could not rewrite the scope or content of their obligations by agreement. Likewise, at common law, innkeepers and common carriers had a set of relatively rigid duties that they owed to their customers.[61]

The normative role of freedom of contract in the market argument is limited. Some proponents of freedom of contract have argued for a general principle allowing a presumptively unfettered power to impose legal obligations on oneself.[62] However, if contract law exists primarily to support markets, then freedom of contract is limited to the context of market exchange. The market argument does not support a general power of imposing legal obligations on oneself or consensually disclaiming the legal duties owed by others to oneself. Rather, the focus should be on the way in which freedom of contract promotes market exchange. Regimes such as the Roman law or the early common law, which allow for security of exchange without freedom of contract, create rigidity in transactional structures. Roman lawmakers in effect decided what all contracts of partnership or bailment were to look like. This rigidity, however, limits the extent of market activity. As markets expand, the information available to lawmakers on the sorts of problems for which contracts provide solutions diminishes.[63]

The point here is analogous to the defense of the price mechanism mounted by Friedrich Hayek in the 1930s and 1940s.[64] Hayek's opponents in those debates were central planners who insisted that benevolent government bureaucrats could generate the optimal allocation of resources. Hayek insisted that the information constraints faced by such planners were insurmountable. In a complex market, most of the information necessary to create beneficial and useful social practices is widely dispersed among market participants. The only way this dispersed information can be incorporated into transactional structures is to allow individual contracting parties to author their own obligations. This information simply is not available to lawmakers. In the absence of freedom of contract, then, the fit between transactional structure and the needs of market participants is limited by the foresight of the lawmakers.

The history of economic development in the Middle East provides an example of this problem. Lively debate takes place among economic historians about the extent to which Islam promoted or retarded economic development. On one hand, Islam provides a favorable ideology for merchants. Unlike Christianity, Islam does not have a powerful anticommercial tradition. Muhammad was a merchant, and neither the Qua'ran nor the hadith of the Prophet evidence hostility toward trade and commerce.[65] During the early centuries of Islam, Muslim lands were among the most economically advanced on the planet.[66] On the other hand, a fair argument can be made that certain rigidities in Islamic law contributed to economic stagnation during the Ottoman period. Under classical Islamic law, all partnerships were necessarily at-will relationships, terminable unilaterally by any party at any time.[67] "Every additional partner thus increased the risk of premature termination by raising the probability of a partner dying, or simply opting to withdraw, before fulfillment of the contract."[68] As a result, partnerships tended to be small, usually only two merchants cooperating for a single trading voyage.[69] It would have been relatively easy to incentivize investment for larger enterprises by simply placing a covenant in the partnership agreement forbidding a partner from withdrawing his capital from the venture for a fixed period of time. Islamic law, however, while providing security of contract, would simply not allow the parties to author such an agreement. Not surprisingly, large-scale firms did not develop in the Middle East in the early modern period, even as they began to emerge in Western Europe.

As we shall see in the final chapter of this book, none of these principles—security of exchange, sanctity of contract, and freedom of contract—are absolute. There are times when it makes sense to relieve parties of their obligations under a contract. There are times when it makes sense to limit the ability of market participants to impose legal obligations on themselves. Finally, there are times when the terms in a contract should be modified absent the mutual consent of the parties. Taken together, however, security of exchange, freedom of contract, and sanctity of contract should provide the basic structure for a market-sustaining law of contracts.

CHAPTER THREE

The Moral Consequences of Well-Functioning Markets

This chapter sets forth the normative heart of the market argument. It can be stated very simply. Well-functioning markets lead to morally desirable outcomes. They inculcate moral habits that support liberal societies. They provide a framework for peaceful and productive cooperation in the face of the pervasive pluralism of contemporary society. They generate wealth, which can have an ameliorative effect on a host of evils. Thus, well-functioning markets are worthy objects of political care. They are sufficiently desirable that they justify the existence of specialized bodies of law that strengthen and extend them. This is what contract law should do.

Markets and the Liberal Virtues

Unease with the idea of virtue is part of the basic DNA of modern political thought. Liberalism emerged in the seventeenth century in reaction to an older vision based on Aristotle as interpreted by the medieval church. For Aristotle, virtues are attributes of the excellent human soul. Human excellence was defined by a comprehensive vision of the purpose of life. In the *Nichomachean Ethics,* he wrote:

> Since then [politics] makes use of the other practical sciences, and since it further ordains what men are to do and from what to refrain, its end must include the ends of the others, and must be the proper good of man.[1]

This good required the cultivation of virtues. Virtue was a functional excellence, a set of acquired habits, dispositions, and characteristics that allowed one to perform a given task well. Conceiving of human life as having a definite goal defined virtue in terms of the acquired attributes that would allow one to achieve that end. "The virtues, then, come neither by nature nor against nature, but nature gives the capacity for acquiring them, and this is developed by training."[2] This training was to be part of the task of politics: the cultivation of the virtues necessary for human excellence.

By the seventeenth century, however, the comprehensive vision of the medieval synthesis was cracking under the pressure of reformation, newly assertive secular authorities, and challenges to Aristotelian epistemology. Liberalism emerged as an ideology for a society marked by religious pluralism. In contrast to the older vision of human excellence, liberalism was less ambitious, promising peace and protection from an assertive state rather than perfection of the soul. Much of contemporary political philosophy reinforces this reticence because of its fixation on moral pluralism. According to one oft-invoked distinction, obligations can be divided between the good and the right.[3] The good refers to comprehensive systems such as religious theologies. The right, in contrast, refers to the basic demands of living respectfully in a pluralistic society and includes things such as rights to bodily security and freedom. Laws should embody the right but be neutral on questions of the good. On this view, virtue implies a vision of the good about which the law should remain silent.

For some liberals, ideas of virtue are dangerous. Humans do not have a uniquely correct end. At most, our goal is a form of self-authorship that is diverse, contingent, and without any fixed end. Cultivating virtue is perverse because it prescribes a particular ideal of life to the exclusion of others. This stunts the project of self-authorship. But even liberals who are agnostic about self-authorship as the highest good may be suspicious of political virtue talk.[4] When pluralism is an irreducible reality, there are prudential reasons for constraining the moral ambitions of the law. Debates over which vision of the good the law should adopt will be inconclusive and destructive. If one vision triumphs in the law, resentment by the losers will undermine the legitimacy that legal institutions require to function. Far better for politics to remain agnostic as individuals remain committed to their own comprehensive visions.[5]

Debates over sexual morality illustrate these issues. For some, pornography is an impediment to a well-ordered soul.[6] Others affirm erotica as liberating, a way of exploring one's sexual identity.[7] These views rest on differing visions of a well-lived human life. For a liberal, such questions are beyond the competence of politics. The law should not have a particular view of sexuality's relationship to the good.[8] Hence, the law may regulate pornography to combat the exploitation of children but may not do so to advance a particular view of sexual morality.[9]

Virtue also is not often associated with markets. Commerce, we are told, makes people selfish and insensitive to others because markets enshrine acquisitiveness as the dominant human impulse. Ebenezer Scrooge is the quintessential "man of business."[10] At the heart of this view is an unease with the profit motive. In Plato's *Republic,* merchants are identified with the lowest part of the soul—the appetites—while the higher aspects of the soul—spiritedness and reason—are associated with nonmarket callings, namely warriors and rulers.[11] The market is thus a threat to the well-ordered soul. Just as philosopher kings should rule businesspeople, in a virtuous soul, the appetitive concerns of commerce are subordinated to the higher demands of honor and reason. Echoes of this moral hierarchy continue. For example, during the 2008 presidential campaign, Barack Obama contrasted the selflessness of public service to the mercenary spirit of private gain, repeatedly telling the story of how he pursued a higher calling as a political activist despite pressure to pursue a commercial career.[12] As in Plato's ideal city, Obama presented a world in which the profit motive relegated commercial actors to a moral status inferior to that of public servants.

At times, the moral impact of the market is seen in darker terms. In the movie *Wall Street*, Gordon Gecko, the moral embodiment of capitalism, insists that "greed is good" and pursues his own projects with a ruthless disregard for the welfare of others.[13] Even more chilling is the character of Michael Corleone in *The Godfather*.[14] The movie portrays the transformation of an idealistic World War II veteran into the brutal heir of his father's criminal empire. Ultimately, he arranges the murder of his brother when the logic of the family business demands it. Michael justifies his crimes by insisting, "It isn't personal, it's business." The implication is that business represents an amoral realm, a place where the demands of personal virtue have no claim. The dramatic coherence of Michael's use of the term *business* testifies to a set of moral assumptions about markets.[15] Commerce makes men bad.

There is also a softer line of criticism. Even if commerce does not produce monsters, it does produce a cramped set of habits, beliefs, and affections. Sinclair Lewis's novel *Babbitt* captures this view.[16] Babbitt is a model businessman. He works hard to turn a profit. He is also an aesthetic and moral pygmy. He has no appreciation of art or culture. His views are vapid and conformist, his morality hypocritical.[17] He is the grotesque spiritual product of commerce.[18]

These pessimistic views of the relationship between virtue, liberalism, and markets are mistaken. Liberalism requires certain virtues, and markets can inculcate them. As others have pointed out, hostility to virtue mistakenly identifies the perfectionist politics of Aristotle and the idea of virtue.[19] While Aristotle is difficult to square with the limited moral ambitions of liberalism, his is not the only way of relating virtue and politics. Virtue is a functional excellence. Aristotle's perfectionism focuses on the task of being human. Virtue, however, can be relevant to any task. It is simply a set of acquired characteristics that allows one to achieve a particular goal.[20] Liberal virtues are the traits that allow one to function successfully in a liberal society. Hence, even if politics is agnostic on the nature of human excellence, there are many liberal tasks that require virtues. As Peter Berkowitz has observed, "Contrary to much conventional wisdom, the liberal tradition not only makes room for virtue but shows that the exercise of virtue is indispensable to a political regime seeking to establish equality and protect freedom."[21]

The pessimistic take on markets' influence on character is similarly mistaken. Critics miss the way that commerce inculcates valuable habits. As a psychological matter, they oversimplify the motives of market participants, reducing them to a monomaniacal desire for monetary gain. The market, however, also disciplines and channels acquisitiveness. Indeed, in the eighteenth century, Montesquieu insisted that commerce had a beneficent effect on individual character. In *The Spirit of the Laws*, he argued that markets made men more peaceful and tolerant, "gentle" in the eighteenth-century idiom.[22] To be sure, partisans of the so-called *doux commerce*[23] thesis did not view markets through entirely rose-colored glasses. Adam Smith had a healthy respect for commerce but worried in the *Wealth of Nations* that the nascent factory system would create a dull-witted mass of workers engaged in mindlessly repetitive tasks, undermining the critical spirit on which self-government depended.[24] Nevertheless, the doux commerce tradition was correct that markets breed virtues that support a liberal polity. Markets require that one consider the point of view of others and alter one's behavior to satisfy their desires. This disposition supports three important liberal virtues. The first is deliberation, the ability to consider an opposing viewpoint. The other two virtues are negative. Markets weaken loyalty to tribe and family, cultivating the ability to relate to strangers according to impersonal criteria. Finally, markets break down aristocratic habits, encouraging people to relate peaceably as equals.

Exchange has two key features. First, it is unanimous. Each party to a market exchange has at least the nominal power to veto the transaction. In contrast, political systems allow action in the face of dissent.[25] In a political debate my goal might be to persuade, but politics provides a mechanism to triumph in the face of my interlocutor's opposition. Democratic outcomes are always premised on the absence of unanimity, although differing decision procedures require greater or lesser levels of consensus.[26] The wishes of at least some members of the polity can be ignored.[27] Not so with exchange. Without the cooperation of my partner, no exchange is possible.

Second, exchange requires that each party pursue the other party's interests to achieve his or her own interests. As Adam Smith observed:

> It is not from the benevolence of the butcher, the brewer, or the baker that we expect our dinner, but from their regard to their own interest. We address ourselves, not to their humanity but to their self-love, and never talk to them of our own necessities but of their advantages.[28]

Exchange thus requires a kind of other-regardingness. To be sure, it is not altruism. Our concern with the advantages of the butcher, the brewer, and the baker is not the love of our neighbors. Exchange does not require such love. Commerce, however, is impossible when I am indifferent to the concerns of my trading partner. In a more aristocratic age, tradespeople were an object of scorn precisely because of the servility that the market imposed on them. Gentlemen possessed the luxury of satisfying their needs while maintaining indifference to others. The tradesman, in contrast, could not afford hauteur because he was dependent on the satisfaction of others' interests for the gratification of his own needs.

The claim that trade promotes other-regardingness will strike some as implausible. For example, some anthropologists claim that in many "primitive" societies, exchange is associated with unscrupulous advantage taking.[29] For instance, among the Pukhtun of Northern Pakistan, there is a practice called *adal-badal* (give and take). As reported by one anthropologist:

> *Adal-badal* is always practiced with non-relatives and affords men a great deal of pleasure as they attempt to get the advantage over their exchange partner.

> A good exchange, in which a man feels he has gotten the better of the deal, is cause for bragging and pride. If the exchange is bad, the recipient tries to renege on the deal or, failing that, to palm off the faulty object on someone unsuspecting. The best partner is someone who is distant spatially and will therefore have little opportunity to complain.[30]

The Pukhtun, however, do not exchange in anything that resembles a well-functioning market. Agriculture rather than trade dominates their economy.[31] Furthermore, economic interactions tend to be mediated through client–patron relationships rather than markets.[32]

In contrast, cross-cultural studies suggest that, as societies become more commercial and less pastoral or agrarian, people are more willing to consider the interests of others.[33] Experiments involving the so-called ultimatum game provide evidence of this relationship.[34] The game involves two players. Player one has a sum of money that she divides between herself and player two. Player two either accepts or rejects the offer. If she accepts it, both players keep the money. If she rejects it, then neither player keeps anything. A purely self-interested individual should give as much as possible to herself and as little as possible to the other player. If the other player is also self-interested, she should accept any division, no matter how paltry. Observed reality, however, is quite different.[35] Players never divide the sum in the way suggested by the rational actor model. Rather, they always offer more than the minimum payment and reject offers that they regard as too low.

Those playing the ultimatum game in societies with well-functioning markets—the United States, Japan, Western Europe, and Israel for example—tend to make a division of around 40 percent to 50 percent.[36] Surprisingly, there is little variation across what are otherwise different cultures. When the game was played among the Machiguenga people of the southeastern Peruvian Amazon, however, the results were very different.[37] The Machiguenga practice a form of subsistence agriculture with relatively little commercial activity. Strikingly, they offer far less than the players from commercial societies. When the experiments were expanded beyond the Machiguenga to other small-scale societies, similar levels of variation were found.[38] Herders who engage in repeated sales of cattle exhibit more prosocial behavior than independent subsistence farmers.[39] Even among the Machiguenga, the more land that a farmer has under cultivation to grow crops for the market rather than for consumption, the larger his offer in an ultimatum game.[40] Contra the pessimists, exchange within a market tends to make people more attentive and responsive to others' points of view.

The capacity to consider others is key to many liberal virtues. John Rawls insists that political justice begins with a two-part conception of human nature. First, people are free and equal moral agents who deliberate over their course in life.[41] Second, moral agents must recognize the identity of others as equal moral agents, pursuing their own courses in their own lives.[42] A similar starting point for liberal conceptions of justice can be found in the Millian maxim that one should be afforded maximum liberty consistent with like liberty for everyone else in society.[43] These formulations help us to think through the demands of justice in a liberal society. The ability to engage in such deliberation is an acquired trait, a virtue. Indeed, according to Locke, in the state of nature, the passions overwhelm deliberation and conscience.[44] It is only by acquiring the ability to see the world through the eyes of another that effective political cooperation is possible. This is precisely the skill demanded of a successful trader. The merchant must of necessity learn to see the world through the eyes of his or her customers. This does not mean, of course, that commerce leads ineluctably to liberalism or even that commercial experience is necessary to reflect about justice. But the habits inculcated by well-functioning markets will make people adept in precisely the feats of imaginative understanding that liberalism requires.

Well-functioning markets also breed moral habits that weaken tribal links and flatten social hierarchies. This can be seen in two areas. The first is the relationship between markets and family loyalty, and the second is the effect of commerce on aristocratic ideas of honor. Contrary to state-of-nature myths, humans have never existed in a condition of presocial individuality, whether of the violent Hobbesian variety or the happy Acadia imagined by Rousseau. Rather, all humans are born into social and biological relationships: a family.[45] The biological basis for the family is kin selection and reciprocal altruism.[46] Like many other animals, humans seem hardwired to favor people who share their genes. They are also evolutionarily predisposed to be more altruistic toward members of their native social group—namely, their families. These biological structures, in turn, are reinforced by a host of social mechanisms from gossip to rules surrounding marriage and inheritance that push people toward favoring kin above others.

For the most part, this is all to the good. Families provide nurture for children, companionship for adults, material support, and even spiritual meaning. Loyalty to kin, however, creates political problems. The institutions of the state should treat all citizens equally. When the norms of kin selection dominate politics, we have pathology. Examples of this pathology include nepotism, tribal strife, and the neglect of impersonal criteria for state action such as the rule of law in favor of familial connections. Francis Fukuyama has labeled this nexus of problems "patromonialism" and identified it as the central impediment to the formation of healthy modern states.[47] Other social theorists have flagged the same issue. Douglas North, John Joseph Wallis, and Barry Weingast, for example, have argued that the transition to healthy liberal democracy involves a shift from what they call "natural orders" to "open access orders."[48] The key difference between these orders is the presence or absence of impersonal relationships. In natural orders, a relatively small elite governs society on the basis of personal relationships. Access to wealth, power, and other social goods is limited to those with connections to the elite. In an open access order, in contrast, personal relationships give way to impersonal rules.

Families are not organized as markets. Commerce with intimates is possible but delicate. Family relationships dominated by exchange are not happy. Likewise, patrimonial relationships are not commercial but rather take the form of patron and client. Certainly, some vestiges of patrimonialism can survive in well-functioning markets, as in the case of family firms. Market competition, however, tends to punish family firms that cling too tightly to the norms of patrimonialism to the exclusion of commercial logic.[49] Those who live within well-functioning markets will of necessity develop the habit of interacting with strangers not as foreigners beyond the family or tribe but as customers, suppliers, employees, and other impersonal roles.

Families are not the only social structures that must be chastened for liberal democracies to function properly. One of the hallmarks of a liberal regime is hostility to aristocracy. Although liberal orders need not be radically egalitarian, they do require at a bare minimum that formal distinctions based on class or caste be broken down sufficiently that their social power does not overwhelm liberal institutions. Consider the way in which ideas of honor undermine liberal democracy. At the heart of this ethos is a social hierarchy in which inferiors must show due deference to their betters.[50] The resulting tensions surrounding respect can prove destructive when paired with democratic politics. The case of Mathew Lyon and Roger Griswald, congressmen in the 1790s, provides an example of the problems that an ethos of honor can pose for the practice of democracy.[51] In a heated debate, Lyon spat in Griswald's face. The House of Representatives took up the issue but voted not to expel Lyon. Griswald responded by beating Lyon on the floor of the House with a stick, while Lyon defended himself with a set of fireplace tongs. By caning Lyon—as opposed to challenging him to a duel—Griswald was using the violent vocabulary of honor to make a deliberate and well-understood statement of contempt. Caning was how a gentleman responded to an insult from an inferior.[52] More than a half century later, Senator Charles Sumner attacked the pro-slavery views of Congressman Preston Brooks's father-in-law. Brooks interpreted Sumner's speech as an attack on the honor of his family and used the vocabulary of stylized violence to show his contempt for the Massachusetts senator by beating him unconscious with a heavy stick on the Senate floor.[53]

Markets, on the other hand, tend to replace the "manly" virtues of aristocracy with the more peaceable habits of tradespeople. For some this is unfortunate. Thomas Carlyle, for example, lamented the effects of commerce, writing in 1840 of bygone times:

> For, in one word, *Cash Payment* had not then grown to be the universal sole nexus of man to man; it was something other than money that the high then expected from the low, and could live without getting from the low. Not as buyer and seller alone, of land or what else it might be, but in many sense still as soldier and captain, as clansman and head, as loyal subject and guiding king, was the low related to the high. With the supreme triumph of Cash, a changed time has entered.[54]

Writing in the 1830s, Alexis de Tocqueville took a more optimistic view, noting that the commercial ethos in the United States tended to undermine aristocracy and promote democracy. He wrote, "As soon as work seems to all citizens an honorable necessity for the human race and is always clearly performed, at least in part, for payment, then the wide gap which used to separate the different professions in aristocratic societies disappears."[55] He continued:

> American servants do not believe that they are degraded for working since everyone around them is working. They do not feel humiliated by the idea of receiving a wage, for the President of the United States also works for a salary. He is paid for giving orders much as they are paid for obeying them. In the

United States, professions are more or less laborious, more or less lucrative but never higher or lower. All honest occupations are honorable.[56]

Tellingly, the decline of dueling in the United States was intimately linked with the rise of commercial society. "The older code of honor with its emphasis on gentlemanly touchiness about perceived slights and insults was replaced by a more commercial vision of honor centered on personal honesty and trustworthiness."[57]

A liberal political order requires that certain habits of mind and action—virtues—be widely distributed among the citizenry. Citizens must peacefully deliberate within a system of impersonal institutions in ways that imaginatively consider the perspectives of others. Commerce breeds habits that support these virtues by forcing market participants to consider one another's needs and desires while breaking down patrimonial and aristocratic impulses. In short, well-functioning markets inculcate liberal virtues.

Markets and Moral Pluralism

In 1533 Jan Beuckelszoon, a Dutch religious seeker, heard a new variant on the Christian gospel known as Anabaptism.[58] Rather than waiting patiently for God to bring the promised millennium of the Book of Revelation, the preacher insisted that God's elect needed to establish the New Jerusalem. Known as Jan of Leyden, Beuckelszoon traveled to the city of Munster to preach Anabaptism. Shortly after Jan began teaching, the local bishop entered the city with 2,000 soldiers to arrest him. The populace expelled the troops, and less than a month after his arrival, Jan controlled the city. Everyone was required to convert to Anabaptism or face expulsion from the city in the dead of winter. Meanwhile, the bishop besieged the city. Jan was crowned king of Israel, and, citing the Bible, he instituted polygamy and concubinage. He also armed his followers—including women—and began sorties against the encircling troops. Two refugees from the city showed the besiegers how to breach its walls, and on June 25, 1535, the bishop entered Munster.[59] The bishop had Jan tied to a stake and flayed alive with red-hot iron tongs. Jan's tongue was pulled out, and he was finally finished with a dagger after the crowd—hardened as were the denizens of the sixteenth century to such things—began to sicken from the smell of his agony.[60]

Munster was one of the opening skirmishes in the wars of religion that tortured Europe until the Peace of Westphalia in 1648. For more than a century, Catholic and Protestant armies battled in France, the Low Countries, England, Scotland, Ireland, Switzerland, Austria, and, above all, in Germany.[61] Hundreds of thousands died in battle, and large areas were reduced to starvation. Of course, the wars were never entirely about religion. The Protestant Cromwell's invasion of Catholic Ireland had as much to do with long-standing English ambitions as religion. Likewise, by the end of the Thirty Years War, the Catholic Cardinal Richelieu supported Protestants to advance Gallic interests in Germany. Despite the messy realities of geopolitics, however, the sixteenth- and seventeenth-century European wars, with their savage brutality, have seared themselves into Western memory as the catastrophe that comes of wedding moral and religious fervor to power politics.

In a sense, liberal democracy is a response to the wars of religion. Thomas Hobbes wrote *The Leviathan* in the shadow of the brutality of the English Civil War, which pitted Puritans against high Anglicans and Catholics. A generation later, John Locke penned the ur-text of English-speaking liberalism, *The Second Treatise on Government,* during the denouement of the religious wars in England, when the realm's Protestant elite expelled its final Catholic monarch. The shadow cast by the wars of religion reaches the present. Writing about contemporary politics, the philosopher Robert Audi argues:

> Religion can . . . be a divisive force in democratic politics. The impulse to pursue the Ultimate Good, particularly in an authoritative context and with the support of others sharing the same religious outlook, can lead to a tendency, conscious or unconscious to dominate others. A holy cause can sanctify extreme measures.[62]

Likewise, Martha Nussbaum begins her account of religious freedom in America by tracing its roots back to the wars of religion. "The first half of the seventeenth century saw bloody explosions of religious violence in both Britain and continental Europe. Most early American colonists came to the New World in flight from religious persecution."[63]

In a secular society, however, religion is not the only source of potentially dangerous conflict. The first half of the twentieth century saw totalizing secular ideologies of the left and right replace religious fervor. Movements such as Nazism and communism offered complete visions of the ultimate good, identifying it with the triumph of racial purity or a Utopian dictatorship of the proletariat. In both cases, the result was human carnage on a scale that dwarfed the wars of religion.[64]

One of the hallmarks of modern society is moral pluralism. Long gone is the assumption that society can be structured by a single moral orthodoxy commanding universal assent. In the traditional telling, that dream died when Martin Luther nailed his ninety-five theses to the door of Wittenberg Cathedral. Many would reject the Protestant-centrism of this story today, but few would deny that modern societies exhibit high levels of moral and religious pluralism. Indeed, some political philosophers have expanded the original concern with cosmic religious politics to all politics based on comprehensive moral beliefs, whether sacred or secular.[65]

If the wars of religion represent moral pluralism in its most pathological form, then a society in which people with sharply differing beliefs peacefully cooperate represents the liberal ideal. Liberal theorists have proposed various ways of achieving this ideal. One popular strand of thinking insists that appeals to comprehensive ideas of the good should be treated as *per se* illegitimate in public life. Ronald Dworkin, for example, has argued that liberalism's "constitutive morality is a theory of equality that requires official neutrality amongst theories of what is valuable in life."[66] Likewise, John Rawls has insisted on the need for "public reason," which forswears appeals not only to religion but comprehensive systems of secular morality.[67] The goal of this rhetorical abstemiousness is twofold. First, as a conceptual matter, abstaining from appeals to such comprehensive beliefs will lead to conclusions that more closely adhere to an ideal of justice in which all citizens are treated with respect, regardless of moral or religious beliefs. Second, by avoiding appeals to the good, the acrimony of political debate can be lessened. If all sides agree that only reasons based on a thin conception of public morality are acceptable, then they are less likely to feel resentment and alienation when their own thick moral vision fails to dominate.

Whatever the merits of public reason as a theory, it does not reflect actual practice in liberal democracies.[68] Religion has not been banished from the public sphere. In the United States, many of the most important political movements have had religious elements. Examples include abolitionism, prohibition, the civil rights movement, the pro-life backlash against *Roe v. Wade,* and debates over gay rights.[69] Likewise, many of the most enduring pieces of U.S. political rhetoric have drawn on religious ideas and imagery. Two examples will suffice. In his second inaugural address, Abraham Lincoln suggested that America's suffering in the Civil War was divine retribution for the national sin of slavery.[70] In his 1963 "I Have a Dream" speech, Martin Luther King Jr. framed the struggle for black equality as a matter of Christian salvation and redemption. Borrowing language from the Bible, he preached, "I have a dream that one day every valley shall be exalted, every hill and mountain shall be made low, the rough places will be made plain, and the crooked places will be made straight, and the glory of the Lord shall be revealed, and all flesh shall see it together."[71]

The apparently neutral categories of public reason have also not delivered public life from violent debate. Indeed, in some cases, they have exacerbated it. The legacy of *Roe v. Wade* provides an example.[72] For pro-life advocates, an unborn child is a human being, an innocent person deserving of protection even at the cost of his or her mother's freedom after conception. For pro-choice advocates, a fetus cannot be equated to a person. Doing so is a pretext for restricting the basic freedom over one's own body. Furthermore, because restrictions on abortion necessarily act on the bodily integrity of women but not men, they also undermine sexual equality. The Supreme Court, however, has insisted that its decisions on abortion represent a neutral resolution of the issue.

> Where, in the performance of its judicial duties, the Court decides a case in such a way as to resolve the sort of intensely divisive controversy reflected in *Roe* and those rare, comparable cases, its decision has a dimension that the resolution of the normal case does not carry. It is the dimension present whenever the Court's interpretation of the Constitution calls the contending sides of a national controversy to end their national division by accepting a common mandate rooted in the Constitution.[73]

Yet, despite these appeals to the supposedly neutral categories of constitutional law, abortion has been one of the most contentious issues in U.S. politics. Those who see the Court's decisions as a defeat do not accept the legitimacy and neutrality of the Court's decisions.

The conceptual continence of public reason is not the only way in which liberalism manages moral pluralism. Liberal democracies also rely on institutional structures.[74] For example, regular elections allow one side to win and get some of what it wants. Any electoral victory, however, is temporary. The next election holds out to the losers the hope of future victory. This reconciles them to their current time in the wilderness.

Likewise, legislatures impose on competing factions the necessity of achieving at least limited consensus. A final institutional mechanism is to limit the reach of politics by removing certain issues from the political agenda. Hence, for example, the religion clauses of the First Amendment manage religious pluralism by limiting the ability of the state to suppress a disfavored creed or exalt a favored sect over its competitors.[75] Likewise, constitutional rights to freedom of speech, press, and association provide an outlet for dissent.[76] Rights to privacy, such as those announced by the Supreme Court, shield certain decisions and aspects of life from majority decisions.[77] All these rights try to limit the reach of politics in its most coercive form. The hope is that we create a space where clashing moral and religious factions can peacefully coexist without the persistent fear among followers of being branded as heretics and persecuted.

Considerable acrimony continues notwithstanding these institutions. Elections are notorious incubators of extremism even among those who are disposed toward moderation.[78] Likewise, legislative politics frequently generates more partisan jockeying than consensus building. Finally, free speech may not be the social panacea of liberal dreams. Evidence supporting the hope that reasoned debate will tend to moderate extreme beliefs is thin at best. We tend to approach political or moral discussions as a contest in which there are winners and losers.[79] People presented with arguments that they cannot refute are likely to see themselves as losers in the exchange and go searching for better ammunition to use next time. They are unlikely to simply change their beliefs in the face of reasoned objections. Indeed, political debate tends to make people more extreme, pushing them toward the starkest and least nuanced versions of their previous beliefs.[80] Likewise, the public articulation of frustrations, rather than serving as a safety valve, often deepens a sense of grievance and makes one less likely to cooperate with those beyond the borders of one's wronged tribe.[81]

I offer this pessimistic assessment of liberalism's response to moral and religious pluralism for two reasons. First, public reason and constitutional arrangements alone are inadequate mechanisms for managing moral pluralism. This does not mean that they should be abandoned. Whatever the merits of public reason in its most aggressive formulation, our political culture clearly functions better for not being dominated by theological disputes between irreconcilable religious factions. Likewise, despite the acrimony and polarization generated by elections, legislative politics, and public debate, the bloodless rhetorical conflict of a mature liberal democracy—for all its ugliness—is to be preferred to the blood-soaked streets of Munster. Liberal politics alone cannot provide a sufficient framework of cooperation for a society with deep moral disagreements. It is simply unreasonable to hope that elections and political debate will generate sufficient consensus to pursue all the collective goals that we might have.

Second, markets are a powerful alternative to politics for pursuing collective projects with those whom we might disagree violently with on moral, religious, or political issues. Albert Hirschman has observed that the preclassical theorists of the market saw commerce as harnessing people's interests to control their passions.[82] One can think of intense convictions as a kind of passion that pushes a believer toward extremes. Market participants, however, do not appeal to the passions, convictions, and deepest beliefs of those with whom they deal. Rather as Adam Smith observed, market actors "appeal only to their regard to their own interest."[83] In offering a means by which people cooperate with those whose beliefs they otherwise despise, markets provide powerful incentives to control the very forces that disturb the sleep of liberal theorists. One can see the effectiveness of this approach by considering the relative ease with which those who have sharply differing religious, political, and moral convictions work peacefully with one another as employees of a private corporation or contracting partners in a market exchange. The appeal to the interests proves far more powerful than an appeal to the rhetorical abstemiousness of public reason, and the institutions of market exchange in many ways provide a superior context for pluralistic cooperation to that offered by political institutions such as elections, legislations, or legally entrenched rights.

This is because markets require both more and less agreement than political forms of organization. Consider two different sets of explosions that illustrate the differences between political and commercial cooperation. The first occurred on the night of February 13, 1945.[84] At 10:13 P.M. British Lancaster bombers lumbered into the skies over Dresden and began dropping high explosives on the city. The bombs ripped the roofs off buildings, scattering wood and other flammable debris through the streets. A few minutes later, the first incendiary bombs began to fall. They ignited the kindling set by the earlier explosive bombs, and the hundreds of small fires rapidly merged. Within forty-five minutes, a gigantic column of fire consumed the center of the city. Eventually the fire created hurricane-force winds that pulled people and debris into the center of the expanding inferno. The next day, B-17 bombers from the U.S. Eighth Air Force hit the city, again setting massive fires. Twenty-five thousand German civilians were killed.

The second explosion occurred on October 30, 1994.[85] Since 1919, the Sears Merchandise Center stood on Roosevelt Boulevard in northeastern Philadelphia. It was one of the largest buildings in the city, and its clock tower and neogothic façade even managed to generate some local affection as a landmark. By the early 1990s, however, the building had come to the end of its life. A real estate development firm purchased the property and hired two companies to clear the site.[86] The demolition experts carefully wired the building with 12,000 pounds of high explosives, placed so that the building would implode on itself without damaging neighboring property. The demise of the building became a community event. A local newspaper sponsored a competition to raise money for a fund that helps the children of police officers killed in the line of duty, and Crystal Melody Lee, a 28-year-old booking agent, won the privilege of pressing the plunger that set off the explosives.[87] It was the largest private demolition in history.[88]

Both the destruction of the Sears Merchandise Center and the firebombing of Dresden were huge collective enterprises requiring thousands of people. They rested, however, on very different levels of moral agreement and responded in different ways to moral pluralism. On one level, the attack on Dresden required intense moral consensus. Marshalling the resources necessary to build planes and explosives and then deliver them across hundreds of miles of hostile airspace required national mobilization and international unity between Britain and the United States. In contrast, the destruction of the Sears Merchandise Center was less fraught. A few residents voiced wistful memories about the building to reporters, but there was no widespread opposition to its destruction.[89] Those involved in the intricate process of its demolition shared no strong sense of moral purpose. In short, the demolition of the Sears Merchandise Center lacked anything like the intense sense of moral purpose that lay behind the British and U.S. airmen who dropped bombs on Dresden.

The two efforts also responded in markedly different ways to moral disagreement. The destruction of Dresden resulted from the ideological rivalry between Nazism's totalitarian vision of racial purity and the Anglophone commitment to liberal institutions and a geopolitical order dominated by the North Atlantic democracies. In the end, this disagreement was mediated on a vast scale using fire and high explosives. In a less dramatic way, the unity within the U.S. and British war machines was also mediated by force. Despite widespread support for the war in the United

States after Pearl Harbor, the economic machine that produced the bombs and B-17s that destroyed Dresden was ordered by government fiat as wartime regulators took over large swaths of U.S. industry.[90] Likewise, draftees filled the militaries that dropped the bombs, and even volunteers found themselves subject to discipline where disobedience to orders could be met with lethal force.

Those who carried out the destruction of the Sears Merchandise Center had far less coercive capacity at their disposal to deal with moral disagreement. To be sure, had a local architectural heritage activist chained herself to the building in an attempt to stop its destruction, the owners could have employed the police to eject her. Well-functioning markets are not entirely devoid of coercion, which may be necessary to specify property rights, limit predation, and enforce contracts. However, equating such coercion with the kind of force at the disposal of the Allied powers that fire-bombed Dresden fails to appreciate a difference in scale so massive as to amount to a qualitative chasm. In contrast to the airmen and victims of the Dresden bombings, none of whom could defect from their assigned roles, all of the participants in the Sears Merchandise Center explosion had a relatively easy way of abstaining from the project. There was no need to fine, imprison, shoot, or fire-bomb those who did not wish to be involved in the demolition of the building.

Well-functioning markets thus have much to recommend them as a liberal institution. Economic interests provide a motive for cooperation that does not require intense moral consensus, and markets provide a context in which that cooperation can occur without the *Sturm und Drang* and widespread coercion that accompanies even democratic politics. As already noted, participation in well-functioning markets tends to breed moral habits. Among these is a disposition to put aside political, moral, or religious concerns when engaged in market transactions. This does not mean, of course, that decisions within the marketplace are unconnected with participants' broader moral visions. The person who buys local because of opposition to national corporations is combining moral deliberation and market exchange. It is difficult, however, for such moral concerns to dominate market exchange. An examination of politically motivated boycotts, perhaps the quintessential example of an attempt to structure market exchange around moral concerns, shows the limitations of such an approach.

Most boycotts are unsuccessful. In 1997, for example, the Southern Baptist Convention, concerned by Disney's gay-friendly corporate policies and its production of antireligious movies, called on the nation's 15 million Southern Baptists to boycott the company.[91] Superficially, the boycott looked threatening. Disney's core market consists of families with young children, and the Southern Baptist Convention claimed to command the attention of many such families. Yet after eight years, the Southern Baptist Convention quietly abandoned the boycott, insisting that its "voice had been heard."[92] Disney, however, reported that it had seen no discernible effect from the boycott and had not changed any of the policies that had motivated the Southern Baptist Convention to take action in 1997. In July 2012, gay rights activists called for a boycott of Chick-fil-A restaurants because the company's vice president supported groups opposed to same-sex marriage.[93] The boycott, however, was met with countercalls by religious conservatives to buy Chick-fil-A.[94] In the end, the company negotiated a settlement with gay rights activists, but this apparent victory for the boycott came only after Joe Moreno, a Chicago alderman, threatened the company with adverse government action.[95] In other words, it was the involvement of a government official that made the Chick-fil-A boycott successful.

Historically, the most successful boycotts have involved either government action or some other mechanism for overcoming the collective action problems that doomed the Southern Baptist Convention's attempts to pressure Disney.[96] During the years leading to the American Revolution, for example, opponents of British policy boycotted English merchants. They were successful in obtaining a repeal of objectionable laws, but maintaining the boycott required vigilante violence against merchants who continued to trade with Britain.[97] Likewise, divestment in South Africa by multinational corporations spurred the final collapse of Apartheid in that country, but such divestment was accompanied by congressional legislation punishing the Praetorian regime.[98] Even the iconic Montgomery bus boycott, which brought Martin Luther King Jr. to national prominence and marked the launch of the mass civil rights movement in the South, was not ultimately resolved by naked economic pressure. Rather, the bus company insisted that it was required to segregate by Alabama law, state prosecutors soon brought actions against Rosa Parks and King for violating various laws, and ultimate victory came for the boycotters when the Supreme Court declared de jure discrimination in interstate transportation unconstitutional.[99]

The political ineffectiveness of pure boycotts illustrates the power of well-functioning markets. For those who are eager to change the world by pressuring businesses, the difficulty of mounting a successful boycott is unfortunate. From a broader perspective, however, the robustness of market cooperation in the face of political, moral, and even religious disagreements is deeply heartening. We need not rely on the imperfect mechanisms of public reason and democratic institutions to generate cooperation in the face of moral pluralism. It is enough to offer the butcher and the baker one's patronage in return for food. As Jules Coleman has trenchantly observed:

> Markets maximize social interaction without individuals first being required to agree upon fundamental social values or to share a conception of the good or of the constitutive elements of the good life. The market is a particularly appropriate form of rational organization under certain sets of empirical circumstances, including heterogeneity of values, cultural diversity, geographic dispersion, and the like. In such communities markets contribute to social stability. That is their attraction to liberal political theory. In addition, to the extent that the preference for stability is itself rational in such communities, markets are a rational form of cooperation. Though based on the principles of individual rationality, the market is itself a way in which individuals give expression to a prior commitment to cooperate.[100]

To Coleman's assessment of the market, I would add that habitual involvement in the market breeds such a disposition to cooperate. Those who are socialized into the norms of a well-functioning market are likely to feel that there is something gauche about inquiring into the religious or moral beliefs of the supermarket cashier and refusing patronage on the basis of his or her answer. Likewise, people who habitually participate in the market are likely to find it entirely natural and unremarkable that they often buy and sell with those holding radically different conceptions of the ultimate good. Upon a moment's reflection, however, this rather blasé attitude toward market cooperation is remarkable in light of the violent confrontation to which such clashing moral beliefs give rise elsewhere. It is a thing to be cherished and supported.

Wealth

Some societies are rich and some are poor. In the United States, for example, the top income for households in the middle income range for 2009 was $61,801 per year.[101] In contrast, just over 81 percent of Madagascar's population subsisted on less than $1.25 per day in 2010.[102] In other words, a middle-income family in the United States had more than 135 times the income of most Malagasy. Such jaw-dropping statistics can be multiplied indefinitely by anyone who can access the World Bank's website.[103] The numbers have a human face. Economist William Easterly gives the example of nine-year-old Amaretch, an Ethiopian girl who rises each day at 3:00 A.M. to collect as much firewood as she can hold on her back before making the daylong trek into Addis Ababa to sell it, returning exhausted each night with some money to add to the family's coffers.[104] She told BBC reporters:

> I don't want to have to carry wood all my life. But at the moment I have no choice because we are so poor. All of us children carry wood to help our mother and father buy food for us. I would prefer to be able to just go to school and not have to worry about getting money.[105]

In contrast, even people at the bottom of the socioeconomic spectrum in the United States can expect, by Ethiopian standards, an extremely large income.[106]

Poverty has been the norm in human history. Determining such statistics is necessarily speculative, but the best estimates suggest that when Caesar Augustus ruled the Roman Empire, the average gross domestic product (GDP) per capita in Western Europe was $576, in 1990 dollars.[107] This meant that, in terms of material prosperity, the Roman Empire stood at roughly the same level as the West African country of Ghana, which, according to the International Monetary Fund, had a per capita GDP of $576 in 1993.[108] The Roman Empire was the world's economic bright spot in the year 1. World per capita GDP stood at just $467. The world remained poor for a very, very long time. A thousand years later, per capita world GDP had actually fallen to $450, and it only managed to inch up to $567 over the next five centuries.[109] Except for the increase associated with rises in population, as a global average there was very little economic growth from the time of the Caesars to the Battle of Waterloo. From 1500 to 1820, the rate of growth of global GDP per capita was an astonishingly small 0.04 percent.[110] Over the last few centuries, however, something unprecedented in human history has happened: sustained economic growth. Globally, from 1820 to 1992, the growth in per capita GDP has been 1.21 percent, a number that doesn't sound particularly impressive but which represents a thirtyfold increase over the rate of growth for the previous three centuries. Furthermore, because that number is a global average, it actually understates the magnitude of the material change that has happened in those countries that have achieved sustained economic growth.

It began gradually in England and the Netherlands. The Dutch had achieved modest growth by the end of the seventeenth century.[111] By the mid-eighteenth century, key technological breakthroughs—notably the steam engine and the spinning jenny—were made in Britain, but their full implementation was delayed by the chronic European warfare that culminated at Waterloo in 1815. By 1820, however, the economic revolution was in full swing. In 1820, per capita GDP in the United Kingdom was $1,756 in 1990 dollars. Within fifty years it doubled, doubling again by the outbreak of World War I.[112] During the nineteenth century, other North Atlantic countries, most notably the United States, began to follow Britain's example. Beginning in 1867, Japan also experienced massive economic growth, an example followed after World War II by other East Asian countries. The final result was the pattern of developed and undeveloped countries that we see today.

A huge and controversial literature examines how the West became rich and why some nations today enjoy such material abundance while others languish in extreme poverty. Geography, culture, and political institutions have all been offered as explanations.[113] Adjudicating these conflicting claims is beyond the scope of this book. Rather, I make the more modest claim that well-functioning markets are a necessary condition for the creation of sustained economic growth. This can be seen by considering one plausible alternative explanation for the economic success of the North Atlantic nations: the domination and exploitation of non-Western peoples by Europeans after 1492. The savagery of European expansion is undeniable. The appearance of Portuguese warships in the Indian Ocean in 1497, for example, marked the end of centuries of largely peaceful commerce, as Vasco De Gama engaged in systematic looting and extortion from present-day South Africa to India. Even more destructive was the conquest of the New World. In 1500, Mexico had a population of about 7.5 million and an estimated GDP of $3.1 billion in 1990 dollars.[114] After less than a century of Spanish conquest and domination, the population had fallen to 2.5 million and GDP was a mere $1.1 billion.[115] For all the human and economic destruction wrought in the New World, however, Spain reaped virtually no long-term economic benefit. The central goal of Spanish administration was to extract silver. The Spanish crown used this money to fight a series of expensive wars in Europe. Much of the New World silver ultimately found its way to China in exchange for luxury goods. That which remained in Europe caused inflation. Spain stagnated economically, and, for all its wealth, the Spanish crown became a serial debt defaulter. Tellingly, the economic big bang came not in the sixteenth century but in the nineteenth century.[116] To be sure, the nineteenth century was also an era of imperial expansion. The scramble for colonies, however, came in the second half of the century, after sustained economic growth was well under way. It also proved economically expensive, a luxury that could only be indulged in by wealthy powers rather than a path to riches for those who were upwardly mobile.[117]

The historical timing of sustained growth suggests that the process of market exchange itself was more powerful than conquest. One way of thinking about this is to look at the process of entrepreneurship.[118] Well-functioning markets created incentives for people to experiment and innovate because they provided customers for new ventures.[119] Entrepreneurs, in turn, created new goods and services in order to prosper in the market.[120] It is not simply that they delivered existing goods and services with marginally greater efficiency. Rather, entrepreneurship was a mechanism for discovering entirely new and better ways of living.[121] Thus, the telephone was not simply a more efficient version of the telegraph, which itself was far more than simply a marginally faster version of the letter. By providing a social space in which entrepreneurship thrived, the rise of well-functioning markets facilitated this discovery.[122]

Economists differ sharply on what can be done to improve the lot of poor nations. Jeffrey Sachs, for example, has argued that the end of global poverty lies within power of developed nations, which need only muster the will to devote sufficient resources to aid development.[123] William Easterly, in contrast, sounds a pessimistic note, arguing that aid has been prolific and ineffective, if not destructive.[124] Both agree, however, that well-functioning markets are key to economic growth. Sachs writes, "When the preconditions of basic infrastructure . . . and human capital . . . are in place, markets are powerful engines of development."[125] Easterly, in the midst of a biting critique of Western efforts to impose free markets in the former Soviet Union through top-down shock therapy, insists, "The free market *is* a universally useful system."[126] Both agree that markets alone cannot eliminate poverty.[127] Both insist, however, that markets are the drivers of sustained economic growth.[128]

One might acknowledge that markets are an effective mechanism for generating wealth but deny that wealth is morally desirable. For example, the New Testament declares that "it is easier for a camel to go through the eye of a needle than for a rich man to enter the kingdom of God,"[129] and ascetic moralists from the Buddha to Saint Francis of Assisi have insisted that riches, rather than being a path to happiness and enlightenment, are morally perverse. In more recent years, egalitarians responding to normative defenses of economic theories of law have insisted that wealth cannot be a moral value. Most famously, Ronald Dworkin insisted not only that wealth is not a value but that it cannot even be a component of value.[130] Dworkin's argument is worth considering more deeply because it is the most ambitious and sustained effort in contemporary legal theory to dismiss the normative value of wealth.

Dworkin's target was Richard Posner's idea of wealth maximization as a guiding norm for the law.[131] Dworkin's argument takes the form of two basic claims. The first is that a society in which resources are taken from A and given to B solely because B is willing to pay more for the resources cannot for that reason be deemed better.[132] Dworkin is attacking the idea that social wealth, measured in terms of willingness to pay, is itself a component of value.

> This position holds that if society changes so that there is more wealth then that change is in itself, at least *pro tanto,* an improvement in value, even if there is no other change that is also an improvement in value, and if the change is in other ways a fall in value.[133]

Dworkin was testing the idea that wealth is a value independent of its effect on anything else. He concludes that it cannot meet this exacting standard. His second claim is that if wealth is pursued as the sole normative criterion for law on instrumental grounds, then we cannot assume that maximizing wealth will necessarily lead to better social outcomes independent of wealth. After all, seeking to maximize wealth might result in a legal regime that creates perverse distributional outcomes that leave the poor worse off or have other morally undesirable outcomes.[134] Because of diminishing marginal utility to wealth, Dworkin even imagines that increasing the income of the wealthy might be morally sterile on utilitarian grounds.[135]

Dworkin's argument is either mistaken or beside the point. To take up the latter point first, Dworkin is mainly responding to a very strong claim about wealth maximization—namely, that legal institutions should be arranged so that resources are placed in the hands of those who are willing to pay the most for them and that this should be the exclusive normative goal of the law. This is an extreme position, and other than a few essays written by Richard Posner in the late 1970s, it is not clear that any legal theorist has ever espoused it.[136] In responding to this very strong claim, Dworkin sets up a dizzyingly demanding standard for a moral desideratum. He demands that to be a "value" something must be desirable "just in itself and apart from its costs or other good and bad consequences."[137] While it is certainly true that wealth fails to meet such a standard, the same is true of most other values. For example, a norm of social equality does not seem to satisfy this criterion. We may be able to discover an ultimate good valuable in and of itself without reference to anything else, but insisting on the discovery of such a philosophical lodestone before defending something as sufficiently desirable to warrant the attention of the law is absurd.

The more fundamental problem with Dworkin's argument, however, is that his critique of wealth pursued for instrumental reasons is historically and empirically impoverished. If we take him to be making only the claim that wealth maximization as a single master norm might be replaced by some more pluralistic attempt to advance other goals, then his point is well taken but banal. Dworkin, however, seems to be making a stronger claim—that we have no reason to suppose that the brute increase in social wealth will lead to other desirable outcomes. As he points out, it is certainly possible to imagine situations in which such increases in social wealth could be entirely captured by a small group in a way that would leave no one better off. This, however, is not a normatively significant point. Rather, the question is whether increases in social wealth have *actually* led to morally desirable outcomes with sufficient frequency across time and space to conclude that fostering the markets that make such wealth possible is a worthy goal for lawmakers. Stated in these terms, the case for markets and the wealth that they create is overwhelming.

Prosperity relieves material suffering. This can be seen most dramatically by looking at health and disease. Consider two diseases—malaria and AIDS—that have decimated sub-Saharan Africa, the world's poorest region. Malaria is caused by the *Plasmodium* parasite carried by *Anopheles* mosquitoes.[138] An infected person initially will have chills, fever, and vomiting. Eventually, the fever intensifies, resulting in coma and death. The World Health Organization estimates that, in 2010, there were 219 million cases of malaria worldwide. Yet despite the virulence and prevalence of the disease, "only" 660,000 died of malaria in 2010. Furthermore, these deaths were highly concentrated among children in sub-Saharan Africa. This is because malaria is easily prevented and fully treatable. *Anopheles* mosquitoes mainly bite at night. Sleeping under a cheap mosquito net prevents most infections. The disease is easily cured by quinine, a drug that can be cheaply manufactured either synthetically or from the bark of cinchona trees. In other words, the children claimed by malaria in Africa die because their societies lack the resources to deliver very low-cost drugs.[139]

AIDS in sub-Saharan Africa has been even more deadly. The disease is caused by a virus that attacks the immune system. The body is unable to fight off the pathogens that are constantly suppressed by a healthy person. About one in twenty adults in sub-Saharan Africa was infected with AIDS in 2012. A staggering 69 percent of the world's AIDS sufferers live in the region. Since its appearance three decades ago, AIDS has killed about 25 million people. The disease cannot be cured, but through a cocktail of antiviral drugs, its effects can be contained.[140] Generic manufacturers of the drugs can provide the treatment for as little as $1 per day.[141] In 2011, about 1.2 million adults and children in Africa died of AIDS.[142] As in the case of malaria, the problem is not medical but economic. Those with the disease and their societies lack the resources to deliver the antiviral drugs.[143]

Malaria and AIDS kill the poor because the poor do not have access to relatively cheap drugs. Health care requires material resources—resources that impoverished and disease-wracked countries such as Malawi lack. This, however, gets at only part of the necessity of wealth. International efforts to suppress malaria have garnered much success in the last decade. The disease kills about half the number that it killed as recently as 2005.[144] Quinine is a simple drug that has been used for more than a century. The antivirals that treat AIDS, however, cannot be distilled from tree bark. They require intense and expensive programs of research and development. All of this requires a massive commitment of resources to medical research. The basic research behind such drugs simply is not possible in a poor society, even if that society does have the ability to manufacture and deliver quinine.[145] The misery inflicted by AIDS and Malaria simply cannot be mitigated without wealth. The same is true of countless other diseases.

Wealth also tends to improve conditions for marginalized members of society. For example, women's access to formal legal rights closely correlates with a society's wealth. Most low-income countries restrict the ability of women to own land, and there are no countries with a per capita income above $20,000 per year that place any restrictions on property rights by women.[146] Likewise, low-income nations are far more likely to discriminate against women in child custody proceedings and under inheritance laws.[147] The benefits of increasing social wealth to women are not confined to formal legal rights. For example, econometric studies find that the execution of women as witches correlates strongly with poverty.[148] Similar correlations exist historically between economic growth and the increasing status of women. Economic growth in the United States and the United Kingdom, for example, produced first economic rights, such as the end of coventure, and then political rights, such as the ability to vote and hold public office.[149] In short, one of the best predictors for a society where women have low status and are poorly treated is poverty.

Perhaps counterintuitively wealth is often good for the natural environment. Wealthier countries seem to be more likely to protect endangered species and wildlife more generally. For example, Madagascar, Papua New Guinea, and Bangladesh—poor countries with relatively large coastlines—have all set aside less than 1 percent of their territorial waters as marine preserves.[150] Wealthy countries such as Germany, Australia, and the United States, in contrast, have set aside a significant portion of their territorial waters as natural reserves.[151] It is true that wealth tends to increase populations, and with them pollution. Likewise, those in wealthier societies engage in more economic activity, which often has a negative impact on the environment. The relationship between wealth and pollution, however, is complex. For example, middle-income countries tend to emit more carbon dioxide per capita unit of GDP than do low-income countries. In concrete terms, in 2009, low-income countries on average emitted 0.24 kilograms of carbon per $1 of GDP per capita. Middle-income countries emitted more than double that figure: 0.56 kilograms of carbon per $1 of GDP per capita. High-income countries, however, were more energy efficient. Those in the Organisation for Economic Co-operation and Development, a club for rich countries, averaged just 0.3 kilograms of carbon per $1 of GDP per capita, and countries in the European Union pushed the number to 0.23 kilograms, below the low-income country average.[152]

Despite greater energy efficiency, total carbon dioxide emissions increase with wealth. The same is not true, however, of other pollutants. In 1995, Gene M. Grossman and Alan B. Krueger looked at the connection between per capita GDP and air and water quality.[153] They found "no evidence that environmental quality deteriorates steadily with economic growth."[154] Rather, they discovered a series of inverted U-shaped graphs for a variety of pollutants—what became known as the environmental Kuznets curve.[155] Poor countries initially have low levels of pollution. As they develop, pollution rises, but at some point—estimated at roughly $8,000 of GDP per capita by Grossman and Krueger—pollution levels begin falling.[156] Subsequent research found a similar relationship between wealth and automotive lead emissions, automotive hydrocarbon emissions, toxic waste exposure, indoor air pollution, and various other air and water pollutants.[157] The precise mechanisms behind the environmental Kuznets curve are disputed. Pessimists insist that richer countries simply export their pollution overseas to less developed countries. However, over time, the height of the curve gets lower, which is inconsistent with this theory and suggests that, compared to the past, developing countries today are emitting fewer pollutants before reaching the point at which they become cleaner.[158] A more plausible explanation is that as societies become wealthier, the trade-off between pollution and growth shifts in favor of the environment, resulting in pressure for tighter regulatory standards. Interestingly, there is also evidence that firms embedded in competitive markets tend to become more efficient, polluting less. Hence, privately owned factories in China pollute significantly less than their state-owned counterparts.[159]

Examples of other morally desirable outcomes that are correlated with wealth could be multiplied endlessly.[160] Of course, well-functioning markets and the wealth that they produce, standing alone, are not sufficient to deliver health, increased political stability, better treatment of women and minorities, improved environmental conditions, or a host of other desirable outcomes correlated with wealth. Rather, my claim is that poverty makes everything worse. One needn't believe that wealth is a good in and of itself or even that it is a panacea for social ills to see that material prosperity makes the amelioration of many evils more tractable. Even if one believes in an aggressively redistributive state pursuing egalitarian economic outcomes, there still must be some economic surplus to take from the rich and give to the poor. Experience suggests that such surpluses are more likely to be generated by well-functioning markets than by any other means that humanity has been able to discover thus far. Furthermore, there are certain kinds of desirable goods—such as retroviral treatments for AIDS—that can only be developed by societies where massive wealth can be devoted to basic research and other long-term projects. If poverty makes everything worse, then wealth makes everything easier. In short, the wealth generated by commerce is morally desirable, because it is a necessary condition for much of what we find morally desirable in modern society. Given that basic truth, their ability to generate wealth provides a reason that well-functioning markets should be supported and extended.

CHAPTER FOUR

Contract Law, Efficiency, and Morality

This chapter forms a bridge between the normative defense of markets offered in the previous chapter and the discussion of legal doctrine in the remaining chapters. It presents arguments about the relationship between the market argument and the two dominant theoretical approaches to contract law theory: efficiency analysis and promissory or autonomy theories. Although I reject these approaches as currently formulated, both efficiency and deontological morality can support markets. It is in this role as market facilitators that they should be employed in the specification of contract law. The market can act as a theoretical fulcrum balancing the competing claims of both approaches. Neither is pursued for its own sake; each can be discarded as a criterion for contract law when it subverts or fails to support market exchange.

Markets, Efficiency, and Contract Law

In the market argument, markets are not valued for their efficiency. Rather, legal rules that create efficient incentives are to be desired because they promote markets. Markets facilitate peaceful cooperation and coexistence in a pluralistic society. Markets inculcate social habits that are important for the maintenance of liberal societies. They are not valuable in and of themselves, but they do deliver a bundle of moral goods of sufficient value to justify legal institutions such as contract that serve to strengthen and expand commerce.

Markets also generate wealth. To the extent that the idea of efficiency means something like the elimination of waste or the effective use of resources to generate wealth, then I have no quarrel with the claim that markets are efficient and should be valued for this reason. Markets more effectively order the production of goods and services than do rival systems of economic organization, and societies that turn over the bulk of production to markets will be wealthier than those societies that do not. As an empirical matter, wealthier societies exhibit a host of desirable features, and for that reason the generation of wealth is a legitimate goal—one that makes markets desirable and justifies a market-sustaining law of contracts.

When legal theorists use the term *efficiency*, however, they are not using it in the ordinary sense. Rather, efficiency is a term of art. Indeed, *efficient* can have three possible meanings: Pareto superiority, Pareto optimality, and Kaldor-Hicks efficiency. Ultimately, these ideas of efficiency do not provide powerful normative reasons for action. An allocation is Pareto optimal if we cannot reallocate resources to make any person better off without making at least one person worse off. On its own, Pareto optimality has no normative significance. If a heartless glutton steals food from a starving child, the allocation is Pareto optimal. The food cannot be returned to the child without making the glutton worse off. The world in which the glutton eats the stolen food has nothing to recommend it. Prohibiting improvements in the starving child's lot when it involves depriving the thieving glutton of his gains is perverse.

The other concepts of efficiency also fail as normative criteria. State of affairs A is Pareto superior to B if at least one person is made better off in A and no one is made worse off than in B. Initially, this seems attractive. We increase utility without troubling trade-offs between individuals.[1] The problem with Pareto superiority, however, is that it is impossible to satisfy. Every transaction makes someone worse off and so the conditions for Pareto superiority cannot be met.[2] Imagine a sociopath who enjoys the suffering of children. A starving child discovers forgotten pirate treasure that rescues her from destitution. Pareto superiority withholds approval from the child's good fortune because the sociopath, having lost the amusement of her suffering, is worse off. Even unobjectionable transactions, such as the purchase of a farmer's crop, could place upward pressure on the price of grain, thereby making other purchasers marginally worse off.[3]

Kaldor-Hicks efficiency relaxes the demands of Pareto superiority in a bid to be normatively useful. A is Kaldor-Hicks efficient to B if it is possible for those who are made better off by the shift from B to A to fully compensate those who are made worse off and still reap some benefit. A Kaldor-Hicks efficient shift is thus potentially Pareto superior, but compensation need not actually be paid. Hence, the discovery of lost treasure would be blessed by Kaldor-Hicks efficiency as long as the sociopath could be paid from the child's windfall enough to be indifferent to her good fortune. There is no need that the child actually pay the sociopath. It is sufficient that she be able to do so.

Unsurprisingly, law and economics generally invokes Kaldor-Hicks efficiency.[4] Equally unsurprising, Kaldor-Hicks efficiency has been criticized.[5] On one hand, some object to how Kaldor-Hicks efficiency trades off the welfare of one individual against another.[6] Of course, this is what makes it more tractable than Pareto superiority. By making such tradeoffs, however, Kaldor-Hicks efficiency, according to the argument, "fails to take seriously the difference between persons."[7] Kaldor-Hicks efficiency is also indifferent to distributive questions. The rich may take from the poor as long as the surplus in the resulting distribution is—in theory—sufficient to compensate the now further impoverished losers.[8] Obviously, distributive questions are important for egalitarians, but even those unmoved by the ideal of equality are not truly indifferent to such concerns. Suppose that a single individual, call him Scrooge, happened to value every resource just $1 more than every other member of society. It would thus be efficient for Scrooge to take resources from others until they had no resources at all. Not even someone comfortable with inegalitarian distribution would favor Scrooge getting everything and Tiny Tim (and everyone else) getting nothing. Kaldor-Hicks efficiency, however, cannot criticize this result.[9] Proponents of efficiency have sought to respond. Louis Kaplow and Steven Shavell argue that welfare should always trump concerns for fairness.[10] They note, however, that many people have a taste for fairness such that they prefer moderately egalitarian outcomes for others.[11] Such outcomes are blessed as increasing welfare.[12] Barak Medina and Eyal Zamir propose a modified version of the efficiency criterion.[13] Rather than focusing exclusively on maximizing welfare, we should subject it to the constraint of weak deontological rights.[14]

Efficiency, however, suffers from deeper problems. The concept of welfare employed by efficiency theorists is problematic.[15] Consider classical utilitarianism. According to Jeremy Bentham, utility consists of pleasure.[16] A moment's reflection reveals the difficulties inherent in Bentham's idea of welfare: How does one measure the magnitudes of pleasures and pain? Are all pleasures commensurable with all pains? And so on. Economics improves on Bentham by decoupling welfare from a particular psychological state. Rather, agents have a set of ordered preferences.[17] Welfare consists of their satisfaction. Rather than quantifying the pleasure that candy gives a child, we simply ask whether the child prefers candy to vegetables. If the answer is yes, then welfare increases when candy displaces vegetables on the dinner table. We need not even observe an agent's rank orderings in the abstract. We can infer them from observed choices. When the child eats candy rather than vegetables, we infer a preference for candy over vegetables. In place of Bentham's intractable quantification of pleasures and pain, we need only observe behavior.

This approach takes preferences as given. The more preferences that are satisfied, the greater the welfare. The greater the welfare, the more desirable a state of affairs. This approach removes our ability to arbitrate the moral desirability of particular preferences. Of course, not all preferences will be satisfied. When the satisfaction of the preferences violates the demands of Kaldor-Hicks efficiency, it is disallowed. It is not, however, disallowed because of any judgment as to the inherent worth of the preference. In theory, every preference is worthy of satisfaction regardless of its content. The only question is how the satisfaction of A's preferences are to be balanced against the satisfaction of B's preferences. The question remains, however, as to why one would want to treat preferences in this way.

Initially, this approach seems to appeal to the idea of liberty, because it respects "private" desires. Only when preferences place costs on others does the theory provide a basis for limiting their satisfaction. It also appeals to the idea of equality because all preferences are equally valued. The theory refuses to treat some preferences as higher or better because of their content. It thus endorses a kind of egalitarianism of desires. In both the argument from liberty and the argument from equality, the theory appeals—if only implicitly—by analogy to liberal institutions that allow citizens to pursue their personal visions of the good life as long as they respect the rights of others.[18]

The analogy, however, does not hold. Consider again the sociopath who enjoys the suffering of children. If we treat the content of preferences as irrelevant, we cannot condemn the sociopath's desires as perverse or immoral. Indeed, they are just as worthy of satisfaction as the starving child's desire for food. Suppose that, to indulge the sociopath's penchant for misery tourism, we confiscate a plane ticket from an aid worker and transfer it to the sociopath. Provided that the sociopath could compensate those harmed by the confiscation for their losses and still derive satisfaction from watching the miserable children, the transfer would be Kaldor-Hicks efficient. Yet a world in which sociopaths are indulged in their desire to enjoy the misery *is, for that reason,* a worse place. Efficiency, however, gives us no basis for making such a judgment.[19]

What, then, is left of the economic analysis of law as a normative matter? One response would be to simply reject it as a dead end. Such a root and branch rejection of efficiency analysis, however, is mistaken. Economic analysis ought to remain an important part of any normative discussion of contract law. As a positive matter, economic analysis is a corrective to the often undertheorized approach to the effect of legal rules taken by lawyers, judges, and scholars. Law creates incentives, and economics identifies assumptions about how agents respond to incentives and rigorously works out their consequences. Positive analysis, however, is distinct from normative analysis. One may subscribe to positive economic analysis without regarding efficiency as normatively desirable. Likewise, one may reject the positive theory favored in the economic analysis of law while still subscribing to some version of welfare maximization.[20] In the market argument, efficiency is instrumentally useful in designing legal rules that extend and strengthen market activity in society. All things being equal, we want an efficient law of contracts because it would better fulfill its purpose of supporting the market. This is a normative rather than a positive use of economic theory, but one that does not treat efficiency as a moral good.

According to Ronald Coase, in a world of zero transaction costs, parties can always bargain to an efficient allocation of resources ex post regardless of the initial allocation ex ante.[21] Coase's primary concern was the problem of externalities.[22] When a firm bears all its own costs, it acts only when the benefits exceed the costs. If, however, its activity imposes costs on others—as when, for example, a factory pollutes the air—its incentives are skewed, and the firm will act even when the costs exceed the benefits. Until Coase, the orthodox solution to this problem was to impose a tax on the business equal to the costs that its pollution imposes on others.[23] However, if the victims of pollution can bargain with the business, no such tax is necessary. The victims will pay a sum of money greater than the benefit that the firm gets from polluting to induce the firm to stop. The only thing that keeps such an outcome from occurring in the real world is the cost of dispersed victims bargaining with the firm. Coase's insight can be coupled with the thought of Adam Smith to understand the role of efficiency in the market argument.

In chapter 3 of *The Wealth of Nations*, Adam Smith observed that "the division of labor is limited by the extent of the market."[24] Normally, Smith's insight is couched in terms of productivity. He gave the example of a pin factory where workers, by specializing in a single stage of pin production, could combine to produce vastly more pins than the sum of their individual outputs.[25] Specialization, however, is far more than a method of more efficient production. Rather, specialization is the precondition for trade itself. Smith gives the example of those living in remote areas. "In the lone houses and very small villages which are scattered about in so desert a country as the Highlands of Scotland," he writes, "every farmer must be a butcher, baker and brewer for his own family."[26] He continues:

> In such situations we can scarce expect to find even a smith, a carpenter, or a mason, within less than twenty miles of another of the same trade. The scattered families that live at eight or ten miles distant from the nearest of them, must learn to perform themselves a great number of little pieces of work, for which, in more populous countries, they would call in the assistance of those workmen.[27]

In the absence of specialization, autarky reigns. The householder of the Highlands produces everything himself. In short, he does not participate in the market.[28]

On the other hand, as transportation costs fall, trade increases and, with it, the extent of the market. Smith writes:

> What goods could bear the expense of land-carriage between London and Calcutta? Or if there were any so precious as to be able to support this expense, with what safety could they be transported through the territories of so many barbarous nations? Those two cities, however, at present carry on a very considerable commerce with each other, and by mutually affording a market, give a good deal of encouragement to each other's industry.[29]

Seashore communities face lower transaction costs in the form of cheap seaborne trade and enjoy the benefits of more extended markets. "It is natural that the first improvements of art and industry should be made where this conveniency opens the whole world for a market to the produce of every sort of labour."[30]

Distance is not the only transaction cost. Legal rules can also create inefficient incentives, thereby raising transaction costs, or they can reduce transaction costs, thereby increasing the scope of market activity.[31] Coase's insight was that it was possible in theory for parties to bargain around a legal regime that inefficiently allocated some resource. Bargaining around an inefficient rule, however, is not costless. It is itself a transaction cost. Hence, even in an environment in which transaction costs are otherwise low, a legal system filled with inefficient rules will increase transaction costs and thereby constrict the scope of market activity.

The market argument thus condemns inefficiency to the extent that it limits the scope of market activity. There are, however, cases in which the inverse is true. Sometimes a commitment to market processes will be inefficient. Imagine the transfer of an asset from A to B that is Kaldor-Hicks efficient. In theory, A and B could enter into a market exchange for the asset, but conducting such an exchange would be costly. It could well be less expensive to forcibly transfer the asset from A to B. Such a transfer would generate the benefits of a Kaldor-Hicks improvement *and* avoid a costly market exchange. Something like this logic is behind the use of eminent domain power to assemble property for economic development.[32] If one believes that the cost of government error is less than the cost of requiring market processes, then efficiency analysis would bless the transaction. The market perspective, however, condemns such a forced transfer *even if it is efficient*, because it replaces the morally desirable market process with the at-best morally sterile act of forced transfer. The bare fact that such a transfer might be Kaldor-Hicks efficient gives us no reason for employing the law to force it.

Consider two efficiency arguments about specific legal doctrines. The first is the doctrine of an easement by necessity.[33] Suppose that A owns Blackacre, a piece of property abutting a public road. A divides Blackacre into two lots and sells the back 40, which does not abut the road, to B. The bargain and the resulting conveyance leaves the new lot—formerly the back 40 of Blackacre—stranded without access to the public road. In this case, courts will give to B an access easement over A's property, even when no such easement was part of the original bargain.[34] This is often done on the fictitious grounds that the parties intended to do so, but there is no reason to suppose this is true, and courts do not require evidence of intent.[35] It is sufficient that such an easement is "necessary" for B's use of the land.[36] It is simply a forced transfer of a property interest "to allocate rights to their highest valuing users, thereby overcoming the need for strategic bargaining."[37]

Replacing market transactions with a forced transfer in this case makes sense if one considers efficiency a normative goal. Market exchange is desirable if it leads to efficient allocations, but if commerce fails to deliver efficient results, then exchange should be replaced by forced transfers. If, however, one is skeptical of the normative credentials of efficiency, then the case for jettisoning exchange is weaker. Markets have a normative value independent of their role as efficient allocators of resources—a value that is lost when the process of exchange is ruthlessly suppressed in the name of Kaldor-Hicks efficiency.

In these cases, the law short-circuits market exchange between the right holder and the initial property holder. An involuntary transaction rather than exchange achieves the desired efficient allocation of resources. The opposite rule, however, need not always be inefficient. In many of these situations, we have what economists call a bilateral monopoly. The right held by A has only one purchaser, B, and the right desired by B can be had from only one seller, A.[38] Bilateral monopolies, however, do not create insurmountable barriers to transacting. Neighbors routinely contract to buy and sell abutting property precisely because it is abutting, or they purchase access easements across one another's land. Yet such negotiations in theory face a bilateral monopoly problem. If we refuse to displace market activity with a forced transfer, parties would face the costs of bargaining, but, as suggested in the previous chapter, this may be a benefit rather than a loss. Market activity is not an unfortunate transaction cost. Rather, it is a positive source of moral goods, such as liberalism sustaining moral habits.

Consider the case of *Voss v. Brown*,[39] decided by the Washington Supreme Court in 1986. Brown acquired a parcel of land adjacent to Voss's land.[40] In the purchase, Brown acquired an access easement across Voss's property, bargaining despite the bilateral monopoly in the market for the easement.[41] Brown then acquired a second parcel of property adjacent to his first parcel but not adjacent to Voss's parcel.[42] Brown began using the easement across Voss's property to conduct improvements on his second parcel, a clear violation of the original deed.[43] When Voss sought an injunction to enforce his right under the grant, however, the Washington Supreme Court refused, in effect expanding Brown's easement at Voss's expense.[44]

The decision is easy to justify on economic grounds. According to the court, the expansion of Brown's easement placed only a de minimis burden on Voss. Without access to Voss's property, however, Brown's second parcel would be worth substantially less. Accordingly, the de facto transfer of property from Voss to Brown, while leaving Voss worse off, was Kaldor-Hicks efficient. Research into the lawsuit, however, reveals a relationship rife with the kinds of pathologies that market exchange can mitigate.[45] The wrangle over the implied easement poisoned the relationship between the neighbors. The owner of the dominant estate refused to discuss his use of his neighbor's property, running construction equipment over the land without his neighbor's consent.[46] For his part, the owner of the serviant estate physically blocked the disputed easement, halting all work on his neighbor's new house.[47] Years later, bitterness over the litigation continued to rankle both parties.[48] Good walls make for good neighbors, but, not surprisingly, the forced transfer of property does not.[49]

Now consider a second kind of efficiency argument. Contracts for the sale of goods frequently involve some period of time between the making of the contract and the buyer obtaining possession of the goods.[50] Often the goods must be transported from the seller to the buyer. Mishaps frequently occur between contract and final delivery. If the warehouse where the goods are stored burns, who bears the loss? What if the ship carrying the goods sinks? May the buyer sue the seller for breach of contract, or are the sunken goods the buyer's problem? The parties to the contract are, of course, free to draft provisions answering these questions, but often they don't, and the law must fill the gap.[51] Traditionally, the law answered these questions by asking whether title to the goods had passed to the buyer.[52] If title had passed, the buyer bore the loss. If not, then the seller bore the loss. As a result, allocation of the risk of loss could turn on such apparently unrelated questions as whether the seller had received a check from the buyer for the goods.[53] The Uniform Commercial Code replaced the search for the passage of title with specific rules. The risk of loss stays with the buyer as long as the goods are in her possession.[54] A complicated set of rules governs cases of loss when the goods are lost while being transported by a carrier.[55] When goods are held by a bailee, the risk of loss passes when the bailee acknowledges "the buyer's right to possession of the goods."[56] In all these cases, the risk of loss lies with the party that can most easily exercise control over the goods, or—alternatively—the risk of loss passes when the buyer acquires the ability to mitigate against the risk of the goods' loss.[57]

Assigning the risk of loss to the party that controls the risk most cheaply is economically efficient. If we assume that most parties are economically rational, then left to their own devices they would likely assign the risk to the party that can bear it at the lowest cost. Relatively few parties, therefore, will object to the allocation of risk supplied by the default rule. Of course, those that do object are free to contract around the rule, negotiating to a different result. By efficiently allocating the risk, however, the rule eliminates the need for investment in such negotiations—an investment that represents a loss from an efficiency perspective. In so doing, it encourages exchange rather than short-circuiting it, however, because it does not require the forced transfer of a valuable right.

The economic analysis of law conceptualizes the cost of bargaining as a waste of resources to be eliminated whenever possible. Taken to its logical extreme, such a stance is deeply hostile to market processes. In theory, a central planner with sufficient information about resources and preferences could allocate all goods and services efficiently without wasting any effort on the messy process of market exchange. On my view, however, the cost of market processes is not a waste. Indeed, much of the social benefit from markets emerges from the process of bargaining and exchange. In the process of give and take and the exchanging of *quid* for *quo,* those with differing beliefs learn to trust and understand one another. When this "wasteful" process is short-circuited by legal fiat, these benefits are lost. Nevertheless, rules that reduce transaction costs *without eliminating the element of exchange* have much to recommend them from a market perspective. Such rules increase the overall scope of market transactions.

Markets, Morality, and Contract Law

The other main approaches to contract are moral, autonomy, or promissory theories.[58] They posit that contract law reflects the duty to keep a promise or the social imperative to recognize the autonomous choices of contracting parties. The relationship between these moral theories and the market argument mirrors the approach to economic efficiency. According to the market argument, contract law should be organized around deontological morality not for its own sake, but to the extent that doing so fosters a morality that supports market exchange. Ultimately, promissory morality is too thin to either justify or specify contract law. Nevertheless, something like the moral stance behind such theories tends to support market exchange, and for that reason it can inform contract law.

In the market argument, the moral basis of contract is mediated through the practice of market exchange. Autonomy or moral theories of contract tend to be unmediated. They posit a relatively tight connection between moral obligations on one hand and legal obligations on the other. A generation ago, for example, Charles Fried argued that promise is the moral foundation of contract law.[59] He did not argue that contract law was tangentially related to promising or that it indirectly supported promissory morality. Rather, he argued that contract law was a legal reflection of promissory morality. The obligation to keep a contract was simply the legal embodiment of the moral obligation to keep a promise.[60] Indeed, for some theorists, the connection between moral ideas and the language of contract doctrine is so palpable that any theory that fails to explain this congruence is for that reason defective.[61]

This reflective approach, however, is mistaken. It raises two problems for contract law theory. The first is normative, and the second is doctrinal. The normative problem is justifying why these particular obligations should be treated not only as moral obligations but also as legal obligations. Often moral obligations are, in the terminology of natural law theory, imperfect. They are morally but not legally obligatory. The doctrinal problem arises when one tries to translate moral obligations into concrete legal rules. Contract law of necessity must resolve innumerable concrete disputes between contracting parties. In many cases, it is by no means clear that the moral principles that contract law supposedly reflects provide any guidance that is sufficiently concrete to resolve actual legal disputes.

Consider first the normative objection. Why should the law seek to enforce moral obligations at all? This objection can take a strong form or a weak form. The strong form rests on the distinction within liberal philosophy between the right and the good. According to this view, liberal societies begin with the brute fact of moral pluralism. The law should be morally neutral, allowing each citizen to decide for him- or herself questions of personal morality and pursue his or her own vision of the good. The law should confine itself to protecting individual rights independent of ideas about the good. According to the strong objection, for example, promissory morality is a matter of personal virtue and cannot be a legitimate legal concern.[62] This does not mean, of course, that contract law is illegitimate, only that it cannot be legitimately defended as enforcing the moral obligation to keep a promise.

Rather than claiming that there is some clearly defined realm of moral demands—the good—that cannot be made legal rules, the weaker version of the objection points out that not all moral obligations are legal obligations. This is true even in legal systems that have no liberal scruples about enforcing morality. For example, under classical Islamic law, there is no sharp distinction between religion and the state. Rather, the Qua'ran equates moral and legal obligation, saying to the faithful, "You are the best nation ever brought forth to men, bidding to honour, and forbidding dishonour, and believing in God."[63] Notice the assumption that the community may forbid wrongful behavior—"dishonour." Even so, Islamic legal theorists have a fivefold categorization of actions: those that are forbidden, those that are discouraged, those that are indifferent, those that are encouraged, and those that are required. Hence, even in the view of the classical sharia, there are moral obligations that are not also coercible legal obligations. Indeed, no one believes that all moral obligations should become legal obligations. One must at least explain why promissory moral obligations should also be legal obligations. Merely demonstrating that there is a moral duty to keep a promise does not demonstrate that there should be a corresponding legal obligation, even if one does not subscribe to a sharp distinction between the right and the good.

Some promissory theorists seek to answer this question. Fried's response is to insist that promises are a matter of the right rather than the good. Promise breaking is a breach of trust, an abuse of another person.[64] This claim, however, does not stand up to closer scrutiny. First, there are abuses of trust that are not legally prohibited, even though they are often more wrenching than a breach of contract. Consider, for example, the person who discovers that her romantic partner has been cheating. While such action might be a grounds for divorce—and thus legal action—for a married couple, for an unmarried couple, there is no legal wrong. Second, not all broken promises violate trust. Consider the habitual promise breaker who is not trusted. It would be odd to say that such a person breaches no moral obligation when, as expected, he breaks his promise. This suggests, however, that the wrong of promise breaking does not lie in the abuse of trust.

The promissory theory of contract also cannot account for universal and unavoidable features of contract law. Under the promissory theory, contractual obligations reflect the self-imposed moral obligations of promises. As Richard Craswell has pointed out, however, only a relatively small portion of contract law doctrine can be plausibly linked to the content of promises.

> Philosophical theories . . .—including the one endorsed by Fried—have no . . . implications for the content of the law's background rules. These theories ground the enforceability of promises on considerations of individual freedom and autonomy, or on the principle of fidelity to one's prior statements or

> commitments. In a nutshell, the fidelity principle is consistent with any set of background rules because those rules merely fill out the details of what it is a person has to remain faithful to, or what a person's prior commitment is deemed to be. Thus, while fidelity may dictate that a promisor must live up to the obligations described by any set of background rules that the law has adopted, it cannot guide the legal system in deciding which background rules to adopt in the first place.[65]

For example, the social conventions that govern promise making might more or less mirror the rules of contract formation. Likewise, doctrines surrounding breach might reflect promissory morality. Repudiation of a contract might reflect norms around promise breaking. Similarly, interpretation of a contract might focus on intended meaning because it tracks the self-imposed obligations of the promisors.

However, much of contract doctrine cannot reflect promissory morality. Morality tells us to keep our promises. Contractual disputes, however, often arise in cases where the agreement is silent. In the face of gaps, the law must of necessity step in, if only with a rule stating that there is no contract. The Uniform Commercial Code, for example, stands ready with rules governing price, delivery, order of performance, and other matters when the contract is silent.[66] Promise keeping, however, provides no guidance in such cases. Other normative concerns must specify the law's substance.

Moral practices such as promise keeping are still important to the market argument. Markets have not only moral effects but moral causes. In *The Protestant Ethic and the Spirit of Capitalism*, Max Weber argued that modern markets resulted from moral beliefs with origins in Calvinism.[67] According to Weber, capitalism requires a combination of hardheaded materialism and otherworldly self-denial. The capitalist cares about accumulating wealth. On the other hand, he must delay consumption and invest capital to generate additional wealth. Catholicism's ascetic tradition celebrated the renunciation of consumption without material accumulation, and a competing tradition tolerated the consumption of the laity without infusing an urge toward accumulation. When Calvinism infused commercial pursuits with the moral force of a religious calling and made the puritanical accumulation of wealth a mark of divine grace, it offered the spiritual prerequisite for capitalism. Or so said Weber.

Weber's thesis has been subject to extensive criticism.[68] While modern capitalism first emerged in Protestant England and Holland, within Weber's Germany, it is difficult to find any evidence of systematic economic differences between Protestant and Catholic regions.[69] Likewise, economists question Weber's implicit assumption that capital accumulation is decisive to economic growth, focusing instead on institutions, technological discoveries, and entrepreneurial innovation.[70] This does not mean that modern theorists have given up on a causal relationship between moral beliefs and well-functioning markets, but there are reasons to treat such theories with suspicion.

First, the cultural explanations for economic outcomes can be an intellectual deus ex machina. For example, the underlying cultures of North Korea and South Korea, East and West Germany during the Cold War, and either side of the city of Nogales, which straddles the United States–Mexico border, do not differ greatly.[71] The wide divergence of economic outcome in each dyad, however, suggests that poor institutions explain relative levels of poverty.[72] On the other hand, when culture does seem economically decisive, we then must explain why places develop one culture rather than another. Culture simply relabels the question. Second, moral beliefs as an explanation for market outcomes creates the danger of assuming that the poor are poor because they are morally inferior while the rich are rich because they are morally superior. Such an assumption flirts with discredited defenses of imperialism that justified Western domination of other societies because Western material superiority was evidence of moral superiority.[73]

Being cautious of moral explanations, however, should not keep us from asking what beliefs best support markets. This is a question of social practice, not moral truth. Moral beliefs—like formal legal rules and informal social practices—affect people's behavior.[74] Just as a regime of property rights may create better incentives for well-functioning markets, we can also ask what kinds of moral beliefs best support commerce.[75] For moral critics of the market, commerce necessarily reduces human relations to what Thomas Carlyle called the cash nexus, extinguishing fellow feeling and social obligation.[76] Without such a narrow morality, commercial society is impossible. Such is the shame of markets, say these critics. For some defenders of the market, however, the narrow, personal wealth maximizer is the hero. She is *homo economicus*, whose decisions will be led by the invisible hand of the market to efficient outcomes. Indeed, when people pursue wider moral agendas in the market, they threaten its beneficent order.[77]

The irony is that markets are a response to the dependence of humans that in turn deepen their interdependence. Societies in which well-functioning markets thrive are not filled with monomaniacal wealth maximizers. Likewise, places filled with rugged individuals bereft of fellow feeling are not, generally speaking, particularly prosperous. Indeed, in societies where moral beliefs seem to closely approximate homo economicus, we do not observe well-functioning markets.

Edward Banfield's famous study of social life in southern Italy provides a classic illustration.[78] Banfield claimed that an ethos he called "amoral familialism" dominated moral life in southern Italy.[79] In the small Sicilian town that he studied, Banfield found loyalty toward family members but narrowly self-interested relations with non-family members. People were constrained only to the extent that they were directly monitored. When monitoring failed, people opportunistically maximized outcomes for themselves and their families. To be sure, the disciple of amoral familialism is not identical to homo economicus. Unlike *homo economicus*, he has a striking loyalty to kin. In interactions with strangers, however, amoral familialism seems to produce behavior that looks very similar to unrestrained individualism and wealth maximization.

The result was the widespread poverty Banfield observed.[80] Southern Italy was not bustling with markets where the invisible hand guided narrowly self-interested actors. Rather, narrow self-interest led to endemic distrust and chronic economic backwardness.[81] Banfield's student Robert Putnam contrasted the economic outcomes in southern Italy with the prosperous and commercially successful north of the country.[82] In place of amoral familialism, Putnam found a society with high levels of trust and cooperation. Rather than taking every opportunity to maximize personal wealth, people willingly abstained from opportunistic behavior.[83] Crucially, according to Putnam, the differences were social rather than institutional, because under the highly uniform legal structure imposed by Rome, northern and southern Italy have identical legal and political systems.[84]

Well-functioning markets require that agents rely on the future actions of others. There is, however, a distinction between trust and mere assurance.[85] Assurance is the confidence I have in your future behavior based on my assessment of your response to external incentives. Suppose I know that you will behave as *homo economicus,* and we have made a contract. I also know, however, that in the event of breach you will have to pay me a sum equal to the costs that your breach imposes on me. In this case, I have the assurance of your performance as long as the cost of performance is less than my costs in the event of breach. My expectations of your future behavior, however, do not arise because I trust in your fidelity.

The crucial difference between trust and assurance is that trust provides me with confidence in your future performance even when you face no external sanctions. Although trust may sound rather ethereal to those who insist on a hardheaded cynicism about human behavior, it is essential to the functioning of a complex, modern market.[86] There are severe limits on the law's ability to monitor and punish malfeasance.[87] Some misbehaviors are difficult to observe, the machinery of the law is expensive to employ, and often bad actors are judgment-proof. These problems become more acute as markets become more complex and extensive. Complexity increases the difficulty of monitoring behavior, particularly in cases involving specialized expertise where nonexperts may find it difficult to understand what specialized workers are doing, let alone spot subtle forms of opportunism.[88] In these situations, the assurance provided by merely institutional constraints is insufficient. We need genuine trust, the kind of trust that comes from the knowledge that others have an internal motivation to avoid opportunistic behavior. For example, development economists have argued that pervasive, small-scale corruption in firms and government acts as a drag on economic growth in many societies. Well-functioning markets die of a thousand cuts, or never emerge to begin with.

The economist David Rose has made this point in terms of what he calls "golden opportunities."[89] These are situations in which one faces a positive payoff from behaving opportunistically and there is zero possibility of detection. In such cases, institutional incentives by definition will fail, because the formal and informal mechanisms that sanction bad actions will not be able to identify bad actors. As markets become more extensive and the firms operating within those markets become larger, golden opportunities become more numerous.[90] This is because in the highly specialized niches that proliferate in well-functioning markets, those tasked with monitoring will frequently lack the specialized knowledge necessary to identify subtle forms of shirking and advantage taking. Yet without specialization and the decentralization of information, highly developed markets are not possible.

The solution is a set of moral beliefs that discourage dishonesty even when the chances of detection are zero.[91] Without such beliefs, there will not be sufficient trust to maintain markets based on specialization and dispersed knowledge. Tellingly, Rose insists that being morally earnest and generally kind is insufficient. Experimental evidence and evolutionary theory suggest that humans evolved to thrive in relatively small groups.[92] Accordingly, humans seem hardwired with instinctive moral responses facilitating cooperation in small groups. We treat members of our own tribe with empathy and concern. We feel guilt about taking advantage of those with whom we have close ties. People who lack these basic moral responses are sociopaths.[93] We find their lack of ordinary moral inhibitions shocking and abhorrent in part because such absences are so rare.[94]

Unfortunately, small-group morality cannot sustain well-functioning markets. There are at least three problems. The first is the limits of empathy.[95] Most people feel guilt when they harm identifiable individuals. On the other hand, when our empathic instincts lack a clear victim, opportunism generates far less guilt. A person who wouldn't steal even a small sum of money from a neighbor might well embezzle a thousand dollars from a large corporation, precisely because, in the case of the corporation, there is no particular individual who is harmed. Rose calls the second problem the "greater good rationalization problem."[96] Suppose that I am faced with a golden opportunity in which only a faceless corporation will bear the costs of my opportunism. I might take advantage of the situation not to enrich myself but rather to do some moral good, such as feeding starving children or funding the fight against injustice. My noble motives, however, produce actions that have many of the same effects as opportunism. Indeed, someone with a highly developed sense of empathy could be *for that reason* less trustworthy in the context of a highly developed market. Finally, there is the human propensity to distinguish between people who are in-group and people who are out-group.[97] We are more likely to avoid opportunism toward those whom we identify as fellow tribe members. Again, this seems to be a hardwired moral propensity, another legacy of our small-group evolutionary origins.

What kind of morality would support markets? First, we need to be relatively indifferent to the tribal identity of the party with whom we contract. Markets do not require anything so morally ambitious as universal fraternity. One can maintain tribal identities and still participate in markets. The trust on which markets depend, however, requires that the obligations flowing out of exchanges not vary according to the in-group or out-group status of counterparties. Second, market participants must feel that their obligations are matters of duty rather than resting on calculations of harm or empathy.[98] Without separating one's sense of moral obligation from one's sense of empathy for an identifiable victim, the highly distributed and impersonal exchange of well-functioning markets will be difficult to maintain. The complex and dispersed nature of markets will create too many opportunities for advantage taking that lack a clearly identifiable victim. Finally, the obligations on which exchange depends cannot be traded off against some greater good that is more tightly bound to our natural sense of empathy.[99] This is because such nobly motivated actions are functionally identical to crass opportunism when it comes to generating trust among market participants. These do not seem to be a natural set of moral responses. Well-functioning markets can place demands on our moral behavior that run counter to intuitions bequeathed to our species by evolution. The moral beliefs demanded by markets seem rather cold and formalistic. Their virtue lies in their ability to support commercial trustworthiness. It is the moral goods of the market—including the effects of market exchange on our other moral habits—that provides an indirect justification for such moral responses.

Initially, looking to the moral preconditions of commerce seems disconnected from the market argument. In the tradition of Max Weber, an account that assigns to moral beliefs pride of place in explaining the trust required by markets is cultural rather than institutional. It is a matter of endogenous preferences rather than exogenous incentives. Law, on the other hand, is perhaps the quintessential example of an incentive-creating institution. An aggressive cultural account might insist that law is largely epiphenomenal. It is at best a reflection of the underlying moral beliefs that are doing all the real work in strengthening and extending the reach of market activity.

There is, however, no logical requirement that cultural explanations exclude institutional explanations. Necessity does not imply sufficiency. More importantly, however, institutions interact with culture, supporting and undermining particular moral beliefs. Law can have an impact on moral beliefs and behavior. Contract law must attend to the moral beliefs that make well-functioning markets possible. The link between trust, moral beliefs, and markets has two important implications for contract law. First, where the morality supporting markets exists, contract law should not undermine that morality. Second, to the extent that it can, contract law should seek to foster the moral beliefs that make markets possible. For example, the law of contracts should enforce promises made in furtherance of commerce in part because doing so will tend to reinforce the moral practice of commercial promise keeping. Likewise, the law should not relieve a party of her obligations under a contract in order to allow the promisor to serve some higher moral purpose, because doing so will tend to undermine the rigid morality of fidelity that tends to support commerce. In such situations, contract law should attend to morality not because it enforces moral obligations, but because it should seek to foster moral practices that support markets.

Because efficiency theories are essentially consequentialist, judging legal rules based on their effects, most legal theorists see them as incommensurable with moral theories that judge legal rules primarily on their correspondence to moral obligations rather than on their effects. Efficiency analysis, we are told, takes an ex ante moral perspective, while promissory and other moral theories of contract take an ex post perspective. Hence, much of the theoretical argument over contract law has taken the form of partisans of one approach or the other defending their preferred normative criterion against attacks.[100] Others have sought to create a pluralistic theory of contract.[101] According to this approach, efficiency and morality are either theories of different things or there is some principle that allows us to rank order them such that we can prefer one approach or the other when they conflict. The market argument is thus a pluralistic theory of contract that seeks to reconcile both efficiency and deontological morality into a single theory. It does not, however, adopt the so-called vertical integration strategy, hierarchically arranging one value above the other.[102] Rather, it sees contract law in terms of supporting a particular morally valuable social practice—namely, market exchange. It then employs both efficiency reasoning and moral reasoning when doing so supports markets, discarding both when they erode contract law's ability to support commerce.

PART II

Part 1 contained the basic normative framework for the market argument offered in this book. I provided a definition of well-functioning markets and argued that they inculcate virtues that support a liberal society and provide a framework for productive cooperation in the face of deep moral, religious, or political disagreements. Finally, I argued that markets should be valued because of the material prosperity that they can generate and the ameliorative effect that prosperity has on a host of social evils. In part 2, we pivot from these highly abstract arguments to specific questions of contract law. My goal is to demonstrate that the market argument has the critical power to generate concrete suggestions on the particulars of legal doctrine. Without such a demonstration, the argument cannot claim to be a theory of contract law in any legally meaningful sense. Of necessity this means that the discussion will become rather more technical. We will examine some of the great set-piece debates in contract law theory, such as the doctrine of consideration, the structure of remedies, and the proper approach to boilerplate agreements. Finally, a discussion of the limits of the market argument considers the ways in which commerce can become pathological. Such pathological markets ought to define the boundaries of contract law. The application of the market argument to concrete legal questions reveals the way that it reorients our thinking about contract law away from questions of individual consent and toward the social process of commerce and the character of the markets that contract law supports.

CHAPTER FIVE

Consideration

The *Restatement (Second) of Contracts* defines a contract as a "promise that the law will enforce or whose performance the law otherwise recognizes as a duty."[1] Some philosophers have denied that contracts are necessarily a species of promises, but provided that we are willing to substitute a term like *agreement* or *commitment* for *promise*, virtually all theorists would agree that contracts are legally enforceable commitments of some kind.[2] As E. Allen Farnsworth has observed, however, "No legal system has ever been reckless enough to make all promises enforceable."[3] As a threshold matter, then, any system of contract law must answer the question of what sorts of commitments the law will enforce. The answers that have been given to that question have varied from promises accompanied by the ritual dismemberment of an animal to written commitments sealed with wax.[4] The modern common law has fixed on the doctrine of consideration as its primary answer. For a promise to become a contract, it must be supported by consideration. "To constitute consideration," according to the Second Restatement, "a performance or a return promise must be bargained for."[5] To use an older formulation, "any benefit conferred by the promisee on the promisor, or any detriment incurred by the promisee, may be a consideration."[6] In other words, contracts consist of promises made as part of a quid pro quo. The law enforces promises that have been bargained for but not those that are a mere *nudum pactum*.

The doctrine of consideration has not been popular among legal theorists. As a doctrinal matter, it has created a host of problems, most notably in the context of contract modifications and gratuitous promises that seem difficult to distinguish in any meaningful way from bargained-for promises. As a theoretical matter, bargain as a concept seems to lack the normative power to justify the legal enforcement of some promises and the exclusion of others from contract. Hence, despite its persistence, consideration has few defenders. The market argument, however, takes a more positive view of consideration. If contract law exists to support markets, then it is natural that bargain and exchange should mark the border between contract and mere promise. The problem with the doctrine of consideration lies in its practical execution rather than its normative orientation.

In place of the current doctrine of consideration, all promises made in furtherance of commercial activity within a market should be presumptively enforceable, regardless of whether there is a quid pro quo. Additionally, promises made outside of the context of a market should be enforced so long as they involve a bargain in fact. Hence, the market argument counsels in favor of enforcing a *nudum pactum* as long as it is given in a commercial context. This rule would deal with the lion's share of cases currently dealt with under the doctrine of promissory estoppel. To the extent that doctrine or ideas of unjust enrichment are used to enforce gratuitous, noncommercial promises, they should be abandoned.

The Problems of Consideration

Since its modern formulation by the classical contract theorists of the late nineteenth and early twentieth centuries, the doctrine of consideration has come under three interrelated attacks. We can call these the coherence of exchange attack, the modification attack, and the gratuitous promise attack. According to the coherence of exchange attack, the doctrine of consideration fails because we are unable to consistently identify whether consideration is present or absent in a particular transaction in any non-question-begging way. According to the modification attack, the requirement that all contracts be supported by consideration plays havoc with parties' expectations and any defensible approach to contract in situations where parties seek to renegotiate their contracts midperformance. Finally, according to the gratuitous promise attack, the doctrine of consideration is underinclusive. There are some promises that seem practically indistinguishable from ordinary commercial bargains, but they cannot plausibly be said to be supported by any kind of consideration. In these cases, the doctrine of consideration seems to unduly restrict the enforceability of commitments.

The first problem created by the doctrine of consideration arises in cases where identifying the existence of a bargain proves difficult. Consider the difficulty of distinguishing between a bargain and a conditional promise. Suppose that I say, "If you come to my office next week, I promise to give you $500." This could be a gratuitous promise to make a gift. The requirement that you come to my office merely states the method by which the gift can be accepted. Furthermore, the condition need not have anything to do with the acceptance of the gift at all. For example, I might promise, "If your house burns to the ground, I will replace it" or "If your daughter gets into law school, I will pay her tuition." In these cases, there is a gratuitous promise, albeit one in which there is no obligation to perform unless the named condition—the burning of the house or the law school acceptance—occurs. On the other hand, my promise, "If you come to my office next week, I promise to give you $500" might be a bargain. Perhaps the promise to pay $500 is conditioned on your coming to my office because that is the deal. We have a quid pro quo in which I promise to pay you $500 in return for which you make the trek to my office. Far from being a gratuitous gift promise with a condition, we have a unilateral contract supported by consideration. In this case, the consideration would be your actually making the journey to my office.

Consider the classic case of *Allegheny College v. National Chautauqua County Bank,*[7] in which Justice Cardozo grappled with this distinction. In 1921, Allegheny College was in the midst of a fund-raising drive when it approached Mary Yates Johnson about making a gift. Johnson agreed to donate $5,000 to the college provided that it use the money to establish a fund named in her memory devoted to those entering the ministry. When Johnson died, her executor refused to pay the promised donation, and the college sued. The question presented was whether the promise made to the college was supported by consideration or whether it was a *nudum pactum*.[8] Cardozo found that the college had undertaken an obligation to create the fund desired by Yates and spend the money on the education of ministers. In so doing, it provided consideration on her promise, which could accordingly be sued on by the college as a valid contract.

The problem with Cardozo's holding is that Yates's promise appears to be a gift rather than a quid pro quo. Certainly, Yates's promise was an act of generosity rather than a bargain. Cardozo's laboring over the doctrine of consideration seems to be a highly motivated attempt to benefit the college by enforcing the promise rather than a good faith effort to locate a bargain in fact. Nowhere in the record recited by Cardozo did the college make any explicit promise to Yates that it would name a fund in her honor or use the funds as she indicated. Before her death, Yates did in fact make a $1,000 payment on the promised $5,000 gift. While the college did use the funds for a scholarship given to a student studying for the ministry, it never established a fund named in Yates's honor. In short, it looks as though the college accepted a gift and then spent the money, albeit in a way that the donor may have expected. Cardozo, however, takes what looks to be a conditional gift and finds in the fact of the condition a set of mutual promises. As Grant Gilmore rather dismissively put the point, "Cardozo delighted in weaving gossamer spider webs of consideration" and "a judge that could find 'consideration' in . . . the Allegheny College case could when he was so inclined find consideration anywhere: the terms had been so broadened as to have become meaningless."[9]

For my purposes here, what is important is not the merits of Cardozo's resolution of the case in *Allegheny College* but the difficulty that it highlights. In some jurisdictions, promises to charitable institutions are enforceable without consideration, making the specific point of law at issue in *Allegheny College* moot.[10] The case does, however, point to the difficulty of identifying the border between bargains and gifts. A defender of the doctrine of consideration might reply that such borderline cases are always with us and the fact that a rule creates difficult cases at the margins cannot count as a criticism of the rule. Furthermore, one might point out that gift promises are relatively rare—legal anomalies that delight law professors but have little relevance to the actual operation of legal doctrine. Fair enough. Consideration, however, creates deeper problems than the coherence of exchange.

The doctrine of consideration has also been drafted into policing the boundaries of legitimate contract modification. The results have not been particularly edifying. Contract modifications require that the law distinguish between two situations. On one hand, when parties enter into a contract, their ability to forecast future events will always be limited. Sometimes things happen that no one contemplated, and the parties wish to modify their obligations. In other cases, the parties' desires and goals may shift in the midst of performance, and they want to change the terms of their deal midstream. On the other hand, when *quid* is exchanged for *quo* over time, parties often find themselves in a vulnerable position. One party may have made transaction-specific investments that will be lost if the other party fails to perform.[11] This situation gives the party that has not yet performed a great deal of power. By threatening breach, she can extract additional benefits from the counterparty. When faced after the fact with a dispute about a contract modification, the law must determine whether the modification represents a reasonable mutual accommodation between the parties or a bit of predatory ex post opportunism. The common law has assigned this task to the doctrine of consideration.

Initially this seems a natural move. Modified promises are promises, and consideration purports to answer for us the question of what promises the law should enforce. It seems unobjectionable, therefore, that it should also answer the question of what modifications the law should enforce. A trio of famous cases involving sailors illustrates the problem. In *Harris v. Watson*,[12] Lord Kenyon was confronted by a case in which a captain promised additional pay to his sailors if they would agree to work the ship while the ship was in heightened danger. "If this action was to be supported, it would materially affect the navigation of this kingdom,"[13] Lord Kenyon opined. Indeed, he supported the rule that the captain should not be required to pay wages to seamen in the event of a lost cargo; otherwise, he wrote, sailors "would in many cases suffer a ship to sink, unless the captain would pay any extravagant demand they might think proper to make."[14] Kenyon's dire prediction of sinking ships seems unlikely given that the seamen might face a very long swim to shore. Nevertheless, he accurately identified the problem of blessing modifications in a situation where the captain was potentially exposed to ex post opportunism by his crew.

Harris v. Watson was decided in 1791. Two decades later, King's Bench was presented with a similar case in *Stilk v. Myrick*.[15] In the course of a voyage from London to the Baltic, two seamen deserted the ship. The captain was unable to hire replacements and promised the remaining crew additional wages if they would agree to work the ship. When the captain refused to pay the additional wages, the crew sued. Lord Ellenborough followed Lord Kenyon in refusing to enforce the promise, but he disagreed with the reasoning in *Harris v. Watson*.

> Here, I say, the agreement was void for want of consideration. There was no consideration for the ulterior pay promised to the mariners who remained with the ship. Before they sailed from London they had undertaken to do all they could under the emergencies of the voyage. They had sold all their services till the voyage should be completed.[16]

A promise to perform what they were already contractually obligated to do could not be consideration on the captain's promise to pay. The attempt to modify the terms of the agreement foundered on the doctrine of consideration. *Stilk v. Myrick* was followed by the federal courts in *Alaska*

Packers' Association v. Domenico,[17] which decided that an attempt by seamen on a voyage from San Francisco to Alaska to renegotiate the terms of their compensation midvoyage failed for want of consideration on the proposed modification.

The application of the doctrine of consideration to modification cases can be criticized on two grounds. First, if our ultimate goal is to identify modifications extorted by ex post opportunism, then it is not clear that consideration is a very good filter. For example, in *Alaska Packers' Association,* the seamen were paid much of their compensation in the form of a two-cent bonus for each fish that they caught.[18] Upon arriving in Alaska, it was alleged that the nets provided for them were damaged and so the voyage would be less profitable than promised. In these circumstances, perhaps a modification of the contract was reasonable in light of the circumstances rather than an act of opportunism by the seamen.[19] In other words, the doctrine of consideration might invalidate modifications where there is no reason to suppose that there has been any abuse or advantage taking by the promisee.

The second objection is that, in the context of modifications, the doctrine of consideration is so malleable that it can always be found if the court wishes to see the modification enforced. Rather than being a bit of mindless formalism generating senseless results, it simply obfuscates the true grounds for the court's decision. Hence, while a promise to perform actions that the promisor was previously obligated to perform could not be consideration on the proposed modification of the agreement, provided the promised performance varied in any particulars from the original performance, consideration could be found. The difference in the two performances sufficed.[20] Likewise, nothing kept the parties who wished to modify their agreement from mutually agreeing to a rescission of their previous contract and, once freed of any contractual obligations, entering into a wholly new agreement on terms modified from those in the original agreement. Once courts realized that such a rescission and novation could be implied in the absence of an explicit agreement, it became relatively easy to bless modifications or damn them, generating consideration or denying its existence depending on the outcome desired by the court.[21] Although courts will still refuse to enforce contractual modifications for want of consideration, the *Restatement (Second) of Contracts* largely ameliorated the effects of the doctrine by validating modifications that are reasonable in light of circumstances not foreseen at the time that the parties entered into the contract.[22] Still, the winding course of the marriage between consideration and modification highlights the contradictions and logical difficulties of the doctrine.

The final doctrinal difficulty created by the doctrine of consideration is its inability to validate contracts whose enforcement seems unobjectionable and desirable. Most famously, of course, the doctrine of consideration refuses to validate promises to make a gift. This, however, is a less grievous fault than some have suggested. The law of consideration does not keep people from making gifts. It simply keeps people from being sued for failing to make gifts that they promised to make. Indeed, there is an argument to be made that the legal enforcement of gifts actually undermines the idea of generosity, because it would mainly matter in those cases where the giver has chosen not to give.[23] It is arguable whether a gift made under the duress of the law remains a gift.[24] Far more troubling are rather ordinary commercial transactions invalidated by the springes of the consideration doctrine despite their similarity to agreements that are uncontroversially treated as contracts.

Consider the case of *Foakes v. Beer*.[25] Julia Beer obtained a judgment against John Weston Foakes for slightly more than £2,000. Foakes and Beer then executed a contract in which Foakes agreed to pay £500 on the debt immediately, with the remainder of the principal to be paid in a series of installments. Beer promised not to execute on the judgment and agreed not to demand payment of interest. After Foakes made the payments promised in the contract, Beer sued for the interest. Foakes raised the contract as a defense, and in due time the case arrived before the House of Lords. The question presented was whether Beer's promise to sue was supported by consideration. The court relied on the seventeenth-century precedent in *Pinnel's Case*,[26] where Lord Coke had held that the payment of a lesser sum could not be consideration on a promise to release a debt of a greater amount, but that something other than a sum of money—"a horse, hawk, or robe"—could be. The outcome in the case makes sense within the strict logic of the doctrine of consideration. Because the promisee gives nothing in return for the release other than what he is already obligated to give, there is no detriment. It is the same problem as *Stilk v. Myrick* but in a different guise.

Outside of the formal logic of the consideration doctrine, however, the outcome makes no sense.[27] Under the logic of *Pinnel's Case*, it is entirely possible to obtain a release from a debt by paying less than the full value of the debt so long as the payment takes the form of a "horse, hawk, or robe" rather than a sum of money. There is no reason, however, to require payment in the form of livestock, pets, or garments rather than cash. Furthermore, there are perfectly good and understandable reasons that someone might accept less than the full amount in satisfaction of a debt. As Arthur Corbin observed:

> It is an error of fact to suppose that one gets no benefit when he gets only that to which he had an existing right. A bird in the hand is worth much more than a bird in the bush. . . . It is likewise error of fact to suppose that performance of a duty is no detriment to the promisee. If this performance is the payment of money, it is money that he might have paid to other persons with greater advantage to himself (and even without doing any legal wrong whatever).[28]

In the absence of duress or some other reason to suppose that the agreement was suspect, it defies any reasonable commercial logic to prohibit the settlement of debts as the parties see fit.

Another problem involves option contracts. It is extremely common in the course of business negotiations for one party to grant an option to another party. For example, after preliminary negotiations, the seller of a piece of land might tell a real estate developer that she will leave an offer open for a brief period while the developer finalizes financing. The promise to hold the offer open constitutes an option, and the common law generally demands that the promise be supported by consideration before it can be recognized as legally binding.[29] In some cases, this requirement presents no difficulty. When the asset in question is substantial, taking it off the market during the period for the option will be potentially costly and the seller will demand compensation. In this case, the quid pro quo is less a formality engaged in to make the promise enforceable than a business reaction to the parties' assumption that the option already is enforceable. However, when the seller does not demand compensation for holding the offer open—as, for example, when holding the property off the market imposes no costs on the seller—the option will be a *nudum pactum*, unenforceable for want of consideration.

It is difficult to see, however, why these promises should not be enforced, and the pressure to enforce them has caused the law to resort to various stratagems to circumvent the consideration requirement. One approach is to enforce the option under the doctrine of promissory estoppel on the grounds that the promisee reasonably relied on the promise.[30] In many cases, there is, no doubt, actual reliance, but one cannot help but suspect that, in many cases, the reliance is fictitious. In the case of the real estate developer who is seeking financing for his project during the term of the option, it is tempting to say that he relies on the promise to keep the option open. In many cases, however, the developer would be seeking financing regardless and would be unable to accept the offer immediately in the absence of financing. In such a case, the option is made not to induce the developer to rely but because the seller believes that it increases the probability that the developer will ultimately accept the offer. The behavior of both the seller and the developer in such cases is reasonable, but it has nothing to do with the idea of reliance. Not surprisingly, the law has developed other fictions to enforce the option without consideration. Most notably, in some jurisdictions, a signed writing that recites the existence of consideration will be enforced, even if no consideration was in fact paid. By refusing to look behind the writing, the law in effect allows the enforcement of gratuitous options.[31]

In addition to its doctrinal peculiarities, consideration has also drawn the ire of contract theorists from across the philosophical spectrum. Autonomy and economic theorists tend to place a high premium on freedom of contract, although for somewhat different reasons. For autonomy theorists, a proper respect for the agency of contracting parties requires that the law honor their intentions without paternalistically second-guessing them. For economic theorists, freedom of contract is important because third-party decision makers generally lack information on what combination of new obligations will increase welfare. The fact that individuals—who generally possess the best information about what will increase their welfare—have chosen a set of obligations provides strong evidence that enforcing the chosen obligations will be beneficial. The doctrine of consideration, however, represents a limitation on freedom of contract. The mere fact that someone has voluntarily promised something is insufficient to make it a contract in the absence of consideration.

Ironically enough, however, those theorists who are skeptical of freedom of contract also tend to be hostile to the doctrine of consideration. Unlike autonomy theorists or economic theorists, these critics are comfortable with denying the prima facie sufficiency of choice as a basis for contractual obligations. Rather, they look to the substantive content of promises as a touchstone of enforcement. Hence, for example, one might wish to enforce only those promises that conform to some substantive ideal of fairness. Alternatively, one might look to the idea of reliance, giving promisees a cause of action because they have suffered some harm rather than out of respect for the promisor's choice. For these theorists, the problem with the doctrine of consideration is not that it limits freedom of contract but that it does so in ways unrelated to their chosen normative criteria.

Charles Fried's attack on the doctrine of consideration provides a classic statement of the critique based on freedom of contract.[32] According to Fried, the doctrine of consideration contains an inherent contradiction. On one hand, the doctrine claims that "only promises given as part of a bargain are enforceable."[33] On the other hand, "whether there is a bargain or not is a formal question only"[34] and can be identified "without looking at motives and content."[35] The first commitment that the law will only enforce promises with bargained-for consideration rests on the idea of limiting freedom of contract. The law "holds that individual self-determination is not a sufficient ground of legal obligation, and so implies that collective policies may after all override individual judgments."[36] The second commitment, however, suggests that the law will not second-guess the substantive content of parties' contracts. In other words, it will respect their freedom of contract. Courts do not inquire into the adequacy of consideration, nor do they ask whether the parties were truly motivated by the bargain or whether they would have been willing to perform in the absence of consideration. According to Fried, the doctrinal difficulties created by consideration flow from the inherent contradiction between these two elements. Hence, he argues that all promises deliberately and fairly made ought to be enforced by the law. "Freedom of contract *is* freedom of promise, and . . . the intrusions of the standard doctrines of consideration can impose substantial if random restrictions on perfectly rational agents."[37]

Fried claimed to have penned *Contract as Promise* in part as a response to Grant Gilmore's attack on classical contract doctrine in *The Death of Contract*.[38] Ironically, however, Gilmore shares with Fried contempt for the doctrine of consideration. According to Gilmore, "it is the fate of contract to be swallowed up by torts (or for both of them to be swallowed up in a generalized theory of civil liability)."[39] Gilmore's claim was both descriptive and normative. Descriptively, he saw the rise of unjust enrichment and promissory estoppel sounding the death knell of a vision of contract based on consideration and party autonomy. Normatively, he thought that classical doctrine was based on laissez-faire economic theory, which "comes down to something like this: If we all do exactly as we please, no doubt everything will work out for the best."[40] He continued, "For good or ill, we have changed all that. We are now all cogs in a machine, each dependent on the other. The decline and fall of the general theory of contract and, in most quarters, of laissez-faire economics may be taken as remote reflections on the transition from nineteenth-century individualism to the welfare state and beyond."[41] Gilmore insisted that detrimental reliance and substantive regulation of transactions for fairness should be the touchstones for contractual liability rather than consideration. Writing less flamboyantly, Patrick Atiyah came to roughly the same conclusion.[42] After offering an exhaustive account of the doctrinal difficulties involved in the idea of bargained-for consideration, he concluded that consideration should mean "a reason for the enforcement of a promise, or even more broadly, a reason for the recognition of an obligation."[43] Chief among these reasons, according to Atiyah, is detrimental reliance, although in general he believes that courts should attend to "changes in social and commercial conditions, and changes in the moral values of the community"[44] rather than the formalities of the consideration doctrine.

Economic theorists have also not been especially enthusiastic about the doctrine of consideration. In an early and influential article, Charles Goetz and Robert Scott argued that one of the main economic purposes of enforcing promises is to maximize the surplus created by the promisor and the promisee in each transaction.[45] This surplus will be a function of the level of investment made by the promisee in reliance on the promisor's performance and the investments made by the promisor in performance and in assuring the promisee of performance. They concluded that, in the context of bargaining, the parties may ex ante reach agreements that will lead to optimal levels of investment on both sides and that bargained-for promises ought to be enforced. In the case of unbargained-for promises, however, the economic case for enforcement is mixed. In some cases, such as donative promises, "extra-legal sanctions against breach are effective," and "the supply of donative promises is likely to be very sensitive to the attachment of legal liability."[46] In other words, donors forgo otherwise desirable promises for fear of litigation costs, and the threat of litigation will provide little in the way of additional assurance performance. In other situations, however, Goetz and Scott suggest that "enforcement of nonreciprocal promises will optimize social benefits when extra-legal sanctions are minimal and the promisor can be encouraged to adapt the form of the promise to the risk of regret."[47] Their argument suggests that, while economic theory has no quarrel with the enforcement of bargains, making bargain a necessary condition for the enforcement of a promise in all cases is unjustified.[48]

Markets and the Boundaries of Contract

The market argument suggests that the basic intuition behind the doctrine of consideration is correct, but that the doctrine must be altered. If the purpose of contract law is to strengthen and sustain well-functioning markets, which crucially include exchanges between strangers, then it seems natural to make bargains the touchstone of contractual liability. Exchange, after all, is the quintessential example of commerce, and if contract exists to serve commerce, then it makes sense to confine it to bargained-for promises. This intuition is based on two correct assumptions and one incorrect assumption. The first is that the enforcement of contracts is a potentially costly activity requiring a special justification. The second correct assumption is that the conceptual core of contract is the commercial agreement. The faulty assumption is that confining enforceable contracts to bargained-for promises will advance these goals. In place of the doctrine of consideration as it now stands, I propose a two-part rule. First, all promises made in furtherance of commercial activity should be presumptively enforceable. Second, bargained-for promises outside of the context of an established market should be presumptively enforceable.

Imposing legal liability on promises and other voluntary commitments is costly, even if one thinks that people should be held to such commitments. First, there is the expense of litigation. Attaching liability creates the possibility of lawsuits, which will then require lawyers and their attendant costs. Second, there is the risk of error by the courts. In some situations, courts will decide cases incorrectly. People will be held to deals to which they did not in fact commit, or courts will misjudge the consequences and meaning of parties' actions, imposing liability in unexpected and unjustified ways. These risks mean that liability should be imposed only when we have substantial reasons for imposing it. We must be convinced that the benefits of liability exceed these costs. Suppose that, like Charles Fried, we generally believe that voluntarily made promises are a good thing and the world is better when such promises are kept. Given such a belief, we would regard a punitive tax imposed on promising as, all things being equal, morally unfortunate. Liability, however, is a kind of tax—a cost imposed on an activity, because, all things being equal, it makes that activity more risky. Hence, even one who believes that the legal obligations of contract ought, in a perfect world, to mirror the moral obligations of promising, might believe that, all things considered, imposing liability on promises is a bad idea given the costs of litigation and judicial error. Indeed, this is a reason that the common law allows parties by agreement to render otherwise enforceable commitments legally unenforceable.[49] This strikes me as a sensible rule and one that has not been challenged by Fried or other promissory theorists.

Why, then, does the market argument require that the law attach liability to at least some commitments? As discussed in previous chapters, well-functioning markets require complex interactions between strangers. In the absence of such interactions, commerce will tend to be relatively simple and confined within groups defined by tribal, religious, or regional identities. This is because complex interactions require relatively high levels of trust. Trust can be generated without the help of law in social situations in which it is relatively easy for individuals to monitor and sanction those who abuse their trust. Consider, for example, a family. In such cases, monitoring is relatively easy. For evolutionary reasons, people are likely mildly predisposed to look out for the interests of those with whom they share genes. Furthermore, people are often socialized into caring for family members. As a result, we rightly tend to expect less opportunistic behavior in family relationships. This does not mean, of course, that opportunism is unheard of in families. Much great literature would be rendered implausible if it were. The close and continuing associations within families, however, make it easier to sanction misbehaving family members using mechanisms ranging from shame to violence. Similar stories about the relative ease of generating trust within tight-knit ethnic or religious groups could be told.

The problem is that many of the benefits of well-functioning markets occur in precisely those cases where people engage in commerce across tribal boundaries. It is in these situations that markets can serve as an institutional context for cooperation in the face of moral pluralism, inculcate liberal virtues, and generate large-scale wealth. Contractual enforcement provides a way of increasing trust between strangers sufficient to allow for commerce across tribal lines. Legal institutions in effect provide the goods delivered by informal social arrangements in smaller, more closely knit communities. Of course, law alone cannot generate the trust that well-functioning markets require. Banks are willing to make substantial loans to strangers in a healthy market in part because they can rely on the enforcement of their contracts. Banks also want information on the borrower's income, assets, and credit history. Furthermore, banks will rely on nonlegal sanctions, such as the effects of a bad credit report, in placing their trust in the borrower. Even so, however, legal enforcement of the agreement is vital to generating this trust, sufficiently vital that it justifies imposing liability even in the face of costly litigation and judicial error.

Given this justification for enforcing contracts, it makes sense to confine contractual enforcement to those agreements that support well-functioning markets. As described above, however, this is not what the current doctrine of consideration does. It denies enforcement to certain agreements—such as gratuitous options made in the context of commercial negotiations—that would seem to be precisely the kind of market transactions that we would wish to enforce if we want to foster trust between strangers. There are, of course, many legal systems that dispense with the doctrine of consideration. Under civil law, an enforceable contract requires *causa* rather than consideration. Although the ideas are related, *causa* is much broader than merely bargained-for exchange. It includes any legitimate motivation for entering into the contract. Hence, a gratuitous option contract would be enforceable at civil law because it has *causa*—the furtherance of trade—even if there is no bargained-for consideration. Likewise, the Convention on Contracts for the International Sale of Goods, to which the United States is a signatory, does not require consideration in order for an agreement to be enforceable.[50] Similarly, several U.S. statutes make certain contracts enforceable without consideration. For example, the Uniform Commercial Code makes modifications to contracts for the sale of goods enforceable without consideration, and the Uniform Premarital and Marital Agreements Act dispenses with consideration for prenuptial agreements.[51]

In place of the doctrine of consideration, the law should presumptively enforce all agreements made in furtherance of commercial activity. This would mean that all agreements or promises made in the context of a market would be enforced. Of course, the force of such a rule would only be presumptive. We might have good reasons—such as indefiniteness or duress—for refusing to enforce some agreements made in the context of a healthy market, just as we have good reasons under current law for refusing to enforce agreements supported by consideration. Such a rule would have a number of attractive features. First, it would eliminate the problems created by gratuitous commercial promises. Such promises would be presumptively enforceable. Hence, for example, a seller who promises to leave an offer open would create a gratuitous option right in the vendee so long as the promise was made in furtherance of economic exchange. There would be no requirement that the promise to leave the offer open be supported by additional consideration. Second, it would make the law of contract coextensive with markets. We would thus align legal doctrine with its justification. We would also no longer use consideration to police issues such as contract modification or the release of indebtedness.

There will, however, be cases where it will be unclear whether a contract has been made in furtherance of economic activity. Consider the contract in *Hamer v. Sidway*,[52] where an uncle promised to pay his nephew $5,000 if the nephew would refrain from drinking, smoking, and gambling until his twenty-first birthday. Under the rule stated in the previous paragraph, it is not clear whether this contract would be enforced. It was not made in furtherance of a commercial transaction and was not made in an established market. Nevertheless, if there was a bargain in fact, then the contract should be enforced. This is because one of the purposes of contract law is to extend well-functioning markets. At the time the contract was made, there might not be a market in promises to refrain from drinking, smoking, and gambling. Were such a market to develop, however, it could have all of the beneficial effects of other well-functioning markets. Exchange outside of the context of an established market and in the presence of mixed or opaque motives can be the first step toward establishing a new market. Hence, the market argument would suggest that bargain may be a sufficient condition for enforcing an agreement even if it is not a necessary condition. By honoring exchanges even outside of the context of established markets, the law can assist in the generation of new markets.

Gifts, Reliance, and Unjust Enrichment

Consideration is not the current common law's sole basis for enforcing promises. Current law also purports to enforce promises based on reliance and in some cases at least based on concerns relating to unjust enrichment or so-called moral consideration. There is also a persistent debate among common law contract theorists about the desirability of enforcing gift promises. Adopting the approach argued for here would have several important consequences that are worth considering. In particular, it would not enforce gift promises. It would not enforce promises based on reliance. Finally, it would not enforce promises based on concerns for unjust enrichment or moral consideration.

First, it would render gift promises unenforceable. Because bargains would be considered a sufficient but not necessary element for the enforcement of a promise, my proposal would enforce gratuitous promises provided that they were made in a commercial setting. However, while some gratuitous promises would be enforced, wholly noncommercial gift promises would not be enforced. For some readers this may be an objection. My response is twofold. First, in the context of true gift promises, we lack a strong reason for enforcing the promise. By a "true gift promise," I mean a promise to make a gift to an individual that the promisor later chooses not to perform. To the extent that we wish gifts to be given and received, it is because we believe that generosity is an important social practice that ought to be recognized by the law.[53] Likewise, we might believe that the giving of gifts should be seen as part of a property owner's right to dispose of her property as she sees fit.[54] These are all reasons why the law should recognize completed gifts, a conclusion with which I have no quarrel. However, the enforcement of gift promises does not involve recognizing acts of generosity. Rather, it involves providing a remedy to a disappointed donee when a donor changes his or her mind. What normative goal would enforcing such promises advance? Surely it cannot be the legal recognition of generosity. The person coerced by the law into giving a gift is not behaving generously.

In some cases, we might wish to enforce gift promises as a way of subsidizing charitable institutions that depend on gifts.[55] I have no quarrel with this approach in principle. The idea would be that the enforcement of gift promises to such institutions is rather like granting them tax-exempt status or the deductibility of donations made to qualifying charities, a nudge by the law in favor of laudable activity.[56] As a matter of policy, however, enforcing all gift promises to charities seems a badly targeted way of supporting the goods provided by nonprofit institutions. For example, some such institutions—the Knights of the Ku Klux Klan for example—may have perverse goals that we have no wish to support. A general rule of enforcing gift promises to nonprofit institutions thus seems rather hamfisted. Regardless, however, this rationale does not provide a reason to enforce gift promises in general.

The second reason that the nonenforcement of gift promises is not a good objection to the approach proposed above is that most of the litigation involving gift promises is not actually an attempt to enforce a promise in the face of breach. Rather, such litigation almost always involves claims against the estate of a dead promisor and is a contest between the promisee and the beneficiaries of her will. Consider the classic case of *Ricketts v. Scothorn.*[57] The case involved a promise made by a grandfather to his granddaughter to pay her $2,000. The grandfather never made the promised gift, but there was every indication that he desired and intended to do so. However, he died without having made the payment, and the granddaughter sued the executor of his estate. The case is always presented as involving the enforceability of the promise and is most famous as an early articulation of the doctrine of promissory estoppel. In reality, however, the case is less about promise making and promise breaking than about whether to enforce the donative commitment of the grandfather after his death. There is, of course, a way that the grandfather could have ensured that his granddaughter received the $2,000 after his death: he could have made her a beneficiary under his will. He failed, however, to comply with the formalities that would have given her a bequest. Seen in this light, the enforceability of the promise has less to do with the law of contracts than with whether we should honor donative intentions that fail to comply with the formalities of a will. There may be perfectly good reasons for relaxing these formalities in cases such as *Ricketts v. Scothorn*, but the opinion does not discuss them. Furthermore, by casting these disputes as contract cases rather than wills cases, we direct our attention away from what seems to be the key policy question posed by the case. By enforcing the grandfather's promise, for example, the court in effect gave the grandfather's bequest to his granddaughter priority over his other heirs and equal treatment with his commercial creditors. If we think of her as the potential beneficiary of a bequest rather than a promisee, however, this special treatment becomes somewhat bizarre, and, in any case, it is wholly undefended in the court's opinion.

Once we eliminate cases involving charitable institutions and claims against the executors of estates, gift promises prove to be a relatively trivial category. The lion's share of the reported cases will fall into one of these two categories. In the first, we have a weak case for enforcing the promise; in the second, the enforceability of the promises implicates questions of succession and testamentary law that are best treated by reference to the policy concerns that animate the law of wills rather than the law of contracts. The cases that remain are vanishingly rare and, for the reasons stated above regarding generosity, are poor candidates for legal enforcement.

The second possible objection has to do with the doctrine of promissory estoppel. Section 90 of the *Restatement (Second) of Contracts* allows a court to enforce "a promise which the promisor would reasonably expect to induce action or forbearance on the part of the promisee . . . and which does induce such action . . . if injustice can be avoided only by enforcement of the promise."[58] Some contract theorists, most notably Grant Gilmore and Patrick Atiyah, have argued that detrimental reliance is *the* basis for contractual liability.[59] (In Atiyah's case, it is also the basis for the moral obligation to keep a promise.[60]) On this view, the central goal of contract law should be to compensate victims who rely on promises to their detriment for the losses caused by breach. One might object to the market-centered theory of enforceability offered above by insisting that it will not protect those harmed by detrimental reliance.

There are two responses to this objection. First, the market-based approach would enforce gratuitous promises made in a commercial context. This would actually encompass the bulk of current promissory estoppel cases, which generally arise out of market transactions such as gratuitous options. Indeed, a number of extensive studies of the decided cases have found that most promissory estoppel cases are less about compensating parties for detrimental reliance than they are about circumventing the consideration doctrine in cases where it produces commercially perverse results. Hence, courts are finding promissory estoppel in the absence of clear evidence of reliance provided that the promises occur in a commercial context where we can infer that the parties intended to be legally bound.[61] A good example of such a case is *Feinberg v. Pfeiffer Co.*[62] Feinberg was a long-time employee of Pfeiffer Company. At a meeting of the board of directors, the company voted to give her an annuity for life upon retirement. Eventually she retired, and subsequently the company refused to pay the annuity. She sued. The promise was without consideration, and she claimed that she eventually chose to quit working in reliance on the promise. It's unclear, however, that she ever in fact relied on the promise at all. Despite her self-serving testimony at trial, she may have retired because she was simply too old to continue working. Indeed, viewing this fact pattern in terms of reliance has potentially perverse results. For example, had Pfieffer simply fired Feinberg, she would have no claim to the annuity. Indeed, this is precisely what happened in the case of *Pitts v. McGraw-Edison Co.*, where the court refused to enforce a promised retirement annuity made at the time that a worker was fired by his employer.[63] Under the market-based approach offered above, the promises to both Feinberg and Pitts would be enforced, regardless of reliance. What would matter was that the companies made the promises in a commercial context in furtherance of economic activity.

The second response is that there is no noncircular way of applying the doctrine of promissory estoppel. According to the *Restatement*, the goal is not to enforce every promise that is relied upon; nor is it to compensate promisees for every investment made in reliance on a promise. Rather, we seek to determine whether the reliance was "reasonable." In other contexts, the common law has recognized that encouraging promisees to rely on promises can be senseless. In the famous case of *Rockingham County v. Luten Bridge Company*,[64] the court denied recovery to a construction firm that built a bridge in the middle of nowhere in reliance on a promise by the county, because the company knew that the county had no intention of performing. Likewise, economic theorists have long recognized the problem of overincentivizing reliance.[65] The commentary to the *Restatement (Second) of Contracts*' section 90 highlights the difficulties:

> The promisor is affected only by reliance which he does or should foresee, and enforcement must be necessary to avoid injustice. Satisfaction of the latter requirement may depend on the reasonableness of the promisee's reliance, on its definite and substantial character in relation to the remedy sought, on the formality with which the promise is made, on the extent to which the evidentiary, cautionary, deterrent and channeling functions of form are met by the commercial setting or otherwise, and on the extent to which such other policies as enforcement of bargains and the prevention of unjust enrichment are relevant.[66]

Notice that in this analysis reliance does no work in picking out which promises should be enforced; rather, we must look to a host of other considerations from commercial settings to unjust enrichment to determine whether the reliance is legally relevant. We do not recognize the legal enforcement of promises because there is reliance. Rather, we recognize reliance because we have decided on other grounds that the promise should be legally enforced. The problem with the reliance theory of contract is not that it is mistaken but that it is not a theory of contract at all. It is a way of labeling promises that we wish to enforce rather than a conceptual mechanism for identifying those promises.

Finally, under current doctrine, courts will sometimes enforce promises made without consideration where unjust enrichment might result from nonenforcement. It is important to distinguish such cases from true cases of restitution or quasi contract. Consider two cases. In *Cotnam v. Wisdom*,[67] a man was severely injured in a streetcar accident. A doctor who arrived at the scene tried to save the unconscious victim, who subsequently died. The doctor presented the man's estate with a bill for services rendered, which the executor refused to pay on the grounds that the dead victim never contracted to pay for the services. The court sided with the doctor. Although in reaching its decision the court spoke in terms of quasi contracts and implied in law contracts, there was no agreement or promise of any kind in the case. In *Webb v. McGowin*,[68] an employee of a lumberyard was permanently disabled while rescuing his employer from a workplace accident, and the employer promised to pay the man an annuity for life.[69] When the employer's estate subsequently refused to pay the promised annuity, the man sued. The defendant claimed, correctly, that there was no bargained-for consideration supporting the promised annuity payment. The court held, however, that, notwithstanding the gratuitous nature of the promise, the defendant should have to pay the annuity. In *Cotnam,* the basis of the liability was not properly contractual at all. Rather, we should see it as flowing from the law of restitution, which, like tort, should be seen as an independent source of civil liability.[70] The market argument says nothing one way or the other about the structure of the law of restitution. It has no quarrel with the outcome of the case in *Cotnam,* but it does not offer any support for that decision either.

The approach to enforceability sketched in the previous section, however, would support enforcement of the promised annuity in *Webb v. McGowin*. The promise was made by an employer to an employee in the context of the market and their commercial relationship. The outcome in *Webb v. McGowin* is, of course, anomalous in terms of the traditional doctrine of consideration because there was no quid pro quo between the employee and the employer. The outcome is generally explained in terms of either a moral obligation on the part of the employer to pay the employee or the necessity of preventing the employer from being unjustly enriched at the expense of the employee. According to the market argument, however, the promise is not enforced for these reasons. Rather, it was rightly enforced because it was made in the context of a healthy market, and its enforcement will serve to strengthen the trust within that market.

The point can be illustrated by contrasting *Webb v. McGowin* with *Harrington v. Taylor*.[71] In *Harrington*, a man was in the midst of a violent argument with his wife when she attacked him with an ax. The wife's friend intervened to rescue the man, turning the ax aside. In doing so, however, the friend was severely injured. The man promised to compensate the wife's friend for her injuries. When he failed to pay as promised, she sued. The court ultimately ruled that the contract was unenforceable for want of consideration. Under the market-based rule offered above, the husband's promise would not be enforced. His promise was not made in furtherance of commerce or in the context of a healthy market. Nor was it a bargain whose enforcement might have led to the creation of a new market. It was in essence a promise to make a gift, albeit a promise motivated by a feeling of gratitude and moral obligation.

The bare fact that he made a promise does not provide a reason for the law to intervene to enforce the husband's commitment. For the reasons given above with regard to gift promises, our collective approbation of generosity and gratitude do not provide reasons for the law to intervene to enforce the promise. One might respond, however, that in justice the wife's friend ought to be entitled to payment for her injury. This may well be the case, but it does not provide any reason for enforcing the husband's promise as opposed to simply making him liable.

Consider two reasons why our sympathies might lie with the wife's friend. First, we might believe that the husband has an obligation to compensate her for her injury. After all, his life was saved because of her sacrifice. He has been enriched at her expense. This is the same intuition that lies behind the law of unjust enrichment. Without taking a position on the ultimate merits of this claim, I would point out that such an obligation is independent of his promise. We don't believe that he owes her because he promised. Rather, we believe that he promised because he owed her. Accordingly, we might wish the law to impose on him an obligation to pay for her injury. This obligation, however, should not turn on whether he happened to make a promise to her. Indeed, the presence or absence of the promise seems irrelevant to our consideration of whether he should have an obligation to pay.

Second, we might believe that the husband should pay the wife's friend because of her loss. The idea here is that the woman has suffered a costly misfortune, and it would be cruel and unjust to simply leave that misfortune where chance happened to let it fall. The intuition here is the same one that underlies social insurance. Either because of concerns about distributive justice or efficient risk bearing, we believe that the cost of the woman's misfortune should be transferred to others. This intuition may be entirely correct, but it does not provide a reason for enforcing the husband's promise to compensate her for her injury. As a matter of distributive justice, there is no reason to suppose that the husband ought to pay for the injury. For example, the husband may be very poor while the wife's friend is very wealthy. In this case, to make the husband the insurer of the woman's injury would be distributionally perverse from an egalitarian perspective. Suppose, however, that the husband is very wealthy and the wife's friend is impoverished. One might then think that the world would be better if he bore some of the cost of her injury. Notice, however, that in this case the fact that he has promised is irrelevant. We ought to make him the insurer of her loss because he is wealthy, not because he promised. One might think that he ought to bear the risk because he was the beneficiary of her action, but this simply restates the unjust enrichment argument already made. Finally, from an efficiency point of view, we would want the risk of her loss to be borne by the party that can manage that risk at the lowest cost. This might be the woman. It might be the husband. It might be some third party, such as the government. The fact that he has promised to pay for her injury, however, does not provide any information on the question of who is the cheapest bearer of the risk. In short, regardless of one's conclusions regarding duties of restitution or the need to shift costly losses, the presence or absence of a promise by the husband is irrelevant. Indeed, examining the question through the lens of enforcing this agreement simply distracts one from the real issues presented by the case—issues that have nothing to do with the law of contracts.

For understandable reasons, the doctrine of consideration has few defenders. Its application has created needless complexity and uncertainty in the law. Notwithstanding its faults, however, the idea of bargained-for consideration gestures toward an important and ultimately correct intuition about the law of contracts. Contract law ought to exist to facilitate the needs of the market, and commerce rightly constitutes the core of contractual liability. The idea that bargained-for consideration should be the touchstone of enforceability for voluntary agreements should be abandoned. There are many instances when enforcing gratuitous promises will serve to increase the trust between strangers upon which well-functioning markets depend. Rather, I argue that the law should presumptively enforce all promises made in furtherance of economic activity. Because we ought to strengthen and extend well-functioning markets, the law should also presumptively enforce bargained-for promises, even outside of the context of an existing market. This is because such bargains might be the basis for some emerging market. As for the other bases for contractual liability under current law—reliance and quasi contract—as well as the recurrent question of gift promises, none of these strike me as providing good reasons for enforcing agreements outside of the context of market exchange. Because most of the promises currently enforced by these doctrines occur within the context of well-functioning markets, my proposed rule would enforce them. However, when were are dealing with cases of pure reliance, pure donative promises, or pure quasi contracts, I do not think we have sufficient reason to enforce otherwise unenforceable promises even if we might wish to impose liability under other bodies of law such as restitution.

CHAPTER SIX

Remedies

For much of the twentieth century, scholarship on contract remedies was obsessed with the measure of damages. The obsession began in 1936 with the publication of "The Reliance Interest in Contract Damages" by Lon Fuller and his student William Perdue.[1] The article set the research agenda for much of the work that followed, earning it a place in the ranks of the most-cited law review articles of all time.[2] Fuller and Perdue's influence came from the framework that they created for classifying contract damages. They noticed that at times courts protect a promisee's expectation in the promisor's performance, awarding damages to put the victim of breach in the position she would have occupied had the contract been performed.[3] In other instances, courts protect the promisee that has exposed herself by relying on the promise, awarding damages to put the victim of breach in the position she would have been in had she not relied on the promise.[4] Finally, in some cases, courts require breaching promisors to disgorge any benefit conferred by promisees.[5] The tripartite classification proved so beguiling that the American Law Institute wrote it into the *Restatement (Second) of Contracts* in a wholly gratuitous section that announces no applicable rule and exists only as an homage to Fuller and Perdue.[6]

Fuller and Perdue, by focusing theoretical attention on the measure of damages, gave the nascent law and economics movement one of its first big openings in the 1970s. At common law, expectation damages are the primary remedy, and Fuller and Perdue labored mightily to explain why this is so.[7] They argued that contract law should compensate the promisee harmed by reliance but concluded, in the kind of contortion that only a law professor could love, that the best way of protecting reliance was to award expectation damages.[8] Legal economists had a more elegant answer.

When a promisor breaches a contract, he deprives the promisee of the benefit of his performance. Performance is costly because of direct investment and foregone opportunities. The insight of the law and economics movement was that at times the cost of performance may exceed the benefits of performance to the promisee. Expectation damages, rather than coercing performance, simply require that promisors internalize the costs of breach to promisees when they make the decision about whether to perform. To quote Jeremy Bentham, damages are a "license in disguise,"[9] pricing rather than prohibiting breach. Thus was born the theory of efficient breach, which defined much of the scholarly debate on contract law in the final third of the twentieth century. Critics of economic analysis of the law have attacked the theory.[10] Law and economic scholars, in turn, have offered their own criticisms and refinements.[11] They have adopted the basic methodological stance of the argument, focusing on damage measures and the incentives they create for investment in performance. Thus has the obsession lived on.

Deciding on the proper measure of damages is important, but the focus on this question has led to the neglect of other aspects of contract remedies.[12] More basic remedial structures in contract law have received little, if any, scholarly attention. Specifically, contract law shares with other private law areas such as torts or restitution two basic features. The first is bilateralism. Damages are paid from breaching defendants to disappointed promisees. The doctrine of privity prevents damages from being paid to anyone other than a promisee, with some limited exceptions for third-party beneficiaries.[13] The law does not allow a stranger to the contract, such as the government, to claim damages. The bilateral structure of contract damages seems natural, but it is by no means clear that it can be justified. As discussed below, for example, many of the economic puzzles of contract damages could be solved if defendants paid a third party rather than the promisee.

The second feature of contract remedies is private standing by plaintiffs. When a promisor breaches a contract, nothing happens unless the promisee chooses to act. No government official monitors contractual performance. Breach is not a crime or a regulatory infraction. Rather, the cause of action against the promisor belongs to the promisee. It is literally a piece of her personal property, what the law labels a chose in action, to do with as she sees fit. She alone has the power to bring suit against the promisor, and if she chooses not to do so—or lacks the resources to sue—then the promisor will face no legal consequences for breach. One could easily imagine alternative systems. We could make breach of contract a crime and empower public prosecutors to punish contract breachers. Alternatively, we could allow someone other than the promisee to bring suit against the promisor. Finally, we could place a duty on the promisee to institute a legal action against the promisor. In place of any of these alternatives, we have a law that empowers victims to act against wayward promisors and leaves plaintiffs in control of any litigation.

As a normative matter, are bilateralism and private standing desirable, or should they be replaced by some other structure? Given how deeply both structures are entrenched in every major system of contract law today, the failure of a normative theory to justify this feature provides a reason to treat it with skepticism. Certainly, normative—as opposed to interpretive—theory is under no conceptual obligation to justify the entirety of the law, and at times fundamental change to legal institutions is justified. Most people, however, have a strong intuition that promisees ought to control the litigation against promisors and that damages should be paid to the plaintiff rather than some party unrelated to the transaction. Such strong prereflective intuitions are an important datum in any normative argument and should only be rejected for compelling and well-articulated reasons. Both autonomy and economic theories of contract have a difficult time justifying bilateralism and private standing.

In contrast, I argue that both bilateralism and private standing let the victims of breach retaliate against contract breachers. Allowing this private but limited retaliation fosters commerce by solving the prisoner's dilemma inherent in contracting over time. Private retaliation, however, is dangerous. It is inherently aggressive, and that aggression must be limited if markets are to provide many of the moral benefits of commerce. Accordingly, unlike primitive legal systems, which allowed attacks on life and limb, we generally limit retaliation to the extraction of money and cap the amount taken to the value of what was promised. An eye for an eye; a tooth for a tooth; an expectation for an expectation.

The Problem of Bilateralism and Private Standing

Neither economic nor promissory theories of contract can offer plausible defenses of bilateralism and private standing. Of course, this is not a fatal objection to either approach if we understand them as normative rather than interpretive theories. However, while both approaches fail to defend bilateralism and private standing, they fail silently. These theorists have not explicitly attacked either structure nor have they defended them. To the extent that both structures seem intuitively attractive as features of private law, the failure of economic and promissory theories to explicitly attack or defend either structure provides a reason for treating both approaches with skepticism.

The failure of efficiency theories begins with the theory of efficient breach. Economic problems with the theory of efficient breach have long been recognized. What has not been clearly acknowledged is the role of bilateralism in those problems. The most important economic objection to the theory is the problem of overreliance.[14] Robert Cooter and Thomas Ulen summarized the economic paradox:

> (1) In order for the promisor to internalize the benefits of precaution, he or she must pay full compensation to the promisee for breach. (2) In order for the promisee to internalize the costs of reliance, he or she must receive no compensation for breach. (3) In contract law, compensation paid by the promisor for breach equals compensation received by the promisee. Therefore, contract law cannot internalize costs for the promisor and the promisee as required for efficiency.[15]

The problem of overreliance can be illustrated with a simple example. Imagine that Jack promises to supply Jill with a widget-making machine, and Jill informs Jack that in reliance on the contract, she will be purchasing a large supply of widget materials to manufacture widgets for the insatiable widget market. Jack then finds that Jane, who is a more efficient widget maker, will offer him an amount for the widget machine such that he can fully compensate Jill and still make a profit. True to the efficient breach theory, Jack reneges on his agreement, Jill successfully sues to recover her expectation damages, and Jack pockets the difference between Jill's damages and the price paid by Jane for the widget-making machine. Unfortunately, one problem mars this otherwise delightful picture of social efficiency: The effort and resources spent in procuring the unused bales of widget materials in Jill's warehouse are a waste. The problem is that, if all is working as the efficient breach theory suggests, once Jack and Jill have contracted, Jill has no incentive to consider the likelihood of Jack's performance. If Jack breaches, Jill will be fully compensated by expectation damages. It would be more efficient, however, for Jill to consider the likelihood of Jack efficiently breaching and structure her reliance accordingly. It is socially wasteful for promisees to act as though their promisors' eyes will never stray to other opportunities after the contract is signed.

Law and economics theorists have long understood this problem and have put on as brave a face as possible.[16] A. Mitchell Polinsky has summarized the situation:

> In general, there does not exist a breach of contract remedy that is efficient with respect to both the breach decision and the reliance decision. With respect to breach, the expectation remedy is ideal, whereas with respect to reliance, the restitution remedy is ideal. Thus, which remedy is best overall depends on whether the breach decision or the reliance decision is more important in terms of efficiency.[17]

What lies at the root of this problem is the bilateral structure of contract damages. By taking this structure for granted, however, the role of bilateralism in the problem of overreliance has been obscured.

One might argue that bilateralism coupled with private standing is a second-best response to the inadequacy of our enforcement technology and defended as such on efficiency grounds. Rather than charging the state itself with an impossible task, enforcement is decentralized by giving aggrieved promisees a private cause of action. Allowing a plaintiff to benefit from a fine imposed on a defendant gives potential plaintiffs an incentive to press their grievances in court, thus policing the conduct of promisors. The problem with this response is that, while it provides a completely plausible reason for dispersing enforcement, it still does not save economic theories from the basic contradiction between efficient breach and efficient reliance.

There is no reason why enlisting private lawsuits to create the proper incentives necessarily implies the particular relational structure of liability that we see in contract law. For example, it seems possible to create a system of optimal contract enforcement based on the model of qui tam statutes. In a *qui tam* action, the successful plaintiff receives a bounty for bringing a lawsuit that serves to enforce a public policy such as honesty in government procurement.[18] There is no requirement that the plaintiff be damaged by the defendant. It is sufficient that the plaintiff have knowledge of the defendant's wrongdoing. Likewise, one could argue that promisees are private attorneys general, seeking efficient levels of sanctions against breaching promisors. Economics, however, suggests that the amount of money that a plaintiff should be able to recover bears no relationship to the magnitude—if any—of the plaintiff's loss.[19] Indeed, there is no requirement that the plaintiff be harmed at all,[20] and most *qui tam* relators have suffered no personal loss at the hands of the defendant.[21] Rather, the amount of money that the plaintiff recovers in a *qui tam* action is set so as to maximize the government's goals: recovery of money defrauded and increased incentives for honesty among government contractors considering the costs imposed by the payment to the plaintiff itself.[22] By analogy, an optimal regime of dispersed contract enforcement would be one where a defendant would pay the full amount of the plaintiff's expectation but where the plaintiff would recoup only an amount sufficient to encourage the optimal level of lawsuits.[23]

Promissory theories have similar difficulties accounting for bilateralism and private standing. Charles Fried's *Contract as Promise* provides a good illustration of the problems. If we fail to hold a promisor to his commitment, argues Fried, "we infantilize him."[24] Respect for the autonomous choice of others, of course, is at the heart of Fried's account of contract.[25] He thus claims that the legal obligation to pay expectation damages in the event of breach simply mirrors a moral obligation to do the same thing. "Since contracts invoke and are invoked by promises," he writes, "it is not surprising that the law came to impose on the promises it recognized the same incidents as morality demands."[26] He goes on to claim that "the connection between contract and the expectation principle is . . . palpable."[27] What, however, is the palpable connection between Fried's "promise principle" and the "expectation principle"?

Fried never explains why the moral obligation to keep a promise implies a moral obligation to pay a sum of money sufficient to put the promisee in the position that she would have been in had the promise been performed. Contrary to his claim, it is by no means obvious that this is true. Suppose I promise my wife that I will pick her up from the airport. I fail to do so, and as a result, she must hire a cab to drive her home. In this situation, what is my moral obligation to my wife? I have clearly made a promise, and I have clearly broken the promise. It is very easy to determine my wife's expectation damages: the cab fare. Does my duty to keep my promise obviously imply a duty on my part to give my wife a sum of money equal to the cab fare? It would certainly be strange were I to do so. A much more natural response would be for me to apologize to my wife for my carelessness or to acknowledge the legitimacy of her feelings of resentment toward me.[28] Of course, this example does not prove that Fried's expectation principle cannot be extracted from his promise principle. It does, however, suggest that appeals to the self-evidence of the connection will not get the job done. There are at least three ways in which the expectation principle might be extracted from the promise principle. In the end, however, none of these approaches are successful.

First, there are cases where the payment of expectation damages is tantamount to performance. The most obvious example is a promise to pay a liquidated debt. If I promise to give you $500 next week, your expectation damages if I fail to tender the promised sum will be exactly $500.[29] Forcing me to pay $500 in expectation damages forces me to perform my obligation. Indeed, this is precisely how the common law writ of debt was understood. It did not award damages for breach of an obligation, but simply forced the obligor to perform. Likewise, any time that an alternative to performance is readily available in the market, giving a disappointed promisee expectation damages will allow her to purchase the equivalent of performance without any loss.[30] Despite its appeal, however, this argument cannot explain the connection between expectation damages and the promise principle in many cases. Most obviously, contracts involving even moderately unique services cannot be analogized to contracts for the sale of a commodity where money forms an almost perfect substitute for performance.

The second possibility is that promissory obligations continue to exist in some sense even after the initial promise has been broken, and it is this residual promissory obligation that creates the duty to pay expectation damages. Consider again my promise to pick up my wife from the airport. What obligations do I now have toward my wife with regard to my promise when I fail to arrive on time?[31] One possibility would be that my obligations are at an end. I am clearly in the wrong because I broke my original promise without good cause. At this point, however, there is no way that I can perform my initial obligation. Although I am now guilty of a moral wrong, I have no further moral obligations associated with my promise. It is finished. But this account of my obligations does not seem to track our ordinary understanding of what we undertake when we make a promise. Rather, it seems to me that when I am late, I have an obligation based on my promise to get to the airport to pick up my wife. Abstracting from this example, we could say that when we break a promise, we continue to have a promissory obligation to provide some sort of reasonable substitute performance.

On this view, expectation damages are simply the continuation of the initial promissory obligation. If I promise to deliver goods to you at a specified time and fail to perform, my promissory obligation has not come to an end. Rather, I remain obligated to do the next best thing or something of the like. Thus, when I pay you expectation damages, I am performing my obligations under the promise, albeit only those residual obligations remaining after I have broken my original promise. The residual obligations theory of expectation damages, however, has its own embarrassments. It is by no means clear that in most cases the residual promissory obligation left in the wake of a broken promise consists of a duty to pay money. Imagine that I am on the way to the airport to pick up my wife at 5:00 P.M., but through my own negligence I left late. At 5:15 P.M., I pull into the arrivals lane at the airport, and when I see my wife waiting at the curb, rather than stopping to pick her up, I roll down the window and toss out a wad of money as I speed by. Few would say that such actions demonstrate a mastery of promissory morality.

Third, one might argue that when promisors make a contract, they are making a promise to pay damages in the event of breach.[32] On this view, the obligation to pay damages is part of the contingent content of what was promised, and the award of damages is thus in effect a form of specific performance. The most powerful objection to this argument is that it is simply mistaken to suppose that most contracting parties do in fact intend to pay damages in the event of breach. The argument is a descendant of the option theory of contract put forward by Holmes, which has garnered the attention of some legal empiricists.[33] While contracting is too ubiquitous an activity for a comprehensive sociological study, we do have reason to suppose that people do not regard contractual obligations as a disjunctive obligation to perform or pay damages.[34]

The second objection is that, as a matter of law, we do not allow the parties to fully control the content of their remedial obligations. It is true that expectation damages are a default remedy only, but it does not follow from this that parties are free to specify any remedy that they wish. Furthermore, the constraint on party control over remedial obligations extends much further than prohibitions on unconscionable remedies such as Shylock's pound of flesh in *The Merchant of Venice*. Strikingly, parties cannot contract into the remedy of specific performance. Likewise, the penalty doctrine places constraints on the content of explicit liquidated damages, limiting them to those that are a reasonable forecast of actual damages.[35]

A promissory theory also faces difficulty making sense of private standing. The most natural argument is that private standing is a decentralized system of enforcement. Notice that this defense works equally well across economic and promissory theories. It bears no unique relationship to the promise principle. For example, efficiency theorists might posit that plaintiffs are paid to incentivize optimal performance. In the case of promissory theories, in contrast, plaintiffs enforce the obligation to perform one's promises. And so on. The pragmatic argument for private standing is ultimately agnostic about the source and shape of the underlying social policies that it vindicates. As already noted, this pragmatic argument has an initial plausibility, but it cannot explain the odd fact that it is only the promisee (or a third-party beneficiary) that is able to bring an action for breach of contract. This is a problem for Fried. It is important to realize that for Fried's theory, the privity doctrine is a key aspect of contract law. Unlike the doctrine of consideration, for example, he does not view it as an unfortunate holdover from more wooly headed times. Rather, for Fried, promises create relational moral duties, and, accordingly, contracts consist of relational legal obligations. He writes, "Promises—and therefore contracts—are fundamentally relational; one person must make the promise to another, and the second person must accept it."[36]

It does not follow from this, however, that Fried has an account of the relationship between his promise principle and private standing. Indeed, in the one place in *Contract as Promise* where he explicitly touches on the issue of private enforcement and moral obligation, his comments seem at least potentially hostile to private standing. Again, in the context of discussing contract formation, he writes:

> Don't say that I can always refuse to enforce the promise, or refuse to scold the promisors for breaking it, or even refuse to feel resentment at the breach. The moral force of a promise cannot depend on whether the promisee chooses to "enforce" the promise. After all, what does it mean to enforce a promise in the moral sphere? I suppose one can demand its performance, but if there is a morally binding obligation under a promise, the existence of the obligation does not depend on a demand by the promisee—nor on his scolding the promisor, nor on his feeling resentment.[37]

This passage suggests that the moral obligation to keep a promise is not contingent on action by the promisee to "enforce" it. Yet the law is indifferent to the breach of contract unless the wronged promisee takes some action.

Justifying Private Standing

My approach to these questions begins with dismembered goats. The fifteenth chapter of Genesis in the Bible records one of the most famous contracts in history. Abram (later renamed Abraham) has left his homeland in Ur and come to the land of Canaan. After defeating a coalition of local kings, Abram has a vision in which God promises the childless patriarch that his decedents will outnumber the stars of heaven and that he will inherit the land of Canaan. The skeptical Abram asks, "O Lord God, how am I to know that I shall possess it?"[38] The text goes on: "[God] said to him, 'Bring me a heifer three years old, a she-goat three years old, a ram three years old, a turtledove, and a young pigeon.' And he brought him all these, cut them in two, and laid each half over against the other."[39] It is, to modern ears, a strange story. Abram doubts God's promise, but his doubts are allayed when God instructs him to dismember three animals. Why does the ritual with the mutilated livestock convince Abram that God's promise is meant seriously? Although the answer is obscure to us, it would have been apparent to an ancient reader. God's response to Abram transforms his promise into a legal covenant by invoking the formality through which such covenants were created in the ancient Near East.[40]

The slaughter of the heifer and the she-goat was an enacted penalty clause.[41] In effect, the parties to a covenant agreed that, in the event that they failed to fulfill their part of the bargain, they should be treated in the same manner as the dismembered animals. Indeed, in Biblical Hebrew, one does not "make a covenant." The phrase is translated more literally as to "cut a covenant."[42] The formality of killing an animal to seal a deal was widespread in the ancient world—appearing, for example, in Babylonian treaties and the agreement dividing Alexander the Great's empire upon his death, when his generals hacked up a dog.[43] Thomas Hobbes notes the form in Leviathan, writing that, "before the time of Civill Society . . . there is nothing can strengthen a Covenant of Peace . . . but . . . [the] Feare as a Revenger of their perfidy. . . . Such was the Heathen Forme, Let Jupiter kill me else, as I kill this Beast."[44]

In part, as Hobbes noted, the ritual invoked the punishment of the gods (an ironic position for the militantly monotheistic Yahweh to take in Genesis 15), but it also may have been embedded in a system of self-help. The relationship is nicely captured in Book III of *The Iliad*, when Priam, the king of Troy, and Agamemnon, leader of the besieging Achaeans, agree to end their war through single combat between champions from either side. They formalize the agreement by slitting the throats of a brace of sheep and pouring their blood, along with wine, on the ground as a libation to the gods. The Trojans and Achaeans then join in a prayer: "Zeus—god of greatness, god of glory, all you immortals! Whichever contenders trample on this treaty first, spill their brains on the ground as this wine spills—theirs, their children's too—their enemies rape their wives!"[45] Notice the prayer not only invokes the wrath of the gods but suggests the legitimacy of violence against oath breakers and their families.[46] In an anarchic world of feuding tribes, this ex ante authorization would have been particularly important because it would allow a disappointed promisee to exact vengeance on a promisor without fear of retaliation by members of the promisor's tribe.[47]

If the ancient sources valorize the right of private retaliation without ambivalence, they also show an interest in limiting retaliation. The most famous example of this concern is found in the Bible. According to the Book of Exodus, the divine law delivered to Moses at Sinai declared: "When men strive together . . . if any harm follows, then you shall give life for life, eye for eye, tooth for tooth, hand for hand, foot for foot, burn for burn, wound for wound, stripe for stripe."[48] Retaliation was limited by a principle of proportionality. To take more than an eye for an eye was to engage in predation. According to the Talmud, the bloody, but limited, retaliation sanctioned by the *lex talionis* was then converted into the payment of money.[49] Likewise, the earliest Germanic and Anglo-Saxon laws contained a schedule of wergild that might be proffered in lieu of blood feud.[50] Indeed, according to nineteenth-century historians, private law itself emerged from attempts to limit the violence of feuding tribes. "Step by step, as the power of the State waxes," wrote Frederick Pollock and Frederic William Maitland, "the self-centred and self-helping autonomy of the kindred wanes. Private feud is controlled, regulated, put, one may say, into legal harness."[51]

Hobbes famously claimed that life in the state of nature was "solitary, poore, nasty, brutish, and short."[52] By the "state of nature," Hobbes meant a world without formal government. His solution to the miserable brutishness of anarchy was Leviathan, an all-powerful state that could compel obedience to law. The alternative to Leviathan, he insisted, was chaos. Few thinkers today endorse Hobbes's frank embrace of absolutism, although a strong assumption continues that Hobbes was correct about anarchy: In the absence of the state, chaos results.[53] History and anthropology, however, reveal that Hobbes was mistaken on this crucial point. As an empirical matter, anarchic systems are not chaotic. Rather, they are filled with social practices that constrain conflict, violence, and predation. The state simply is not the only solution to the Hobbesian problem of man's constant "endeavour to destroy, or subdue one an other."[54]

One of the most common mechanisms for creating order in an anarchic system is the feud.[55] If a member of tribe A harms a member of tribe B, then members of tribe B will retaliate against a member of tribe A. This creates incentives for members of both tribes to avoid predation and to police misconduct by members of their own tribe. Admittedly, the order provided by such a system is brittle and can result in a cycle of violence that is difficult to escape. Most of the time, though, it does not break down. Indeed, as opposed to the vicious anarchy predicted by Hobbes, in many societies where feuds govern, elaborate courtesy and hospitality are the norm.[56]

Human flourishing, however, requires more than simply the absence of predation. It also requires that individuals cooperate with one another. In Hobbes's vision of the state of nature, anyone foolish enough to enter a contract makes himself vulnerable to opportunism:

> For he that performeth first, has no assurance the other will performe after; because the bonds of words are too weak to bridel mens ambition, avarice, anger, and other Passions, without the feare of some coërcive Power; which in the condition of meer Nature, where all men are equall, and judges of the justnesse of their own fears, cannot possibly be supposed.[57]

In a world of simultaneous exchange, of course, contracts are not really necessary.[58] *Quid* is exchanged for *quo*, but there is never an executory obligation to deliver *quid* or perform *quo*.[59] As soon as the element of time is introduced, however, the problem becomes more complicated.

Contracting over time leaves both parties in a classic prisoner's dilemma.[60] Traditionally, scholars have looked to law as a solution to the dilemma.[61] If we have contract law, so goes the argument, Able needn't worry about Baker's defection, because once Baker enters into a legally binding contract, the law will prohibit his defection. This explanation assumes, however, that the state requires parties to perform their contracts. As already noted, the state leaves the question of legal action entirely in the hands of the promisee. In the absence of plaintiff-initiated litigation, Leviathan is indifferent to breach of contract. Accordingly, the story of contract law as a simple prohibition on defection must be modified.

Another solution to the prisoner's dilemma is for disappointed promisees to retaliate against promise breakers. While the classical prisoner's dilemma yields the depressing result of mutual defection when played as a one-shot game between rational actors, a substantial literature demonstrates that when the game is played repeatedly, cooperation develops through a strategy of tit for tat.[62] Each player cooperates until the other player defects, at which point the nondefecting player retaliates by defecting in the next round.[63] The logic behind the strategy is that Able limits the probability of Baker's defection by threatening to punish him should he defect.[64] Ironically, the ability to retaliate provided by a multiround game increases the probability of cooperation and thus reduces the likelihood that retaliation will become necessary.

The problem with the simple tit-for-tat strategy is that it is costly and requires that parties engage in a series of mutual commitments.[65] It cannot provide for cooperation in one-shot scenarios.[66] One must be able to retaliate without a second transaction. Consider again the case of Spartacus discussed in chapter 2. The pirate admiral was able to break his promise to Spartacus with impunity because his navy immunized him from retaliation by the Spartacan army. Ironically, perhaps, it was Spartacus's inability to retaliate that led to the breakdown of cooperation, and some mechanism facilitating attacks would have resulted in greater cooperation (and, one might add, fewer crucified slaves). On the other hand, as the treaty between Agamemnon and Priam from *The Iliad* illustrates, even parties that are violently opposed to one another can reach agreement when it is possible to credibly threaten the other party with retaliation in the event of breach.[67] There is, thus, a sense in which cooperation depends on the ability to retaliate rather than, as Hobbes suggests, its complete suppression.

Of course, retaliation may lead to escalating conflict.[68] If retaliation takes the form of self-help violence, as in the case of feuding Icelandic chieftains or Bronze Age Greeks, the target may fight back. Furthermore, if the legitimacy of the initial attack is not clearly established, then the natural reaction of the attacked party's tribe is to retaliate. The reason is simple: In an anarchic system, the credible threat of retaliation is the best way to avoid unprovoked predation. A retaliatory threat is only credible, however, if one consistently retaliates against apparent wrongs, which is why cultures of honor and vengeance emerged in anarchic societies. Not surprisingly, these societies developed memorable rituals—such as the dismembering of goats—by which retaliation for breach of contract could be distinguished from simple predation. These rituals were attempts to reduce, ex ante, the potential level of ex post violence in the event of retaliation for breach. Over time, societies developed stronger safeguards against the risk of escalating conflict inherent in encouraging permissible retaliation for breach: The extraction of wealth replaced bloodier responses; adjudication came to replace self-help, acting as a gatekeeper to retaliation; and, finally, the scope of even monetary retaliation was limited.[69] In short, rather than completely displacing the world of anarchy, as Hobbes suggested, contract law tames and limits the anarchic mechanism of retaliation without repudiating its basic structure. It solves the problem of opportunism and facilitates the human flourishing made possible by social cooperation.[70] It does this by facilitating retaliation against contract breachers in ways that prevent retaliation from becoming merely predatory.

Given that the prisoner's dilemma created by contracting over time can be solved either through third-party enforcement by the state or by empowering private plaintiffs, why would the market argument counsel in favor of private standing rather than regulatory or criminal enforcement? Despite the apparent distance between the worlds of ancient covenants and modern contract litigation, the notion of contractual liability as consent to retaliation fits comfortably within modern commercial practices. Relational contract theorists have long noted the apparent disjunction between contract doctrine and the actual practices of contracting parties.[71] Contract lawyers often speak as though contracts specify the obligations of parties over the course of a deal, guiding their behavior.[72] But in practice, formal legal contracts often have little to do with the complex process of cooperation and mutual accommodation that characterizes business practice.[73] Contracts are important not because they govern the terms of the deal but because they function as the basis for litigation in the event of a breakdown in the relationship between the parties. Lisa Bernstein, for example, has shown how businesspeople operate under two distinct sets of norms.[74] Relationship-maintaining norms govern ongoing business relationships and are characterized by the informal accommodation and cooperation observed by relational contract theorists.[75] End-game norms come into play when ongoing relationships have broken down.[76] This is when parties invoke their formal contract rights.[77] Put in starker terms, formal contracts often function less as guides for cooperation than as weapons to be used when cooperation breaks down.

This vision of modern practice is consistent with the core structure at work in the ancient covenant rituals. The formal contract exists to specify the conditions under which a promisee may retaliate against a wayward promisor. Likewise, modern practice suggests that it is quite reasonable to suppose that in many—or indeed most—cases, legal contracts exist mainly to facilitate retaliation in the event that relations between the parties break down. The contract does more than this, however. It also radically constrains the ability to retaliate in the end game by specifying the conditions under which A may proceed against B and by limiting the mode of retaliation to litigation. Furthermore, although it may seem odd to speak of litigation as a form of attack on a defendant's wealth or as retaliation by a disappointed promisee, it captures an important reality of modern law. People experience litigation as an aggressive action. Indeed, military metaphors abound in discussions of litigation.[78] Much of this, of course, can be dismissed as lawyerly machismo. Nevertheless, the rhetoric persists because it comports with the inevitably antagonistic and aggressive nature of litigation. When A sues B for breach of contract, he or she makes a decision to attack B through the courts, and one will be hard pressed to find a defendant who does not experience litigation as a form of attack. In this sense, modern litigants are much like the Trojans and Achaeans who battled before Ilium in the wake of Agamemnon's broken covenant.

The Measure of Damages

Viewing the remedial structure of contract law primarily as a limited form of retaliation designed to solve the problem of the prisoner's dilemma inherent in contracting yields some insights into the concrete structure of contract doctrine. It is black-letter law that a so-called penalty clause is unenforceable.[79] Parties are free to specify the amount of money that they must pay in the event of breach, but the amount chosen must be a reasonable estimate of one's actual damages.[80] A liquidated-damages clause that exceeds a reasonable estimate of the parties' actual expectation damages will be deemed a penalty clause.[81] For many theorists, this rule is puzzling.

For promissory theorists, the penalty doctrine is a stark limitation on freedom of contract.[82] If contracts are to be respected because they represent the autonomous choices of the parties, then, unless there are third-party effects, the law ought to be indifferent as to the substantive content of agreements.[83] This content is a matter for the parties to decide, and for the state to restrict or second guess if the choices of private parties fail to show them the respect that they are due. Granted, some promissory theorists, such as Seana Shiffrin, question whether one can make a promise that contemplates its own breach, but this argument suggests that contract law should reject not only the penalty doctrine but the entire notion of liquidated damages.[84] But for those who ground contracts in promissory morality or the autonomy of citizens in a liberal polity, the penalty doctrine constitutes an interpretive embarrassment. Indeed, some autonomy theorists have sought to defend the entire bilateral structure of contract damages as an implied promise to pay money in the event of promise breaking.

Economic theorists, who place a premium on the value of private ordering, likewise have difficulty accounting for the penalty doctrine. Initially, the theory of efficient breach seems to suggest that penalty clauses are undesirable because they overincentivize performance.[85] From an economic point of view, there is nothing per se efficient about the performance of contracts—rather, the parties should perform only when the benefits of performance outweigh its costs.[86] Penalty clauses appear to incentivize performance even when the costs of breach outweigh the benefits of performance. This apparently neat explanation, however, holds true only if the costs of renegotiation are high. It falls apart once the possibility of ex post renegotiation emerges.[87] If a promisor can realize greater returns from breach than performance will realize for a promisee, he can always bargain for a release from his obligations by offering the promisee part of the upside profit from breach. In effect, a promisor can threaten, "Agree to release me, or else I will perform and you won't be able to capture any of the benefits from my breach." Indeed, because penalty clauses commit the promisor to sharing a larger portion of the surplus created by breach opportunities ex post, they may provide an efficient ex ante bargaining tool for promisors who wish to credibly commit to dividing such a surplus with promisees.[88]

One might try to justify the rule on the ground that it protects contracting parties from inconsiderately imposing crushing liability on themselves in the event of breach.[89] For example, some scholars have pointed to the experimental results of behavioral decision theorists, which suggest that humans are prone to systematic errors in how they assess the risk of unlikely events such as breach of contract.[90] Accordingly, courts' willingness to police liquidated-damages clauses can be justified by the need to protect people from their faulty assessments of the risk of paying a penalty.[91]

The problem with this interpretation of the doctrine is that it cannot explain why penalty clauses are singled out for special monitoring.[92] After all, the behavioralist research suggests that people are likely to inaccurately assess the risks associated with events other than contract breach; yet the law normally does not inquire into the substance of contractual terms. For example, if A loans B $10 to be repaid with 10 percent interest in one year, the penalty doctrine would disallow a clause requiring the payment of a fairly trivial additional sum—say $50—if B failed to tender the $11 as promised.[93] It is difficult to see why the law should protect parties from the decision to enter into such relatively harmless agreements. Alternatively, suppose that A loaned an enormous sum of money to B, so enormous that B had little hope of repaying it. Absent fraud or unconscionability, such a contract is legally unobjectionable.[94] The penalty-clause doctrine thus seems, at best, a ham-fisted attempt at paternalism.[95]

In contrast, thinking of contractual liability as a form of retaliation has a simple explanation for the penalty doctrine: Law exists in part to limit the ability of parties to engage in predation against one another. This does not mean that the law eliminates any ability to retaliate against wrongs. Rather, the law civilizes recourse by replacing private violence with private litigation and limiting satisfaction to the extraction of wealth from the party in the wrong.[96] Consider again the covenant between Agamemnon and Priam before the walls of Ilium. The parties consented that, in the event of breach, their throats could be slit, their children enslaved, and their wives raped.[97] The agreement is barbarous and unjust, but the injustice does not reside in the fact that the promisor consented to attack in the event of breach. The barbarity of the agreement lies in the excessive nature of the attack. The advent of contract law limited recourse to retaliation that is proportionate to the wrong inflicted. The law does not allow a party to consent to a disproportionate response because the establishment of a system of private law was fueled by a desire to limit the scope and violence of recourse in the face of wrongs.[98] By insisting on proportionality in retaliation against commercial wrongs, the markets facilitated by contract law "gentle" manners.

This account is consistent with two other aspects of the penalty doctrine. First, law will not honor a liquidated-damages clause that exceeds the value of what was promised; but there is no objection to clauses that limit recourse to less than expectation damages in the event of breach.[99] In effect, parties may declare that they will be satisfied with recourse at less than the full value of what was promised to them.[100] Such subcompensatory recourse is not excessive and therefore is unobjectionable. Indeed, parties are free to disclaim all rights to recourse ex ante by agreeing to otherwise valid contracts that contain clauses disclaiming that they are legally enforceable.[101]

Second, the doctrine does not sweep into its ambit true option contracts, in which parties agree ex ante on a price for the purchase of a release from certain obligations. For instance, so-called pay-or-play contracts are quite common in the film industry and are routinely honored by the courts.[102] Under these contracts, an actor is promised a fixed sum of money—say $1 million—in return for the actor's promise to perform in or refrain from performing in a contemplated film at the movie studio's discretion.[103] If the studio and the actor instead made a bilateral contract where the actor promised to act and the studio promised to hire the actor for a film at the rate of $1 million, a $1 million liquidated-damages clause could be deemed a penalty clause.[104] The actor would have a duty to mitigate her damages by finding another role, and in any case her claim for the lost $1 million under the contract would be offset by the amount saved—in this case, the cost of performing in the movie—as a result of the breach.[105]

From a purely economic point of view, there is no distinction between the pay-or-play agreement and the liquidated-damages clause. Both are options. In contrast, the legal distinction makes sense if the aim of the penalty doctrine is to limit retaliation. The $1 million pay-or-play clause is not meant as recourse in the event of breach; indeed, in refusing to make the movie and tendering $1 million, the studio fully performs its contractual obligations, and there is no breach. On the other hand, when the clause is meant to specify the recourse to be allowed in the event of breach, then the law limits recourse to proportionate damages.

For Fuller and Perdue, the mystery was why the law should award expectation damages rather than reliance damages.[106] Their answer was a rather convoluted story about how expectation damages were the most effective way to protect reliance.[107] As noted above, promissory and economic theorists have offered their own explanations.[108]

Regardless of what one makes of the merits of any of these arguments,[109] they all suffer from a basic problem: The law seldom awards full expectation damages.[110] A host of doctrines ensure that the actual damages awarded to any plaintiff will be less than the value of her expectancy. First, under U.S. law, parties must bear their own legal expenses, which means that in the absence of an attorney's fee clause, a plaintiff will always be undercompensated for the full value of his contractual expectation.[111] Second, damages may only be recovered where they can be calculated with certainty.[112] Real, but uncertain, losses receive no compensation beyond nominal damages.[113] Third, under the rule in *Hadley v. Baxendale*,[114] consequential damages are sharply limited.[115] Those damages that are not foreseeable at the time of contract formation are not recoverable unless they are specially communicated at that time.[116] In at least some jurisdictions, additional consequential damages must also be specially agreed to ex ante.[117] Fourth, in the event of a promisor's breach, a promisee has a duty to mitigate her damages.[118] She must make reasonable efforts to limit the amount that the promisor must pay.[119] Failure to do so results in a reduction of any claim for damages.[120] These limitations present problems for any theory that takes full expectation damages as the correct remedy for breach, because they ensure that full expectation damages are virtually never paid.[121]

As a doctrinal matter, it thus makes more sense to think of expectation damages as a limitation on awards rather than an entitlement in the event of breach. The point is most powerfully illustrated by contemporary doctrine's treatment of claims for reliance damages. According to the *Restatement (Second) of Contracts*, reliance damages are available as an alternative measure for recovery.[122] As a practical matter, plaintiffs are likely to seek reliance damages in those cases where the reliance measure would yield a larger recovery than expectation damages—for example, where a promisee makes a losing contract that the promisor then serendipitously breaches.[123] Courts (and the *Restatement*), however, have been unsympathetic to plaintiffs who attempt to recover the full value of their reliance on a losing contract.[124] Rather, defendants are allowed to provide evidence of what the plaintiff would have lost had the contract been performed, and any award will then be reduced by these avoided costs.[125] The result is that the expectation measure—when it can be determined—operates as an effective limit on the amount of reliance damages that can be recovered.[126]

The structure of expectation damages must be viewed in light of the previously discussed limiting doctrines. Requirements of certainty, limitations on consequential damages, and the like all serve to cabin the recourse available to promisees against breaching promisors.[127] The expectation measure, rather than providing the value of an entitlement, represents an upper limit on recovery. The actual amount that a plaintiff can recover may in practice be considerably less than the full value of his expectation interest. Indeed, plaintiffs are free to sue and ask courts for less than the value of their full expectation damages, and they frequently do so. There is no impediment to such suits. Rather, claims for damages are disallowed when they exceed the expectation measure or fall within one of the other limiting doctrines discussed above.

I conclude this chapter by returning to the bloody covenant rituals of the Bible and Homer. The agreement between Priam and Agamemnon recounted in *The Iliad* ultimately failed. The attempt to limit war through cooperation broke down, fighting resumed, and, after the sack of Troy, Agamemnon returned to Argos. In his Oresteia trilogy,[128] Aeschylus continues the story, recounting how Agamemnon's wife, Clytaemnestra, murdered him in revenge for his earlier sacrifice of their daughter. Clytaemnestra, in turn, was killed by her son Orestes in revenge for the murder of his father. In the final play of the trilogy, Orestes, pursued by the Furies, a vengeful band of outraged demigods, flees to Athens, throwing himself on the mercy of the goddess Athena. The Furies, embodying vengeance, feud, and outraged honor, demand the murderer. Orestes's patron, the god Apollo, calls for the summary expulsion of the Furies from the city, dismissing them as nothing more than agents of senseless violence:

> Go where heads are severed, eyes gouged out,
> where Justice and bloody slaughter are the same . . .
> castrations, wasted seed, young men's glories butchered,
> extremities maimed, and huge stones at the chest,
> and victims wail for pity—
> spikes inching up the spine, torsos stuck on spits.[129]

One might say that Apollo wishes to relegate the Furies to a world where life is "solitary, poore, nasty, brutish, and short."[130]

Athena's response, however, is more measured. She submits Orestes to the judgment of the Athenian court, allowing the Furies to make the case for his punishment. The jury is hung, and Athena reluctantly casts the final vote for acquittal on the grounds that Clytaemnestra's crimes justified Orestes's matricide, enraging the Furies. Their leader insists to Athena that by supplanting vengeance with adjudication, "you have ridden down the ancient laws, wrenched them from my grasp."[131] Athena, however, refuses to cast the Furies from the city. Instead, she invites them to take a hallowed place buried beneath its foundations, an offer the Furies ultimately accept. Athena tells the citizens of her city:

> Neither anarchy nor tyranny, my people.
> Worship the Mean, I urge you,
> shore it up with reverence and never
> banish terror from the gates, not outright.[132]

The title of the final play is *The Eumenides*, which refers to the transformation of the Furies, and literally means "the kindly ones." In the final speech of the play, the women of the city, acting as chorus, sing their praises:

> You great good Furies, bless the land with kindly hearts,
> you Awesome Spirits, come—exult in the blazing torch,
> exult in our fires, journey on.[133]

Contractual liability rests on a sensibility similar to that put forward by Aeschylus. The earliest covenant rituals consisted of consent to violent retaliation in the event of breach. In effect, the parties invited the Furies into their relationship in the hope of creating trust sufficient for cooperation. It was a dangerous expedient that resulted in a fragile cooperation prone to violent breakdown. Hobbes, following Aeschylus's Apollo, insisted that the Furies must be driven from the community by an omnipotent Leviathan. To the extent that modern theories of contract focus their attention exclusively on the way that the law, as a third party, enforces agreements, they rest on a similar sensibility. The common law took a different course. Rather than eliminating private retaliation, the common law tamed and limited it. The Furies, however, remain buried deep within the structure of contractual liability. Damage measures act less as fines or entitlements to compensation than as limits on private retaliation. Indeed, inherent in the notion of money damages is the notion of a limit on retaliation that eliminates the possibility of personal violence. Perhaps most strikingly, contract law does not enforce contracts per se; rather, it empowers disappointed promisees to act against breaching promisors through the courts. In doing so, it fosters commercial cooperation by allowing for the mutual accommodation of trading partners while preserving the threat of retaliation in the event of opportunism. Finally, it limits the extent of aggression inherent in retaliation, assisting in the gentling of manners Montesquieu associated with *doux commerce*.

CHAPTER SEVEN

Boilerplate

In 2001, Apple introduced the iPod, which rapidly became the most popular personal music player in history. Users must install the accompanying iTunes software, which results in a pop-up screen containing the software license; and one must click "I agree" to proceed with the install. Among other things, the contract states that "you also agree that you will not use the Apple Software for . . . the development, design, manufacture or production of missiles, or nuclear, chemical or biological weapons."[1] The notion of weaponizing iTunes is not entirely far-fetched. In August 2006, British authorities arrested a terrorist cell in the United Kingdom. The would-be terrorists planned to blow up ten passenger jets over the Atlantic using bombs detonated using modified iPods.[2] The potential violation of contractual obligations to Apple does not seem to have figured in the calculations of the jihadis. Indeed, like most iPod owners, they probably never read the license before clicking "I agree."

The iTunes license is an example of boilerplate—a complex, preprinted agreement offered on a take-it-or-leave-it basis without negotiation and which is seldom, if ever, read. In all likelihood, the Apple lawyers inserted the restrictions on using iTunes to manufacture weapons of mass destruction because of U.S. laws governing the sale of encryption technology—such as that in the iTunes software—that can be weaponized. Knowing that boilerplate is not going to be read, drafters have inserted more whimsical terms. The boilerplate software license for one company states:

> Should you fail to register any of the evaluation software available through our web pages and continue to use it, be advised that a leather-winged demon of the night will tear itself, shrieking blood and fury, from the endless caverns of the nether world, hurl itself into the darkness with a thirst for blood on its slavering fangs and search the very threads of time for the throbbing of your

> heartbeat. Just thought you'd want to know that. Alchemy Mindworks accepts no responsibility for any loss, damage or expense caused by leather-winged demons of the night, either.[3]

Such jokes, however, point to a serious issue that contract theorists have struggled with for nearly a century. In a modern economy we are constantly entering into contracts defined by complex boilerplate. These contracts are unread and often unreadable by any but the most determined consumer[4] yet are generally enforced as written by the courts.

Boilerplate is ubiquitous for good reason.[5] Just as the mass production of goods dramatically lowered prices and increased living standards, boilerplate agreements allow the mass production of transactions. In complex organizations, managers may not trust employees to negotiate on behalf of the firm. Limiting transactions to preapproved boilerplate terms reduces a firm's agency costs. Boilerplate also allows firms to manage risk by creating a single, predictable legal structure for all their transactions. Despite these and other benefits, however, boilerplate has always concerned judges and contract theorists. The complex contract offered on a take-it-or-leave-it basis that is unread departs from the vision of a negotiated agreement between equals who can be trusted to look after their own interests. This concern is coupled with unease about enforcing contracts that contain terms such as arbitration agreements, choice-of-forum and choice-of-law clauses, disclaimers of warranties, limitations on damages, constraints on the ability of purchasers to use purchased items, and other terms that critics deem to be harsh or unfair.

Ultimately, the concerns with boilerplate center on the role of consent in contract law. To many, the consent of a consumer presented with a boilerplate agreement seems too attenuated to justify its enforcement. The market argument, however, reformulates the role of consent in contract theory and suggests that the critics' focus on consent or its absence in boilerplate agreements is misplaced. In the market argument, consent does not justify the enforcement of contracts. Rather, we enforce contracts because doing so strengthens and extends markets. It is the moral value of markets and commerce that justifies contractual enforcement. Contract law does this by providing both flexibility and certainty in transactional structures, functions served by boilerplate agreements. In this vision, consent serves two subordinate functions. First, it coordinates legal obligations. Second, it is one mechanism among many that constrains abuse by the authors of contractual terms. Enforcing contracts with extremely thin or attenuated consent presents no particular normative challenge for the market argument as long as other mechanisms exist that constrain the authors of contract terms and the bare minimum of consent necessary to avoid conflicting terms is present. Doctrinally, this suggests that, rather than examining whether consumers "meaningfully" consent to boilerplate, we should look at the social context in which these contracts are formed to determine whether other feedback mechanisms constrain contract authors. In principle, the market argument does not condemn the regulation of boilerplate terms based on their substantive content. It is skeptical of this approach, however, not because it threatens personal autonomy but because restrictions on transactional design tend to ossify and stunt well-functioning markets.

The Case against Boilerplate and Some Responses

The legal scholar who launched much of the modern debate on the problems of boilerplate agreements was Friedrich Kessler.[6] His work anticipated later criticisms of boilerplate agreements. The traditional defense of freedom of contract rested on the assumption of "the genuineness and reality of consent" between parties "on a footing of social and approximate economic equality."[7] Such, however, is not the case with boilerplate:

> Standard contracts are typically used by enterprises with strong bargaining power. The weaker party, in need of the goods or services, is frequently not in a position to shop around for better terms, either because the author of the standard contract has a monopoly (natural or artificial) or because all competitors use the same clauses. His contractual intention is but a subjection more or less voluntary to terms dictated by the stronger party, terms whose consequences are often understood only in a vague way, if at all.[8]

Such contracts, he went on to argue, serve to "build up and strengthen industrial empires"[9] and are "effective instruments in the hands of powerful industrial and commercial overlords enabling them to impose a new feudal order of their own making upon a vast host of vassals."[10] Subsequent critics have deepened Kessler's arguments, but none of them have improved on the verve of his language.

The critique of boilerplate takes three forms. The first objection is that, because those who agree to these contracts cannot negotiate over their terms or otherwise do not have meaningful choices, the contracts lack the consent necessary to justify their enforcement. The second objection is that, due to consumer ignorance or irrationality, boilerplate results in inefficient and unduly harsh terms. The final objection is that boilerplate undermines democracy, empowering corporations to become a law unto themselves by avoiding benign regulations and imposing harsh terms on prostrate consumers.

The central argument against the enforcement of boilerplate contracts is that they lack meaningful consent. Several features of boilerplate contracts raise concerns. First, by definition, boilerplate agreements are offered on a take-it-or-leave-it basis. The parties do not negotiate over the terms. Rather, the terms are authored by one party and accepted by the other party. Second, no one reads boilerplate contracts. Thus, those who "consent" to these contracts are ignorant of their terms. Third, boilerplate is often used in situations where there is an inequality of bargaining power. Those making this argument generally do not explain precisely what is meant by bargaining power, but it seems to be some amalgam of greater sophistication and resources on the part of the party that authors the agreement.[11] Sometimes the claim is made that boilerplate contracts are used by monopolists or near monopolists such that consumers lack any meaningful alternative but to agree to the terms.[12] Finally, in some instances, even the bare formality of presenting the promisor with a document to sign is not observed.

So-called browsewrap agreements, in which a website owner asserts that a visitor assents to terms merely because the terms are linked to someplace in the site, provide an example of this last problem.[13] In *Nguyen v. Barnes & Noble, Inc.*,[14] for example, an online retailer sought to compel arbitration based on its website's terms of use. Each page of the site contained a link to the terms at the bottom of the page, but nothing called attention to the link, nor did the pages claim that visitors had agreed to the terms by using the site. However, if one clicked on the link, several pages of boilerplate appeared, which included a clause claiming, "By visiting any area in the Barnes & Noble.com Site . . . a User is deemed to have accepted the Terms of Use."[15] In effect, Barnes & Noble placed terms in the vicinity of consumers and claimed consent based on language contained in the entirely unobserved boilerplate. The court refused to enforce the agreement, noting that "where the link to a website's terms of use is buried at the bottom of the page or tucked away in obscure corners of the website where users are unlikely to see it, courts have refused to enforce browsewrap agreements."[16] In other cases, however, judges have enforced browsewrap agreements when defendants were in fact aware of the terms or even when they were only subsequently informed of their existence.[17] In these cases, the consent to the boilerplate seems attenuated. Increasingly, however, so-called clickwrap agreements are standard.[18] In these cases, the full text of the boilerplate is presented to a customer who must then click "I agree" before being allowed to proceed with the transaction. Courts have uniformly upheld such clickwrap agreements.[19]

Boilerplate is offered on a take-it-or-leave-it basis. Offerees cannot negotiate. Without the ability to negotiate, the meaningfulness of consent is questionable. Or so goes the argument. The problem is that this criticism makes a fetish out of bargaining. Customers can also shop. Both bargaining and shopping are costly, but there is no a priori reason to suppose that one process is more legitimate than the other. Critics point out that often the choice offered by shopping is illusory because all firms offer the same terms.[20] This is pointed to as evidence of bargaining power or collusion. However, it is also consistent with equilibrium in a competitive market where producer surplus is transformed almost entirely into consumer surplus. For example, prices in a competitive market will tend to be the same across all producers, because competition drives price down to marginal cost. In this situation, consumers rather than producers hold the whip hand. Analogously, the same terms across a market may mean that competition has forced firms to offer the most favorable terms consistent with their costs. In short, without more we cannot draw any normatively significant conclusion from the fact that all the producers in a given market offer the same terms on a take-it-or-leave-it basis. Furthermore, research suggests that, at least in some markets—such as software licensing—there is considerable variation across firms as to the terms offered.[21]

A second persistent criticism of boilerplate is that businesses use it to exploit the ignorance of consumers for their own profit. For example, a corporation may have good information about the probability that its products are defective. The background rules of law assign the costs of those defects to the corporation, but a corporation can use boilerplate to shift some of that risk to consumers. Consumers accept the terms either because they do not understand them or because they inaccurately assess the probability of the risk. In the 1960s and 1970s, this concern was phrased in terms of a lack of consumer sophistication.[22] More recently, scholars have used the economic language of asymmetric information and bounded rationality.[23] Such asymmetric information between offerors and offerees can create inefficient transactions. If consumers are inaccurately assessing the costs associated with risk, boilerplate may be creating losses even if consumers are aware of the existence and meaning of terms. They will price these terms but will do so inaccurately.[24]

This argument is a variation on the well-known "lemons problem" first identified by George Akerlof, in which asymmetric information leads to efficiency losses in otherwise competitive markets.[25] In Akerlof's model, losses resulted from pervasive discounting by the purchasers in information-starved markets and adverse selection as "good" sellers withdraw from the market rather than sell their undervalued goods at artificially low prices. The lemons problem, however, presents an opportunity for savvy entrepreneurs. Used car dealerships, for example, can offer legally enforceable warranties as a way of signaling the value of their wares. Such signaling overcomes the information problem, eliminating the loss that would otherwise result, and allows sellers and buyers to divide the resulting surplus. If boilerplate is causing losses—as opposed to transferring wealth from consumers to producers—then it would present a similar opportunity. Rather than offering boilerplate terms that lower costs by destroying value, firms have an incentive to provide consumers with information about the value of their legal rights. This is because once consumers realize that the rights they were previously transferring to firms in return for lower prices are actually worth more than the decrease in price, they ought to be willing to pay a higher price to a firm that does not seek to have consumers waive those rights. In other words, if information asymmetries cause losses, firms can increase profits by overcoming the information asymmetry and then dividing the resulting surplus with consumers.[26]

Margaret Radin has offered a variation on the uninformed consumer argument based on behavioral psychology. Because of cognitive biases, she argues, consumers are likely to underestimate the probability of rare, adverse events.[27] They mistakenly believe that they will never need to avail themselves of various legal remedies and are too ready to contract away these rights through arbitration agreements. Radin gives several examples, including a mother who agreed to an arbitration clause with a safari company.[28] Her child was subsequently attacked and killed by a hyena. In this case, one might argue that the mother fell prey to cognitive biases that led her to underestimate the probably of wild animal attacks and undervalue her legal rights. Enforcing the arbitration agreement in that case would lead to inefficient levels of precaution by the safari company and injustice to the grieving parents.

There are a number of problems with this argument. First, hyena attacks are in fact very rare.[29] The mother's steep discounting ex ante of the value of legal recourse for such an attack cannot be prima facie evidence of cognitive bias and irrational optimism. She may have simply been accurately judging the probability of attack. In concrete terms, ex ante it may be perfectly rational not to worry about litigating hyena attacks. Furthermore, even if the mother was suffering from cognitive biases, such biases often cause people to overestimate certain risks. For example, people consistently assume that highly salient or memorable dangers such as wild animal attacks are far more probable than is the case.[30] Accordingly, cognitive biases may cause people in the mother's situation to be *too* reticent about agreeing to arbitration. Furthermore, contract drafters may be subject to the same cognitive biases that infect consumers. Hence, if people systematically underestimate the occurrence of certain risks, why would contract drafters incur the expense of drafting against eventualities that they (mistakenly) believe will never occur? Indeed, one implication of the symmetrical application of Radin's cognitive bias theory is that contract drafters may devote insufficient resources to drafting against certain eventualities, although Oren Bar-Gill has argued that, in competitive markets, firms that fail to take advantage of consumers' cognitive biases will be driven out of business.[31]

It is worth noting here that the current debate about boilerplate is less about the quality of consent than about the competing merits of traditional tort litigation and arbitration. Much of the litigation over boilerplate involves enforcing arbitration agreements. Many critics believe that arbitration contracts are undesirable because they view the rights provided by the tort regime—such as heavy procedural protections, trial by jury, class-action mechanisms, and punitive damages—to be very valuable.[32] This, however, is a controversial position. Radin, for example, lauds German law's approach to form contracts, but under German law there is no right to trial by jury, no mechanism for class-action lawsuits, and no punitive damages.[33] My point is not to take a side in this debate but merely to point out that it has little to do with contract law per se and more to do with the importance one places on U.S. tort law.

The final argument against the enforcement of boilerplate invokes democracy. On this view, corporations use boilerplate to impose terms on consumers without giving consumers any real choice.[34] Because the terms of the contract are authored by the corporation, enforcing boilerplate amounts to an illegitimate delegation of lawmaking authority to a private business. It displaces the legal rules established by democratic institutions with illegitimate rules imposed for some private and nefarious purpose. The assumption is that legislation by democratic institutions is always more legitimate than lawmaking by market actors. Clearly, important differences exist in the public legitimacy of legislatures and corporations, but we should avoid romanticizing democratic institutions and catastrophizing private rule making.

Broadly speaking, democratic lawmaking is legitimate for three reasons. First, those subject to democratic institutions supposedly consent to the laws that they produce. This is the central conceit of social contract theories.[35] Elections, for example, are mechanisms by which government obtains the consent of the governed. Of course, as theorists from Rousseau to Rawls have pointed out, social contract stories are myths, whether stated in terms of historical event or tacit present consent.[36] As David Hume observed:

> Can we seriously say, that a poor peasant or artisan has a free choice to leave his country, when he knows no foreign language or manners, and lives, from day to day, by the small wages which he acquires? We may as well assert that a man, by remaining in a vessel, freely consents to the dominion of the master though he was carried on board while asleep, and must leap into the ocean and perish, the moment he leaves her.[37]

Likewise, the consent represented by democratic participation is extremely attenuated. Laws bind those who choose not to vote as well as those who voted against those laws. Indeed, compared to the stories of consent told by democratic theory, the consent of consumers to boilerplate contracts is actually far more direct. Consumers are often unaware of the precise meaning or content of the agreements that they sign, but lawmakers—to say nothing of citizens—are often unaware of the precise meaning and content of the laws to which they assent.[38]

The second basis of democratic legitimacy lies in institutions that allow citizens to alter the law. In advanced democracies, however, the ability of lone individuals to influence lawmaking is extremely limited. Some have claimed there is an important difference between a rights-bearing citizen approaching a legislator and a consumer petitioning a corporation.[39] Legislators, however, are under no obligation to meet with constituents. The access that representatives grant to citizens is a matter of prudence rather than a legal duty. On the other hand, customer service departments generally have the authority to make concessions to consumers despite what the formal contracts might say. For example, I have obtained three replacement Kindle e-readers despite limited warranties in the accompanying boilerplate. Although consumers may have no voice in the boilerplate terms, they often have voice in their relationships with corporations.[40] The same is not always true of legislation.

Finally, democratically authored laws are generally taken to be substantively better than alternative rules. Democracy is a feedback mechanism that is supposed to weed out egregiously bad legislation.[41] One need not be entirely cynical about democracy, however, to notice that elections and democratic politics provide imperfect feedback at best. Elections, for example, often turn on events—such as foreign affairs or the business cycle—unrelated to immediate legislative activity. Likewise, the institutional structures of democracy often create perverse incentives.[42] By comparison, the market provides far more immediate feedback to private firms. Actions that harm consumers are likely to drive them away. Unlike elected officials, who face the electorate infrequently, firms face their customers constantly, and, as the high rate of corporate mortality demonstrates, they are often found wanting. To be sure, the feedback mechanisms provided by the market are also imperfect. My point is not that market processes are flawless or even that they are always superior to political processes. Rather, I wish to make the more modest claim that we ought not to romanticize democracy. It is by no means clear that public rule makers will always produce superior outcomes to private rule makers.

Markets, Consent, and Boilerplate

While the criticism of boilerplate has become increasingly sophisticated—if not baroque—the heart of the problem centers on consent. If consumers meaningfully consent to boilerplate terms, then it is far more difficult to question their economic efficiency. Likewise, it is difficult to make extravagant claims about the threat of boilerplate to democracy if such contracts are simply agreements by private individuals. Implicit in all the critiques of boilerplate is the assumption that some robust idea of consent is a necessary condition for the legitimate enforcement of contracts. According to the critics, boilerplate lacks such consent, and the rest of their critique consists of a parade of horribles that follow from compromising on robust contractual consent.

It thus becomes important to understand the role of consent in the market argument. Compared to autonomy or efficiency arguments, consent plays a limited role in the market argument. To be sure, consent is a necessary condition for enforcing a contract, but in the market argument, consent neither justifies enforcement nor marks out welfare-enhancing transactions. Rather, in the market argument, contracts are valuable because they facilitate commerce and extend the reach of markets. It is their beneficial consequences that justify the enforcement of contracts. In this argument, consent plays two subordinate roles. First, it coordinates the legal obligations of market actors while allowing transactional flexibility and experimentation. Second, it is one mechanism among many that constrains the authors of contractual terms. Compared to alternative theories, the market argument places fewer conceptual demands on the idea of consent and is comfortable with the enforcement of contracts where consent is quite attenuated, so long as other conditions are met. To understand the role of consent in the market argument, it is useful to contrast it with the role of consent in alternative theories.

Consent performs important but differing tasks in both efficiency and autonomy theories. For efficiency theorists, the normative goal of contract law is to facilitate the allocation of resources that will maximize collective welfare. In theory, an omniscient central planner could allocate resources by fiat so that the resulting distribution would be efficient.[43] In practice, however, decision makers lack information on whether a new allocation of resources increases or decreases welfare. They require some epistemic marker signaling that a new allocation is desirable. Consent serves this function. We assume that individuals have the best information on what will increase their own welfare and that, in contrast to observing welfare itself, observing consent is relatively easy. Barring third-party effects, the fact that the parties to a transaction mutually consented to the reallocation of resources provides evidence that the resulting distribution increases welfare.

Consent has a different role in autonomy theories. Note that for efficiency theorists, consent is instrumentally useful in solving information problems in maximizing welfare. It is the increase in welfare—not consent per se—that justifies the enforcement of contracts. In contrast, for autonomy theorists, consent provides the justification for contractual enforcement. Our primary concern is not the maximization of welfare but respect for the autonomy of human choices. On this theory, we enforce contracts because for the state to refuse to give effect to the consent of the parties would, in Charles Fried's phrase, "infantilize" them.[44]

Both of these approaches place substantial demands on consent. For an efficiency theorist, consent is about information. It seems reasonable to suppose that using consent as a proxy for individual welfare requires that agents understand the nature of the choices that they are making and their likely consequences. A wholly ignorant choice is a slender reed on which to hang conclusions about the welfare effects of the resulting distribution of resources. Likewise, if we value the autonomous choice of contracting parties, it seems reasonable to insist that consent be meaningful in some sense. If the demands of autonomy are satisfied by merely volitional action regardless of whether the consent is informed or coerced, then autonomy theorists are left in the absurd position of being unable to criticize fraud or threats of violence as impositions on liberty. After all, the defrauded party makes a volitional choice, as does the person who hands over his wallet to a mugger when faced with the choice between "your money or your life." Mere choice can't be enough. Choice requires some level of liberty and understanding to be normatively significant. It thus seems reasonable for the critic of boilerplate to argue that autonomy and efficiency theories have a difficult time justifying the enforcement of boilerplate contracts where offerees are ignorant of their content and would not understand its significance if they did read the fine print.[45] In such cases, clicking "I agree" to unread and (for a layperson) unreadable terms, the critics argue, provides little information about the welfare effects of the resulting redistribution and cannot be seen as an important exercise of individual freedom.

As discussed in chapter 2, contract law supports markets by providing for freedom of contract and sanctity of contract. These principles provide both flexibility and reliability for commercial actors by allowing them to alter the scope and shape of their legal obligations. Contract law, then, credibly commits that legal recourse will be available in the event of breach. Flexibility and consent are not synonymous with each other. For example, imagine a legal rule that empowered every corporation to unilaterally alter all the legal obligations to which it or its customers might be subject. Such a rule would provide a great deal of flexibility but would run roughshod over the idea of consent, because the corporation could unilaterally impose obligations on nonconsenting parties. Likewise, one could have consent with very little flexibility. Consider status-based obligations such as marriage.[46] Until the relatively recent shift toward the enforcement of premarital agreements, the legal obligations associated with marriage were inflexible.[47] The parties to the union did not author the legal incidents of marriage, and as a legal matter every marriage was just like every other marriage. Despite this inflexibility, however, marriage was a nominally consensual relationship.

What, then, is the relationship between consent and flexibility in the market argument? One could imagine a legal system in which the legal obligations surrounding market transactions are inflexible. Indeed, for much of human history, this is precisely how legal systems treated market transactions. The Code of Hammurabi, for example, contains a number of legal rules governing market transactions—for example, what happens when the purchaser of a slave discovers that the slave has the Benu-disease or the allocation of risk in the lease of agricultural land—but it contains nothing remotely resembling a general law of contract. The obligations it sets forth are inflexible.[48] As recently as the late nineteenth century, the typical legal treatise on contact law was organized around discrete and often wildly varying rules for particular transactions, such as leases, sales, and bailments.[49] In other words, market transactions were still dominated by rules defined by the status of the parties rather than the content of their agreement. Each transactional type had a relatively inflexible set of associated legal obligations.

In a world lacking legal flexibility, we would expect there to be markets. Indeed, as long as commerce flowed into the preapproved channels of legally recognized transactions, the law would serve to strengthen and extend markets. Problems, however, arise when market actors confront unforeseen problems or wish to experiment with transactional forms that differ from those hardwired into the legal structure. The Islamic law of partnership contracts provides an example. Classical Islamic law placed restrictions on the terms of partnership agreements, with the result that partnerships could only be easily formed for a single trading voyage.[50] When trade and commerce were of a relatively small scale, this did not present a problem. However, the rigidity of the law made it difficult to create larger, longer-lasting firms. This contributed to the anemic economic growth of Islamic societies in the early modern period, just as Western societies began their long upward spike in productivity. In such cases, the law, through its inflexibility, impedes rather than supports commerce.

The solution to this problem is to allow market actors the flexibility to author their own legal obligations and experiment with new transactional structures. But flexibility creates its own problems and dangers. If market participants can unilaterally alter their obligations, we will soon confront coordination problems. Suppose that, rather than imposing a one-size-fits-all solution when it comes to warranties on the sale of goods, the law allows parties to author their own warranties. Left to their own devices, sellers and buyers will choose different warranty rules to govern the same transaction. Sellers might choose a rule of caveat emptor, while buyers will prefer a regime of strict liability for all defects. By confining the realm of legal flexibility to consent, however, this problem is solved. There is no clash of conflicting warranties authored by buyers and sellers, because we give effect only to terms agreed to by both parties. In short, consent allows the creation of privately authored legal rules without a chaos of conflicting obligations.

Consider the analogy of states in the U.S. federal system or sovereign nations in the international system. We understand both states and sovereign nations as legal agents that have the power to unilaterally impose legal obligations on others—most notably their own citizens. Problems arise, however, if we understand these agents as having the power to unilaterally impose legal obligations on one another. Problems would arise, for example, if a state could proclaim that its officers are free to violate the laws of another state with impunity when visiting that state's territory. The U.S. Supreme Court has stated that:

> Such a claim [i.e., that a state officer is free to violate the laws of another state] necessarily implicates the power and authority of a second sovereign; its sources must be found either in an agreement, express or implied, between the two sovereigns, or in the voluntary decision of the second to respect the dignity of the first as a matter of comity.[51]

Likewise, if a state wishes to impose a duty on another state to act, it must do so via an interstate compact—a contract—with the other state.[52] Similarly, states in the international system can impose specific legal obligations on other states only if those states consent by signing a treaty.[53] Such rules make sense. In their absence, sovereigns could issue conflicting commands to one another, and there would be no legal mechanism for determining which set of rules governed. Similarly, consent controls chaos by coordinating the privately authored obligations that parties seek to impose on each other via contract.

A lack of coordination, however, would not be the only problem with allowing unilateral authorship of legal obligations. We would also be worried about the substantive content of the legal obligations created. This concern could take two forms. First, we might be worried that economically destructive and inefficient transactional forms could persist. Just as the process of organic evolution depends on variation and feedback through the process of natural selection, well-functioning markets also depend on variation and feedback. Most innovations are bad ideas that deserve to die. No one need lament the speedy demise of the Edsel or New Coke. This is true of transactional innovations as well. Inconvenient, high-interest-rate financial products such as pawnshops, installment plans, and layaway purchases, for example, once dominated the consumer credit market. They have receded to the margins because consumers are far less likely to consent to such arrangements when they can turn instead to credit cards, which are more convenient and, in many cases, carry lower real interest rates.[54] Consent thus facilitates the feedback of competition. Transactions that involve needless expense or otherwise make people worse off are weeded out by the process of consent. One need not subscribe to heroic assumptions about the rationality of market actors or the competitiveness of markets to appreciate this point. It is enough to recognize that consent can be a useful mechanism for providing negative and positive feedback about the usefulness of transactional structures.

Second, we might worry that the power to unilaterally author legal obligations would lead to abuse. If I have the power without your consent to alter the obligations that you owe to me, I will be tempted to use my legal power as a tool for predation. In the past, some corporations have been given this power. For example, the Virginia Company was founded in 1606 to generate money from the English claim to North America.[55] The crown granted to the company "the superior managing and direction onelie of and for all matters that shall or may concerne the govermente"[56] of the new colony, giving it the power to make and enforce laws in Virginia. Initially the company focused on reaping the maximum short-term profit through forced labor and draconian restrictions on outside merchants, because there were few mechanisms constraining the company's power.[57] The House of Burgesses was ultimately set up as a feedback mechanism that limited the company's ability to unilaterally impose obligations.[58] Consent can provide a similar constraint on the authors of contractual terms. It places pressure on those who would author predatory legal obligations by requiring that they obtain the consent of their putative victims before putting their scheme into action. Again, it is not necessary to make heroic assumptions about the economic rationality of market actors to concede that consent is one method by which predation can be constrained.

A system providing decentralized flexibility in the authorship of legal obligations—that is, contract—will require some minimal level of consent to those obligations. Without consent, we have a coordination problem with A and B authoring inconsistent legal obligations for each other. In this argument, consent is not providing a justification for contractual enforcement. The justification lies in the value of markets and commerce. Consent is simply necessary to keep the system of decentralized obligation authoring from collapsing into a chaos of conflicting rights and duties.[59] Notice, however, that the level of consent necessary to perform this coordinating function is rather limited. When a consumer confronts an unread screen full of boilerplate and clicks, "I agree," the coordination problem has been solved, even though the consent may be uninformed and otherwise lack the character that someone looking to consent as a justification for contractual enforcement might demand. Indeed, the coordination problem would be solved if I agreed to be bound by unreadable terms, such as those contained in a box that I do not yet have the right to open.[60] All we need is some act of agreement that allows us to identify that terms of the new obligations and the parties to whom they will be applied. A deep understanding of their meaning or robust participation in their authorship is not necessary. This also explains why it makes good sense not to enforce browsewrap contracts where it is difficult to discern any consent at all.

As noted above, however, consent can also serve as a feedback mechanism for weeding out abusive or destructive terms. When considering this second function of consent, the depth of a party's understanding is potentially important. Most people do not read most of the boilerplate contracts that they sign. If anything, this process of agreement without knowledge has only accelerated in recent years, as the ease of contracting on the Internet has massively expanded ordinary consumers' ability to make contracts.[61] Given this situation, we cannot depend on people clicking "I agree" when contract terms flash across their computer screens to effectively police the content of those agreements.

It does not follow, however, that contracts involving such attenuated consent should be unenforceable. Although consent is one feedback mechanism policing the content of boilerplate agreements, it is by no means the only one. Consider the analogy of legislation. Most members of Congress never read the bills on which they vote.[62] Indeed, the legislative text of most laws would be utterly incomprehensible if it were read.[63] Most members of Congress also do not read the committee reports summarizing the legislation.[64] In some cases, laws—even major laws—come to the floor without a committee report or are amended beyond the point of recognition once out of committee. The 1964 Civil Rights Act, for example, passed in the Senate without a committee report.[65] No one, however, seriously questions the legitimacy of a duly enacted statute on the ground that the members of Congress did not read or understand the law they were voting on. Why is this so?

One way that our society might guard against bad laws is to select wise men and women as legislators who study and understand legislation. *The Federalist Papers*, for example, noted the need for "extent of information and stability of character"[66] in members of Congress. Likewise, St. George Tucker, an influential early American jurist, wrote of "wise deliberations and mature decisions" of legislators "founded on correct knowledge of facts."[67] This is, however, not our only—or even our main—way of guarding against bad legislation. Rather, legislators act in a social context that provides feedback mechanisms against bad laws. Lobbyists and pressure groups monitor the minutiae of legislation. The press covers the activities of Congress. Periodic elections can hold legislators responsible for laws. None of these mechanisms is perfect. Nevertheless, it is this broader context, rather than the subjective understanding of legislators, that legitimizes legislation.

The Constitution does not adopt a rule granting validity only to votes accompanied by a full knowledge of the meaning and significance of the votes. Indeed, courts are prohibited from inquiring into whether legislators read or understood the legislation on which they voted. Under current doctrine, they may not even inquire whether legislators in fact cast votes in favor of the legislation. They must simply accept formally enrolled bills as valid.[68] In place of a searching judicial inquiry into legislative consent, we have constitutional provisions that seek to structure the environment in which legislators operate so that it contains multiple feedback mechanisms against abusive or unwise laws. Hence, for example, the First Amendment guarantees the freedom of the press, the right of assembly, and the right of citizens to petition the government.[69] Likewise, the Fifteenth, Nineteenth, Twenty-fourth, and Twenty-sixth Amendments seek to ensure a robust system of electoral feedback.[70]

We can also look at the social context in which boilerplate is written to see whether it contains mechanisms that constrain the authors of contracts and limit abusive or otherwise undesirable terms. In some cases, contracting parties thoroughly read and understand the terms before agreeing to them and are in a position to walk away from the transaction if the terms are objectionable. What makes this situation ideal is not that this consent is somehow more meaningful than the consumer who clicks "I agree" on a pop-up software license without reading it. Recall that in the market argument, the bare fact of consent—meaningful or otherwise—is not what makes the enforcement of contracts desirable. The reason that fully informed consent is desirable is that it would provide a robust feedback mechanism in the authorship of boilerplate terms.

In the real world, of course, people seldom read most of the contracts that they sign, especially when those contracts are long and contain technical clauses governing unlikely events. The common law "duty to read," which binds us to contracts to which we assent regardless of whether the terms are read or understood, tries to create an incentive for nonreaders to exert themselves.[71] Likewise, numerous courts have held that, in order to bind a consumer to a contract, the terms must at the very least be available for inspection.[72] We can think of such a rule as being similar to sunshine laws designed to ensure that citizens have access to the information needed to hold legislators accountable. Likewise, the opportunity to read holds open consent as a possible feedback mechanism constraining boilerplate authors. Hence, for example, the American Law Institute's Principles of the Law of Software Contracts requires that "a standard form [be] reasonably accessible electronically prior to initiation of the transfer at issue" and that "upon initiating the transfer, the transferee has reasonable notice of and access to the standard form before payment or, if there is no payment, before completion of the transfer."[73] A growing body of evidence, however, suggests that bare disclosure of terms has virtually no effect on either consumer behavior or the quality of the terms drafted.[74]

Even in a case where we have ideal conditions, consent will not provide a perfect constraint on the authors of contractual terms. Sometimes people make mistakes and accept terms that in retrospect were not in their best interests. As noted above, however, consent is not the only mechanism that can constrain boilerplate terms. Law and economics scholars have long recognized that in competitive markets, not every consumer needs to study contract terms in order to constrain offerors.[75] So long as there is some group of marginal consumers who pay attention to contract terms, boilerplate authors will compete for these consumers by offering favorable terms. Because in a competitive market, competition occurs at the margin, the nonreading consumers can free-ride on the efforts of the shoppers. Credit cards provide an example of such a dynamic. Many credit card contracts offer various benefits, from cash-back programs to discounts with particular merchants to free insurance products. Any credit cardholder who discovers one of these programs without realizing that it was included in his or her card agreement has benefited from competition for marginal term shoppers.

There are two situations in which competition for marginal shoppers will fail to police boilerplate terms. First, if offerors can distinguish between consumers who shop for terms from those who do not, then the authors of boilerplate can engage in "term discrimination." Just as a seller can sell the same product at a different price to different consumers based on their willingness to pay and thus engage in price discrimination,[76] boilerplate authors will offer contracts with favorable terms to term shoppers and contracts with less favorable terms to nonreaders. In this case, the nonreaders can no longer free-ride on the efforts of the shoppers. Such term discrimination—like price discrimination—is not economically inefficient, but it might raise concerns for those who look to competition to police one-sided terms.

Second, in some markets there may simply be no marginal consumers that shop based on contract terms. We lack detailed empirical studies of contracting for most markets. One exception is online end-user license agreements, where Florencia Marotta-Wurgler has conducted several detailed studies. In one study, she measured the amount of time that people spent on the pages containing contract language.[77] Because the documents are quite lengthy, it was easy to identify consumers who could not possibly have read the terms. The study found that, for all practical purposes, no one reads the agreements. At most, 2 consumers per 1,000 spent any time at all (usually only a few seconds) on the page to read the terms, and there is no way of knowing whether those consumers actually read the terms or were called away from their computers.[78] These results have led some scholars to claim, rather extravagantly, that there simply are no marginal consumers who shop for terms.[79] This goes beyond the evidence. Outside the context of online contracting for software, we know that there are consumers who shop for at least some contract terms, either by reading the fine print or through intermediaries who provide information on contract terms. Examples include those who shop for credit cards based on bonus point plans or fees, or consumers who scrutinize warranty terms for cell phones or automobiles.[80] Nevertheless, it is surely true that we cannot assume that such marginal consumers always exist. In some markets and for some terms, there simply isn't anyone shopping.

Even in markets where no contract offerees are reading the terms, however, other forms of competition may police boilerplate contracts for abuse. For example, if firms can reduce their costs by pushing the cost of risk onto consumers, it does not follow that the firms will be enriched at the expense of customers. In a competitive market, economic theory suggests that prices will be driven down to marginal cost. If boilerplate reduces costs to firms, any resulting rents should ultimately be dissipated as price reductions to consumers. Notice that this argument does not assume that consumers are even informed about the content of boilerplate contracts. They could be wholly ignorant of the contents of the contracts, as we know they are in some markets. Rather, the argument assumes only that consumers respond to prices and that firms compete with one another on price. Neither of these premises requires that we make heroic assumptions about the cognitive capacity of consumers. The argument is not that consumers price risk but only that firms cannot capture long-term rents by lowering their own costs. Lower costs lead eventually to lower prices. It is difficult to determine whether there is empirical evidence that this is happening. Marotta-Wurgler's research finds no meaningful differences in the price of software based on differences in the friendliness of boilerplate to consumers.[81] This suggests that consumers are not shopping for terms. Her research, however, does not look for any correlation between end-user license agreement terms and the profitability of firms. Hence, it does not tell us whether firms are reaping supracompetitive rents by snookering consumers with artfully crafted boilerplate or if some firms are simply less efficient than other firms.[82]

One might, however, object to arguments based on price competition on a variety of grounds other than skepticism that it is occurring. First, boilerplate will still have distributive effects; they will simply be intraconsumer rather than between consumers and corporations. Consider, for example, a mandatory arbitration agreement. Ex post, such an agreement might result in more money to the corporation and less to the consumer involved in a dispute with the corporation.[83] However, over time, competition will transform these rents into lower prices for all consumers. Hence, the boilerplate makes some consumers (those who bought at lower prices and had no dispute with the corporation) better off at the expense of other consumers (those who bought at the lower prices and had a dispute with the corporation).[84]

Boilerplate coupled with price competition will also—all things being equal—tend to transform certain kinds of nonmonetary or partially nonmonetary rights into the single metric of cash. For example, the tort system exists to provide victims of torts with monetary compensation, but it does more than this. It also gives citizens a way to exercise their agency by allowing them to act against those that wrong them and hold them accountable before the public courts.[85] Contractual provisions limiting liability or the ability of tort victims to act against tortfeasors in court will tend to transform such rights into lower prices. If one believes that all goods are commensurable and their values can be rendered into cash equivalents, then this transformation should not be especially troubling. On the other hand, if one believes in a more pluralistic idea of human goods, then monetizing all such claims in the form of lower prices may be problematic.[86] Notice, however, that this is less an objection about boilerplate than an objection to *any* effort to exchange noncommensurable legal rights for cash.

The feedback mechanisms discussed above—competition for marginal shoppers and price competition—both focus on the moment of contract formation, and how consumers manifesting less than fully informed consent may nevertheless collectively constrain the authors of boilerplate. There are moments other than formation, however, in the life of a contract when feedback mechanisms constrain the power of boilerplate authors. Contract scholars have long recognized that it is a mistake to think about contracts solely in terms of their formal content.[87] Frequently, contracts are embedded in ongoing relationships between the parties characterized by a significant amount of give and take that ignores formal contractual language. The same is true of businesses that are repeat players in the market and value their reputation. Indeed, formal contracts frequently do not govern ongoing relationships between the parties. Rather, they are meant only to lay out so-called end-game norms that govern the breakdown of relationships.[88] Similarly, firms may disclaim legal liability to consumers in situations where reputational sanctions force them to provide recourse not because they are limiting the remedies of wronged consumers but because they wish to avoid courts that cannot detect opportunistic behavior by consumers.[89]

In such situations, reputational sanctions constrain firms' behavior. It is not in the interest of companies to assert their full legal rights under a contract, because doing so will generate a negative reputation. Given the amount of money that firms spend on matters such as trademarks and advertising, it is clear that reputation is extremely important to many companies. Furthermore, the existence of third parties that provide information on companies to consumers, including information on contract terms, suggests that firms risk customer goodwill if they treat consumers badly, regardless of the contract terms. For example, many websites allow consumers to compare credit cards, including such contract terms as interest rates, fees, and reward points. Some of these sites are advertising vehicles for credit card companies. Others, however, such as NerdWallet.com, tout their status as "unbiased" and "independent." Douglas Baird has observed that "sellers are unlikely to invoke fine print, and when they do, it often doesn't help them" because of adverse reputational consequences.[90] Likewise, research into warranties in the automobile industry, which had resulted in the famous boilerplate case of *Henningsen v. Bloomfields Motors, Inc.*,[91] found that manufacturers generally settled disputes regardless of boilerplate terms. "Fear of adverse publicity and loss of good will, a nonlegal sanction," the author wrote, "has no doubt had its effect on manufacturers."[92]

Dealing with Boilerplate

The market argument relocates the place of consent in our theory of contractual enforcement. Consent no longer functions as a primary justification for the enforcement of contracts. Rather, it serves to coordinate the process of decentralized obligation authoring that contract law facilitates and is one possible mechanism among many for constraining foolish or predatory terms. Informed consent, however, is neither a necessary nor a sufficient condition for the legitimate enforcement of a contract.[93] The coordination problem may be solved by a bare manifestation of consent without any real understanding of the terms, and we need not worry about abusive terms in such an agreement provided that the social context in which it is made and performed provides other mechanisms for policing overreaching. Current doctrine's approach to boilerplate, however, is largely fixated on the idea of consent, as are the most prominent suggestions for reform. This focus is mistaken. Rather than looking for informed or meaningful consent and refusing to enforce a contract when it is absent, we should look to social context without worrying a great deal about whether those who sign boilerplate agreements read or understand their content.

Consider Section 211 of the *Restatement (Second) of Contracts*, which states:[94]

> When the other party has reason to believe that the party manifesting such assent would not do so if he knew that the writing contained a particular term, the term is not part of the agreement.[95]

This rule seeks to limit the actual manifestation of a party's consent to a boilerplate agreement with some notion of what the party's real consent would have been had he actually read and understood the terms of the contract. There are two problems. First, how is a court or jury to determine ex post what a party would or would not have consented to in a hypothetical world ex ante? This problem is particularly acute because litigation over boilerplate generally does not involve terms shocking in themselves—"an equal pound of your fair flesh, to be cut off and taken in what part of your body pleaseth me"[96]—but terms assigning remote risks ex ante that happen to in fact occur ex post. In such a case, who can say whether the person would have refused the agreement if she had been aware of the assignment of risk for an extremely unlikely event? Furthermore, with complex terms, it may make no sense to ask whether the person would have consented had he known of the terms, for the simple reason that he would not have understood their meaning had he been aware of them.

The second problem is that it is unclear why the absence of hypothetical consent should matter. If consent is what justifies the enforcement of a contract, then the real question is whether the boilerplate was consented to with the required degree of understanding. If the contract was not consented to in a meaningful way, then it ought not to be enforced. The fact that it might have been consented to in some hypothetical world should not matter if actual consent is the touchstone of contractual legitimacy. As Ronald Dworkin has observed in another context, "A hypothetical contract is not simply a pale form of an actual contract; it is no contract at all."[97] If actual consent is the fount of contractual legitimacy, Dworkin's conclusion seems inescapable. Likewise, if some attenuated notion of consent is sufficient to justify the enforcement of some of the terms in cases where there is actual—albeit less than fully informed—consent, why should some hypothetical absence of consent be allowed to defeat real consent with regard to some terms? This is important, because Section 211 contemplates the enforcement of boilerplate terms of which the promisor is unaware.[98] Once consent has been given and that consent is sufficient to justify enforcing some not fully understood term, then it seems odd to say that actual consent can be defeated by a hypothetical withholding of consent. One suspects that in this analysis the discussion of hypothetical consent or the hypothetical absence of consent is vacuous. It is simply a stand-in for picking out terms that courts or commentators find objectionable not because of the presence or absence of consent but because of their substantive content.

Another approach is to enforce only the terms of which a consumer is subjectively aware and resolve all other questions using contract default terms, regardless of what is contained in the boilerplate.[99] Courts should enforce these terms because they are genuinely consented to and represent a "real" contract. The default terms are to be preferred to the boilerplate terms because they have the imprimatur of democratic legitimacy. The problem with this approach is that it centralizes the control of transactional structures in judicial or legislative decision makers. This would make it difficult for firms and other market actors to mass-produce complex transactional structures that deviate substantially from the form that judges deem fair and reasonable. This is hardly an insuperable impediment to markets, but it does eliminate much of the variation and experimentation that make contract law valuable. As the example of the ossification of Islamic commercial law shows, it also holds out the danger of substantially burdening commerce.[100] The preference for default terms rests in large part on the assumption that judges and other lawmakers are well placed to design transactions for market actors. It is far from clear, however, that this sunny assessment of judicial and legislative capacity can be justified. As one commercially sophisticated judge has observed, "The courtroom . . . is not a boardroom. The judge is not a business consultant."[101]

Another alternative is simply to insist that the attenuated consent given to boilerplate terms is sufficient to justify their enforcement. Randy Barnett gives the example of a friend who says, "Whatever it is that you want me to do, write it down and put it into a sealed envelope, and I will do it for you."[102] There is nothing conceptually challenging about such a commitment, and there is no reason to suppose that the friend in this case has not in fact made a commitment even though he is necessarily ignorant of its content. The consumer who agrees to an unread software license is in the same position. It is as though she had agreed to be bound by the unread terms contained in a sealed envelope. Indeed, Barnett explicitly defends the outcomes in cases such as *Hill v. Gateway 2000, Inc.*[103] and *ProCD v. Zeidenberg,*[104] where the court held a consumer to the terms of boilerplate that he could not read at the time of agreement. Barnett reasons that "what is true of terms unread because of rational ignorance, is also true of terms unread because they are supplied later."[105] He nevertheless concludes that while one can assent to unread—and even unreadable—terms, those who sign boilerplate contracts cannot be held to terms that are "radically unexpected."[106] Barnett supports this claim by insisting that the actual social meaning of the act of clicking on "I agree" is "I agree to be bound by everything that I haven't read except that which is radically unexpected." This claim, however, seems strained. It is entirely possible, for example, that consumers believe they will be held to every term in the boilerplate to which they agree without reservation and are simply taking their chances. Barnett's escape hatch to liability seems less grounded in the social meaning of consent than in an unwillingness to enforce unduly harsh or bizarre terms.

There is another problem with Barnett's approach. He is surely correct to argue that there is nothing illogical or conceptually difficult about consenting to obligations that one does not fully understand. However, this misses the nature of the criticism of the consent involved in boilerplate contracts. The criticism is not that applying the term *consent* to the consumer who clicks "I agree" to an unread software license is some kind of conceptual or logical mistake that misunderstands the meaning of the idea of consent.[107] Rather, the complaint is that this consent is too attenuated to justify contractual enforcement. Elsewhere, Barnett argues that consent does not justify enforcement where there is a "lack of ability to assert meaningful assent."[108] The question is thus not whether parties can consent to unread and perhaps incomprehensible terms but why the fact that they have so consented should be treated as "meaningful assent." Barnett clearly is not willing to bless every volitional manifestation of consent with contractual liability, but he fails to articulate where one places the threshold of meaningfulness that he assumes the person who has accepted unread boilerplate to have crossed.

The market argument suggests that the search for meaningful consent should be abandoned. Consent is less central to the justification of contractual liability than these approaches suggest, and the focus on consent distracts our attention from the factors on which we should be focusing. Of course, consent is not irrelevant. We should not impose contractual liability in the absence of an objective manifestation of consent, because to do otherwise is to risk a chaotic world of conflicting and incoherent obligations. However, the consent necessary to solve this coordination problem need not be particularly well informed. The agreement to unread terms sealed in an envelope is sufficient. The fact that this minimal level of consent is present, however, does not mean that our inquiry into the enforceability of an agreement should be at an end. Rather, once the threshold question of consent and coordination has been answered, we should focus our attention on the social context in which agreement takes place to ensure that there are sufficient feedback mechanisms to constrain the authorship of abusive or predatory contract terms.

The most common doctrinal rout of attack against boilerplate, especially in the context of arbitration agreements, is procedural unconscionability.[109] Arthur Leff, who coined the term, defined procedural unconscionability in terms of "bargaining naughtiness,"[110] and the cases have tended to focus on issues around the quality of consent. Thus, courts have looked askance at the absence of bargaining over contract terms and the inability of consumers to understand technical aspects of particular provisions. Likewise, judges have pointed to the imbalance in sophistication between corporate drafters and the consumers to whom they offer boilerplate.[111] Indeed, some courts have flirted with the idea that consumer boilerplate is per se procedurally unconscionable because of such concerns.[112] The focus on these and other supposed bits of bargaining naughtiness is mistaken. Rather, courts should examine the social context in which boilerplate is authored, accepted, and performed. In particular, courts should concern themselves with whether feedback mechanisms are in place that constrain the authors of boilerplate.

If parties read, understand, and dicker or shop all the terms, then consent itself will provide the feedback. We might require that parties ex ante have access to a copy of the boilerplate as a prophylactic rule to make such feedback via consent easier, but strictly speaking such access is not a necessary condition for legitimate contractual enforcement and is unlikely in itself to be a particularly useful feedback mechanism.[113] Certainly, the mere fact that boilerplate terms can or cannot be read before a transaction is completed should have little normative significance. On the other hand, when boilerplate terms are offered in a market, they ought to be presumptively enforceable. Generally, price competition and the scramble for marginal term shoppers should produce powerful enough feedback mechanisms. If the party attacking the enforcement of boilerplate terms, however, can plausibly demonstrate that there is no competition for marginal shoppers in the market, then the burden should shift to the party seeking enforcement of the boilerplate to show that he or she is constrained in the performance of the contact. Where there are repeat players who regularly negotiate with consumers ex post—for example, through customer service departments with the authority to waive contract terms—then courts can conclude that authors of boilerplate remain subject to meaningful constraints. On the other hand, when the offerors of boilerplate deal with consumers on a one-shot basis and lack any meaningful reputation in the market, then courts should treat the enforcement of boilerplate terms with much greater suspicion.

Boilerplate accompanied by bare price competition presents a difficult case. Absent antitrust concerns, most firms will offer boilerplate in the context of markets where they compete on price.[114] If boilerplate lowers costs to firms, we would expect those cost savings to be passed on to consumers as lower prices even if consumers do not read or understand the terms. As noted above, one might still be concerned with problems of asymmetric information in markets with price competition. If transaction costs are sufficiently low, such asymmetries should not be a problem because those with good information have an incentive to profit by informing those with bad information. However, where the costs of credibly disclosing information to consumers are high and the profits available from educating them are low, bare price competition will be insufficient to police boilerplate terms. Finally, if one concludes that certain kinds of rights are incommensurable with money, then the disclaimer of such rights in boilerplate should not be enforced.[115]

On the whole, the market argument takes a permissive stance toward the enforcement of boilerplate. Generally speaking, boilerplate contracts should be enforced provided that there is some minimal level of formal consent. In policing these agreements, courts should abandon the search for meaningful consent or, in the absence of such consent, the search for hypothetical consent. Rather, they should look to the social context in which contracts are made and performed to determine whether there are feedback mechanisms that police overreaching, abuse, and incompetence. Where such mechanisms are absent, courts should refuse to enforce the terms. Where they are present, courts should enforce the contract without worrying about the meaningfulness of consent. This framework is ultimately procedural. It is designed so that courts can be agnostic about the value of the substantive content of boilerplate agreements when determining whether they should be enforced.

Much of the concern with boilerplate agreements, however, is not procedural but substantive. While courts and commentators express concern about the absence of bargaining and contracts of adhesion, their primary concern is with the terms rather than the way the contracts are formed. In the end, these concerns are less about boilerplate than about the limits of contract law itself. Since the nineteenth century, the common law has been extremely skeptical of substantive regulation of contractual terms in the absence of some evidence of diminished consent. Normatively this concern is most often justified in terms of respecting the autonomy interests of the parties. The market argument, however, does not view contract as primarily an expression of individual autonomy. It thus provides no principled objection per se to regulating contracts based on their content.[116] My concern with such regulation is not that it threatens individual liberty but that lawmakers are frequently ignorant about transactional structures and too quick to see sharp dealing in any departure from what they assume a transaction should look like. They also have been insufficiently attentive to the way that rigid limitations on freedom of contract have undermined well-functioning markets. This cautious stance, however, is not a principled objection to content-based regulation. Indeed, under some circumstances, everyone—even the most committed libertarian defender of contract—believes that otherwise valid contracts should not be enforced purely on the basis of their content.[117] That is the topic to which we turn in the final chapter of this book.

CHAPTER EIGHT

Pernicious Markets and the Limits of Contract Law

On the whole, this book has taken a celebratory stance toward commerce and markets. I have argued that markets serve at least three important moral purposes. They instill certain virtues that support a liberal political system. They provide a social context for peaceful and productive cooperation between those with differing visions of the good life and differing tribal identities. Finally, markets generate wealth, which has an ameliorative effect on a host of social evils. Well-functioning markets are one of humanity's great social and moral achievements. Contract law should be grounded in this optimistic assessment of the value of markets. We ought to enforce contracts not because of the demands of economic efficiency narrowly construed or to respect individual autonomy but because contract is quintessentially the law of the marketplace and by enforcing contracts we strengthen and extend markets.

Not all markets, however, deserve the praise that I have heaped on commerce. Markets can be evil. Just as well-functioning markets have important moral consequences, pernicious markets can cause harm, destroy valuable social and personal goods, and invade aspects of life that should be separated from commerce. In the final chapter of the book, I turn to markets in their pernicious inflection. To acknowledge that markets can be pernicious does not undermine the basic normative claims of the market argument advanced in this book. Rather, pernicious markets mark the limits of contract law. If contract law ought to be structured to support well-functioning markets because such markets are morally valuable, it follows that, when markets are pernicious, the justification for contract law fails—or at the very least weakens dramatically. The market argument thus accounts for the universal limitations that we observe in all legal systems on the enforcement of contracts. It also focuses our attention on the question that we must ask in order to understand the limits of contract law: When are markets pernicious?

The Limits of Contract Law

No system of contract law has ever enforced all voluntary agreements. Every existing system of law has deemed certain kinds of transactions beyond the bounds of legal enforcement. The dominant theories of contract law do a poor job of justifying such restrictions. For autonomy theories, restrictions on contractual freedom seem to undermine the goal of respecting the choices of contracting parties. This approach suggests that contracts should be enforced because they were chosen rather than because of their substantive content. Yet all systems of law refuse to enforce some contracts solely on the basis of their content. Some theorists have seen in these limiting doctrines a regulatory or distributive stance toward contractual activity. This argument, however, makes little sense given how institutionally ill-suited contract law is for playing a regulative or distributive role. The market approach offers, I shall argue, a better way of thinking about the limits of contract law.

In the common law, doctrines such as unconscionability and contracts void for violating public policy have always limited contractual freedom. For a promissory or autonomy theory, such doctrines are suspect at best. They seem to be foreign intrusions into the libertarian purity of contract.[1] If we justify the law of contracts primarily in terms of enforcing promises or respecting autonomous choice, then any time we refuse to enforce a promise or disregard a contract that was freely chosen, we seem to be ignoring the moral foundations of the law. As a normative matter, this intuition counsels in favor of limiting these doctrines as much as possible or tying them back to some notion of duress or other imperfection of choice.[2] Refusing to enforce a freely chosen contract purely on the basis of its content is anathema to such theories. The content of contracts should be left to the parties and ought not to be the concern of the law.

On the other side of the ideological spectrum are theorists who see contract law as largely regulative.[3] They eagerly point to the persistence of such doctrines as contracts void for public policy as evidence that contract law has been about controlling behavior all along.[4] By casting contract law in regulative terms they seek to undermine freedom of contract as part of a broader effort to justify the legitimacy of the modern regulatory state.[5] On this view, attacking the idea that contracts reflect the self-authored obligations of contracting parties is an important premise in rejecting laissez-faire economics.[6] The problem with this approach is that whatever its divergence from a system of pure autonomous choice, contract law is not a particularly good instrument for suppressing or even regulating behavior. A similar criticism can be leveled at those who seek to achieve distributive goals via contract law.[7] For example, the enforcement of boilerplate agreements has been criticized on the grounds that doing so tends to benefit powerful and wealthy corporations at the expense of weak and impecunious consumers.[8] This result, critics argue, is distributionally perverse. In a just society, the law should transfer wealth from the corporations to the consumers rather than vice versa. Even if we accept the questionable economic description on which this argument is premised, however, contract law seems a poor vehicle for redistributing wealth. Other institutions—notably the taxing and spending power of the state—are far more effective mechanisms for redistributing wealth.

In this book I have argued that the normative goal of contract law is to support well-functioning markets. Contract law does not exist primarily to advance individual autonomy by allowing parties to author their own legal obligations. Rather, it allows parties to impose legal obligations on themselves when doing so supports practices and institutions—commerce in the market—that deliver a set of goods that are sufficiently desirable morally to justify government support. Contract law should be oriented toward supporting well-functioning markets. The phrase "well-functioning markets" is deliberately chosen. In chapter 2, I was careful to differentiate the idea of a well-functioning market from the economists' ideal of a perfectly competitive market. Well-functioning markets are not defined by the conditions necessary for optimal economic efficiency. Rather, they are defined by conditions necessary to deliver a particular set of moral goods: cooperation, certain virtues, and wealth. Not all markets, however, are well functioning. Indeed, some markets are pernicious.

Consider the Atlantic slave trade, which flourished from the fifteenth to the nineteenth centuries.[9] The commerce in African slaves ultimately resulted in the kidnapping and immiseration of 14 million people. Of those, an estimated 1.8 million died on the trek to the African shore where they were sold to European slavers. Another 1.8 million died during the Middle Passage from Africa to the Americas. Still another 1.5 million died during the first year of labor on American plantations. The majority of the remaining 9 million lived their entire lives as slaves.[10] The victims of this commerce were ripped from any familiar social context, humiliated, tortured, transported in brutal conditions thousands of miles, and then forced to work under inhuman conditions until they died. Originally, the slave trade was organized primarily through a series of crown-granted monopolies such as the Royal African Company. In the closing decades of the seventeenth century, the English slave trade opened to private entrepreneurs when the courts declared the crown-granted monopolies illegal.[11] By 1712, the operation of the slave trade had been turned over entirely to private entrepreneurs. Thereafter, the commerce thrived. Indeed, the so-called golden age of the slave trade, from 1700 to 1808, corresponded to the period in which the traffic was largely in private hands. Of all the slaves shipped from Africa to the New World over the course of the centuries that the Atlantic slave trade thrived, more than two-thirds were shipped during this period, 40 percent of whom were carried by American and English ships taking advantage of the hostility of the common law toward attempts by the government to monopolize the trade.[12]

The Atlantic slave trade is one of the great moral catastrophes of history. Its scale and the brutality of its conditions, for example, dwarf other instances of human slavery.[13] Unlike tragedies such as the Holocaust or the mass murders perpetrated by Stalin, Mao, and Pol Pot, the slave trade was fundamentally a market atrocity. To be sure, slavery was inevitably intertwined with war and geopolitics, but ultimately the slave trade was a commercial venture carried out in an international market by merchants and entrepreneurs as a business venture. It provides the best historical example of a pernicious market. Whatever benefits the commerce in humans might have conferred on merchants or planters, it cannot erase the human misery and degradation wrought by the slave trade. Given the evils of such a market, the law should not have supported it. Accordingly, one should not enforce contracts for the sale of slaves. Notice, however, that refusing to enforce contracts for the sale of slaves would not have been an effective mechanism for abolishing slavery. To say that withholding contractual enforcement from slavery-related contracts would not have ended the slave trade does not deny the widespread complicity of commercial actors in the slave trade. Rather, I am making the practical point that pernicious markets can thrive without the legal support of contract law. Such markets may be smaller than they would be in the presence of contractual enforcement, but contract law is a poor tool for suppressing a market. The abolition of the slave trade ultimately required the aggressive intervention of the Royal Navy at the height of its power in the early nineteenth century. This doesn't mean that the law should enforce contracts for the sale of slaves. In the case of the slave trade, the justification for contract law simply runs out, even if withholding contractual enforcement would not have abolished the slave trade. For the market argument, there is no compromise here on normative principles. Indeed, the enforcement of slaving contracts and the extension of such a pernicious market would be foreign to the market argument offered in this book.

The question of paternalism runs through most discussions of the limits of contract law. Charles Fried, for example, suggests that if we refuse to enforce a contract because it might be bad for the party making it, we have "infantilized" that party.[14] As stated by Michael J. Trebilcock, paternalism presents:

> The question . . . [of] whether we can always be confident that exchanges that appear to reflect parties' present preferences are really in their own best interest or, even if we believe they are not, whether the collectivity through its legal instrumentalities is entitled to substitute its judgments for the individuals involved.[15]

This is surely an important question, but the market argument suggests that it may have less to do with contract law than the contemporary debate assumes. The question of paternalism is clearly implicated when the law prohibits parties from voluntarily entering into a transaction. If we are Kantian liberals like Fried, we are concerned that such actions fail to respect the sanctity of individual choice. If we are economic welfarists, we are likely to think that the fact that the parties agreed to the contract means that it increases their welfare in the sense of satisfying their revealed preferences. As the example of the slave trade suggests, however, contract law does not really present to us the question of whether to prohibit a transaction.

Consider the example of gambling contracts. Las Vegas is famous for its casinos, and gambling is legal in the Silver State. Nevertheless, contracts creating gaming debts will not be enforced in Nevada.[16] Asked to reconsider its common law rule against enforcing gaming contracts, the state supreme court noted in 1980 that, "despite the fact that gambling, where licensed, is legal in Nevada, this court has long held that debts incurred, and checks drawn, for gambling purposes are void and unenforceable" and refused to reverse its previous precedents.[17] Nevada does not take a paternalistic attitude toward gambling. If its citizens (or visitors from other states) wish to gamble, Nevada does not prohibit them from doing so. It does not follow from this, however, that Nevada must enforce their contracts. As the Nevada Supreme Court recognized, the question of paternalism is separate from the question of contractual enforcement. The litigant calling on the state to enforce a contract is not asking to be left free from interference in his or her private decisions. Rather, he or she is asking that the government act to support the market that will be strengthened by the enforcement of the contract. That market and the choices within it, however, can exist in the absence of contractual enforcement, as the thriving gaming industry of Nevada illustrates. Contractual enforcement presents only the question of whether the state should strengthen and extend the market.

This does not commit the market argument to a regulative vision of contract law. The ability of contract law to suppress pernicious markets is sharply limited. Consider the problem of cartelized markets in which companies collude to raise prices against consumers. In the nineteenth century, as a matter of the common law of contracts, certain kinds of agreements in restraint of trade were unenforceable.[18] Despite the refusal of the courts to enforce such agreements, however, monopolistic cartels continued to exist, relying on mechanisms other than legally enforceable contracts to coordinate price-fixing schemes.[19] Accordingly, in 1890 Congress passed the Sherman Anti-Trust Act.[20] The law categorically banned all contracts "in restraint of trade."[21] Such agreements were rendered legally void, but more importantly, merely entering into such a scheme now became a federal crime. The Sherman Act made such contracts a misdemeanor, and under current law the crime is a felony that can carry a $100 million fine and up to ten years in prison.[22] In place of the milder disapproval of the law of contracts, the Department of Justice could now jail price fixers.[23] The stronger sanctions of the criminal law, in turn, were more effective at suppressing cartelized markets.

In dealing with the limits of contract law, we need some theory—or a set of theories—that will allow us to identify pernicious markets. It is worth pausing at this point to note that one may disagree with the particular account of pernicious markets that I offer in this chapter and still accept the basic premise of this book. Perhaps you identify pernicious markets using a different set of criteria than those offered here. These are difficult questions, and reasonable people will likely disagree. However, if you are constructing a theory of pernicious markets to identify the limits of contract law, you have accepted the basic argument of this book: that contract law exists to support markets when markets are normatively desirable and remains normatively justified only so long as the markets it supports are morally desirable. Once those markets cease to be practices worthy of social support, the rationale for contractual enforcement collapses and contract law should step aside.

Philosophers that have considered the moral limits of markets have tended to cast their arguments as responses to defenses of the market based on either libertarian notions of freedom or economic defenses of efficiency.[24] They have argued for the inadequacy of the negative concept of liberty relied on by libertarian defenses of the market and attacked the notion of welfare inherent in economic defenses of the market. Often this critique is tied to a broader metaethical point about the proper way of making normative judgments. Both Margaret Radin and Elizabeth Anderson, for example, take aim at the idea of commensurability inherent in the reductionism of welfare economics. Anderson insists on value pluralism, arguing that, although we can make choices between competing values, this does not imply that in doing so we are employing a single metric of welfare.[25] Radin makes a similar argument in the name of philosophical pragmatism rather than value pluralism, insisting that moral analysis should be kept closely tied to actual experience and our particular historical circumstances. That experience, she claims, is inconsistent with the notion that we use a single rubric of welfare when making practical judgments.[26] These authors assume that efficiency analysis marks the domain of the market and that in demonstrating the realms in which efficiency analysis does not work they have demonstrated the moral limits of the market.

The defense of the market developed in this book, however, rests on neither libertarian ideals of freedom nor economic notions of welfare. To the extent that it is persuasive, it suggests that critics of the market are mistaken to assume that in identifying the limits of efficiency analysis (or perhaps the idea of negative liberty) we have identified the proper contours of the market. It also means that many of their arguments are not particularly useful in thinking about the limits of the market when we understand commerce as being valuable for reasons independent of economic efficiency or libertarian choice.

Broadly speaking, markets can be pernicious in three ways. First, markets may have undesirable consequences. Some markets may harm those engaged in the trade, or it may produce effects that harm others. Second, as discussed in chapter 3, markets rest on and instill certain moral habits—a kind of mercantile ethos. This ethos has many social virtues and provides one of the reasons that the law should support markets through the enforcement of contracts. Nevertheless, a mercantile ethos is not appropriate for all aspects of life. Markets may become pernicious when they involve the injection of mercantile values into contexts and practices where those values are destructive. Third, there are certain kinds of goods or actions whose character is changed when they are traded in a market, resulting in the loss of a value that can be maintained only by ensuring that such goods or services are not distributed in a market.

Of course analyzing whether the law should support any particular market by enforcing contracts made in that market is difficult. In some cases, all three evils may be present in the same market. In this situation, we may be fairly confident that the law should not enforce the contracts in question. We may even want the criminal law to step in to suppress the market entirely. In other cases, however, the mere fact that the market may be pernicious in one of these ways does not mean that the law should refuse to enforce contracts made in the market. First, the market may have enormous benefits that we would be unwilling to forgo despite some of its pernicious characteristics. Second, in some cases, refusing to enforce contracts may make the market even more pernicious—for example, by driving it underground and encouraging people to use extralegal violence to solve the problems of trust and coordination normally dealt with by contract law.[27] Finally, the evils of the market in question might be best dealt with by some other body of law. In such a case, supporting the market with contractual enforcement need not be pernicious and doing so can deliver the kinds of moral goods discussed in this book.[28]

Markets with Harmful Consequences

Some markets have particularly harmful consequences. This statement is deliberately vague. I do not have a particular theory of harm to offer, and I acknowledge the difficulty of formulating a conception of harm.[29] The market argument does not rest on a single metric of value—for example, welfare as the satisfaction of revealed preferences. If it did, it would be a simple matter to conceptualize markets as harmful when they generate inefficiency. It may be that the moral goods—certain virtues, peaceful cooperation, and wealth—delivered by markets can be understood in terms of a single rubric, such as utility conceptualized as something other than the naked satisfaction of preferences. It may ultimately rest on a pluralistic understanding of values. I have tried to keep the arguments put forward in this book agnostic on such deep metaethical issues. But however one understands harm, when markets are harmful, we have a good reason for withholding contractual enforcement.

The Atlantic slave trade was clearly a harmful market. It rested on the mass deprivation of human liberty. It encouraged a huge investment in economic activity where most of the costs were externalized onto nonconsenting parties, creating a strong prima facie case for its economic inefficiency.[30] It bred habits of brutality and cruelty in those engaged in the trade. Most dramatically, it organized kidnapping, torture, and coerced labor on a massive scale, inflicting misery on millions of victims and their families. By virtually any reckoning, it was a harmful market that the law should not have supported through contractual enforcement. Notice that the basic idea that contract should not be used to support a harmful market can be deployed using multiple conceptions of harm—misallocation of resources, moral degeneration, and human suffering—and that as the catalog of harms multiplies, the case against contractual enforcement strengthens.

Sometimes the harmful consequence of enforcing a contract is the way that doing so would change the structure of a market. Consider two examples. First, the law has long treated contracts in restraint of trade with suspicion. So-called noncompete agreements restrict the ability of employees to set up rival businesses. At common law, such agreements would not be enforced unless they were geographically and temporally limited. One justification often given was that enforcing an unlimited noncompete agreement would force the promisor into destitution. As the U.S. Supreme Court put it in 1873, the law is concerned with "the injury to the party himself by being precluded from pursuing his occupation, and thus being prevented from supporting himself and his family."[31] This justification, however, is not particularly persuasive. If a shoemaker promises not to exercise his craft when he leaves the employ of his boss, it does not follow that he will be destitute, only that he will not make his living as a shoemaker.[32] However, such noncompete clauses will restrict the level of commerce in shoes—in effect, limiting the scope of the market and the benefits that it can provide. According to the U.S. Supreme Court, the result of enforcing unlimited noncompete contracts would be "injury to the public by being deprived of the restricted party's industry."[33] On this rationale, the reason for not enforcing the contract is that doing so will make the market broader and more robust. The harm in enforcing the contract is harm to the health of the market itself.

The doctrine of unconscionability has often been defended in terms of imperfect consent by contracting parties or a paternalistic need to protect weak individuals from their own poor choice to enter into harsh or one-sided contracts.[34] Arthur Leff famously referred to this as "bargaining naughtiness."[35] However, in reality, many of these cases involve an unwillingness to enforce contracts that courts believe will result in a harmful market.[36] Consider the case of *Discover Bank v. Superior Court*, decided by the California Supreme Court in 2005.[37] The case addressed whether an arbitration contract in which consumers waived their right to participate in a class-action lawsuit or class-action arbitration was unconscionable. The court concluded that such contracts were unenforceable. Although the court expressed concern about the fact that such waivers were often included in "a consumer contract of adhesion . . . [with a] party with superior bargaining power,"[38] the court's decision was not ultimately based on concerns with whether consent was meaningful or the need to protect consumers from themselves.[39] Rather, the court's concern was that such waivers would allow sellers to engage in numerous acts of small-scale fraud. In contrast, "a class action by consumers produces several salutary byproducts, including a therapeutic effect upon those sellers who indulge in fraudulent practices [and] aid to legitimate business enterprises by curtailing illegitimate competition."[40] In this argument, the virtue of class-action suits—and the evil of enforcing contracts that suppress them—lies in their effects on the character of merchants and the nature of the market in which they operate. The ultimate merits of *Discover Bank* are debatable, but the case illustrates the way in which the link between contracts and markets can inform unconscionability analysis.[41]

There are also many markets that are harmful, but where the harm can be dealt with through other bodies of law. The most obvious examples are markets that create costs or harms to third parties. For example, markets in food, chemicals, and pharmaceuticals can produce harmful pollution that has unexpected results. To take one bizarre example, in the Potomac River basin, veterinary pharmaceuticals used in agriculture have caused smallmouth bass to develop both male and female sex organs, threatening fish populations.[42] One response to the harm caused by these markets would be to conclude that we lack a good reason for enforcing contracts to buy or sell food, chemicals, or pharmaceuticals. Given the enormous benefits that society reaps from such markets, however, such a response would be absurd. It makes far more sense to regulate the conduct within the market that is harmful rather than to withhold contractual enforcement. This analysis suggests that, in many cases, withholding contractual enforcement from a market will not make sense; doing so makes sense only when the kind of transaction at issue can be shown to have great harms and few benefits. Whatever the ultimate merits of its decision, the court in the *Discover Bank* case was engaging in the proper kind of analysis by focusing on the particular effects of class-action arbitration waivers rather than refusing enforcement of credit card contracts because of the problem of class-action waivers.

The Commercial Ethos in Noncommercial Settings

Markets instill certain moral habits and require certain moral attitudes. We might be concerned about supporting markets that involve the injection of these attitudes into contexts where we find them inappropriate. Something like this concern has been voiced in objections to commodification. Commodification refers to two interrelated attitudes.[43] First, something is fully commodified when it is treated as entirely fungible with some other thing. Second, full commodification involves reducing the entirety of something's value to its cash price. An example of something that is fully commodified might be an exchange-traded futures contract.[44] Every pork belly future is a perfect substitute for another pork belly future with the same terms. The clearinghouse function of the exchange eliminates even the variation of counterparty risk. Likewise, a pork belly future's value can be expressed entirely in cash. Indeed, upon settlement of the contract, no pork bellies change hands. An amount of cash equal to the difference between the contract price and the market price changes hands. The danger of commodification arises when aspects of people's basic humanity are treated as commodities. According to philosophers who are critical of commodification, this can create a slippery slope in which humans are treated as commodities.[45]

As the example of the slave trade illustrates, the fear that humans will be fully commodified is not without substance. Ultimately, however, the idea of commodification is less useful in thinking about the limits of markets than its proponents suggest. First, complete commodification is actually relatively rare. Consider wage labor. Marx was one of the first theorists to explicitly argue for the evils of commodification by claiming that wage labor coupled with industrialization transformed the proletariat into a fungible input of production, dehumanizing the workers.[46] Marx's description, however, is a far-from-accurate picture of all or even most labor relationships.[47] It certainly is not the case that the mere fact that labor is bought and sold in a market leads inevitably to the commodification of laborers. Employers cannot treat their workers as fungible gears in a huge machine. As discussed in chapter 4, the possibilities for shirking and other forms of petty opportunism that cannot be monitored are extremely common in all but the simplest kinds of organizations.[48] Rather, employers necessarily rely on the honesty and good faith of workers in order to operate. In other words, employers must see workers as moral agents rather than disposable commodities if they hope to create anything but the simplest possible firms. To be sure, in commercial relationships, money is part of what motivates actors, and often other concerns will be subordinated to the pursuit of profit. This, however, is not the same thing as the complete commodification described by Marx and feared by modern critics of the market.

Margaret Radin, a prominent theorist of commodification, acknowledges this fact. She sees commodification as a continuum with complete commodification at one pole and complete noncommodification at the other pole.[49] Relatively few situations involve complete commodification. Her worry, however, is that partial commodification puts us on a slippery slope to complete commodification. This argument, however, has the problems inherent in all slippery-slope arguments.[50] Radin suggests, for example, that the enforcement of surrogacy contracts will lead to a world in which women are completely commodified, with every female characteristic from race and hair color to IQ priced and commodified in the surrogacy market.[51] We no longer need to speculate about the social effects of surrogacy agreements. Such contracts will be honored in at least some states, and we now have more than a generation of experience with their effects.[52] The dystopian, commodified future feared by Radin has not materialized. Other objections can be raised about surrogacy contracts, but a slippery slope to complete commodification does not seem to be one of them.[53] Other claims that markets will lead to a slippery slope of complete commodification should be treated with similar skepticism.

The fear that markets push relentlessly toward a world of universal fungibility and cash valuation rests on a misunderstanding of how markets function. Critics often see the market through simplified neoclassical models in which agents are single-minded profit maximizers that value every choice in terms of a cash equivalent. This is not a particularly good description of economic models, and it certainly is not a good description of how markets actually operate. Indeed, as discussed extensively in chapter 4, markets among such agents would be extremely difficult to maintain. In actual markets, people do not behave as single-minded profit maximizers, and their interactions involve substantial levels of trust based on the assumption that one's counterparties have internalized certain standards of ethical behavior. Deviations from profit-maximizing behavior are not aberrations from some internal ideal of the market. Rather, they are necessary conditions for the existence of widespread commerce.

Commodification also is not a particularly useful idea because it focuses our attention on the objects being traded rather than the process of trade itself. Eighteenth-century writers such as Montesquieu and Adam Smith used the term *commerce* when discussing the market. The choice of word is revealing. Commerce is a social process that happens between individuals. They understood that commerce was a particular kind of activity and that many of the important questions about markets focused on the effect of that activity on habits and the moral structure of our interactions with others. In chapter 3, I argued that the effects of this process are largely positive. But as Montesquieu acknowledged, it is not universally so. "Commerce," he wrote, "corrupts pure mores," giving the example of how proximity to commerce made the ancient Gauls effete and allowed Germanic tribes to triumph over them.[54] On this view, the real danger of commerce is not that it will lead us to see every object as a commodity. Indeed, few of the objects exchanged in the market are seen as pure commodities in the sense that worries critics of commodification. Rather, the danger is that commerce will cause us to see every social interaction as an occasion to truck and barter.

Imagine that I invited friends to my house for dinner. As they arrived, I informed them that I would be charging them for the meal we were about to consume. At the conclusion of the evening, I presented each of my guests with an itemized bill for the food that they had eaten and demanded payment. There are several ways that we could understand what is wrong with my behavior. According to the commodification theory, what is wrong here is that I am viewing food as a commodity. Food, however, is bought and sold in the market constantly, and there is no reason this is particularly pernicious. For example, we might say that the problem is that selling food in the market leads me to commodify food, which constitutes a misunderstanding of the nature of food. In other words, I am mistreating the food by commodifying it. This seems implausible. Surely what is gauche about my behavior is not how I am treating the food but how I am treating my friends. I am treating them as customers rather than guests. Notice that there is nothing about treating someone as a customer that is pernicious or dehumanizing. When I sit down in a restaurant, I am treated as a customer—treatment that can coexist quite comfortably with a friendly and humane relationship with my server. Indeed, the interaction with the server may be morally valuable, bringing me into positive and productive contact with a stranger outside of my ordinary tribal circle. What is wrong with my dinner party is not some evil of the customer–proprietor relationship. Rather, it is that I have injected mercantile values and commercial modes of interaction into a setting where they do not belong.

This is a problem that Montesquieu recognized. In Book 20 of the *Spirit of the Laws* he wrote:

> The spirit of commerce produces in men a certain feeling for exact justice, opposed on the one hand to banditry and on the other to those moral virtues that make it so that one does not always discuss one's own interests alone and that one can neglect them for those of others. By contrast, total absence of commerce produces the banditry that Aristotle puts among the ways of acquiring. Its spirit is not contrary to certain moral virtues; for example, hospitality, so rare among commercial countries, is notable among bandit people.[55]

Commerce encourages one to think in terms of the justice of one's interactions—Have I been cheated? Have I treated my customer honestly?—but tends to crowd out impulses toward generosity.[56] When my friends arrived at my house for dinner, they understood that I was offering them a gift, perhaps one that might create a reciprocal obligation to invite me over for dinner at some point in the future but something quite different than a sale. Note that this tendency does not mean that commerce is evil. As Montesquieu notes, commerce tends to reduces predation—"banditry"—and facilitate a sense of justice. Furthermore, societies with strong norms of hospitality are not necessarily desirable, because the norms may arise in response to chronic levels of violent conflict and weak institutions for dealing with it.[57]

Following this analysis, the law should be anxious about enforcing contracts in ways that extend the market—and with it the habits and practices of commerce—into areas of life where traditionally noncommercial norms have dominated. One area where the law has clearly displayed anxiety about the extension of contract is the family. Hence, courts have refused to enforce contracts offering contingency fees or bonuses for attorneys and others who procured a divorce for a client.[58] Other courts have refused to enforce contracts in which a man promised to support or marry a woman if she would agree to divorce her husband in favor of the promisor.[59] Similar contracts will not be enforced if the woman is single but the man is married.[60] For many years, the common law courts refused to enforce contracts that attempted to alter the rights of parties upon divorce.[61]

The concern with contracting around marriage continues despite the relaxation of many of the old doctrines and the general willingness to enforce prenuptial agreements. In the famous case of *Posner v. Posner*, the Florida Supreme Court enforced a prenuptial agreement limiting a wife's claim for alimony upon divorce, breaking with earlier cases refusing to enforce contracts that "intended to facilitate or promote divorce."[62] In reaching its conclusion, however, the court acknowledged the old unease, stating, "At the outset we must recognize that there is a vast difference between a contract made in the market place and one relating to the institution of marriage."[63] The law has evolved in response to these concerns. For example, the Uniform Premarital and Marital Agreements Act creates a number of special defenses to liability on prenuptial agreements.[64] Parties must have independent legal counsel when making the contract or formally waive such counsel.[65] Likewise, to make a valid agreement the legal rights being given up must be prominently stated, and the assets of each spouse, the claim on which one is bargaining away, must be disclosed.[66]

Premarital agreement law is based on the assumption that a prospective spouse presented with a premarital contract is being asked to bargain away his or her rights to equitable distribution of marital property upon divorce. This bargaining dynamic creates an awkward and dangerous situation. In negotiating the terms of the premarital contract, the interests of the parties are adverse. On the threshold of marriage, however, there are likely to be high levels of trust and optimism. Writing in another context, Elizabeth Anderson has observed, "A kind exploitation occurs when one party to a transaction is oriented toward the exchange of gift values, while the other party operates in accordance with the market norms of commodity exchange."[67] This situation exists when the mercantile practices of bargaining and contract are injected into the very different context of lovers on the threshold of marriage. This situation creates a temptation for the wealthier prospective spouse to take advantage of his or her poorer partner by getting him or her to sign away claims on future assets and income without providing full disclosure of the value of what is being lost. Likewise, the law fears that in the midst of prenuptial optimism, men and women underestimate the likelihood of divorce and inconsiderately give up valuable rights that they erroneously believe they will never wish to exercise.

One's concern about contracting around marriage will hinge on the extent to which one views commercial bargaining as foreign to marriage. This concern will likely be culturally contingent on one's understanding of marriage. Consider the example of Muslim marriages, which have become the subject of litigation in the United States.[68] In Islam there is no concept of sacraments. One becomes married by signing a contract. Furthermore, under Islamic law, the contract must include certain terms, including a *mahr* or *saddaq*, which is a sum of money that the husband promises to confer on the wife in the event of divorce. Not surprisingly, bargaining over the size of the *mahr* is an expected element of becoming married. In this context, unlike the social script envisioned by the Uniform Premarital and Marital Agreements Act, bargaining is not a foreign intrusion of mercantile values into an arena where they are likely to run counter to the parties' expectations. For this reason, the market argument suggests we should be less concerned with the enforcement of *mahr* contracts, provided they are interpreted correctly, than we are with the enforcement of ordinary premarital agreements.[69] To the extent that one regards the contractual model of Muslim marriages as inferior to the romantic model of marriage in which bargaining is a foreign intrusion, then one might wish to refuse enforcement of *mahr* contracts so as not to support an undesirable model of marriage. But given the deep religious convictions and cultural identities tied up in the Muslim model of marriage, such a move strikes me as unwise and unnecessary. It is, however, a stance that recognizes an important aspect of what is at issue in defining the limits of contract law: the allocation of market values across different spheres of life.

Markets and the Destruction of Value

Sometimes exchanging a good or service in the market transforms it in a way that destroys its value. This is similar to but ultimately different from the idea of commodification discussed above. As articulated by critics, the problem with commodification is that it suggests the ultimate commensurability of all values through a cash price.[70] Alternatively, they argue that property can in some sense be an extension of personhood, so that the commodification of certain goods and services undermines personhood.[71] The argument I wish to make is less philosophically ambitious. It's not that the sale of certain things in a market commits some metaethical mistake of commensurability or threatens the humanity of property owners. Rather, it is that much of the value of certain goods simply ceases to exist when they are traded in a market.

Consider a verdict rendered by a judge. The value of the verdict comes from two sources. First, it ends some conflict by providing a definitive decision—or at least that is the hope. Second, it decides the conflict on the basis of a warrant that confers on it some legitimacy. Hence, in legal proceedings, judges are expected to decide cases in accordance with law. In an arbitration proceeding, an arbiter is expected to render her decision in accordance with the rules mutually agreed to by the parties. When a judge or arbiter sells a verdict, however, much of the value of the verdict is destroyed. First, such a judgment loses the warrant of its legitimacy because it is no longer decided according to law. The same is true when an arbiter sells a verdict rather than applying the rules agreed upon by the parties. Given the way in which a verdict acquires legitimacy, there is no legitimate way a verdict can be sold. Notice that what is problematic here is not that a verdict is a form of property so tightly connected to personhood that its commodification undermines someone's humanity. Nor is the problem one of mistaken commensurability. The problem is not that justice, for example, is something that we cannot put a dollar value on. (Indeed, people regularly do so when they hire arbiters, lawyers, and the like.) The problem is that a market in verdicts is inherently destructive of the value of verdicts. There is simply no reason to enforce a contract to sell verdicts, because doing so destroys the value of what is sold.

Consider another example. In 1919, the Chicago White Sox faced the Cincinnati Reds in the World Series.[72] The White Sox were not a happy team, and the players universally despised the club's owner, Charles Comiskey, for his miserliness. Under Major League Baseball's Reserve Clause, players had to accept the low salaries offered by Comiskey or leave professional baseball. League rules also prohibited rival teams from bidding up salaries.[73] (Baseball is famously exempt from antitrust laws, and courts were willing to enforce the Reserve Clause).[74] A syndicate of gamblers approached the players, eight of whom agreed to throw the series to the Reds in exchange for money. Eventually news of the fix got out. Fans were outraged. The players were indicted for fraud in 1920, but they escaped conviction. The newly appointed commissioner of baseball banned the eight players implicated in the scandal from professional baseball for life.

What is wrong with fixing a baseball game? The so-called Black Sox were indicted for fraud, but most of those outraged by their acts were ordinary fans who had wagered nothing on the games. Was the harshness of the commissioner's response motivated by a desire to protect gamblers? It seems unlikely. Rather, in throwing the game, the Black Sox transformed the World Series from a competition to something else—a farce, a simulation of a baseball game. There is no way in which the outcome in a baseball game can be bought and sold while remaining an athletic competition. Making victory in the World Series an object of commerce transformed the game and destroyed much of its value.

This argument should be differentiated from arguments that claim a good is somehow cheapened or tarnished by market exchange, even if it is not transformed. Consider the example of awards or prizes. The Oscars are supposed to be awarded by the Academy of Motion Picture Arts and Sciences to actors and filmmakers who have, in the judgment of their professional peers, produced something of notable excellence. The award would cease to function this way if one could pay to have an Oscar awarded. However, the Academy also requires that recipients promise not to sell the golden statues they are awarded.[75] The argument against selling the award does not apply to the physical statues themselves. Much of the value of these statues lies in their history and the aesthetic value of the statues as physical objects. One might worry that selling the statues somehow cheapens them, but when Michael Jackson purchased the statue awarded in 1940 for Best Picture to the producer of *Gone with the Wind* for $1.54 million, he did not change the nature of the award given decades before.[76] Such an argument rests on the mistaken belief that there is something inherently suspect or degrading in commerce. This book emphatically rejects those assumptions. Commerce is not mean or low or dirty. An engagement ring provides another example. Suppose a woman pays a man to give her an engagement ring unaccompanied by a marriage proposal. The fact that the transaction was a sale destroys much of the value of the ring, because an engagement ring acquires most of its value by being allocated based in love and commitment, not commerce.[77] There is, however, nothing about buying and selling diamond rings that degrades them. Hence, when a jeweler sells an engagement ring he does not destroy its value; although this transaction cannot create the value that comes by giving a ring as part of a marriage proposal.

This problem is not confined to the world of gifts, games, and awards. Markets are systems of allocation based on price and consent. Any time the value of a good is tied up in how it is allocated, its value can be destroyed when it is allocated by a market. Accounting firms and credit rating agencies provide prosaic examples. We can think of these agencies as providing a good in the form of a clean audit report or a bond rating. The value of these goods arises from the way they are awarded. In the case of clean audit reports, the accountants are supposed to distribute them based on a professional review of a company's books.[78] In the case of a ratings agency, the firm is supposed to make a disinterested judgment about a bond's possibility of default.[79] Of course, auditing services and rating services are bought and sold in the market, a fact that often leads consumers to doubt their value.[80] Nevertheless, in theory, the outcome of the report or rating—as opposed to the audit itself— is not supposed to be for sale. When it was revealed, for example, in 2001 that Enron had in effect been purchasing favorable audit reports from Arthur Andersen, the accounting firm collapsed.[81] As in the case of the Black Sox, much of the evil of Arthur Andersen's actions lay in fraud.[82] However, once it was known what the firm was doing, it was no longer engaged in fraud. It was merely selling valueless audit reports, which were valueless precisely because they were sold.

The relationship between these kinds of pernicious, value-destroying markets and contract law is ambiguous. In cases infused with fraud, the question is simple. If Arthur Andersen contracted with Enron to provide a clean audit report, then Enron should not be able to sue for breach if Arthur Andersen declines to do so. Notice, however, that in this case the outcome is overdetermined. Enforcing such a contract creates a market that not only diminishes the value of audit reports but harms those that rely on fraudulent audit reports to make investment decisions. In cases where there is no fraud or other harm to third parties, the issue becomes more ambiguous. We might think of such value-reducing markets as unobjectionable. For example, because of the well-known lemons problem, the sale of a new car destroys part of its value, as demonstrated by the price differential between new and nearly new cars.[83] Nevertheless, enforcing contracts for the sale of new cars is unobjectionable.

Contract law should refuse to enforce such value-destroying agreements in two cases. The first is where virtually all of the value of the good is destroyed when it is sold. Contract law is provided by the community, and the expenses of enforcement are borne in part by the public. Thus, providing support for markets that generate virtually no value is a poor use of society's resources. However, these are situations in which such contract suits are unlikely to arise for the simple reason that it is unlikely that these markets will arise. Few people, for example, try to create legally binding contracts in which they seek to purchase friendship or love—a good that seems to cease to exist if it is purchased.[84] The second situation is the class of cases where we fear that the purchased version of the good will crowd out the more valuable, unpurchased version. Imagine that half of the games in professional baseball were rigged. If fans knew which games were rigged and which were not, they might be able to value them accordingly. Perhaps games could be bought and sold in the American League but not in the National League. On the other hand, if this information is opaque, then fans will likely discount the value of all baseball games, including those that are genuine athletic contests. The problem here is not fraud but uncertainty. Indeed, it is similar to the lemons problem identified with used cars.[85] In such cases, it makes good sense to not support the market for thrown baseball games.

In the end, however, the case for nonenforcement of contracts for the exchange of goods whose value lies in nonmarket distribution is weak. There are relatively few goods whose value is tied exclusively to their method of distribution. This is why we are untroubled by contracts for the sale of engagement rings, even though we understand that purchasing an engagement ring for oneself without an accompanying engagement to be married misses much of the value of such a ring. We enforce the sale contract because the value of diamond rings doesn't lie exclusively in how they are distributed. World Wrestling Entertainment, the sports league formally known as the WWF, provides a second example. The contests between the wrestlers in these matches involve flamboyant costumes, copious trash talk, and very little in the way of actual athletic competition. Rather, matches are carefully choreographed in advance, winners and losers are chosen to maximize drama—and with it revenue to the league—and wrestlers who depart from approved scripts for the matches are punished. All the fans, however, understand what is happening. They realize they are watching a simulacrum of athletic competition rather than the real thing. The same is true of the Harlem Globetrotters' 8,829 victories in exhibition games between 1971 and 1995, generally with a designated stooge team. The fact that victory and defeat had been bargained for in advance did not degrade the sport, because no one thinks they are watching a real basketball game. The Globetrotters provided a spectacle rather than a competition. These examples, however, suggest that, in many cases, what is being sold when non-market-distribution goods are sold is actually something that everyone understands to be different from the real thing, but nevertheless worthwhile for what it is. Twinkies are not fine pastries, but that does not keep them from being fine Twinkies.

Contracts ought to be enforced to support well-functioning markets—that is, markets that deliver liberal virtues, peaceful cooperation, and wealth. If markets fail to deliver these goods but instead become pernicious, then we lack a good justification for enforcing the contracts that sustain those markets. In this case, withholding contract enforcement is not an apostasy from the libertarian purity of contract law or even an exercise in paternalism. We should not enforce contracts simply because people desire to impose legal obligations on themselves and a respect for personal autonomy requires that we accede to their wishes. Contractual enforcement is not a purely private matter. Rather, contract law is a public institution that ought to serve the public purpose of sustaining markets. To say that contract law is a public institution, however, is not to concede that it should be thought of as a mechanism for regulating the behavior of contracting parties. Contract law simply isn't well suited for controlling or suppressing behavior. Hence, when the state prohibits individuals from ingesting recreational drugs, it may be behaving paternalistically, but when it refuses to enforce a contract between drug dealers, it is not. In the latter case, we refuse contract enforcement because we do not believe that markets in recreational drugs ought to be strengthened and extended, even if denying enforcement cannot suppress such markets.

Well-functioning markets thus mark out the limits of contract law. Markets can turn pernicious in at least three ways. First, they can cause harm, as when commerce generates pollution. Second, they can involve the injection of commercial values into areas of life where such values are inappropriate, such as in the context of family relations. Finally, some goods derive their value from the way in which they are distributed and lose their value when they are distributed commercially rather than, say, on the basis of some notion of merit or affection. Of these three problems, the second provides the strongest case for refusing to enforce contracts. Harmful markets often have great benefits in addition to their harms. The best response is generally to suppress the harm directly by regulating behavior rather than through shrinking the market by refusing to enforce contracts. Likewise, goods that lose their value if they are commercially distributed generally will not be bought and sold without deception. A company only pays for a clean audit report if it thinks that markets will be fooled. There is no open market in clean audit reports because they have no value. On the other hand, there are some goods—such as victories by the Harlem Globetrotters—that lose value when distributed commercially but nevertheless continue to have sufficient value in their degraded form as to create demand. Generally speaking, we have no reason not to enforce such contracts. Hence, while the market argument is conceptually quite comfortable with limiting contractual enforcement, in practice it counsels in favor of cabining doctrines such as unconscionabilityor contracts void for violating public policy.

Conclusion

This book has tried to answer a simple question: What justifies contract law? The answer I give is the same answer that Shakespeare gives in *The Merchant of Venice*:

> The Duke cannot deny the course of law;
> For the commodity that strangers have
> With us in Venice, if it be denied,
> Will much impeach the justice of the state,
> Since that the trade and profit of the city
> Consisteth of all nations.[1]

We have contract law because it makes the Rialto possible. We "cannot deny the course of law" in providing recourse for breach of contract because the commodity of strangers is morally valuable. Both the wealth and the liberal character of the city require that commerce be strengthened and extended by enforcing contracts.

Although contract law is the quintessential law of the market, this fact has played a minor role in the philosophy of contract law. Rather, noneconomic theorists of contract law have tended to focus on promissory morality and individual autonomy in spinning their justifications for contract. This approach has the strange effect of rendering markets theoretically invisible in their accounts of the law. It is as though the role of contract law in supporting commerce is an accidental by-product of the law rather than its central goal. In practice, contract law overwhelmingly deals with matters of commercial exchange. This is not some accident of the way in which our society happens to use promissory morality. Rather, the support of commerce lies at the normative heart of contract law.

The moral philosophers of contract law, however, are correct to treat the normative credentials of economic efficiency with suspicion. While I share with economic theorists a healthy appreciation for the power of markets, ultimately economic efficiency in and of itself is not morally significant. Markets and commerce, however, are morally important. Their significance does not lie in the satisfaction of revealed preferences but in the way that markets structure individual characters and social interactions. Commerce breeds habits of mind—virtues—that support a liberal society. Markets provide a framework for peaceful cooperation across the fault lines of race, culture, religion, and politics that puts the much-vaunted pluralism of democratic political institutions to shame. Finally, well-functioning markets are the greatest engine of material prosperity that humanity has yet discovered. The miserly piling up of treasure may have nothing to recommend it morally, but wealth is the precondition for much of what is valuable in modern society. It has an ameliorative effect on a host of evils, and there are few social problems that are not made more intractable by poverty. Contract law strengthens and extends markets. It is commerce on the Rialto and its virtues that justify that law.

The claim that contract law exists to foster commerce has theoretical and critical bite. Theoretically, by placing the market at the center of the philosophy of contract law, we are able to understand how the competing claims of autonomy and efficiency theories ought to interact. Neither promissory morality nor economic efficiency provides a sufficient normative justification for contract law. However, both concerns can underwrite well-functioning markets. Exchange in the market as an ongoing social practice thus provides a fulcrum on which to balance the competing claims of both theories. Efficiency and deontological morality should specify the rules of contract law when they support the strengthening and extension of market exchange but should be discarded when they undermine it. In its critical guise, the market argument suggests that we reformulate the rules governing contract formation, the law's treatment of boilerplate contracts, and how we understand the limits of contract law. On all these issues we should be asking whether contract law supports the extension of well-functioning markets. When it ceases to do so, the normative justification for contract runs out and the law of contracts should step aside.

Notes

Preface

1. See Nathan B. Oman, "Unity and Pluralism in Contract Law," *Michigan Law Review* 103, no. 6 (2005): 1483–1506; Nathan B. Oman, "Corporations and Autonomy Theories of Contract: A Critique of the New *Lex Mercatoria*," *Denver University Law Review* 83, no. 1 (2005): 101–45; Nathan B. Oman, "The Failure of Economic Interpretations of the Law of Contract Damages," *Washington and Lee Law Review* 64 (2007): 829–75.

2. Compare Oman, "Failure of Economic Interpretations" (arguing in favor of infusing corrective justice into theories of contract law) with Nathan B. Oman, "Consent to Retaliation: A Civil Recourse Theory of Contractual Liability," *Iowa Law Review* 96 (2011): 529–79 (offering a civil recourse–based theory of contractual liability); Nathan B. Oman, "Why There Is No Duty to Pay Damages: Powers, Duties, and Private Law," *Florida State Law Review* 39 (2011): 137–61 (arguing that civil recourse is a superior account of private law to corrective justice). Professor Curtis Bridgmen once said that my thinking on contract law reminded him of the man who was discovered on a deserted island worshiping in a makeshift chapel. Down the beach several hundred yards was another small shelter. When asked about it, the man responded, "Oh, that's where I used to go to church." The punch line is a fair indictment of my thinking.

3. See Nathan B. Oman, "Markets as a Moral Foundation for Contract Law," *Iowa Law Review* 98 (2012): 183–230.

4. Portions of chapter 6 were previously published as Oman, "Failure of Economic Interpretations"; Oman, "Consent to Retaliation"; Nathan B. Oman, "Promise and Private Law," *Suffolk University Law Review* 45 (2012): 935–60.

5. See Roy Kreitner, "Multiple Markets and the Justification of Contract," *Iowa Law Review Bulletin* 98 (2013): 20–27.

Chapter One

1. The legal themes in *The Merchant of Venice* have long made it a perennial favorite with the law reviews. See, for example, Kenji Yoshino, "The Lawyer of Belmont," *Yale Journal of Law and the Humanities* 9 (1997): 183–216 (examining the character of Portia as an ideal of the legal advocate); Ken Masugi, "Race, the Rule of Law, and the Merchant of Venice: From Slavery to Citizenship," *Notre Dame Journal of Law, Ethics and Public Policy* 11 (1997): 197–224 (examining Abraham Lincoln's reading of the play as a tragedy about slavery and race); Michael Jay Willson, "A View of Justice in Shakespeare's *The Merchant of Venice* and *Measure for Measure*," *Notre Dame Law Review* 70 (1995): 695–726 (examining the view of justice at issue in Portia's resolution of Shylock's contract with Antonio); and Roberto Mangabeira Unger, "The Critical Legal Studies Movement," *Harvard Law Review* 96 (1983): 622–23 (discussing the differing legal worlds of Venice and Belmont in the play).

2. William Shakespeare, *The Merchant of Venice*, in *The Complete Works: The New Pelican Text*, eds. Stephen Orgel and A. R. Braunmuller (New York: Penguin Books, 2002), 285, I.i.161.

3. Ibid., I.i.9.

4. Ibid., I.i.42.

5. Ibid., I.i.177.

6. Ibid., I.iii.139–46.

7. See Christopher Marlowe, *Doctor Faustus and Other Plays*, eds. David Bevington and Eric Rasmussen (New York: Oxford University Press, 2008).

8. Shakespeare, *The Merchant of Venice*, I.iii.63–64.

9. Ibid., I.iii.102.

10. See generally John Thomas Noonan, *The Scholastic Analysis of Usury* (Cambridge, MA: Harvard University Press, 1957).

11. See Gen. 30:31–43.

12. Shakespeare, *The Merchant of Venice*, I.iii.90.

13. Deut. 23:20 (RSV).

14. See David Graeber, *Debt: The First 5,000 Years* (London: Melville House, 2012), 287–90 (discussing medieval Jewish debates over usury).

15. See Noonan, *The Scholastic Analysis of Usury*, 101 (discussing the formulation of the exception by the medieval canon lawyers).

16. Shakespeare, *The Merchant of Venice,* I.iii.127–29.

17. Ibid., I.i.130–32.

18. See Simon Armitage, trans., *Sir Gawain and the Green Knight* (New York: W. W. Norton, 2013) (1300s) (telling the story of a knight who struggles to keep an oath made to his enemy despite the challenges of keeping his word). I am grateful to Rosalynde Welch for bringing this example to my attention.

19. Shakespeare, *The Merchant of Venice,* III.iii.24–31.

20. Ibid., IV.i.38–39.

21. Ibid., IV.i.211–13.

22. Ibid., IV.i.215–19.

23. See William Shakespeare, *The Merchant of Venice, A Longman Cultural Edition*, ed. Lawrence Danson (New York: Longman, 2004), x.

24. For background on the case, see David Harris Sacks, "The Promise and the Contract in Early Modern England: Slade's Case in Perspective," in *Rhetoric and Law in Early Modern Europe*, eds. Victoria Ann Kahn and Lorna Hutson (New Haven, CT: Yale University Press, 2001), 28–53.

25. During the reign of Queen Elizabeth I, which ended in 1603, King's Bench was known as Queen's Bench. To avoid confusion, I refer simply to King's Bench regardless of who was sitting on the throne.

26. Sacks, "The Promise and the Contract," 31.

27. See generally A. W. Brian Simpson, *History of the Common Law of Contract: The Rise of the Action of Assumpsit* (Oxford: Clarendon Press, 1975) (providing an account of medieval contract law and the rise of the action of assumpsit). See also J. H. Baker, *An Introduction to English Legal History*, 4th ed. (London: Butterworths LexisNexis, 2011), 317–61 (summarizing the early history of the common law of contract); David Ibbetson, *A Historical Introduction to the Law of Obligations* (New York: Oxford University Press, 1999), 126–53 (recounting the rise of the action of assumpsit).

28. See A. W. Brian Simpson, "The Place of Slade's Case in the History of Contract," in *Law, Liberty, and Parliament*, by Allen D. Boyer (Indianapolis: Liberty Fund, 2004), 70, 77 ("The locus classicus upon the difference of practice is Edwards v. Burre (1573) where Wray J. explained the then state of the law. He said that in King's Bench proof of the debt is sufficient, 'car le dette est assumption en ley'").

29. See Simpson, "The Place of Slade's Case" (summarizing the pre–*Slade's Case* law as being "that the common law does not allow a man to have an action on the case if another action is available; presumably the King's Bench judges thought that the implied promise [i.e., the legal fiction allowed in King's Bench that every action in assumpsit on a debt involved a second promise to pay the debt] to distinguish the causes of action").

30. See Sacks, "The Promise and the Contract," 34–35 (discussing wager of law).

31. Ibid., 35. Cf. Peter T. Leeson, "Ordeals," *Journal of Law and Economics* 55, no. 3 (August 1, 2012): 691–714 (arguing that, in the context of close-knit medieval communities with a strong set of theological beliefs, ordeals constituted an effective and efficient method of fact finding).

32. Writs other than *assumpsit* and *debt* existed for the enforcement of formal agreements such as written promises made under seal.

33. See Simpson, "The Place of Slade's Case," 71 ("[The Court of Exchequer Chamber] habitually reversed the judgments of the King's Bench in cases of indebitatus assumpsit, following the Common Pleas view of the law, but the King's Bench

stuck to its guns, with the result that there was an unseemly conflict between the courts").

34. Slade's Case, 76 Eng. Rep. 1072 (K.B. 1602).

35. See Sacks, "The Promise and the Contract," 37 ("The rise of the action on the case in assumpsit in King's Bench is itself part of this market-driven process").

36. Ibid. ("By the beginning of the sixteenth century, common lawyers and judges, especially those connected with King's Bench, felt considerable concern about their loss of business to the equity jurisdictions and prerogative courts—no trivial matter in area of rapid inflation").

37. Todd S. Lowry, "Lord Mansfield and the Law Merchant: Law and Economics in the Eighteenth Century," *Journal of Economic Issues* 7, no. 4 (1973): 605–22 (quoting C. H. S. Fifoot, Lord Mansfield 7 (1936)).

38. Pillans v. Van Mierop, 97 Eng. Rep. 1035, 1038 (K.B. 1765).

39. See generally Charles Fried, *Contract as Promise: A Theory of Contractual Obligation* (Cambridge, MA: Harvard University Press, 1981).

40. See, for example, Stephen A. Smith, *Contract Theory*, Clarendon Law Series (New York: Oxford University Press, 2004); Seana Valentine Shiffrin, "The Divergence of Contract and Promise," *Harvard Law Review* 120 (2007): 708–53 (arguing that promissory morality provides an outer boundary for legitimate forms of contract law); Randy E. Barnett, "A Consent Theory of Contract," *Columbia Law Review* 86 (1986): 269–321 (arguing that consent rather than promissory morality provides a normative grounding for contract law); Andrew Gold, "A Property Theory of Contract," *Northwestern University Law Review* 103 (2009): 1–62 (arguing that contract law can be grounded in a neo-Lockean conception of property rights).

41. Compare Richard A. Posner, *Economic Analysis of Law*, 8th ed. (New York: Aspen Publishers, 2010), 115–82 (discussing contract law) with Russell Korobkin, "Behavioral Economics, Contract Formation, and Contract Law," in *Behavioral Law and Economics*, ed. Cass R. Sunstein (New York: Cambridge University Press, 2000), 116–43 (discussing contract from a behavioral law and economics perspective).

42. Compare Louis Kaplow and Steven Shavell, *Fairness versus Welfare* (Cambridge, MA: Harvard University Press, 2002) (arguing that welfare should be the sole determinant of legal policy) with Barak Medina and Eyal Zamir, *Law, Economics, and Morality* (New York: Oxford University Press, 2010) (arguing that efficiency analysis can and should be restrained by a deontological morality).

43. See Fried, *Contract as Promise*, 21.

44. Ibid.

45. Ibid., 36.

46. See, for example, Peter Benson, "The Unity of Contract Law," in *The Theory of Contract Law: New Essays* (Cambridge: Cambridge University Press, 2006), 118 (arguing that the doctrines of contract law instantiate a set of formal imperatives arising out of the transfer of moral entitlements).

47. See Gold, "A Property Theory of Contract," 3 ("This Article offers a new, rights-based theory of contract obligation that builds on ownership concepts. It suggests that the right to performance of a contract is best understood as a special type of property—property to the promisor's future actions")

48. Ibid., 31 ("Principles of just acquisition clarify how a promisee can acquire ownership of a promisor's performance. In turn, this analysis demonstrates that a variety of legal doctrines, including the objective interpretation of contracts, the requirement of consideration, and the standard expectation remedy, are all justifiable in transfer terms").

49. Ibid., 8.

50. See generally Dori Kimel, *From Promise to Contract: Towards a Liberal Theory of Contract* (Portland, OR: Hart, 2005).

51. Cf. Joseph Raz, "Promises in Morality and Law," *Harvard Law Review* 95 (1982): 916–38.

52. See Kimel, *From Promise to Contract*, 65.

53. Ibid., 78.

54. See generally Daniel Markovits, "Contract and Collaboration," *Yale Law Journal* 113 (2004): 1417–1518; see also Daniel Markovits, "Making and Keeping Contracts," *Virginia Law Review* 92 (2006): 1328 ("the morality of agreements grows out of the value of the relation that agreements engender between promisors and their promisees"). Markovits goes so far as to identify contract's power to connect strangers as the highest instantiation of the moral practice of promising more generally. See Daniel Markovits, "Promise as an Arm's-Length Relation," in *Promises and Agreements: Philosophical Essays*, ed. Hanoch Sheinman (New York: Oxford University Press, 2011), 313–14 ("Promise's highest form will be achieved not in personal promises . . . but in promises among strangers, that is among parties whose engagement arises entirely at arm's length. Contract may be understood as the legal elaboration of arm's-length promising").

55. See Ronald Coase, "The Problem of Social Cost," *Journal of Law and Economics* 3 (1960): 1–44.

56. See Richard A. Posner, *The Economics of Justice* (Cambridge, MA: Harvard University Press, 1981), 4–5 (arguing that common law judges tend to decide cases to "bring the economic system closer to the results that would be produced by effective competition").

57. See Robert Cooter and Thomas Ulen, *Law and Economics*, 6th ed. (Boston: Pearson/Addison Wesley, 2012), 291–92 (discussing the idea of a perfectly specified contract and its relationship to the specification of contract law).

58. Edmund Burke, *Reflections on the Revolution in France*, ed. J. C. D. Clark (Stanford, CA: Stanford University Press, 2001), 220.

59. See Shakespeare, *The Merchant of Venice*, I.iii.27.

60. Ibid., I.iii.29–32.

61. See Unger, "The Critical Legal Studies Movement," 622–23.

62. I am grateful to Roy Krietner for bringing this issue to my attention in relationship to my argument. See Roy Kreitner, "Multiple Markets and the Justification of Contract," *Iowa Law Review Bulletin* 98 (2013): 20, 22–24 (discussing the American legal realists in relationship to my argument that markets provide a moral basis for contract law). See also Nathan B. Oman, "Markets as a Moral Foundation for Contract Law," *Iowa Law Review* 98 (2012): 183 (setting forth the argument to which Krietner is responding).

63. Karl N. Llewellyn, "What Price Contract? An Essay in Perspective," *Yale Law Journal* 40 (1931): 704, 717.

64. George K. Gardner, "An Inquiry into the Principles of the Law of Contracts," *Harvard Law Review* 46 (1932): 1–43.

65. See John Rawls, *A Theory of Justice*, rev. ed. (Cambridge, MA: Belknap Press, 1999); Stephen Mulhall and Adam Swift, *Liberals and Communitarians* (Cambridge, MA: Blackwell, 1992) (noting "the commonplace observation that the publication of Rawls's *A Theory of Justice* was the single most important stimulus to the renaissance of political theory during the 1970s and 1980s").

66. See James E. Herget, *American Jurisprudence, 1870–1970: A History* (Houston: Rice University Press, 1990), 158 ("The works of James and Dewey were known to legal thinkers as evidenced by citations in the scholarly literature. Perhaps more important, a popularized but significant pragmatic perspective gradually penetrated the thinking of the time and became a part of the personal credo of many leaders of American society from Theodore Roosevelt to Roscoe Pound").

67. The impatience goes back to Hart. See H. L. A. Hart, "American Jurisprudence through English Eyes: The Nightmare and the Noble Dream," *Georgia Law Review* 11 (1977): 977 ("Seen from afar it appears to many English jurists not to have advanced legal theory far or to have added much to the stock of valuable jurisprudential ideas").

68. See John Maynard Keynes, *The General Theory of Employment, Interest, and Money* (New York: Harcourt Brace, 1935) (setting forth Keynes's general theory several years after FDR had already begun implementing his New Deal).

69. See Amity Shlaes, *The Forgotten Man: A New History of the Great Depression* (New York: Harper Perennial, 2008), 47–84 (discussing the progressive intellectual background of Roosevelt's brain trust).

70. See Gardner, "An Inquiry into the Principles of the Law of Contracts," 42 ("To the twentieth-century lawyer the idea of contract is of steadily diminishing importance. Questions of administration, of personal liberty and status, of the relations of the state to business enterprise and to private property, bulk relatively larger every year. It is not impossible that we are reverting to a form of economic organization in some respects similar to the feudal system as it existed before western civilization first expanded its frontiers").

71. Kreitner, "Multiple Markets and the Justification of Contract," 21.

72. This is, of course, not entirely true. For example, much of the philosophical analysis of promise keeping rests on the Rawlsian idea that promising is a social

practice that produces certain benefits and that one becomes obligated to follow the rules of just social practices from which one benefits. See generally John Rawls, "Two Concepts of Rules," *Philosophical Review* 64, no. 1 (January 1, 1955): 3–32 (discussing how social practices such as promising might create moral obligations).

73. See generally E. Allan Farnsworth, *Farnsworth on Contracts*, 3rd ed., vol. 1 (New York: Wolters Kluwer Law & Business, 2004), 75–198 (summarizing the common law of contract formation).

74. See Nightingale v. Bridges, 89 Eng. Rep. 496 (K.B. 1689) (invalidating the grant of judicial power to the Royal African Company to enforce its own monopoly against independent slave traders, thus opening up the African slave trade to private entrepreneurs). See also William A. Pettigrew, "Free to Enslave: Politics and the Escalation of Britain's Transatlantic Slave Trade, 1688–1714," *William and Mary Quarterly*, 3rd Series, 64, no. 1 (January 1, 2007): 3–38 (describing the transition from a slave trade dominated by a crown monopoly to one dominated by private entrepreneurs).

Chapter Two

1. See Daniel Defoe, *Robinson Crusoe*, ed. John Richetti (London: Penguin Classics, 2003); Abu Bakr Muḥammed bin Ṭufail, *Journey of the Soul: The Story of Hai bin Yaqz'ān*, trans. Riad Kocache (London: Octagon Press, 1982).

2. See Aldona Jonaitis, ed., *Chiefly Feasts: The Enduring Kwakiutl Potlatch* (Seattle: University of Washington Press, 1991).

3. Adam Smith, *The Wealth of Nations*, ed. C. J. Bullock (New York: Barnes & Noble, 2004), 11.

4. Indeed, there is evidence of at least the capacity for exchange among higher primates. In experiments with humans, chimpanzees demonstrate the ability to trade food, including evidence of a conscious strategy of maximizing their gains from trade. See Lous Lefebve, "Food Exchange Strategies in an Infant Chimpanzee," *Journal of Human Evolution* 11, no. 3 (1982): 195–204. Although chimps can be taught to trade, they do so only in captivity. Wild chimps do not truck and barter. See ibid., 201 ("Food exchange can be thus added to the growing list of sophisticated abilities great apes show in captivity but do not use in the wild").

5. Some scholars argue that trade first emerged as an important human behavior prior to the migration of *Homo sapiens* out of Africa around 125,000 years ago. See Sally McBrearty and Alison S. Brooks, "The Revolution That Wasn't: A New Interpretation of the Origin of Modern Human Behavior," *Journal Human Evolution* 39 (2000): 453–563. There is even some evidence that anatomically modern humans traded with Neanderthals. See Ivor Karavenic and Fred H. Smith, "The Middle/Upper Paleolithic Interface and the Relationship of Neanderthals and Early Modern Humans in the Hrvatsko Zagorje, Croatia," *Journal of Human Evolution* 34 (1998): 223–48.

6. In a sense, it is simply an iteration of the old Sorites paradox in philosophy. One grain of sand is not a heap, nor is two or three grains of sand. At some point, however, a heap clearly exists even if it is difficult to identify the precise point at which it does. So, too, with the piling up of exchanges within society to form markets. See generally Dominic Hyde, "Sorites Paradox," in *The Stanford Encyclopedia of Philosophy*, ed. Edward N. Zalta (Stanford, CA: Metaphysics Research Lab, Winter 2011), http://plato.stanford.edu/archives/win2011/entries/sorites-paradox/.

7. See generally Richard S. Dunn, *Sugar and Slaves: The Rise of the Planter Class in the English West Indies, 1624–1713* (Chapel Hill: University of North Carolina Press, 1972), esp. chaps. 2 and 3.

8. See, for example, 13 S.C. Stat. 271, No. 4730 (1865) (declaring persons of color were "not entitled to social or political equality with white persons").

9. Edward McPherson, *The Political History of the United States of America during the Period of Reconstruction*, 2nd ed. (Washington, DC: Solomons & Chapman, 1875), 29 (quoting the North Carolina legislature's March 10, 1866, "act 'concerning negroes, and persons of color, or of mixed blood' ").

10. Civil Rights Act of 1866, 14 Stat. 27-30 (codified as amended at 42 USC § 1981).

11. See David N. Mayer, *Liberty of Contract: Rediscovering a Lost Constitutional Right* (Washington, DC: Cato Institute, 2011), 34 (discussing the relationship between the 1866 Civil Rights Act and the adoption of the Fourteenth Amendment).

12. See Richard A. Epstein, *Forbidden Grounds: The Case against Employment Discrimination Laws* (Cambridge, MA: Harvard University Press, 1995), 126–27 (discussing the various civil rights statutes of the 1960s as breaking down a quasi-governmental cartel by whites designed to systematically cripple black participation in the market).

13. See Daron Acemoglu and James A. Robinson, *Why Nations Fail: The Origins of Power, Prosperity, and Poverty* (London: Profile Books, 2012), 16–19 (discussing the structure of extractive Spanish institutions in the conquered Inca empire).

14. Batsakis v. Demotsis, 226 S.W.2d 673 (Tex. Ct. App. 1949).

15. See Stephen A. Smith, *Contract Theory*, Clarendon Law Series (New York: Oxford University Press, 2004), 331–37 (discussing conceptual difficulties with the idea of voluntariness in contract law).

16. See Timothy O'Connor, "Free Will," in *The Stanford Encyclopedia of Philosophy*, ed. Edward N. Zalta (Stanford, CA: Metaphysics Research Lab, Fall 2014), http://plato.stanford.edu/archives/fall2014/entries/freewill/.

17. See generally Robert Nozick, "Coercion," in *Socratic Puzzles* (Cambridge, MA: Harvard University Press, 1997), 15–44; J. Roland Pennock and John W. Chapman, eds., *Coercion*, Nomos 14 (Chicago: Aldine-Atherton, 1972).

18. There are less-stark examples of poorly functioning markets. For example, in cases involving utilities, where there is a natural monopoly, participants have a difficult time avoiding transacting with the utility. This is not an example of a well-functioning market, although clearly, utilities present both dangers and benefits.

To say that a market is not well functioning is not to say that it cannot be valuable or that it ought to be suppressed. It is merely to say that it does not generate the benefits associated with well-functioning markets. If all markets took the form of interactions with public utilities, it is by no means clear to me that their support would justify a legal institution such as contract law. Such markets, however, are the exception rather than the norm.

19. This does not mean that coercion isn't a concern. Coercion can be a wrong in and of itself, regardless of its effect on the structure of the market. Furthermore, a society with endemic coercion will likely have poorly functioning markets. In downgrading the importance of voluntariness for the market argument, I mean only to claim that, for purposes of this argument—and therefore for purposes of justifying contract law—it is not necessary that every market transaction meet an exacting standard of voluntariness for us to nevertheless conclude that the market delivers important moral goods and therefore deserves legal support.

20. See generally Priya Basu, *Improving Access to Finance for India's Rural Poor* (Washington, DC: World Bank, 2006).

21. Shaheel Rafique, "Implications of Information Credit for Policy Development in India for Building Inclusive Financial Sectors," *Asia-Pacific Development Journal* 13, no. 1 (2006): 105.

22. See Basu, *Improving Access to Finance for India's Rural Poor*, xvi.

23. See Muhammad Yunus, *Banker to the Poor: Micro-Lending and the Battle against World Poverty* (New York: Public Affairs, 2008), 46–50.

24. Basu, *Improving Access to Finance for India's Rural Poor*, 2.

25. See Amy Chua, *World on Fire: How Exporting Free Market Democracy Breeds Ethnic Hatred and Global Instability* (New York: Anchor Books, 2004), 23–48 (discussing ethnic Chinese trade diasporas).

26. According to the World Bank, ethnic Chinese control 500 of the largest public corporations in Southeast Asia, with total assets in excess of $2.5 trillion. See Darryl Crawford, "Chinese Capitalism: Cultures, the Southeast Asian Region and Economic Globalisation," *Third World Quarterly* 21, no. 1 (2000): 69, 77.

27. The overseas Chinese, of course, are far from being the only modern trade diaspora. See "The Magic of Diasporas: Immigrant Networks Are a Rare Bright Spark in the World Economy. Rich Countries Should Welcome Them," *The Economist*, November 19, 2011, http://www.economist.com/node/21538742.

28. Although it must be noted that, until the advent of Zionism in the nineteenth century and the export of European anti-Semitism to the region by the Nazis in the 1930s and 1940s, the Middle East was consistently more hospitable than Christendom toward Jews. See Bernard Lewis, *Semites and Anti-Semites: An Inquiry into Conflict and Prejudice* (New York: W. W. Norton, 1999), 199 (describing Arab anti-Semites as increasingly relying on anti-Semitic writings from Europe, including the Protocols of the Elders of Zion, which was not published in the Middle East until 1926, and not by an Arab Muslim until 1951).

29. As one historian put it:

> In an environment of risk, in which information flowed slowly and opaquely and commercial legal enforcement was weak, access to credit was essential for successful trading. Credit was dependent on trust, and it was this that intertwined networks of consanguinity, religion, and culture—among Scots and Quakers as well as Jews—sustained particularly well.

Adam Sutcliffe, "Jewish History in an Age of Atlanticism," in *Atlantic Diasporas: Jews, Conversos, and Crypto-Jews in the Age of Mercantilism, 1500–1800*, eds. Richard L. Kagan and Philip D. Morgan (Baltimore: Johns Hopkins University Press, 2009), 18, 24.

30. See Timur Kuran, *The Long Divergence: How Islamic Law Held Back the Middle East* (Princeton, NJ: Princeton University Press, 2011), 189–90.

31. See Chua, *World on Fire*, 32–33 (describing multiple instances of Chinese massacre at the hands of the Spanish and Vietnamese).

32. Roughly stated, this is the result of the first fundamental theorem of welfare economics, which is that, at competitive or Walrasian equilibrium, a market will be efficient. See generally Kenneth J. Arrow and Gerard Debreu, "Existence of an Equilibrium for a Competitive Economy," *Econometrica* 22, no. 3 (1954): 265–90 (offering the first formal proof for this claim).

33. Indeed, one of the great virtues of the price system is that it enables people to act on widely dispersed information that they do not—and cannot—consciously apprehend. See generally F. A. Hayek, "The Use of Knowledge in Society," *American Economic Review* 35, no. 4 (1945): 519–30 (arguing that attempts at central economic planning are doomed to failure because central planners cannot take advantage of the dispersed social information necessary for reasonable social decisions, while the price system harnesses that information and signals it to market participants).

34. See John Joseph Wallis and Douglass C. North, "Measuring the Transaction Sector in the American Economy, 1870–1970," in *Long-Term Factors in American Economic Growth*, eds. Stanley L. Engerman and Robert E. Gallman (Chicago: University of Chicago Press, 1992), 121.

35. See generally Dan Ariely, *Predictably Irrational: The Hidden Forces That Shape Our Decisions* (New York: Harper, 2008) (summarizing work in behavioral economics suggesting that human decision making frequently falls short of the demands of perfect rationality).

36. See generally Frank Machovec, *Perfect Competition and the Transformation of Economics* (New York: Routledge, 1995) (discussing the role of the idea of perfect competition in the history economic thought).

37. Debra Satz, *Why Some Things Should Not Be for Sale: The Moral Limits of Markets* (New York: Oxford University Press, 2010), 7. In fairness, it must be added that contemporary economists have developed highly sophisticated arguments and models that do not purport to describe the working of all markets but focus instead

on the structure of highly specific kinds of exchange. Satz's critique is more powerful when applied to efficiency defenses of the market, where the good of market activity is reduced to a single metric—namely, the satisfaction of preferences. I discuss this issue at greater length in chapter 4.

38. See generally Roy Kreitner, "Multiple Markets and the Justification of Contract," *Iowa Law Review Bulletin* 98 (2013): 20–27 (criticizing the market argument for being insufficiently attentive to the plurality of markets).

39. See Lon L. Fuller, *The Morality of Law*, rev. ed., Storrs Lectures Series (New Haven, CT: Yale University Press, 1969), 46–48 (discussing the necessary generality of legal institutions).

40. This leaves open the question of whether it makes sense to have a single law of contracts or many different laws of contract, depending on the kind of market we are discussing. This is an issue that I have dealt with elsewhere. See generally Nathan B. Oman, "A Pragmatic Defense of Contract Law," *Georgetown Law Journal* 98 (2009): 77, 79–86 (summarizing the arguments in favor of fragmenting the law of contracts into multiple legal fields); Brian Bix, *Contract Law: Rules, Theory, and Context* (New York: Cambridge University Press, 2012), 147–61 (same). I have argued that a general law of contracts is to be preferred to narrower bodies of specialized law, because such a body of law reduces the incentives of special interest groups to invest in capturing the law. See Oman, "A Pragmatic Defense of Contract Law," 90–94.

41. See Kreitner, "Multiple Markets and the Justification of Contract," 20, 25 ("So much rests . . . on that seemingly modest qualifier, 'well-functioning' ").

42. Leo Tolstoy, *Anna Karenina*, trans. Richard Pevear and Larissa Volokhonsky (New York: Penguin Classics, 2004), 1.

43. David Graeber, *Debt: The First 5,000 Years* (London: Melville House, 2012), 229. Notwithstanding this characterization, however, there was a great deal of market activity in the Roman world. See generally Peter Temin, *The Roman Market Economy* (Princeton, NJ: Princeton University Press, 2013); David Jones, *The Bankers of Puteoli: Finance, Trade and Industry in the Roman World* (Stroud, UK: Tempus, 2006).

44. Duncan Kennedy, "The Stages of the Decline of the Public/Private Distinction," *University of Pennsylvania Law Review* 130 (1982): 1349, 1352.

45. Cass R. Sunstein, *Free Markets and Social Justice* (New York: Oxford University Press, 1997), 5.

46. Smith, *The Wealth of Nations*, 19.

47. See Herodotus, *The Histories*, trans. C. C. Macaulay (New York: Barnes & Noble Classics, 2004), 255–56; see also William J. Bernstein, *A Splendid Exchange: How Trade Shaped the World* (New York: Atlantic Monthly Press, 2008), 21–22 (discussing the background of the story in Herodotus).

48. Hernando De Soto, *The Mystery of Capital: Why Capitalism Triumphs in the West and Fails Everywhere Else*, repr. ed. (New York: Basic Books, 2003), 4.

49. I borrow this tripartite scheme from Richard Epstein, although I put it to a use different than his. See Richard A. Epstein, "Contracts Small and Contract Large: Contract Law through the Lens of Laissez-Faire," in *The Fall and Rise of Freedom of Contract*, ed. F. H Buckley (Durham, NC: Duke University Press, 1999), 25, 28.

50. Of course, even in cases of apparently simultaneous exchange, questions of future obligations can arise. Warranties provide the most obvious example. Even if A exchanges cash for widgets with B, what happens if the widget subsequently explodes because of some defect? Can A get her cash back? Is there some other consequence as a result of the previous agreement, such as damages or a duty of repair on B's part?

51. See generally Barry S. Strauss, *The Spartacus War* (New York: Simon & Schuster, 2009).

52. Plutarch, "Crassus," in *Plutarch's Lives*, ed. Arthur Hugh Clough, trans. John Dryden and James Atlas, vol. 1 (New York: Modern Library, 2001), 731.

53. Ibid., 732 (describing how the Crassus killed 12,300 Spartacans).

54. See Nathan B. Oman, "Consent to Retaliation: A Civil Recourse Theory of Contractual Liability," *Iowa Law Review* 96 (2011): 529, 531 ("When promisors hacked up a goat [to seal a bargain], they consented to be hacked up in like manner should they breach").

55. See generally David Stasavage, "Cities, Constitutions, and Sovereign Borrowing in Europe, 1274–1785," *International Organization* 61, no. 3 (2007): 1274 (discussing sovereign debt and sources of borrower credibility).

56. See, for example, Mauricio Drelichman and Hans-Joachim Voth, *Lending to the Borrower from Hell: Debt, Taxes, and Default in the Age of Philip II* (Princeton, NJ: Princeton University Press, 2014) (detailing abusive borrowing by Philip II of Spain and generally discussing borrowing by European monarchies).

57. Niall Ferguson, *The Cash Nexus: Money and Power in the Modern World, 1700–2000* (New York: Basic Books, 2001), 111–15 (discussing the development of the British securities market during the seventeenth and eighteenth centuries).

58. See Barry Nicholas, *An Introduction to Roman Law* (Oxford: Clarendon Press, 1962), 185–87 (detailing typical terms in societas, Roman partnership agreements).

59. See, for example, ibid., 167–91 (discussing predetermined obligations associated with common Roman contracts, including those for sale of goods, personal services, and debt).

60. In some cases, such as innkeepers and common carriers, the law limited the ability of actors to refuse contracting with customers. See generally Joseph Singer, "No Right to Exclude: Public Accommodations and Private Property," *Northwestern University Law Review* 90 (1996): 1283–1497.

61. See W. M. R., "Negligence-Innkeepers-Liability for Loss of or Injury to Goods of Guest," *Texas Law Review* 6 (1928): 545 (citing multiple common law cases supporting the "prevailing view" that "the innkeeper [was] liable for all loss of or injury to the goods of the guest, except when caused by an act of God, . . . or negligence of the guest himself").

62. Randy Barnett, for example, has argued that there ought to be a general ability to consensually alienate virtually all of one's rights, although he believes that certain rights are inalienable. Randy E. Barnett, "A Consent Theory of Contract," *Columbia Law Review* 86 (1986): 269–321; Randy E. Barnett, "Contract Remedies and Inalienable Rights," *Social Philosophy and Policy* 4, no. 1 (1986): 179–203.

63. See Hayek, "The Use of Knowledge in Society," 519–20 ("The peculiar character of the problem of a rational economic order is determined precisely by the fact that the knowledge of the circumstances of which we must make use never exists in concentrated or integrated form, but solely as the dispersed bits of incomplete and frequently contradictory knowledge which all the separate individuals possess"); for example, Oman, "A Pragmatic Defense of Contract Law," 77, 102 ("[Lawmakers] do not know what the 'best' construction contracts would look like, and given the multiplicity of differing contexts, goals, concerns and constraints faced by builders, it probably does not even make sense to think about a 'best' construction contract").

64. See Hayek, "The Use of Knowledge in Society," 528–30 and n. 1 (identifying key voices and perspectives in the "socialist calculation debate" taking place in the 1920s through the 1940s).

65. Graeber, *Debt*, n. 2, at 275 ("From the beginning, Islam had a positive view toward commerce. Mohammed himself had begun his adult life as a merchant; and no Islamic thinker ever treated the honest pursuit of profit as itself intrinsically immoral or inimical to faith").

66. See Marshall G. S. Hodgson, *The Venture of Islam, Volume 1: The Classical Age of Islam* (Chicago: University of Chicago Press, 1974), 21–26 (discussing the growth of political and economic systems in the Middle East during latter centuries of the first millennium).

67. See Kuran, *The Long Divergence*, 64–66 (discussing the Islamic law of partnership).

68. Ibid., 64.

69. Ibid., 65–67 (discussing trading partnerships in seventeenth-century Constantinople).

Chapter Three

1. Aristotle, *Nicomachean Ethics*, trans. F. H. Peters (New York: Barnes & Noble, 2004), I.3 at 1094a.

2. Ibid., II.1 at 1103a.

3. See John Rawls, *A Theory of Justice*, rev. ed. (Cambridge, MA: Belknap Press, 1999), 395–96 (discussing the distinction between the right and the good). See also Stephen Mulhall and Adam Swift, *Liberals and Communitarians* (Cambridge, MA: Blackwell, 1992), 31–33 (same).

4. John Rawls, "The Idea of Public Reason Revisited," *University of Chicago*

Law Review 64 (1997): 765, 775 (explaining the distinction between moral doctrines and liberal political principles).

5. Stephen Macedo, *Liberal Virtues: Citizenship, Virtue, and Community in Liberal Constitutionalism* (New York: Oxford University Press, 1990), 3 ("Government ought not to try to make people virtuous, liberals tend to say, it ought only to provide for equal freedom, order, security, and a few other widely acceptable public goods").

6. See Robert P. George, *In Defense of Natural Law* (Oxford: Clarendon Press, 1993), 186 (arguing that the need to censor pornography stems not from its propensity to shock and offend but from its tendency to corrupt and deprave); Catharine A. MacKinnon, *Only Words* (Cambridge, MA: Harvard University Press, 1993), 9, 62 (contending that pornography is sex abuse that warps a consumer's perception of women).

7. See Nadine Strossen, *Defending Pornography: Free Speech, Sex, and the Fight for Women's Rights* (New York: Scribner, 1995), 161–78 (characterizing pornography as a safe alternative to unsafe sex and one that dissolves social barriers and empowers the women who choose to consume and create it).

8. Cf. Lawrence v. Texas, 539 U.S. 558, 582 (2003) ("Moral disapproval . . . is an interest that is insufficient to satisfy rational basis review under the Equal Protection Clause").

9. See Sable Commc'ns of California, Inc. v. F.C.C., 492 U.S. 115, 126 (1989) ("Sexual expression which is indecent but not obscene is protected by the First Amendment"); New York v. Ferber, 458 U.S. 747, 764 (1982) ("There are, of course, limits on the category of child pornography which, like obscenity, is unprotected by the First Amendment").

10. Charles Dickens, *A Christmas Carol and Other Christmas Books*, ed. Robert Douglas-Fairhurst (New York: Oxford University Press, 2006), 9.

11. Plato offers his theory of the soul in Book IV of the *Republic.* See Plato, *The Republic of Plato*, trans. Allan David Bloom, 2nd ed. (New York: Basic Books, 1991), 97–125. Elsewhere, he writes of merchants, "They progress in money-making, and the more honorable they consider it, the less honorable they consider virtue. Or isn't virtue in tension with wealth, as though each were lying in the scale of a balance, always inclining in opposite directions?" Ibid., 228. See also Joshua I. Weinstein, "The Market in Plato's Republic," *Classical Philology* 104, no. 4 (October 2009): 439–58.

12. See, for example, Barack Obama, "A New Era of Service: Speech at the University of Colorado, Colorado Springs," *Rocky Mountain News*, July 2, 2008.

13. See Oliver Stone, dir., *Wall Street* (Twentieth Century Fox, 1987).

14. See Francis Ford Coppola, dir., *The Godfather* (Paramount Pictures, 1972).

15. In the romantic comedy, *You've Got Mail,* Corleone's line from the Godfather is picked up by Tom Hanks's character, who destroys the business of the character played by Meg Ryan, upending her life, and justifies his apparently heartless

attitude toward her suffering by insisting, "It isn't personal. It's just business." See Nora Ephron, dir., *You've Got Mail* (Warner Brothers, 1998).

16. See generally Sinclair Lewis, *Babbitt* (New York: Harcourt Brace, 1922).

17. According to Sinclair's citation for the 1930 Nobel Prize in Literature: "Babbitt probably approaches the ideal of an American popular hero of the middle class. The relativity of business morals as well as private rules of conduct is for him an accepted article of faith, and without hesitation he considers it God's purpose that man should work, increase his income, and enjoy modern improvements. He feels that he obeys these commandments and therefore lives in complete harmony with himself and society." Erik Axel Karlfeldt, "Award Ceremony Speech," (Presentation speech presented at the Nobel Prize in Literature 1930, December 10, 1930), http://www.nobelprize.org/nobel_prizes/literature/laureates/1930/press.html.

18. Amity Shlaes, *The Forgotten Man: A New History of the Great Depression*, repr. ed. (New York: Harper Perennial, 2008), 61–62 (discussing the perception of Babbitt among progressive critics of capitalism; "The thinkers of the 1920s loved Babbitt because he supplied them with a goal. They would be everything he was not: urban, bohemian, anti-money, idealist").

19. See Peter Berkowitz, *Virtue and the Making of Modern Liberalism* (Princeton, NJ: Princeton University Press, 1999), 7–15.

20. Ibid., 24–27.

21. Ibid., 7.

22. See Charles de Secondat Montesquieu, *The Spirit of the Laws*, eds. Anne Myers Cohler, Basia Carolyn Miller, and Harold Samuel Stone, Cambridge Texts in the History of Political Thought (Cambridge: Cambridge University Press, 1989), 338–54.

23. Sweet commerce.

24. See Adam Smith, *The Wealth of Nations*, ed. C. J. Bullock (New York: Barnes & Noble, 2004), 781–82.

25. See, for example, Kenneth J. Arrow, *Social Choice and Individual Values*, 1st ed. (New York: John Wiley & Sons, 1951), 46–60 (proving the Impossibility Theorem, which demonstrates an incompatibility between the doctrine of voters' sovereignty and that of collective rationality).

26. See, for example, Alexander Hamilton, John Jay, and James Madison, *The Federalist: A Commentary on the Constitution of the United States*, ed. Robert Scigliano (New York: Modern Library, 2001), No. 58 (Madison) (comparing the relative costs and benefits of requiring a simple majority for a quorum).

27. It is worth noting that this assumption is present even in deliberative theories of liberalism, in which the ability to justify a position to every member of the community is made the *sine non qua* of political legitimacy. See, for example, Bruce A. Ackerman, *Social Justice in the Liberal State* (New Haven, CT: Yale University Press, 1980), 8–10 (discussing "conversational constraint" as a legitimating device in liberal theory). Generally, the retreat from full unanimity is finessed in one of

two ways. Either the range of institutional arrangements subject to the exacting standards of universal assent is sharply limited, or the members of the community to whom the justification is addressed is limited either to those who are "reasonable" or to idealized as opposed to actual citizens. Both strategies are on display in Rawlsian liberalism, in which the supposedly universally justified principles of justice apply only to the "basic structure" and in which the arguments are addressed either to the subset of the community with "reasonable" comprehensive belief systems or else to the entirely fictitious inhabitants of the "original position."

28. Smith, *The Wealth of Nations*, 12.

29. See David Graeber, *Debt: The First 5,000 Years* (London: Melville House, 2012), 29–34 (providing examples of predatory bartering).

30. Ibid., 33–34 (quoting Charles Lindholm, *Generosity and Jealousy: The Swat Pukhtun of Northern Pakistan* [New York: Columbia University Press, 1982, 116]). Indeed, David Graeber, riffing off Smith's claim about humanity's innate propensity to "truck and barter," notes that the words, "like their equivalents in French, Spanish, German, Dutch, and Portuguese, literally meant to 'trick, bamboozle, or rip off.' " Ibid., 34. *The Oxford English Dictionary* reports that the word *barter* is a derivative of the now-defunct English word *barrat*, which meant "to quarrel, strive, or brawl." See "Barter," *Oxford English Dictionary* (New York: Oxford University Press, 1989); "Barrat," *Oxford English Dictionary* (New York: Oxford University Press, 1989).

31. See Charles Lindholm, *Generosity and Jealousy: The Swat Pukhtun of Northern Pakistan* (New York: Columbia University Press, 1982), 24 ("These shops are a recent development in the village. Previously, the only shop was that of the goldsmith. All other services were supplied either in traditional shares or by itinerant tradesmen from Kabul").

32. Ibid., 114 ("One form of exchange relation is a recent innovation due to the intrusion of the money economy into Swat. This is the relationship of employer to employee. Previously, Pukhtun confused this relationship with that of a master-servant or patron-client, and therefore refused to demean themselves by seeking jobs").

33. See generally Joseph Henrich et al., "In Search of Homo Economicus: Behavioral Experiments in 15 Small-Scale Societies," *American Economic Review* 91, no. 2 (2001): 73; Joseph Henrich et al., " 'Economic Man' in Cross-Cultural Perspective: Behavioral Experiments in 15 Small-Scale Societies," *Behavioral and Brain Science* 28, no. 6 (2005): 795.

34. See Eython Weg and Vernon Smith, "On the Failure to Induce Meager Offers in Ultimatum Games," *Journal of Economic Psychology* 14, no. 1 (2003): 17–18 (explaining the ultimatum game and its empirical history).

35. Ibid., 18–19 (finding evidence of nongreedy, egalitarian ultimatum behavior in numerous studies).

36. Joseph Henrich, "Does Culture Matter in Economic Behavior? Ultimatum Game Bargaining among the Machiguenga of the Peruvian Amazon," *American*

Economic Review 90, no. 4 (2000): 973, 975 (citing studies by Camerer and Thaler (1995) and Roth (1995) to demonstrate that the mean offer among experimental subjects from industrialized societies averages between 40 percent and 50 percent and that the group's modal offer is 50 percent).

37. Henrich et al., "'Economic Man' in Cross-Cultural Perspective," 795, 799.

38. Ibid., 802. Researchers found that two variables predict prosocial behavior. The first was the payoff to cooperation within the society. The Lamalera people, for example, inhabit a small island in eastern Indonesia and subsist in large part from hunting sperm whales, an intensely cooperative activity. In contrast, the Machiguenga live largely autarkic lives within their immediate families. Groups such as the Lamalera, which experience high returns for cooperation, show higher levels of prosocial behavior. The other predictor is the level of market interaction within the society. Ibid., 808.

39. Ibid., 811 ("Farmers rejected offers more frequently than herders").

40. Ibid., 810.

41. See Rawls, *A Theory of Justice*, 130–32.

42. Ibid.

43. John Stuart Mill, *On Liberty* (Mineola, NY: Dover Publications, 2002), 22 ("The only freedom which deserves the name is that of pursuing our own good, in our own way, so long as we do not attempt to deprive others of theirs, or impede their efforts to obtain it").

44. Berkowitz, *Virtue and the Making of Modern Liberalism*, 80–81 (citing John Locke, "Some Thoughts Concerning Education," in *Some Thoughts Concerning Education and of the Conduct of the Understanding* 25, 29, 32–34 (eds. Ruth W. Grant and Nathan Tarcov 1996)).

45. Although the precise structure that families take has varied dramatically across time and space, in every human society of which we are aware there are family structures. See generally E. Anthony Wrigley, "Reflections on the History of the Family," *Daedalus* 106, no. 2 (Spring 1977): 71.

46. See generally Mary Jane West Eberhard, "The Evolution of Social Behavior by Kin Selection," *Quarterly Review of Biology* 50, no. 1 (March 1, 1975): 1–33; Jonathan Haidt, *The Righteous Mind: Why Good People Are Divided by Politics and Religion*, 1st ed. (New York: Pantheon, 2012).

47. See Francis Fukuyama, *The Origins of Political Order: From Prehuman Times to the French Revolution* (New York: Farrar, Straus and Giroux, 2011), 439 (providing a succinct summary of Fukuyama's theory of patrimonialism).

48. See Douglass C. North, John Joseph Wallis, and Barry R. Weingast, *Violence and Social Orders: A Conceptual Framework for Interpreting Recorded Human History* (New York: Cambridge University Press, 2009), 18–27 (providing a succinct summary of the theory of transitions from natural states to open access orders).

49. See Luis F. Andrade, Jose M. Barra, and Heinz-Peter Elstrodt, "All in the Familia," *McKinsey Quarterly* special ed., no. 4 (2001): 81 ("Empirical evidence

suggests that there is some truth to the common observation that the first generation builds the company, the second preserves it, and the third squanders it. In fact, fewer than 15 percent of family-owned businesses survive under family control beyond the third generation").

50. Frank Henderson Stewart, *Honor*, 1st ed. (Chicago: University of Chicago Press, 1994), 54–63 (explaining "horizontal honor," the respect that one gets from a group of peers called the "honor group," and distinguishing it from "vertical honor," the status and public esteem that one gains by virtue of one's place in a social hierarchy from those below one on the social ladder); Nathan B. Oman, "The Honor of Private Law," *Fordham Law Review* 80 (2011): 47 (same).

51. The fight between Lyon and Griswald is recounted in Joanne B. Freeman, *Affairs of Honor: National Politics in the New Republic* (New Haven, CT: Yale Nota Bene, 2002), 173–75.

52. Ibid., 172 (discussing the social meaning of canning within the culture of honor).

53. The incident is recounted in David Herbert Donald, *Charles Sumner* (New York: Da Capo Press, 1996), 291–97. See generally Bertram Wyatt-Brown, *Southern Honor: Ethics and Behavior in the Old South* (New York: Oxford University Press, 1982) (discussing the culture of honor in the antebellum South).

54. Thomas Carlyle, *Chartism*, 2nd ed. (London: Chapman and Hall, Strand, 1891), 58.

55. Alexis de Tocqueville, *Democracy in America*, ed. Isaac Kramnick, trans. Gerald Bevan (New York: Penguin Books, 2002), 640.

56. Ibid.

57. Oman, "The Honor of Private Law." See also Alison L. LaCroix, "To Gain the Whole World and Lose His Own Soul: Nineteenth-Century American Dueling as Public Law and Private Code," *Hofstra Law Review* 33 (2004): 501–69 (discussing the history of dueling in the United States); C. A. Harwell Wells, "The End of the Affair? Anti-Dueling Laws and Social Norms in Antebellum America," *Vanderbilt Law Review* 54 (2001): 1805–47 (same).

58. The Anabaptists eventually became today's Baptists.

59. See George Huntston Williams, *The Radical Reformation* (Philadelphia: Westminster Press, 1962), 380 ("[Two refugees] deserted and betrayed one of the gates of the town to the Bishop").

60. Ibid., 381 ("[Beuckelszoon was] condemned and tortured with red-hot tongs on a platform for all to see in Munster on 22 January 1536. [His] seared bod[y] was placed in [an] iron [cage] and suspended from the tower of St. Lambert's Church").

61. See generally Diarmaid MacCulloch, *The Reformation: A History* (New York: Viking, 2004), 469 (discussing how "the Catholic struggle to hold the line against Protestantism brought . . . misery to millions of Europeans," highlighted by 15 to 40 percent of the German population dying due to war between 1618 and 1648).

62. Robert Audi, *Religious Commitment and Secular Reason* (New York: Cambridge University Press, 2000), 3–4.

63. Martha Craven Nussbaum, *Liberty of Conscience: In Defense of America's Tradition of Religious Equality* (Princeton, NJ: Basic Books, 2008), 34. The accuracy of Nussbaum's historical claim can be doubted. Certainly, the earliest English colonists in Virginia and the Carolinas did not come to America fleeing religious persecution. What is striking, however, is the way in which she identifies the religious conflicts of Reformation and counter-Reformation as the antithesis of the modern liberal society that she wishes to defend.

64. See, for example, Anne Applebaum, *Gulag: A History of the Soviet Camps* (London: Allen Lane, 2003), 580–85 (estimating that, from 1929 to 1953, Stalin imprisoned 28.7 million, and citing estimates that between 10 and 20 million died in gulags between 1918 and the 1980s); Donald Bloxham, *The Final Solution: A Genocide* (New York: Oxford University Press, 2009), 1 ("Between 5,100,000 and 6,200,000 Jews were murdered during the Second World War, an episode the Nazis called the 'final solution of the Jewish question'").

65. See Steven D. Smith, *The Disenchantment of Secular Discourse* (Cambridge, MA: Harvard University Press, 2010), 65 ("From any of these more critical perspectives [of political philosophers], the sort of distinctively 'moral' discourse practiced in academic and legal contexts is almost predestined to produce an unedifying spectacle. Unmoored from its subject matter, necessarily trading on suppressed premises and commitments, such discourse is inherently deceptive and deficient").

66. Ronald Dworkin, *A Matter of Principle* (Cambridge, MA: Harvard University Press, 1985), 203.

67. John Rawls, *Political Liberalism* (New York: Columbia University Press, 1993), 213 ("As an ideal conception of citizenship for a constitutional democratic regime, [public reason] presents how things might be, taking people as a just and well-ordered society would encourage them to be. It describes what is possible and can be, yet may never be, though no less fundamental for that").

68. See Smith, *The Disenchantment of Secular Discourse*, n. 30, at 24–38 (discussing divergence between modern political debate and the idealizations of liberal philosophers).

69. See Stephen L. Carter, *The Culture of Disbelief: How American Law and Politics Trivialize Religious Devotion* (New York: Anchor Books, 1994), 227–32 (discussing the role of religion in various social and political movements in U.S. history).

70. Lincoln said: "Fondly do we hope, fervently do we pray, that this mighty scourge of war may speedily pass away. Yet, if God wills that it continue until all the wealth piled by the bondsman's two hundred and fifty years of unrequited toil shall be sunk, and until every drop of blood drawn with the lash shall be paid by another drawn with the sword, as was said three thousand years ago, so still it must

be said 'the judgments of the Lord are true and righteous altogether.'" Abraham Lincoln, "Second Inaugural Address," March 4, 1865 (The Avalon Project, Yale Law School), http://avalon.law.yale.edu/19th_century/lincoln2.asp.

71. Martin Luther King Jr., "I Have a Dream," August 23, 1963 (The Avalon Project, Yale Law School), http://avalon.law.yale.edu/20th_century/mlk01.asp. Compare Isaiah 40:4 ("Every valley shall be lifted up, and every mountain and hill be made low; the uneven ground shall become level, and the rough places a plain").

72. 410 U.S. 113 (1973). John Rawls identified constitutional adjudication as a primary example of public reason. Rawls, *Political Liberalism*, 216 ("[Public reason] in a special way to the judiciary . . . in a constitutional democracy with judicial review. . . . The court's special role makes it the exemplar of public reason").

73. Planned Parenthood of Southeastern Pennsylvania v. Casey, 505 U.S. 833, 867 (1992).

74. See Jeremy Waldron, *The Dignity of Legislation* (New York: Cambridge University Press, 1999), 2–3 (discussing the value of legislative institutions).

75. See U.S. Const. amend. I ("Congress shall make no law respecting an establishment of religion, or prohibiting the free exercise thereof").

76. See Whitney v. California, 274 U.S. 357, 375 (1927) (Brandeis, J. concurring) ("[Those who won our independence] believed that freedom to think as you will and to speak as you think are means indispensable to the discovery and spread of political truth; that with them, discussion affords ordinarily adequate protection against the dissemination of noxious doctrine; that the greatest menace to freedom is an inert people").

77. See, for example, Griswold v. Connecticut, 381 U.S. 479, 484 (1965) ("Specific guarantees in the Bill of Rights have penumbras, formed by emanations from those guarantees that help give them life and substance. Various guarantees create zones of privacy. The right of association contained in the penumbra of the First Amendment is one, as we have seen [where privacy is protected from governmental intrusion]").

78. Travis N. Ridout and Kathleen Searles, "It's My Campaign I'll Cry If I Want To: How and When Campaigns Use Emotional Appeals," *Political Psychology* 32, no. 3 (2011): 454–55 (researching U.S. Senate races and finding "that there are some systematic patterns to the use of specific emotional appeals in political campaigns, though the use of some appeals, such as anger, is much more predictable than the use of other appeals, such as pride or enthusiasm").

79. See Cass R. Sunstein, *Going to Extremes: How Like Minds Unite and Divide* (New York: Oxford University Press, 2009), 21–68 (surveying various studies on the polarizing impact of debate between individuals with differing moral or political viewpoints).

80. Ibid., 51 ("While we have hoped that mixed groups, confronted with balanced information, would polarize less, the opposite is sometimes true").

81. Ibid., 114–15 ("One of the characteristic features of feuds is that members of feuding groups tend to talk to only one another, or at least listen only to one

another, fueling and amplifying their outrage, while solidifying their impression of the relevant events").

82. See Albert O. Hirschman, *The Passions and the Interests: Political Arguments for Capitalism before Its Triumph* (Princeton, NJ: Princeton University Press, 1977), 16–20 (discussing several theorists who advocate "the idea of harnessing the passions of men, of making them work toward the general welfare").

83. Smith, *The Wealth of Nations*, 22.

84. See Randall Hansen, *Fire and Fury: The Allied Bombing of Germany 1942–1945* (New York: Doubleday, 2008), 253–54 (describing the bombing of Dresden).

85. Lea Sitton, "An Explosive Finale for Giant Sears: A Landmark Will Go as It Came: In Record-Setting Fashion," *Philly.com*, October 24, 1994, http://articles.philly.com/1994-10-24/news/25874324_1_sears-implosion-explosives (detailing implosion preparations and providing a history of the building).

86. Ibid. (documenting the Rubin Organization's and Engineered Demolition's roles in the implosion); Frank Dougherty, "Buildup Is on for Sears Blast," *Philly.com*, October 14, 1994, http://articles.philly.com/1994-10-14/news/25875038_1_plunger-implosion-roosevelt-boulevard (documenting the role of Mercer Wrecking Recycling).

87. Joanne Sills, "She'll Have a Blast: Woman, 28, Wins Sears Implosion Contest; $2,190 Raised for Hero Scholarship Fund," *Philly.com*, October 27, 1994, http://articles.philly.com/1994-10-27/news/25871056_1_sears-building-roosevelt-boulevard-contest (detailing how Ms. Melody Lee won the contest).

88. Sitton, "An Explosive Finale" ("[The Sears Merchandise Center] is to be the site of the biggest implosion ever").

89. Sills, "She'll Have a Blast" (quoting a Philadelphia resident who thought the building "should come down. It's standing there and nobody's using it and someone will set it on fire. So, take it down").

90. David M. Kennedy, *Freedom from Fear: The American People in Depression and War 1929–1945* (New York: Oxford University Press, 1999), 619–44 (discussing extensive wartime regulation of the U.S. economy).

91. See "Southern Baptists Vote for Disney Boycott," *CNN.com*, June 18, 1997. Among the movies that drew the Southern Baptist Church's ire was Miramax's 1994 film *Priest*, which chronicled the turmoil of a Catholic priest's involvement with a gay lover. See Antonia Bird, dir. *Priest* (Miramax Films, 1994); Miramax had been acquired by Disney in 1993.

92. See M. Alex Johnson, "Southern Baptists End 8-Year Disney Boycott," *MSNBC.com*, June 22, 2005.

93. See Teresa Welsh, "Should Cities Boycott Chick-fil-A over Gay Marriage?" *U.S. News & World Report*, July 27, 2012, http://www.usnews.com/opinion/articles/2012/07/27/should-cities-boycott-anti-gay-marriage-chick-fil-a (documenting the vice-president's interview and the resulting criticism from mayors of several major cities).

94. See Lawrence B. Glickman, "Chick-fil-A Day a Reminder That Boycotts Often Backfire," *Bloomberg*, August 3, 2012, http://www.bloomberg.com/news/2012

-08-03/chick-fil-a-day-a-reminder-that-boycotts-often-backfire.html ("On Aug. 1 [days after calls to boycott Chick-fil-A], thousands of people flocked to the [Chick-fil-A] restaurants, many of them braving long lines and midsummer heat, to make a political statement. As a result . . . Chick-fil-A had a 'record-setting day' in terms of sales").

95. Lucas Grindley, "Angry Alderman Again Threatens to Stop Chick-fil-A from Expanding to Chicago Neighborhood," *Advocate.com*, September 23, 2012, http://www.advocate.com/business/2012/09/23/angry-alderman-again-threatens-stop-chick-fil-expanding-chicago-neighborhood (discussing Moreno's claims about Chick-fil-A's "potentially illegal business standards.").

96. See generally Mancur Olson, *The Logic of Collective Action: Public Goods and the Theory of Groups* (Cambridge, MA: Harvard University Press, 1971), 5–53 (providing a classic discussion of collective action problems).

97. See T. H. Breen, *The Marketplace of Revolution: How Consumer Politics Shaped American Independence* (New York: Oxford University Press, 2004), xv–xvii (discussing boycotts in the American Revolution); Edmund Morgan, *The Stamp Act Crisis: Prologue to Revolution* (Chapel Hill: University of North Carolina Press, 1953), 150–64 (discussing violence and the boycotts surrounding the Stamp Act).

98. See generally Comprehensive Anti-Apartheid Act of 1986, PL no. 99-440, 100 Stat. 1086, Oct. 2, 1986.

99. See Gayle v. Browder, 352 U.S. 903 (1956). For a full account of the legal maneuvering and denouement of the Montgomery bus boycott, see Randall Kennedy, "Martin Luther King's Constitution: A Legal History of the Montgomery Bus Boycott," *Yale Law Journal* 98 (1989): 999–1067.

100. Jules L. Coleman, *Risks and Wrongs* (New York: Oxford University Press, 1992), 5.

101. This is the figure for the top household income when the population is divided by income into five tranches and one looks at the third—that is, the middle—tranche. The data are available online at http://www.census.gov/compendia/statab/cats/income_expenditures_poverty_wealth/household_income.html.

102. World Bank data can be downloaded online at http://data.worldbank.org.

103. Try it some time. The site has interactive graphs as well as the ability to download raw data in spreadsheet format. See http://data.worldbank.org.

104. See William Easterly, *The White Man's Burden: Why the West's Efforts to Aid the Rest Have Done So Much Ill and So Little Good* (New York: Penguin Press, 2006), 1.

105. See "Photo Journal: Ethiopian Wood Collector," *BBC News*, n.d., http://news.bbc.co.uk/2/shared/spl/hi/picture_gallery/04/africa_ethiopian_wood_collector/html/1.stm.

106. Top household income for the bottom fifth of U.S. households in 2009 was $20,453. See United States Census Bureau, "Household Income," *2012 Statistical*

Abstract of the United States (Washington, DC: U.S. Census Bureau), http://www.census.gov/compendia/statab/cats/income_expenditures_poverty_wealth/household_income.html. Per capita income in Ethiopia in 2009 was $340 or about 93 cents per day. See "Ethiopia," World Bank, Washington, DC, n.d., http://data.worldbank.org/country/ethiopia.

107. See Angus Maddison, *Contours of the World Economy 1–2030 a.d.: Essays in Macro-Economic History* (New York: Oxford University Press, 2007), 70. Maddison has also tried to estimate per capita income in different regions of the Roman Empire, which he posits ranged from a high of $600 per capita in Egypt to $400 in the barbarian regions immediately abutting the Empire's borders. See ibid., 53.

108. International Monetary Fund data are available through Google's public data aggregator. Information on Ghana is available at http://www.google.com/publicdata/explore?ds=k3s92bru78li6_.

109. Maddison, *Contours of the World Economy*, 70.

110. Angus Maddison, *Monitoring the World Economy, 1820–1992* (Washington, DC: Development Centre of the Organisation for Economic Co-operation and Development, 1995), 20.

111. See Deirdre N. McCloskey, *Bourgeois Dignity: Why Economics Can't Explain the Modern World* (Chicago: University of Chicago Press, 2010), 10–15 (discussing the "bourgeois revaluation," that occurred in Holland during the seventeenth and eighteenth centuries).

112. See Maddison, *Monitoring the World Economy*, 196.

113. See Jared Diamond, *Guns, Germs, and Steel* (New York: W. W. Norton, 1997) (arguing that the favorable geographic location of Western Europe determined its economic dominance thousands of years before the beginning of recorded history); David S. Landes, *The Wealth and Poverty of Nations: Why Some Are So Rich and Some So Poor* (New York: W. W. Norton, 1999) (arguing that culture has been decisive in fostering economic development); Daron Acemoglu and James A. Robinson, *Why Nations Fail: The Origins of Power, Prosperity, and Poverty* (London: Profile Books, 2012) (arguing that the incentives created by legal and political institutions determine economic outcomes).

114. See Maddison, *Contours of the World Economy*, 378–79.

115. Ibid.

116. In fairness, however, much of the economic expansion of the Dutch was built on the Dutch East India Company, which pursued a ruthless policy of military domination and exploitation in what is today Indonesia. Likewise, British expansion in the early industrial revolution was fueled in large part by the textile industry, which was dependent in its early years on cotton provided by enslaved labor in the United States. Slavery, however, does not seem to have been a necessary or sufficient condition for Britain's economic expansion. Slavery was widely practiced in North America for more than a century before Britain began to experience massive

sustained economic growth. Likewise, the demise of slavery in North America after 1865 did not halt industrial and economic expansion in Britain.

117. See Nathan Rosenberg and L. E. Birdzell, *How the West Grew Rich* (New York: Basic Books, 1987), 17–18 ("The eighteenth- and nineteenth-century history of most imperialist countries makes their economic growth seem more a cause of imperialism, stimulating overseas political adventures in the irresponsible exercise of new-found economic power, than its result").

118. See James M. Buchanan and Viktor J. Vanberg, "The Market as a Creative Process," in *The Philosophy of Economics: An Anthology*, ed. Daniel M. Hausman, 3rd ed. (New York: Cambridge University Press, 2008), 378–98.

119. Ibid., 389–90.

120. Ibid., 391.

121. Ibid.

122. Ibid., 389.

123. See generally Jeffrey D. Sachs, *The End of Poverty: Economic Possibilities for Our Time* (London: Allen Lane, 2005).

124. See generally Easterly, *The White Man's Burden.*

125. See Sachs, *The End of Poverty*, 3.

126. Easterly, *The White Man's Burden*, 72.

127. For example, ibid., 77 ("Nor are markets of much help to those who are now very poor—after all the poor have no money to motivate any market Searchers to meet their needs."); Sachs, *The End of Poverty*, 3 ("Without [infrastructure and human capital] markets can cruelly bypass large parts of the world, leaving them impoverished and suffering without respite").

128. Sachs, for example, offers a defense of sweat shops against rich-world protesters who insist that they should pay higher wages or be shut down. "The sweat shops," he writes, "are the first rung on the ladder out of extreme poverty." Sachs, *The End of Poverty* 165.

129. Matthew 19:24 (RSV).

130. Dworkin, *A Matter of Principle*, 342 ("I do not mean whether the gain in wealth is overridden by the cost in justice or in equal treatment, or in anything else, but whether the gain in wealth is, considered in itself, any gain at all. I should say, and I think most people would agree that [a society in which there are gains in wealth] is not better in any respect").

131. See Richard A. Posner, *The Economics of Justice* (Cambridge, MA: Harvard University Press, 1981), 13–119 (discussing how the concept of efficiency as wealth maximization "is an adequate concept of justice that can plausibly be imputed to judges, at least in common law adjudication"); Richard A. Posner, "Utilitarianism, Economics, and Legal Theory," *Journal of Legal Studies* 8 (1979): 103–40.

132. Dworkin, *A Matter of Principle*, 341–42.

133. Ibid., 242.

134. Ibid., 249–51 (discussing what Dworkin refers to as instrumentalist defenses of wealth maximization).

135. Ibid., 260 (discussing why diminishing marginal utility to wealth suggests that wealth maximization will not maximize utility).

136. Posner himself subsequently abandoned the claim. See Richard A. Posner, "The Problematics of Moral and Legal Theory," *Harvard Law Review* 111 (1998): 1669–70 and n. 62 (rejecting his earlier arguments in favor of wealth maximization).

137. See Dworkin, *A Matter of Principle*, 246.

138. The information on malaria is from World Health Organization, "Media Centre: Malaria," *October 2015*, http://www.who.int/mediacentre/factsheets/fs094/en/.

139. See Sachs, *The End of Poverty*, 7 ("More than one million African children, and perhaps as many as three million, succumb to malaria each year [in 2005]. This horrific catastrophe occurs despite the fact that the disease is partly preventable . . . and completely treatable").

140. See *World Health Organization*, "Media Centre: HIV/AIDS," November 2015, http://www.who.int/mediacentre/factsheets/fs360/en/.

141. See Sachs, *The End of Poverty*, 7–9 (describing the availability of generic antiviral drugs).

142. *Foundation for AIDS Research*, "World-Wide Statistics" (New York: amfAR, July 2015), http://www.amfar.org/about-hiv-and-aids/facts-and-stats/statistics--worldwide/.

143. See Sachs, *The End of Poverty*, 8–9 (describing an HIV/AIDS ward in a Malawi hospital where 450 people were crammed into a ward with a 150 beds and, without treatment, awaited death).

144. See World Health Organization, "Media Centre: Malaria"; Sachs, *The End of Poverty*, 7.

145. See Hugh J. Field and Erick De Clercq, "Anti-Viral Drugs: A Short History of Their Discovery and Development," *Microbiology Today* 31 (2004): 58–61 (providing a history of the long process of research leading to the discovery and manufacture of antiviral drugs). It is worth noting that the discovery of quinine also involved investment in scientific and medical research, albeit on a smaller scale. During the nineteenth century, European countries used some of the wealth created by the industrial revolution to fund systematic research on tropical diseases, in large part so that Europeans could more effectively colonize Africa and Asia. See Acemoglu and Robinson, *Why Nations Fail*, 48–53 (discussing the history of research into tropical diseases such as malaria).

146. See Matthias Doepke, Michèle Tertilt, and Alessandra Voena, "The Economics and Politics of Women's Rights," SSRN Scholarly Paper (Rochester, NY: Social Science Research Network, December 1, 2011), 6–7, http://papers.ssrn.com/abstract=1973883. Forschunginstitut zur Zurkunft der Arbeit/Institute for the Study of Labor, Discussion Paper no. 6215.

147. Ibid., 7–8.

148. See Edward Miguel, "Poverty and Witch Killing," *Review of Economic Studies* 72, no. 4 (2005): 1153–72 (Tanzania); Emily Oster, "Witchcraft, Weather and Economic Growth in Renaissance Italy," *Journal of Economic Perspectives* 18, no. 1 (2004): 215–28 (Italy).

149. Doepke, Tertilt, and Voena, "The Economics and Politics of Women's Rights," n. 123, at 32.

150. The data are available from the World Bank, http://data.worldbank.org.

151. The numbers are 40 percent for Germany and 28 percent for the United States and Australia. There are also many middle-income nations with substantial marine preserves. Ecuador, for example, has set aside 70 percent of its territorial waters. See ibid.

152. The data are available in spreadsheet format through the World Bank's website (http://data.worldbank.org).

153. See Gene M. Grossman and Alan B. Krueger, "Economic Growth and the Environment," *Quarterly Journal of Economics* 110, no. 2 (May 1995): 353–77.

154. Ibid., 353.

155. See Arik Levinson, "The Ups and Downs of the Environmental Kuznets Curve" (Orlando, FL: UCF/Centre Conference on the Environment, 2000) (discussing the origins of the term and the resulting literature). The original Kuznets curve posited that, during the early stages of development, growth was accompanied by increases in inequality but that as societies became wealthier, inequality began to decrease. See Simon Kuznets, "Economic Growth and Income Inequality," *American Economic Review* 45, no. 1 (March 1, 1955): 1–28. The curves plot pollution on the y axis and per capita gross domestic product on the x axis. The inverted U plot arises because pollution initially rises with increases to per capita GDP and then at some point begins to fall.

156. See Grossman and Krueger, "Economic Growth and the Environment," 369 ("We find for most indicators that economic growth brings an initial phase of [environmental] deterioration followed by a subsequent phase of [environmental] improvement . . . . The turning points for the different pollutants vary, but in most cases they occur before a country reaches a per capita income of $8000").

157. See F. G. Hank Hilton and Arik Levinson, "Factoring Environmental Kuznets Curve: Evidence from Automotive Lead Emissions," *Journal of Environmental Economics and Management* 35 (1998): 126–41; Matthew E. Kahn, "A Household Level Environmental Kuznets Curve," *Economics Letters* 59, no. 2 (1998): 269–73; Pingo Wang et al., "A Risk-Based Environmental Kuznets Curve for US Hazardous Waste Sites," *Applied Economics Letters* 5, no. 12 (1998): 761–63; Shubham Chaudhuri and Alexander S. P. Plaff, "Household Income, Fuel Choice, and Indoor Air Quality: Microfoundations of an Environmental Kuznets Curve," *Columbia University Economics Department Working Paper* (New York: Columbia University, 1998); David F. Bradford, Rebecca Schlieckert, and Stephen H. Shore, "The Environmental Kuznets Curve: Exploring a Fresh Specification," NBER

Working Paper 8001 (Cambridge, MA: National Bureau of Economic Research, November 2000).

158. See Susmita Dasgupta et al., "Confronting the Environmental Kuznets Curve," *Journal of Economic Perspectives* 16, no. 1 (Winter 2002): 147–68 (reviewing the debates over the environmental Kuznets curve).

159. Ibid., 155.

160. See Benjamin M. Friedman, *The Moral Consequences of Economic Growth* (New York: Knopf, 2005).

Chapter Four

1. See J. J. C. Smart and Bernard Williams, *Utilitarianism: For and Against* (Cambridge: Cambridge University Press, 1973), 141 (discussing problems with inter personal comparisons of utility); Amartya Sen, "Interpersonal Comparisons of Welfare," in *Choice, Welfare, and Measurement* (Cambridge, MA: MIT Press, 1982), 264 (same).

2. See Amartya Sen, "The Impossibility of a Paretian Liberal," in *Choice, Welfare, and Measurement* (Cambridge, MA: MIT Press, 1982), 285 (discussing the demandingness problem of Pareto superiority as a social choice mechanism).

3. See Richard A. Posner, *Economic Analysis of Law*, 8th ed. (New York: Aspen Publishers, 2010), 17–18 (discussing the effect of transactions on prices and Pareto optimality).

4. See, for example, Richard Posner, *Economic Analysis of Law*, 1st ed. (Boston: Little, Brown, 1972), 17 ("The less austere concept of efficiency mainly used in this book [is] called the Kaldor-Hicks concept of efficiency, or wealth maximization"); Robert Cooter and Thomas Ulen, *Law and Economics*, 6th ed. (Boston: Pearson/Addison Wesley, 2012), 47–48 ("Dissatisfied with the Pareto criterion, economists developed the notion of a potential Pareto improvement (sometimes called Kaldor-Hicks efficiency)").

5. Another, unrelated, objection to Kaldor-Hicks efficiency is the claim that, under certain circumstances, it is circular. It is possible to move from A to B while satisfying the requirements of Kaldor-Hicks and then move from B to A while again satisfying Kaldor-Hicks. This problem is known as the Scitovsky paradox. In these conditions, Kaldor-Hicks is not simply mistaken as a normative criterion but is vacuous. See Jules L. Coleman, *Markets, Morals and the Law* (New York: Oxford University Press, 1988), 104, 110–11 (discussing the Scitovsky paradox as an objection to the Kaldor-Hicks efficiency criterion); Tibor Scitovsky, "A Note on Welfare Propositions in Economics," *Review of Economic Studies* 9 (1941): 77 (explaining the paradox at length).

6. See, for example, Ronald Dworkin, "Why Efficiency?" *Hofstra Law Review* 8 (1979): 563–90.

7. See John Rawls, *A Theory of Justice*, rev. ed. (Cambridge, MA: Belknap Press, 1999), 30 (criticizing utilitarian moral theory more generally).

8. Remember that there is no requirement under Kaldor-Hicks efficiency that any such compensation actually be paid. It is enough that it could potentially be paid.

9. Of course we could impose a duty of compensation on Scrooge, in which case he would be enriched by only $1, and Tiny Tim and the rest of us would be no worse off. Kaldor-Hicks efficiency, however, provides no justification for such a compensation principle.

10. See generally Louis Kaplow and Steven Shavell, *Fairness Versus Welfare* (Cambridge, MA: Harvard University Press, 2002).

11. Ibid., 21 ("We further note a particular source of well-being that has special relevance to our book, namely, the possibility that individuals have a taste for a notion of fairness, just as they may have a taste for art, nature, or fine wine. For example, an individual might derive pleasure from knowing that vicious criminals receive their just deserts (independent of the anticipated effects of punishment on the incidence of crime) or that legal rules reflect a favored conception of fairness").

12. Ibid. ("In such cases, satisfying the principal of fairness enhances the individual's well-being, just as would satisfying his preference for wine").

13. See generally Barak Medina and Eyal Zamir, *Law, Economics, and Morality* (New York: Oxford University Press, 2010).

14. Ibid., 257 ("We nevertheless maintain that certain deontological restraints apply to contracting behavior and that incorporation of deontological constraints with economic analysis of contract law may be fruitful").

15. For a general discussion of the idea of welfare employed by economic theorists, see Daniel M. Hausman and Michael S. McPherson, *Economic Analysis, Moral Philosophy and Public Policy* (Cambridge: Cambridge University Press, 2006), 118–34; see also Allen E. Buchanan, *Ethics, Efficiency, and the Market* (Totowa, NJ: Rowman & Allanheld, 1985), 26–31.

16. Jeremy Bentham, *An Introduction to the Principals of Morals and Legislation* (New York: Oxford University Press, 1996), 2 ("By utility is meant that property in any object, whereby it tends to produce benefit, advantage, pleasure, good, or happiness, (all this in the present case comes to the same thing) or (what comes again to the same thing) to prevent the happening of mischief, pain, evil, or unhappiness to the party whose interest is considered; if that party be the community in general, then the happiness of the community; if a particular individual, then the happiness of that individual").

17. Economists also assume that preferences are transitive. If A is preferred to B and B is preferred to C, then A must be preferred to C. If the ordinal ranking of preferences is not transitive, then problems of circularity arise, and it is difficult to claim that the satisfaction of A increases welfare relative to the satisfaction of B. After all, B would be better than C, which would in turn be better than A.

18. See, for example, John Stuart Mill, *On Liberty* (Mineola, NY: Dover Publications, 2002), 8 ("That the only purpose for which power can be rightfully exercised over any member of a civilized community, against his will, is to prevent harm to others"); Stephen Mulhall and Adam Swift, *Liberals and Communitarians* (Cambridge, MA: Blackwell, 1992), 25–34 (summarizing the liberal case in favor of neutrality toward perfectionist theories of the good).

19. Rejecting the bare satisfaction of preferences as normatively significant does not mean that the state should punish or control preferences. It may be unwise to commit to the state superintendence over the preferences of its citizens for other reasons. Doing so would create many opportunities for intentional and unintentional abuse. It may be impossible in a pluralistic society to generate the legitimacy needed for political institutions to carry out such a task. See generally John Rawls, "The Idea of Public Reason Revisited," *University of Chicago Law Review* 64 (1997): 765–66 ("A basic feature of democracy is the fact of reasonable pluralism—the fact that a plurality of conflicting reasonable comprehensive doctrines, religious, philosophical, and moral, is the normal result of its culture of free institutions" [footnotes omitted]). Likewise, respect for human liberty may require that we leave others free to pursue their own desires as long as they leave us free to pursue ours. See Mill, *On Liberty*, 18 ("The sole end for which mankind are warranted, individually or collectively in interfering with the liberty of action of any of their number, is self-protection. That the only purpose for which power can be rightfully exercised over any member of a civilized community, against his will, is to prevent harm to others"). None of these arguments rests on the idea that one must treat all preferences as equally valuable. We might not trust government officials with the power to monitor and control citizens' choices in entertainment. It would be very strange, however, to say that this is valuable precisely because it lets sociopaths enjoy the spectacle of suffering. Likewise, we might be unable to generate widespread legitimacy for a state with the power to oversee the pleasures of the sociopath. It does not follow that such state is better *because* sociopaths will more fully enjoy the misery of others. Finally, one might believe that it would be a moral evil to interfere with the sociopath's liberty merely to observe suffering. This needn't imply, however, that the sociopath's liberty is valuable precisely because it allows him to enjoy the suffering of children.

20. Cass Sunstein, for example, is a proponent of both behavioralist social science hostile to neoclassical economic *and* of the cost benefit analysis of legal rules, which is essentially an attempt to operationalize the idea of Kaldor-Hicks efficiency. See Cass R. Sunstein, ed., *Behavioral Law and Economics* (New York: Cambridge University Press, 2000); Cass R. Sunstein, *The Cost-Benefit State: The Future of Regulatory Protection* (Chicago: American Bar Association, 2003).

21. See generally Ronald Coase, "The Problem of Social Cost," *Journal of Law and Economics* 3 (1960): 1.

22. Ibid. ("This paper is concerned with those actions of business firms which have harmful effects on others").

23. See Arthur Cecil Pigou, *The Economics of Welfare*, Palgrave Classics in Economics (New York: Palgrave Macmillan, 2013), 192 ("It is, however, possible for the State if it so chooses, to remove the divergence in any field by 'extraordinary encouragements' or 'extraordinary restraints' upon investments in the field. The most obvious forms which these encouragements and restraints may assume are, of course, those bounties and taxes").

24. Adam Smith, *The Wealth of Nations*, ed. C. J. Bullock (New York: Barnes & Noble, 2004), 15.

25. Ibid., 3–5 (discussing pin factories).

26. Ibid., 15.

27. Ibid.

28. Strikingly, his independent existence means that he lacks also the moral benefits of the market. Hence, while the Lowland Scots of Glasgow and Edinburgh, where Smith spent most of his life, were notable merchants, exhibiting the commercial virtues that he exalted in his works, the Highland Scots were notable for their hierarchical and clannish political structure and the ferocity of their warriors toward outsiders. See, for example, C. R. Fay, *Adam Smith and the Scotland of His Day* (New York: Cambridge University Press, 1956), 10–11 (reproducing a letter sent by one of Smith's contemporaries to government officials in London arguing that the Highlands chief export should be fighting men for Britain's imperial wars).

29. Smith, *The Wealth of Nations*, 17.

30. Ibid.

31. See Alan Schwartz and Robert E. Scott, "Contract Theory and the Limits of Contract Law," *Yale Law Journal* 113 (2003): 609 ("Inefficient [contract law] defaults only raise transaction costs unnecessarily").

32. See Richard Allen Epstein, *Takings: Private Property and the Power of Eminent Domain* (Cambridge, MA: Harvard University Press, 1985), 5 ("There are transaction costs, holdout, and free-rider problems that are almost insuperable when the conduct of a large number of individuals must be organized. To this problem, the proper response is the power to force exchanges upon payment for public use. The eminent domain solution shows how a government can be organized to overcome the twin problems of aggression and provision of public goods").

33. See generally William B. Stoebuck and Dale A. Whitman, *The Law of Property*, 3rd ed. (St. Paul, MN: West, 2000), 447–49 (describing easements implied from necessity).

34. See, for example, Gacki v. Bartels, 859 N.E.2d 1178, 1185–86 (Ill. App. Ct. 2006) ("In order to claim an easement by necessity, the plaintiff must present evidence that his property and the defendants' property were owned by a common grantor, that the properties were severed, and that at the time of severance his parcel became landlocked"); Wiliam C. Haak Trust v. Wilusz, 949 N.E.2d 833, 836–37 (Ind. App. 2001) (explaining Indiana's doctrine of easement by necessity); Bickel v. Hansen, 819 P.2d 957, 960–61 (Ariz. Ct. App. 1991) (explaining Arizona's doctrine of easement by necessity).

35. Put in more technical terms, the doctrine of easement by prescription is not treated as an exception from the strictures of the Statute of Frauds and the parole evidence rule in which a contract in fact is enforced despite the formal restrictions of the law. The doctrine does not require proof of any actual agreement. See Stewart E. Sterk, "Neighbors in American Land Law," *Columbia Law Review* 87 (1987): 65–68 (summarizing objections to the intent-based justification for the rule).

36. See Stoebuck and Whitman, *The Law of Property*, n. 54 at 447 ("[The] essential elements [of an easement implied from necessity] are: (1) a conveyance (2) of a physical part only of the grantor's land . . . and (3) after severance of the two parcels, it is 'necessary' to pass over one of them to reach any public street or road from the other").

37. Sterk, "Neighbors in American Land Law," 57.

38. See Douglas Laycock, *Modern American Remedies: Cases and Materials*, 4th ed. (New York: Aspen Publishers, 2010), 383 ("A common source of high transaction costs is bilateral monopoly. Bilateral monopoly exists when the parties have no alternative but to deal with each other. . . . There [is] no market alternative to guide [the parties'] bargaining behavior, and they might have great difficulty reaching agreement").

39. 715 P.2d 514 (Wash. 1986).

40. *Id.* at 515.

41. *Id.*

42. *Id.*

43. *Id.* at 515–16.

44. *Id.* at 518.

45. See generally Elizabeth Samuels, "Stories out of School: Teaching the Case of Brown v. Voss," *Cardozo Law Review* 16 (1995): 1451.

46. Ibid., 1465–68.

47. Ibid., 1484–86.

48. Ibid.

49. Cf. Robert Frost, "Mending Wall," in *The Poetry of Robert Frost*, ed. Edward Connery Lathem (New York: Holt, Rinehart & Winston, 1969), 13 ("Good fences make good neighbors").

50. See James J. White and Robert S. Summers, *Uniform Commercial Code*, 5th ed. (St. Paul, MN: West Group, 2000), 178–94 (explaining the risk of loss provisions in Article 2 of the Uniform Commercial Code).

51. See UCC § 2-509(4) ("The provisions of this section [i.e., the section on risk of loss] are subject to contrary agreement of the parties").

52. See White and Summers, *Uniform Commercial Code*, 180 ("The prior law [to Article 2], section 22 of the Uniform Sales Act, provided in general that only the party who had title or property in the goods also had the risk of loss").

53. Ibid., 182 ("Under the Uniform Sales Act . . . title—and therefore risk—would often jump to the buyer after the goods had become identified to the contract even though they were still in the seller's position").

54. See UCC § 2-509(3) ("The risk of loss passes to the buyer on his receipt of the goods if the seller is a merchant; otherwise the risk passes to the buyer on tender of delivery").

55. The allocation turns on whether the contract calls for delivery to a specific destination or simply delivery by carrier to the buyer. In the first case, risk of loss passes to the buyer upon delivery of goods to the carrier. In the second, it passes upon delivery of the goods to the buyer. See UCC § 2-509(1).

56. See UCC § 2-509(2).

57. For a general discussion of the efficiency of the UCC's risk of loss terms, see R. S. G., "Risk of Loss in Commercial Transactions: Efficiency Thrown into the Breach," *Virginia Law Review* 65, no. 3 (April 1979): 557–72.

58. See Andrew Gold, "A Property Theory of Contract," *Northwestern University Law Review* 103 (2009): 8 (defining an "autonomy theory . . . as a theory on contracts that focuses on justice between the parties to a contractual dispute, rather than focusing on the broader prospective effects of a chosen contract doctrine"); Nathan B. Oman, "Unity and Pluralism in Contract Law," *Michigan Law Review* 103 (2005): 1483–84 ("Most contracts scholars take one of two basic approaches. On one side stand those who, while acknowledging the usefulness of the new theoretical tools, remain unconverted to any of them . . . . On the other side are those who declare that 'theory works.' The problem with pragmatism, they assert, is that ultimately it fails to provide either illumination or concrete conclusions").

59. See generally Charles Fried, *Contract as Promise: A Theory of Contractual Obligation* (Cambridge, MA: Harvard University Press, 1981).

60. Ibid., 1 ("The promise principal, which in this book I argue is the moral basis of contract law, is that principal by which persons may impose on themselves obligations where none existed before").

61. See Stephen A. Smith, *Contract Theory*, Clarendon Law Series (New York: Oxford University Press, 2004), 133 ("The idea behind the transparency objection is not merely that judges do not write like economists or that the economic reasoning judges use is less sophisticated than that used by professional economists. The objection, rather, is that legal arguments are essentially about individual rights and individual responsibility rather than about efficiency or any related concept").

62. See Randy Barnett, "Some Problems with Contract as Promise," *Cornell Law Review* 77 (1991): 1022–33.

63. A. J. Arberry, trans., *The Koran Interpreted* (New York: Simon & Schuster, 1996), 87.

64. See Fried, *Contract as Promise*, 16.

65. Richard Craswell, "Contract Law, Default Rules, and the Philosophy of Promising," *Michigan Law Review* 89 (1989): 489–529, 490.

66. See, for example, UCC § 2-305 (2011) (price) and UCC §§ 307-08 (delivery order or performance).

67. Max Weber, *The Protestant Ethic and the Spirit of Capitalism*, ed. Richard

Swedberg (New York: W. W. Norton, 2009), 49–66 (drawing a causal link between Calvinism and modern capitalism).

68. See R. H. Tawney, *Religion and the Rise of Capitalism* (New York: Harcourt Brace, 1926) (providing the seminal early criticism of Weber's book); see, for example, Ephraim Fischoff, "The Protestant Ethic and the Spirit of Capitalism: The History of a Controversy," *Social Research* 11, no. 1 (February 1, 1944): 53–77 (surveying early scholarly criticism of the Protestant ethic); Jacques Delacroix and François Nielsen, "The Beloved Myth: Protestantism and the Rise of Industrial Capitalism in Nineteenth-Century Europe," *Social Forces* 80, no. 2 (December 1, 2001): 545 ("Five different empirical tests based on the Common Interpretation, a widespread and seemingly reasonable interpretation of Weber's Protestant Ethic, failed to supply it with substantial support").

69. See Niall Ferguson, *Civilization: The West and the Rest*, 1st ed. (New York: Penguin Press, 2011), 262–63 (noting that empirical studies "have tended to cast doubt on Weber's underlying argument that the direction of causation ran from religious doctrine to economic behavior"). See also Davide Cantoni, "The Economic Effects of the Protestant Reformation: Testing the Weber Hypothesis in the German Lands," Barcelona GSE Working Paper 524 (Barcelona Graduate School of Economics, 2010) (studying 276 German cities between 1300 and 1900 and unable "to reject the null hypothesis of no effect of Protestantism" on economic growth); Delacroix and Nielsen, "The Beloved Myth."

70. See, for example, Douglass C. North, *Understanding the Process of Economic Change (Princeton Economic History of the Western World)* (Princeton, NJ: Princeton University Press, 2005), 162–63 (discussing economic growth and noting that "the maintenance of institutions that permit trial and error experiments to occur" is the "best recipe" for sustained economic growth "in the world of continual novel change"); ibid., 155 (noting that intellectual and technological innovation is a necessary, but not sufficient, condition to economic growth).

71. See Daron Acemoglu and James A. Robinson, *Why Nations Fail: The Origins of Power, Prosperity, and Poverty* (London: Profile Books, 2012), 49–53 (discussing cultures that are geographically proximate yet economically disparate).

72. Ibid., 372 ("Nations fail today because their extractive economic institutions do not create the incentives needed for people to save, invest, and innovate. Extractive political institutions support these economic institutions by cementing the power of those who benefit from the extraction").

73. See, for example, J. A. Hobson, *Imperialism: A Study* (New York: Cosimo Classics, 2005), 155 (1902) ("It is desirable that the earth should be peopled, governed, and developed, as far as possible, by the races which can do this work best, i.e. by the races of highest 'social efficiency'; these races must assert their right by conquering, ousting, subjugating, or extinguishing races of lower social efficiency").

74. See David C. Rose, *The Moral Foundation of Economic Behavior* (New York:

Oxford University Press, 2011), 59 ("I posit that in most cases what keeps us from behaving opportunistically, even in circumstances in which we believe there is no chance of being caught, is that we know we will feel guilty if we do so").

75. Ibid., 63 ("Which moral values matter most for achieving the condition of general prosperity?").

76. Thomas Carlyle, *Chartism*, 2nd ed. (London: Chapman and Hall, Strand, 1891), 61 ("O reader, to what shifts is poor Society reduced, struggling to give some account of herself, in epochs when Cash Payment has become the sole nexus of man to men!").

77. Cf. Milton Friedman, "The Social Responsibility of Business Is to Pursue Profits," *New York Times Magazine*, September 13, 1970 ("The difficulty of exercising 'social responsibility' illustrates, of course, the great virtue of private competitive enterprise—it forces people to be responsible for their own actions and makes it difficult for them to 'exploit' other people for either selfish or unselfish purposes. They can do good—but only at their own expense"). Similarly, markets are frequently associated with individualism and self-reliance. For libertarians, this is precisely their attraction. Markets, in contrast to the collective ethos of the state, are an arena more compatible with a proper appreciation for independent, individual choice. Critics of markets, from communitarians to socialists, have essentially the same assessment of the effects of commerce. They speak of the alienation inherent in the marketplace and the atomized and lonely individuals that it produces.

78. Edward C. Banfield, *The Moral Basis of a Backward Society* (Glencoe, IL: Free Press, 1958).

79. Ibid., 10 ("This inability [within a small village] to concert activity beyond the immediate family arises from an ethos—that of 'amoral familism'—which has been produced by three factors acting in combination: a high death rate, certain land tenure conditions, and the absence of the institution of the extended family").

80. Ibid., 33 ("Most people in Montegrano [the subject village of Banfield's study] are desperately poor").

81. Ibid., 10 ("The extreme poverty and backwardness [observed in Montegrano] . . . is to be explained largely . . . by the inability of the villagers to act together for their common good or, indeed, for any end transcending the immediate, material interest of the nuclear family").

82. Robert D. Putnam, Robert Leonardi, and Raffaella Nanetti, *Making Democracy Work: Civic Traditions in Modern Italy* (Princeton, NJ: Princeton University Press, 1993), 6 ("The central question posed in our [book] is this: What are the conditions for creating strong, responsive, effective representative institutions? The Italian regional experiment [examining various cultures spanning 870 latitudinal kilometers in Italy] offers an unparalleled opportunity for addressing this question").

83. Ibid., 178 ("The difficulty of solving dilemmas of collective action in this Hobbesian equilibrium means that society is worse off than in a cooperative

outcome. . . . Thus, the importance of social capital (to inhibit opportunism, cheating, and shirking) increases as economic development proceeds. This may help explain why the gap between the civic North and the uncivic South has widened over the last century").

84. Ibid., 7–16 (discussing how the author's research methodology enabled him to clearly identify a link between civic community and economic welfare).

85. See Toshio Yamagishi, *Trust: The Evolutionary Game of Mind and Society (The Science of the Mind)* (Tokyo: Springer, 2011), 26 ("If we keep using the same word 'trust' to describe both expectations of benign intentions based on evaluations of someone's character or behavioral disposition on the one hand, and expectations of his benign behavior based on his self-interest on the other, our discussion will be hopelessly confused. . . . I am proposing . . . to adopt another term—assurance . . .—to distinguish the two aspects of trust. Assurance . . . in this sense is the aspect of the expectations of someone's benign behavior that is rooted in the evaluation of his self-interest"). See also Rose, *The Moral Foundation of Economic Behavior*, n. 137, at 161–68 (surveying literature on various theories of trust).

86. There is a large scholarly literature on the sources of trust and its importance. For an introduction, see Francis Fukuyama, *Trust: The Social Virtues and the Creation of Prosperity*, 1st ed. (New York: Free Press, 1996).

87. See, for example, Nathan B. Oman, "Markets as a Moral Foundation for Contract Law," *Iowa Law Review* 98 (2012): 183, 215 ("[T]he law of contracts does not 'enforce' contracts in the sense of requiring a breaching party to perform via an order of specific performance. . . . [Additionally], the law of contracts does not 'enforce' contracts in the sense of insuring that breaches of contract are sanctioned by the state. Rather, contract law is a species of private law, which means that rather than enforcing primary obligations it empowers wronged parties to act against those that have breached their obligations"). See also Nathan B. Oman, "Consent to Retaliation: A Civil Recourse Theory of Contractual Liability," *Iowa Law Review* 96 (2011): 543 ("Contractual liability consists of ex ante consent to retaliation in the event of breach—a retaliation limited and civilized through litigation").

88. See Rose, *The Moral Foundation of Economic Behavior*, 15–16 ("The gains from specialization are directly related to the size of groups within which economic activity occurs. . . . Size worsens the problem of opportunism by intensifying commons dilemma incentives associated with opportunism and by increasing the localization of knowledge, which increases opportunities . . to engage in third-degree opportunism").

89. Ibid., 6 ("When a person believes there is no chance of being detected if he behaves in an opportunistic manner, we have an instance of what Robert Frank calls a 'golden opportunity.' . . . Golden opportunities to engage in third-degree opportunism are by definition beyond the reach of institutional mechanisms that work through external incentives").

90. Ibid., 8 ("Golden opportunities to engage in third-degree opportunism frequently arise in large group contexts because of the very specialization that occasions them").

91. Ibid., 16 ("Prudential restraint will not impede opportunism in the case of golden opportunities [which frequently occur in large, specialized markets]. Only moral restraint can do so, most likely through feelings of guilt").

92. See Jonathan Haidt, *The Righteous Mind: Why Good People Are Divided by Politics and Religion*, 1st ed. (New York: Pantheon, 2012), 77 ("For millions of years, our ancestors' survival depended upon their ability to get small groups to include them and trust them, so if there is any innate drive here, it should be a drive to get others to think well of us"); Michael Shermer, *The Mind of the Market: Compassionate Apes, Competitive Humans, and Other Tales from Evolutionary Economics* (New York: Times Books, 2007), 11 ("Overwhelming evidence from numerous fields now shows that fairness evolved as a stable strategy for maintaining social harmony in our ancestors' small bands, where cooperation was reinforced and became the rule while freeloading was punished and became the exception").

93. See, for example, Martha Stout, "The Ice People," *Psychology Today* 38 (2005): 72, 74 (describing sociopaths as "amoral and uncaring").

94. Ibid., 76 (discussing the rates of sociopathy among various populations, noting "the Western world's average [is] 4 percent," whereas in Taiwan, sociopathy exists in about 0.10 percent of the population).

95. See Rose, *The Moral Foundation of Economic Behavior*, 16 ("[The] natural reluctance to harm others is inadequate for supporting the full development and efficient operation of a market economy. The reason why is that group size weakens our natural reluctance to refrain from harming others").

96. Ibid. ("While moral tastes that comport with principled moral restraint solve the empathy problem, doing so is only a necessary condition for supporting genuine trust behavior because one can feel even guiltier about failing to take positive moral actions. To solve this 'greater good rationalization problem,' the obedience of moral prohibitions against negative moral actions (which combats opportunism) must take precedence over the obedience of moral exhortations for positive moral action").

97. See Shermer, *The Mind of the Market*, 12 ("As a social primate species, we evolved to display within-group amity and between-group enmity").

98. See Rose, *The Moral Foundation of Economic Behavior*, 127 ("Because of the empathy problem, harm-based moral restraint is insufficient in large group settings, so moral restraint must also be principled in nature. But even principled moral restraint is insufficient. . . . So to make unconditional trustworthiness possible, something must structure the individual's value system in a way that produces principled moral restraint in conjunction with the lexical primacy of obedience of moral prohibitions . . . [a quality] I shall call an ethic of duty-based moral restraint").

99. Ibid., 133 ("There is no particular reason why our hardwired moral sensibilities will be up to the task of fully supporting the development and operation of a market society. There certainly is little evidence—anecdotal or otherwise—to support such a claim").

100. See generally Smith, *Contract Theory*.

101. See, for example, Jody S. Kraus, "Reconciling Autonomy and Efficiency in Contract Law: The Vertical Integration Strategy," *Noûs* 35 (January 1, 2001): 420–41; Jody S. Kraus, "Legal Theory and Contract Law: Groundwork for the Reconciliation of Autonomy and Efficiency," *Social, Political, and Legal Philosophy* 1 (2002): 385–446; Jody S. Kraus, "Philosophy of Contract Law," in *The Oxford Handbook of Jurisprudence and Philosophy of Law*, eds. Jules L. Coleman and Scott J. Shapiro (New York: Oxford University Press, 2002), 815–67. I have tried my own hand at such theories in the past. See Oman, "Unity and Pluralism in Contract Law"; Nathan B. Oman, "The Failure of Economic Interpretations of the Law of Contract Damages," *Washington and Lee Law Review* 64 (2007): 829–75.

102. See Kraus, "Reconciling Autonomy and Efficiency in Contract Law," 422 (defining the "vertical integration strategy").

Chapter Five

1. Restatement (Second) of Contracts § 1.

2. See, for example, Michael Pratt, "Contract, Not Promise," *Florida State Law Review* 35 (2008): 801–16; Randy Barnett, "A Consent Theory of Contract," *Columbia Law Review* 86 (1986): 269–321.

3. E. Allen Farnsworth, *Farnsworth on Contracts*, 3rd ed., vol. 3 (New York: Wolters Kluwer Law & Business, 2004), 13.

4. See Nathan B. Oman, "Consent to Retaliation: A Civil Recourse Theory of Contractual Liability," *Iowa Law Review* 96 (2011): 534–40.

5. Restatement (Second) of Contracts § 71(1).

6. Oliver Wendell Holmes, *The Common Law*, ed. Mark DeWolfe Howe (Boston: Little, Brown, 1993), 227.

7. 159 N.E. 173 (N.Y. 1927). The case has long been a chestnut for contracts teachers and has garnered much commentary over the years. For a summary, see Curtis Bridgeman, "Allegheny College Revisited: Cardozo, Consideration, and Formalism in Context," *University of California, Davis Law Review* 39 (2005): 158–66.

8. The case also raised the questions of whether the promise could be enforced under the doctrine of promissory estoppel or due to a special public policy in favor of charitable institutions that supported the enforcement of gift promises to colleges. As a promissory estoppel case, *Allegheny College* is difficult to defend, because it is very difficult to determine that the college engaged in any action in

reliance on Yates's promise other than accepting an initial $1,000 payment on the promised gift.

9. Grant Gilmore, *The Death of Contract* (Columbus: Ohio State University Press, 1995), 69.

10. See, for example, Salsbury v. Northwestern Bell Tel. Co., 221 N.W.2d 609, 613 (Iowa 1974) ("It is more logical to bind charitable subscriptions without requiring a showing of consideration or detrimental reliance"); *In re* Estate of Lipsky, 256 N.Y.S.2d 429, 431 (Sur. Ct. 1965) ("A review of the authorities would indicate that the trend of judicial decision during the last century has been towards the enforcement of charitable pledges almost as a matter of public policy").

11. See, for example, Oliver E. Williamson, "Transaction-Cost Economics: The Governance of Contractual Relations," *Journal of Law and Economics* 22, no. 2 (October 1979): 233–61.

12. (1791) Peake 102.

13. *Id.* at 103.

14. *Id.*

15. 170 Eng. Rep. 1168 (1809 K.B.).

16. *Id.* at 1169.

17. 117 F. 99 (9th Cir. 1902).

18. *Id.* at 100.

19. See Deborah I. Thready, "A Fish Story: Alaska Packers' Association v. Domenico," *Utah Law Review* 2000 (2000): 185–221 (providing background on the facts of the case); Charles J. Goetz and Robert E. Scott, "The Mitigation Principle: Toward a General Theory of Contractual Obligation," *Virginia Law Review* 69 (1983): 1007 n. 106 (discussing Alaska Packers).

20. The rule is generally credited to Lord Coke. See Pinel's Case, 5 Coke Rep. 117a. See also King v. Deuluth, Missabe & Northern Railway, 63 N.W. 1105 (Minn. 1895) (a contractors promise to complete on time notwithstanding the failure of a condition excusing performance was consideration), United States v. Stump Home Specialties Mfg., 905 F.2d 11117 (7th Cir. 1990) (Posner, J.) (substitution of a fixed- for a variable-rate interest provision can be sufficient consideration). See Farnsworth, *Farnsworth on Contracts*, 524 (discussing the rule).

21. See, for example, Schwartzreich v. Bauman-Basch, 131 N.E. 887 (N.Y. 1921) (employer and employee rescinded a previous contract and substituted a new agreement with higher compensation). See Farnsworth, *Farnsworth on Contracts*, 1:525 (discussing the rule).

22. See Ballard v. Parkstone Energy, LLC, 522 F. Supp. 2d 695, 710 (S.D.N.Y. 2007) ("For a contract to be modified by a course of conduct, 'any change in an existing contract must have a new consideration to support it'") (quoting *Estate of Anglin v. Estate of Kelley*, 705 N.Y.S.2d 769, 772 (N.Y. App. Div. 2000)); Schwinder v. Austin Bank of Chicago, 809 N.E.2d 180, 189 (Ill. App. Ct. 2004) ("Under Illinois law, a valid modification of a contract must satisfy all the criteria essential

for a valid original contract, including offer, acceptance, and consideration"). The *Restatement (Second) of Contracts* largely ameliorated the effects of the doctrine by validating modifications that are reasonable in light of circumstances not foreseen at the time that the parties entered into the contract. Restatement (Second) of Contracts § 89(a) ("A promise modifying a duty under a contract not fully performed on either side is binding [] if the modification is far and equitable in view of circumstances not anticipated by the parties when the contract was made").

23. See Eric A. Posner, "Altruism, Status, and Trust in the Law of Gifts and Gratuitous Promises," *Wisconsin Law Review* 1997 (1997): 567 ("Much gift-giving that is socially valuable derives its value from its role in nonlegal relationships, and therefore efforts to regulate it with the law would reduce its value"). Cf. Joseph Smith Jr., trans., *The Book of Mormon* (Salt Lake City, UT: Church of Jesus Christ of Latter-day Saints, 1981), Moro. 7:8 ("For behold, if a man being evil giveth a gift, he doeth it grudgingly; wherefore it is counted him the same as if he had retained the gift").

24. In fairness, most of the cases involving gift promises arise in the context of litigation between promisees and the executors of the estates. The classic fact pattern involves A, who makes the promise of a gift to B. A then dies, and the executor of A's estate, in pursuance of her fiduciary obligations to A's heirs, refuses to make the gift promised to B. B then sues. In this context, however, the law provides a very simple mechanism by which A can commit to a gift to B after A's death: A can make B an heir in his will. Because wills are revocable, this mechanism preserves the gift as an act of generosity rather than a legal obligation and avoids the problem of the donative intention somehow foiled by an indifferent law.

25. 9 App. Cas. 605 (H.L. 1884).

26. 5 Coke Rep. 117a.

27. The decision, however, is not entirely without its supporters. See Janet O'Sullivan, "In Defense of Foakes v. Beer," *Cambridge Law Journal* 55, no. 2 (1996): 219–28.

28. Quoted in P. S. Atiyah, *Essays on Contract*, repr., with a new chapter (Oxford: Clarendon Press; New York: Oxford University Press, 1990), 190.

29. Compare James Baird Co. v. Gimbel Bros., Inc., 64 F.2d 344, 346 (2d Cir. 1933) ("An offer for an exchange is not meant to become a promise until a consideration has been received, either a counter-promise or whatever else is stipulated") with Drennan v. Star Paving Co., 333 P.2d 757, 759 (Cal. 1958) ("There is no evidence that defendant offered to make its bid irrevocable in exchange for plaintiff's use of its figures in computing his bid. . . . In sum, there was n[ot] an option supported by consideration").

30. See Mahoney v. Delaware McDonald's Corp., 770 F.2d 123, 127 (8th Cir. 1985) ("We conclude that the magistrate [judge] did not err in applying the doctrine of promissory estoppel to the facts in this case. Mahoney could have allowed his option on the subject property to lapse. He acted further and purchased the building only when assured by Baringer that 'we have a deal'"); *Gimbel*, 64 F.2d

at 346 ("The doctrine of 'promissory estoppel' is to avoid the harsh results of allowing the promisor in such a case to repudiate, when the promisee has acted in reliance upon the promise").

31. See Restatement (Second) of Contracts § 87(1)(a) ("An offer is binding as an option contract if it is in writing and signed by the offeror, recites a purported consideration for the making of the offer, and proposes an exchange on fair terms within a reasonable time"). According to the official commentary on the section: "A recital in a written agreement that a stated consideration has been given is evidence of that fact against the party to the agreement, but such a recital may ordinarily be contradicted by evidence that no such consideration was given or expected. . . . In cases within Subsection (1)(a), however, the giving and recital of consideration performs a formal function only." Ibid. at § 87(1)(a) cmt. c.

32. See generally Charles Fried, *Contract as Promise: A Theory of Contractual Obligation* (Cambridge, MA: Harvard University Press, 1981), chap. 3.

33. Ibid., 33.

34. Ibid.

35. Ibid., 34.

36. Ibid., 35.

37. Ibid.

38. Ibid., Preface.

39. Gilmore, *The Death of Contract*, 103.

40. Ibid.

41. Ibid., 104.

42. See generally P. S. Atiyah, *Promises, Morals, and Law* (Oxford: Clarendon Press, 1982); P. S. Atiyah, *The Rise and Fall of Freedom of Contract* (Oxford: Clarendon Press; New York: Oxford University Press, 1985).

43. Atiyah, *Essays on Contract*, 241.

44. Ibid., 239. Atiyah suggests that "intent to create legal relations" might serve as a new touchstone for formation and writes as though he accepts this as a reasonable test. He then goes on to write, however, that "whether unrelied-upon gratuitous promises should ever be rendered enforceable seems to me a very dubious proposition, and even if the principle is conceded, such promises are difficult to generalize about in advance, because so much depends on the context out of which they arise." Ibid., 242.

45. See Charles J. Goetz and Robert E. Scott, "Enforcing Promises: An Examination of the Basis of Contract," *Yale Law Journal* 89, no. 7 (1980): 1261–1322.

46. Ibid., 1304.

47. Ibid., 1287.

48. In his treatise on the economic analysis of law, Richard Posner offers a half-hearted defense of the doctrine of consideration, suggesting that it may serve evidentiary and cautionary purposes as well as determining opportunistic modifications and litigation over vague or trivial agreements. See Richard Posner, *Economic*

Analysis of Law, 8th ed. (New York: Wolters Kluwer, 2011), 124. Elsewhere, however, he laments the problems created by consideration and asks "why the law doesn't simply make available a form for making binding promises without requiring consideration." Ibid., 123.

49. Balfour v. Balfour [1919] 2 K.B. 571, 578, 579-80 ("For the reasons given by my brethren it appears to me to be plainly established that the promise here was not intended by either party to be attended by legal consequences"); Restatement (Second) of Contracts § 21 ("Neither real nor apparent intention that a promise be legally binding is essential to the formation of a contract, but a manifestation of intention that a promise shall not affect legal relations may prevent the formation of a contract").

50. See United Nations Convention on Contracts for the International Sale of Goods (CISG), 19 I.L.M. 668, Arts. 14–24 (1980) (discussing rules of contract formation).

51. See UCC § 2-209(1) ("An agreement modifying a contract within this Article needs no consideration to be binding"); Uniform Premarital and Marital Agreements Act § 6 ("The agreement is enforceable without consideration").

52. 27 N.E. 256 (N.Y. 1891). For a more detailed and skeptical reading of the facts in the case, see Douglas G. Baird, *Reconstructing Contracts* (Cambridge, MA: Harvard University Press, 2013), 36–43.

53. See James Gordley, *The Philosophical Origins of Modern Contract Doctrine* (New York: Oxford University Press, 1993), 14–15 (summarizing philosophical arguments about the virtue of liberality).

54. See Posner, "Altruism, Status, and Trust in the Law of Gifts and Gratuitous Promises," 593–95 (arguing that the law's different treatment of gift transfers as opposed to gift promises can be explained by the greater need to protect reliance on property rights as opposed to promises).

55. See Restatement (Second) Contracts § 90(2) ("A charitable subscription . . . is binding under Subsection (1) without proof that the promise induced action or forebearance").

56. See Jewish Federation of Cent. New Jersey v. Barondess, 560 A.2d 1353, 1354 (N.J. Super. Ct. 1989) ("The real basis for enforcing a charitable subscription is one of public policy—that enforcement of a charitable subscription is a desirable goal. . . . There is also a practical reason for enforcing charitable subscriptions: 'Lightly to withhold judicial sanction from such obligations would be to destroy millions of assets of the most beneficent institutions in our land, and to render such institutions helpless to carry out the purposes of their organization' " [citations omitted]); see also Hamilton Cnty. Assessor v. SPD Realty, LLC, 9 N.E.3d 773, 775 (Ind. T.C. 2014) ("Indiana Code § 6–1.1–10–16 requires the showing of a charitable purpose to [be tax-exempt to] ensure that the benefit conferred by the exemption both relieves the government of a cost that it would otherwise bear and does not primarily serve a commercial profit motive").

57. 77 N.W. 365 (Neb. 1898).

58. Restatement (Second) of Contracts § 90(1).

59. See Gilmore, *The Death of Contract*; Atiyah, *The Rise and Fall of Freedom of Contract*; Atiyah, *Essays on Contract*.

60. See Atiyah, *Promises, Morals, and Law*.

61. See Daniel A. Farber and John H. Matheson, "Beyond Promissory Estoppel: Contract Law and the 'Invisible Handshake,'" *University of Chicago Law Review* 52 (1985): 903–47; Randy E. Barnett and Mary E. Becker, "Beyond Reliance: Promissory Estoppel, Contract Formalities, and Misrepresentation," *Hofstra Law Review* 15 (1987): 443–97.

62. 322 S.W.2d 163 (Mo. App. 1959).

63. 329 F.2d 412 (6th Cir. 1964).

64. 35 F.2d. 301 (4th Cir. 1929).

65. See William P. Rogerson, "Efficient Reliance and Damage Measures for Breach of Contract," *RAND Journal of Economics* 15, no. 1 (April 1, 1984); Steven Shavell, "Damage Measures for Breach of Contract," *Bell Journal of Economics* 11 (1980): 466. For a summary of the literature and issues involved, see Nathan B. Oman, "The Failure of Economic Interpretations of the Law of Contract Damages," *Washington and Lee Law Review* 64 (2007): 829–75.

66. Restatement (Second) of Contracts § 90 cmt. b.

67. 104 S.W. 164 (Ark. 1907).

68. 168 So. 196 (Ala. App. 1936).

69. The reported case does not designate McGowin as Webb's employer, but he was in fact the owner and president of the lumber company. See Myanna Dellinger, "J. Greeley McGowin, 80 Years Ago," *ContractsProf Blog*, September 1, 2005, http://lawprofessors.typepad.com/contractsprof_blog/2005/09/j_greeley_mcgow.html.

70. For example, the law of restitution has its own set of restatements and has been subject to extensive scholarly elaboration. For an authoritative introductory treatment see Peter Birks, *Unjust Enrichment* (New York: Oxford University Press, 2005).

71. 36 S.E.2d 227 (N.C. 1946).

Chapter Six

1. L. L. Fuller and William R. Perdue, "The Reliance Interest in Contract Damages, Pt. 1," *Yale Law Journal* 46 (1936): 52–96; L. L. Fuller and William R. Perdue, "The Reliance Interest in Contract Damages, Pt. 2," *Yale Law Journal* 46 (1936): 373–420.

2. See Fred Shapiro and Michelle Pearse, "The Most-Cited Law Review Articles of All Time," *Michigan Law Review* 110 (2012): 1490 (finding that Fuller and Perdue's article was the 26th most-cited law review article in history).

3. Fuller and Perdue, "The Reliance Interest in Contract Damages, Pt. 1," 53–54.

4. Ibid.

5. Ibid.

6. The section reads:

> Judicial remedies under the rules stated in this Restatement serve to protect one or more of the following interests of a promisee: (a) his "expectation" interest . . . , (b) his "reliance interest" . . . , or (c) his "restitution interest."

Restatement (Second) of Contract § 344. The section itself gives no actual rules, and nowhere else in the *Restatement* is there a section that exists only to announce "purposes" as opposed to offering definitions or rules. That otherwise careful drafters such as Robert Braucher and E. Allen Farnsworth would include such an odd section in what was meant to be a statement of legal doctrine testifies to the massive influence of Fuller and Perdue's framing.

7. Fuller and Perdue, "The Reliance Interest in Contract Damages, Pt. 1," 53.

8. Ibid., 73–75.

9. Jeremy Bentham, "Last Epigrams and Sayings," in *A Bentham Reader*, ed. Mary Peter Mack (New York: Pegasus, 1969), 359, 363.

10. Peter Benson, "Contract," in *A Companion to Philosophy of Law and Legal Theory*, ed. Dennis Patterson (Cambridge, MA: Wiley-Blackwell, 1996), 24 (summarizing contemporary debates over the theory of contract law); James Gordley, "Contract," in *The Oxford Handbook of Legal Studies*, eds. Peter Cane and Mark Tushnet (New York: Oxford University Press, 2003), 3 (same); Jody S. Kraus, "Philosophy of Contract Law," in *The Oxford Handbook of Jurisprudence and Philosophy of Law*, eds. Jules L. Coleman and Scott J. Shapiro (New York: Oxford University Press, 2002), 687 (same).

11. See, for example, Robert Cooter, "Unity in Tort, Contract, and Property: The Model of Precaution," *California Law Review* 73 (1985): 11–19 (arguing that the expectation measure provides an incentive to a promissee to overrely or rely on promises to a greater extent than is efficient); Aaron S. Edlin, "Cadillac Contracts and Up-front Payments: Efficient Investment under Expectation Damages," *Journal of Law, Economics and Organization* 12 (1996): 98 (discussing the phenomenon of expectation damages causing overinvestment); Aaron S. Edlin and Stefan Reichelstein, "Holdups, Standard Breach Remedies, and Optimal Investment," *American Economic Review* 86, no. 3 (June 1, 1996): 487–91 (offering economic proof that expectation damages do not promote efficiency); Lewis A. Kornhauser, "Reliance, Reputation, and Breach of Contract," *Journal of Law and Economics* 26, no. 3 (October 1, 1983): 693 (arguing that, without reliance, the rule of law produces damages that are not Pareto optimal); William P. Rogerson, "Efficient

Reliance and Damage Measures for Breach of Contract," *RAND Journal of Economics* 15, no. 1 (April 1, 1984): 47–48 (noting that expectation and reliance damages produce inefficient results); Steven Shavell, "Damage Measures for Breach of Contract," *Bell Journal of Economics* 11, no. 2 (October 1, 1980): 472 (discussing the problems of breach in reaching Pareto efficiency); Steven Shavell, "The Design of Contracts and Remedies for Breach," *Quarterly Journal of Economics* 99, no. 1 (February 1, 1984): 124–27 (describing the relationship between efficient breach and the Pareto-efficient production contract).

12. A voluminous literature on specific performance also exists.

13. See, for example, Mahalsky v. Salem Tool Co., 461 F.2d 581, 584 (6th Cir. 1972) ("[There is] no remedy for . . . an action in contract absent privity").

14. Shavell, "Damage Measures for Breach of Contract," 472.

15. Robert Cooter and Thomas Ulen, *Law and Economics*, 6th ed. (Boston: Pearson/Addison Wesley, 2012), 233.

16. See generally Shavell, "Damage Measures for Breach of Contract," 472.

17. A. Mitchell Polinsky, *Introduction to Law and Economics*, 2nd ed. (Boston: Little, Brown, 1989), 38.

18. Patricia Meador and Elizabeth S. Warren, "False Claims Act: A Civil War Relic Evolves into a Modern Weapon," *Tennessee Law Review* 65, no. 2 (Winter 1998): 459.

19. A. Mitchell Polinsky and Yeon-Koo Che, "Decoupling Liability: Optimal Incentives for Care and Litigation," *RAND Journal of Economics* 22, no. 4 (December 1, 1991): 563 ("The optimal award to the plaintiff may be less than or greater than the optimal payment by the defendant").

20. As noted by Cooter and Porat, optimal incentives may require payments to a third party. See generally Robert Cooter and Ariel Porat, "Anti-Insurance," *Journal of Legal Studies* 31 (2002): 203.

21. Dan L. Hargrove, "Soldiers of *Qui Tam* Fortune: Do Military Service Members Have Standing to File *Qui Tam* Actions under the False Claims Act?" *Public Contract Law Journal* 34, no. 1 (Fall 2004): 51 (stating that *qui tam* relators can obtain "a bounty for their information, even if they [have] not suffered an injury themselves").

22. Ibid., 92 ("Congress's ultimate public policy goal in amending the [False Claims Act] in 1986 was to deter fraud and recover the Government's money").

23. Presumably, this is the level at which the marginal social cost of litigation (including the cost of inefficient reliance) is exactly equal to the marginal social benefit from more efficient incentives for the breach of contract. There seems to be no particular reason why this optimal level of reward for plaintiffs should correspond exactly to the optimal level of the fine imposed on defendants.

24. Charles Fried, *Contract as Promise: A Theory of Contractual Obligation* (Cambridge, MA: Harvard University Press, 1981), 21.

25. Ibid., 14–17 (arguing that promissory morality arises from the liberal value of respect for personal autonomy).

26. Ibid., 21.

27. Ibid.

28. Cf. Peter F. Strawson, "Freedom and Resentment," *Proceedings of the British Academy* 48 (1962): 1–25 (arguing breach of moral obligations can give rise to morally justified feelings of resentment).

29. I am assuming, of course, that there are no consequential damages or issues with the time value of money.

30. Expanding on this basic idea, Melvin Eisenberg, for example, has argued that expectation damages function as a de facto form of specific performance. See Melvin A. Eisenberg, "Actual and Virtual Specific Performance, the Theory of Efficient Breach, and the Indifference Principle in Contract Law," *California Law Review* 93 (2005): 977.

31. Clearly, I would have all sorts of moral obligations to my wife in this situation that have nothing to do with my promise to pick her up. For the purpose of this argument, I am setting these obligations aside and focusing purely on my promise. As my wife would be quick to point out, however, even if the account of residual promissory obligation that I lay out in the text is mistaken, I still have an obligation to pick up my wife from the airport simply because of our relationship. Hence, I have an obligation not because I promised her but because I am her friend, lover, and husband.

32. See Jody S. Kraus, "The Correspondence of Contract and Promise," *Columbia Law Review* 109 (2009): 1603–49 (offering an account of contract remedies rooted in promissory morality).

33. See Oliver Wendell Holmes, *The Common Law*, ed. Mark DeWolfe Howe (Boston: Little, Brown, 1993), 236 ("The only universal consequence of a legally binding promise is, that the law makes the promisor pay damages if the promised event does not come to pass. In every case it leaves him free from interference until the time for fufilment has gone by, and therefore free to break his contract if he chooses").

34. See generally Tess Wilkinson-Ryan and Jonathan Baron, "Moral Judgment and Moral Heuristics in Breach of Contract," *Journal of Empirical Legal Studies* 6 (2009): 405–23 (reporting survey research finding that people tended to moralize contract breaches rather than view breach as the exercise of an option not to perform).

35. Another possibility is that expectation damages simply punish promisors for breach. They serve some retributive function, punishing the promisor for wrongdoing as a way of showing proper respect for the promisor's autonomous choice. Admittedly, such an account strays somewhat further from the promise principle than the two proposed above, but it would still rest firmly within the effort to get promises performed or at least respected.

This account, however, faces at least two problems. First, it does not explain expectation damages. If damages merely act as a punishment for breach, then why should the amount of the punishment exactly match the value of the promisee's expectation? A pure retributive version of the damages-as-punishment theory might justify expectation damages on some talionic principle. The idea would be that the punishment should be proportionate to the crime—an eye for an eye, a tooth for a tooth, an expectation for a promise.

The damages-as-punishment theory, however, cannot explain why damages should be paid to the promisee. The purpose of the fine is to sanction a wrongdoer. Once the wrongdoer has been sanctioned, the idea of sanctioning provides us with no further reason that the money paid as a sanction should go to the victim. Indeed, in the case of most criminal fines, the money goes to the state rather than to victims. One might try to justify the payment to promisees as a pragmatic way of creating decentralized enforcement, but, as I have explained at length elsewhere, such an argument fails to explain doctrines such as privity that make it impossible for anyone other than the promisee (or a third-party beneficiary) to obtain damages. See Nathan B. Oman, "Consent to Retaliation: A Civil Recourse Theory of Contractual Liability," *Iowa Law Review* 96 (2011): 560–63; Nathan B. Oman, "The Failure of Economic Interpretations of the Law of Contract Damages," *Washington and Lee Law Review* 64 (2007): 851–54.

36. Fried, *Contract as Promise*, 45.

37. Ibid., 41.

38. Genesis 15:8 (RSV) (internal quotation marks omitted).

39. Ibid., 15:9–10.

40. See Robert Davidson, *Genesis 12–50* (Cambridge: Cambridge University Press, 1979), 45 ("From the one other Old Testament reference (Jer. 34: 18–20) and extra-biblical parallels, it seems that the rite was a form of dramatized curse. The parties as they walked between the severed halves were in effect saying, 'May God do so to me if I violate this solemn agreement.' "); Ze ev W. Falk, *Hebrew Law in Biblical Times: An Introduction*, 2nd ed. (Provo, UT: Brigham Young University Press, 2001), 89 ("In the patriarchal age the parties used to kill an animal as a sign of the punishment to befall the person who broke the covenant").

41. Genesis 15:8 (RSV).

42. See G. Johannes Botterweck, Helmer Ringgren, and Heinz-Josef Fabry, eds., *Theological Dictionary of the Old Testament*, vol. 7 (Grand Rapids, MI: Eerdmans, 1995), 351 (discussing the meaning of the Hebrew term *karat* in the context of covenant making).

43. See Binns L. Elliott, *The Book of the Prophet Jeremiah: With Introduction and Notes*, Westminister Commentaries (London: Methuen, 1919), 262 n. 19 (discussing the dismembering of the dog among Alexander the Great's generals); Bruce Vawter, *On Genesis: A New Reading*, 1st ed. (Garden City, NY: Doubleday, 1977), 211–12 (providing the Babylonian examples).

44. Thomas Hobbes, *Hobbes: Leviathan: Revised Student Edition*, ed. Richard Tuck (New York: Cambridge University Press, 1996), 99.

45. Homer, *The Iliad*, repr. ed. (New York: Penguin Books, 1991), 138.

46. Charles Fensham describes the legitimacy of violence following breach: "On a breach of covenant punishment must follow. The curses of the gods in the extrabiblical material is a deterrent, but not an actual punishment. . . . Direct punishment on the breach of covenant [as opposed to a lawsuit] is probably the only one which could have been used by Near Eastern kings." F. Charles Fensham, "Malediction and Benediction in Ancient Near Eastern Vassal-Treaties and the Old Testament," *Zeitschrift fur Alttestamentliche Wissenschaft,* 74 (1962): 7–8.

47. Indeed, the Bible records at least one case in which a promisor explicitly agreed to violence by the promisee in the event of breach. During the invasion of Canaan recounted in the Book of Joshua, the Israelites send two spies into the city of Jericho, where they are hidden and assisted by a prostitute named Rahab. Rahab and the spies exchange oaths, but the spies insist that, "if you tell this business of ours, then we shall be guiltless with respect to your oath which you have made us swear," meaning that when the Israelites sacked the city, they would be within their rights to kill Rahab and her family. Joshua 2:20 (RSV) (internal quotation marks omitted).

48. Exodus 21:22–25 (RSV).

49. See William Ian Miller, *Eye for an Eye* (New York: Cambridge University Press, 2005), 63–68 (discussing rabbinic interpretation of the *lex talionis*).

50. See Frederick Pollock and Frederic William Maitland, *The History of English Law: Before the Time of Edward I*, 2nd ed. (Cambridge: Cambridge University Press, 1968), 47–48 (discussing wergild and composition in early Anglo-Saxon law).

51. Ibid., 31. Modern historians have questioned the seemingly neat narrative of organic progression put forward by Pollock and Maitland, noting that litigation coexisted in many early societies less as a substitute for the blood feud than as alternative mode of attack in the conflict between persons and clans. See, for example, Miller, *Eye for an Eye*, 119–21; but see Pollock and Maitland, *The History of English Law*, 47 (noting that feud and "the semi-judicial arbitration of wise men" coexisted in medieval Iceland).

52. Hobbes, *Leviathan*, 89.

53. An example of this presumption's hold is expressed by the Tenth Circuit: "To empower each individual to decide whether the particular law is worthy or runs against the individual's private beliefs would necessarily produce a lawless society and chaos. Quite apart from the fact of invalidity of such a system, it has no practical social value. Such a government would fail in a very short time, for carried to its logical conclusion it is anarchy and revolution." *United States v. Ogle*, 613 F.2d 233, 241 (10th Cir. 1979).

54. Hobbes, *Leviathan*, 87.

55. See generally M. L. J. Hardy, *Blood Feuds and the Payment of Blood Money in the Middle East* (Beirut: Catholic Press, 1963) (discussing Arab society's longstanding customs following instances of violent death or injury).

56. See Frank Henderson Stewart, *Honor*, 1st ed. (Chicago: University of Chicago Press, 1994), 88–90 (discussing the obligations that honor culture of the Bedouins imposed on hosts to defend their guests against hostility and contrasting it with early European norms). Montesquieu makes a similar point, noting that "hospitality, so rare among commercial countries, is notable among bandit people." Charles de Secondat Montesquieu, *The Spirit of the Laws*, eds. Anne Myers Cohler, Basia Carolyn Miller, and Harold Samuel Stone, *Cambridge Texts in the History of Political Thought* (Cambridge: Cambridge University Press, 1989), 339.

57. Hobbes, *Leviathan*, 96.

58. In subsistence economies without common exchanges, however, the social practice of agreement and trade can be underdeveloped to a surprising degree. In early medieval Iceland, William Miller writes of "how difficult it might be, in the absence of a market economy and its accompanying mercantile assumptions, to transact without ill-feeling." William Miller, *Bloodtaking and Peacemaking* (Chicago: University of Chicago Press, 1990), 84.

59. Of course, this is an oversimplification. Even in a world of purely simultaneous exchange, disputes can arise out of agreements. For example, if Able exchanges a widget with Baker for cash, and the widget subsequently proves defective, Baker may complain to Able. Some mechanism would be necessary to resolve their dispute. Even in a world of caveat emptor, we would need some rule to tell us that caveat emptor is the standard.

60. See Avinash Dixit, *Lawlessness and Economics: Alternative Modes of Governance* (Princeton, NJ: Princeton University Press, 2004), 14–15 (discussing the famous holdup problem faced in executory contracts). As Dixit notes, "This is like a prisoner's dilemma except that only the second player has the opportunity to make an extra private gain, therefore it is often called a one-sided prisoner's dilemma." Ibid., 16.

61. See, for example, Herbert Hovenkamp, "Rationality in Law and Economics," *George Washington Law Review* 60, no. 2 (January 1992): 312 ("The prisoners' dilemma is simply a situation in which the costs of bargaining or of enforcing the resulting contract are very high"); D. K. Osborne, "Cartel Problems," *American Economic Review* 66, no. 5 (December 1, 1976): 836 ("A prisoners' dilemma can be resolved satisfactorily by an enforceable contract"); Alan Schwartz, "Contracting about Bankruptcy," *Journal of Law, Economics, and Organization* 13 (1997): 128 ("The prisoners' dilemma thus vanishes if the prisoners can write an enforceable contract not to confess"); G. Richard Shell, "Trade Legalism and International Relations Theory: An Analysis of the World Trade Organization," *Duke Law Journal* 44 (1995): 835 ("Binding, rule-oriented trade adjudication is an enforcement mechanism by which states solve a multiparty 'prisoner's dilemma' arising out of trade contracts" [footnote omitted]).

62. See generally Robert Axelrod, *The Evolution of Cooperation*, rev. ed. (New York: Basic Books, 2006), 27–54 (explaining success of tit-for-tat strategy—for

example, matching the cooperate/defect decision made by one's opponent in the previous round—in multiround prisoner dilemma "tournaments").

63. Ibid., 31.

64. Ibid., 36–37.

65. Ibid., 37–38.

66. The threat of refusing to deal can itself discipline defection, provided that the returns on future cooperation are greater than the returns that can be generated from investing the proceeds of a one-time defection. See Dixit, *Lawlessness and Economics*, 16–17 (discussing the "grim-trigger strategy").

67. See Homer, *The Iliad*, 128–44 (discussing a treaty between the Trojans and the Achaeans).

68. Robert Bates provides the following trenchant summary of the problem:

> When the threat of retaliation works, the private provision of coercion can produce peace, as Evans-Pritchard argued; but the behaviors and beliefs that supply peace also encourage behavior that increases the likelihood of violence. In such societies, private warriors populate public places; people bearing arms and intimating their willingness to employ them strut in the boulevards and cluster in the marketplace. Public places are populated with provocateurs; where families are honor-bound to protect their own, hot-tempered youths find protection against the consequences of brazen behavior. Interactions thus take place in a volatile ambience of honor and impudence; young hotheads move to the fore; and a culture of machismo permeates the society. . . . Provocative acts become commonplace—but also uncommonly dangerous because they can unleash violent reprisals.

Robert H. Bates, *Prosperity and Violence: The Political Economy of Development*, new ed. (New York: W. W. Norton, 2001), 46.

69. As the scope of retaliation was limited and the possibility of escalation was reduced, the rituals surrounding contract formation have become considerably less colorful.

70. This argument, of course, does not rest on the notion that all forms of social cooperation are good. Indeed, doctrines such as the law's refusal to recognize illegal or immoral contracts can be understood as a refusal to facilitate pathological forms of cooperation.

71. Ian MacNeil notes:

> All the standard texts on English law reflect a notion that the law of contract litigation is a relatively neat and logical structure of rules. I believe[] this idea to be inaccurate. . . . Contract law is hardly a neat and logical structure of rules, but like all law a social instrument designed to accomplish the goals of man.

Ian MacNeil, *The Relational Theory of Contract: Selected Works of Ian MacNeil*, ed. David Campbell (London: Sweet & Maxwell, 2001), 6; see Stewart Macaulay, "Non-Contractual Relations in Business: A Preliminary Study," *American Sociological Review* 28 (1963): 64 ("Some businessmen object that in such a carefully worked out relationship one gets performance only to the letter of the contract. Such planning indicates a lack of trust and blunts the demands of friendship, turning a cooperative venture into an antagonistic horse trade").

72. Renaud v. Simmons, 254 S.W.2d 418, 419 (Tex. Civ. App. 1952) ("The contract specifies the obligations of the parties in detail").

73. Stewart Macaulay describes this reality: "[The lawyers] complained that businessmen desire to 'keep it simple and avoid red tape' even where large amounts of money and significant risks are involved. One stated that he was 'sick of being told, "We can trust old Max," when the problem is not one of honesty but one of reaching an agreement that both sides understand.'" Macaulay, "Non-Contractual Relations in Business," 58–59.

74. Lisa Bernstein, "Merchant Law in a Merchant Court: Rethinking the Code's Search for Immanent Business Norms," *University of Pennsylvania Law Review* 144 (1996): 1796 (describing the difference between relationship-preserving norms and end-game norms).

75. Ibid. (defining relationship-preserving norms as "the norms that transactors choose to follow when they cooperatively resolve disputes among themselves and want to preserve their relationship").

76. Ibid. (noting that end-game norms are "the norms that transactors would want a third-party neutral to apply in a situation where they were unable to cooperatively resolve a dispute and viewed their relationship as being at an end-game stage").

77. As Bernstein notes: "Merchants behave in ways that reflect an implicit understanding of the distinction between end-game and relationship-preserving norms and . . . they do not necessarily want the RPNs [relationship preserving norms] they follow during the cooperative phase of their relationship to be used to resolve disputes when their relationship is at an end-game stage." Ibid., 1798.

78. James B. Beam Distilling Co. v. Georgia, 501 U.S. 529, 542 (1991) (plurality opinion) ("fight their own battles by litigating before victory was certain"); Torres-Rosario v. United States, Civil No. 07-1282, 2010 WL 174884, at *4 (D.P.R. Jan. 13, 2010) ("Petitioner was faced with a seemingly uphill battle at trial"); OneBeacon Ins. Co. v. Parker, Kern, Nard & Wenzel, No. 1:09-cv-00257 AWI GSA, 2009 WL 2914203, at *2 (E.D. Cal. Sept. 9, 2009) ("Defendant moved to stay the instant action, asserting that it will be required to 'fight a two-front litigation war' because Plaintiff here seeks to adjudicate facts that are the subject of the underlying action"); Lock v. Encompass Ins. Co., No. 07-CV-14257, 2009 WL 804151, at *1 (E.D. Mich. Mar. 25, 2009) ("During the trial, a battle of the experts ensued"); Peavey

Elecs. Corp. v. Baan U.S.A., Inc., 10 So. 3d 945, 950 (Miss. Ct. App. 2009) (en banc) ("following what the trial court described as an 'all out war' of litigation").

79. See Restatement (Second) of Contracts § 356 (setting forth the penalty-clause doctrine).

80. Ibid.

81. Ibid.

82. See Ugo Mattei, "The Comparative Law and Economics of Penalty Clauses in Contracts," *American Journal of Comparative Law* 43 (1995): 433 ("The coherence of penalty clauses ban with the underlying philosophy of freedom of contract is questionable, and the issue is frequently raised both in judicial opinion and in the academic literature").

83. See Randy E. Barnett, "A Consent Theory of Contract," *Columbia Law Review* 86 (1986): 286; Fried, *Contract as Promise*, 105; Stephen A. Smith, *Contract Theory*, Clarendon Law Series (New York: Oxford University Press, 2004), 246–47.

84. See Seana Valentine Shiffrin, "The Divergence of Contract and Promise," *Harvard Law Review* 120 (2007): 734–36.

85. See, for example, Polinsky, *Introduction to Law and Economics*, 31–34 (detailing why the expectation remedy leads to an efficient outcome in breach-of-contract cases).

86. See Polinsky, *Introduction to Law and Economics.*

87. See generally Richard Craswell, "Contract Remedies, Renegotiation, and the Theory of Efficient Breach," *Southern California Law Review* 61 (1988): 629–70 (arguing that, given the possibility of renegotiation ex post, there is no reason to suppose that expectation damages represent a uniquely efficient way of internalizing the costs of breach).

88. Cooter and Ulen, *Law and Economics*, 260–61.

89. See Lake River Corp. v. Carborundum Co., 769 F.2d 1284, 1289 (7th Cir. 1985) (Posner, J.) ("On this view the refusal to enforce penalty clauses is (at best) paternalistic—and it seems odd that courts should display parental solicitude for large corporations").

90. See, for example, Melvin Aron Eisenberg, "The Limits of Cognition and the Limits of Contract," *Stanford Law Review* 47 (1995): 211–59.

91. Robert Hillman has written:

> These cognitive phenomena and the predictions they generate about contract parties' decision making both help to explain the judicial response to liquidated damages provisions and tend to confirm the appropriateness of the current aggressive judicial approach to the issue. The parties view contract breakdown as a remote possibility, fail to focus on it, and, to the extent that they do think about breach, seek a fair remedial package. Because of the lack of paradigmatic bargaining with respect to liquidated damages provisions and because of their potential, due to unanticipated circumstances,

> to generate penalties and windfalls contrary to the parties' intentions, courts do and should enthusiastically police liquidated damages provisions.

Robert A. Hillman, "Limits of Behavioral Decision Theory in Legal Analysis: The Case of Liquidated Damages," *Cornell Law Review* 85, no. 3 (March 2000): 732.

92. Ibid., 735 ("Why should judges single out liquidated damages for this treatment? What contract term would be safe from this attack? Aggressive use of this reasoning to question contract enforceability could therefore undermine contract law's goals of certainty and predictability, which may be better served by the traditional objective theory of assent").

93. See Restatement (Second) of Contracts § 365 cmt. a (1981).

94. Ibid. §§ 162, 208.

95. See Lake River Corp. v. Carborundum Co., 769 F.2d 1284, 1289 (7th Cir. 1985) (Posner, J.) ("Since little effort is made to prevent businessmen from assuming risks, these reasons are no better than makeweights").

96. See Benjamin Zipursky, "Civil Recourse, Not Corrective Justice," *Georgetown Law Journal* 91 (2003): 695–756.

97. Homer, *The Iliad*, 128–44.

98. See John Locke, *Two Treatises of Government*, ed. Peter Laslett (New York: Cambridge University Press, 1989), 324; John C. P. Goldberg, "The Constitutional Status of Tort Law: Due Process and the Right to a Law for the Redress of Wrongs," *Yale Law Journal* 115 (2005): 602 (arguing that allowing civil recourse for tort actions limits the cycle of escalating violence and vengeance that would result from extralegal recourse); Zipursky, "Civil Recourse, Not Corrective Justice," 736 ("Indeed, an earmark of our civil legal system is that it does not involve violent remedies, but civil remedies; it does not involve punishment").

99. See Restatement (Second) of Contracts § 356 cmt. d ("A term that fixes as damages an amount that is unreasonably small does not come within the rule stated in this Section, but a court may refuse to enforce it as unconscionable under the rule stated in § 208").

100. See Rose & Frank Co. v. J. R. Crompton & Bros., [1925] A.C. 445 (H.L.) (holding that courts should honor an agreement expressly disclaiming a right to recourse to damages in the event of breach).

101. Ibid.

102. See, for example, Welch v. Metro-Goldwyn-Mayer Film Co., 254 Cal. Rptr. 645 (Ct. App. 1988) ("The contract included a standard 'pay or play' clause, under which the studio could terminate Welch from the film at any time, but was obligated to pay her the full contract price, unless she failed to fulfill her contractual obligations"), vacated, 782 P.2d 594 (Cal. 1989).

103. Victor P. Goldberg, "Bloomer Girl Revisited or How to Frame an Unmade Picture," *Wisconsin Law Review* 1998 (1998): 1070–82.

104. See Lynch v. CIBY 2000, No. CV 97-9022, 1998 U.S. Dist. LEXIS 23496, at *3 (C.D. Cal. Aug. 13, 1998) (refusing to rule a pay-or-play clause a penalty clause because the plaintiff chose one of two options for performance rather than breaching).

105. See, for example, Restatement (Second) of Contracts § 347.

106. Fuller and Perdue, "The Reliance Interest in Contract Damages, Pt. 2," 53.

107. Ibid., 73–75.

108. Polinsky, *Introduction to Law and Economics*, 31–34 (detailing why the expectation remedy leads to an efficient outcome in breach-of-contract cases).

109. And there is reason to be skeptical of all of them. See Smith, *Contract Theory*, 409–13 (discussing the shortcomings of autonomy and transfer accounts of expectation damages); Oman, "The Failure of Economic Interpretations of the Law of Contract Damages," 851–53 (discussing the shortcomings of efficiency theories of expectation damages).

110. See Robert A. Hillman, "Contract Lore," *Journal of Corporation Law* 27 (2002): 507 ("Contracts people continue to report that the goal of expectancy damages is to make injured parties whole. The reality is dramatically different. A large set of remedial rules often limits the recovery of injured parties to well below expectancy" [footnote omitted]).

111. See Richmond Am. Homes of Colo., Inc. v. United States, 80 Fed. Cl. 656, 673 (2008); Restatement (Second) of Contracts § 344.

112. See Restatement (Second) of Contracts § 352.

113. Ibid.

114. 156 Eng. Rep. 145 (Ex. 1854).

115. Restatement (Second) of Contracts, § 351.

116. Restatement (Second) of Contracts, § 352.

117. See, for example, Morrow v. First Nat'l Bank of Hot Springs, 550 S.W.2d 429 (Ark. 1977) (adopting the tacit-agreement version of the *Hadley* rule).

118. See Restatement (Second) of Contracts § 350.

119. Ibid.

120. Ibid.

121. See Oman, "The Failure of Economic Interpretations of the Law of Contract Damages," 872 (noting that, due to the limitations on damages, full expectation damages are virtually never awarded).

122. See Restatement (Second) of Contracts § 349.

123. See E. Allan Farnsworth, *Farnsworth on Contracts*, 3rd ed., vol. 1 (New York: Wolters Kluwer Law and Business, 2004), 805–8 (discussing the situations in which plaintiffs generally ask for reliance damages rather than expectation damages).

124. See Restatement (Second) of Contracts § 349.

125. *Id.*

126. See Michael B. Kelly, "The Phantom Reliance Interest in Contract Damages," *Wisconsin Law Review* 1992 (1992): 1772 (arguing that the availability of

reliance damages simply shifts the burden of proof and that expectation damages operate as an upper limit on recovery).

127. Ibid., notes 119–29 and accompanying text (summarizing the various doctrinal limitations on full expectation damages).

128. I am grateful to Josh Chafetz for bringing to my attention the connection between Aeschylus's Oresteia and civil recourse. Any errors in interpretation, of course, remain mine.

129. Aeschylus, *The Oresteia*, trans. Robert Fangles (New York: Penguin Books, 1984), l. 183–88.

130. Hobbes, *Leviathan*, 89.

131. Aeschylus, *The Oresteia*, 267.

132. Ibid., 262.

133. Ibid., 276.

Chapter Seven

1. See Apple Inc. Software License Agreement for iTunes § 9, http://images.apple.com/legal/sla/docs/iTunes.pdf.

2. See "Agent Infiltrated Terror Cell, U.S. Says," *CNN.com*, August 11, 2006, http://www.cnn.com/2006/US/08/10/us.security/index.html. On the use of iPods in the plot, see "Terrorist Plot Said to Have Involved Apple iPod as Detonator," *Macdailynews.com*, August 10, 2006, http://macdailynews.com/2006/08/10/terrorist_plot_said_to_have_involved_apple_ipod_as_detonator/; LC Angell, "Report: Terrorists Planned to Use iPod as Detonator," *iLounge.com*, August 10, 2006, http://www.ilounge.com/index.php/news/comments/report-terrorists-planned-to-use-ipod-as-detonator/.

3. Quoted in Mark A. Lemley, "Terms of Use," *Minnesota Law Review* 91 (2006): 470 n. 36.

4. In the discussion that follows, I refer to boilerplate authors as corporations and offerees as consumers, because this is the situation that has generated the most concern. Obviously, "consumers" often includes firms in addition to individuals. Likewise, individuals might choose to use boilerplate contracts for their business.

5. Todd Rakoff provided a thorough discussion of these benefits over three decades ago that remains an excellent summary. See Todd D. Rakoff, "Contracts of Adhesion: An Essay in Reconstruction," *Harvard Law Review* 96 (April 1983): 1173–274.

6. See Friedrich Kessler, "Contracts of Adhesion—Some Thoughts about Freedom of Contract," *Columbia Law Review* 43 (1943): 629–42. Kessler was a German scholar who fled to the United States from Germany in 1934 to avoid Nazi persecution because his wife was Jewish. At the time that he wrote his famous article he was a professor at Yale Law School. In fairness, other scholars had previously examined

the issue. See, for example, Karl N. Llewellyn, "Book Review," *Harvard Law Review* 52 (1939): 700–705. As early as 1917, Nathan Isaacs pointed to boilerplate as an example of the evolution of contract into status, building on the work on Henry Maine and Roscoe Pound, but the contemporary debate begins with Kessler. See Nathan Isaacs, "The Standardizing of Contracts," *Yale Law Journal* 27 (1917): 34–48.

7. Kessler, "Contracts of Adhesion," 630.

8. Ibid., 632.

9. Ibid.

10. Ibid., 640.

11. See, for example, Williams v. Walker-Thomas Furniture Co., 350 F.2d 445 (D.C. Cir. 1965) (refusing to enforcing a cross-collateralization agreement entered into by an unsophisticated consumer).

12. See, for example, Kessler, "Contracts of Adhesion," 632. Given that relatively small firms operating in competitive markets often use boilerplate, it is difficult to take the concerns with monopoly seriously as a general theory of boilerplate. As two prominent legal economists have observed, "An older, and pretty well discredited, scholarly literature thought the absence of bargaining power showed that the seller must have monopoly power, enabling him to foist on consumers whatever terms he liked." Lucian A. Bebchuk and Richard A. Posner, "One-Sided Contracts in Competitive Consumer Markets," in *Boilerplate: The Foundation of Market Contracts*, ed. Omri Ben-Shahar (New York: Cambridge University Press, 2007), 4.

13. For an extensive and critical discussion of Internet contracting, see Nancy S. Kim, *Wrap Contracts: Foundations and Ramifications* (New York: Oxford University Press, 2013).

14. 763 F.3d 1171 (9th Cir. 2014).

15. *Id.* at 1174.

16. *Id.* at 1177. The court in this case was careful to note, however, that: "Were there any evidence in the record that Nguyen had actual notice of the Terms of use or was required to affirmatively acknowledge the Terms of Use before completing his online purchase, the outcome of this case might be different. Indeed, courts have consistently enforced browsewrap agreements where the user had actual notice of the agreement." *Id.* at 1176. See, for example, Be In, Inc. v. Google Inc., 2013 WL 5568706 (N.D. Cal. 2013) (refusing to enforce a browsewrap contract); In re Zappos.com Inc. Customer Data Security Breach Litigation, 893 F.Supp.2d 1058 (D. Nev. 2012) (refusing to enforce a browsewrap arbitration agreement); Van Tassell v. United Marketing Group, LLC, 795 F.Supp.2d 770, 786 (N.D. Ill. 2011) (refusing to compel arbitration when plaintiff "disputes that she ever saw the Conditions of use when making purchases"); Specht v. Netscape Communications Corp., 306 F.3d 17 (2d Cir. 2002) (Sotomayor J.) (refusing to enforce a browsewrap contract).

17. See Southwest Airlines Co. v. BoardFirst, LLC, 2007 WL 4823761 (N.D. Tex. 2007) (enforcing a browsewrap contract after a cease and desist letter from

the plaintiff informed the defendant of the existence of the contract); Register.com, Inc. v. Verio, Inc., 356 F.3d 393 (2d Cir. 2004) (finding that browsewrap contracts may be enforced when the defendant is aware of the terms); Ticketmaster Corp. v. Tickets.com, Inc., 2003 WL 21406289 (C.D. Cal. 2003). See also Lemley, "Terms of Use," 472–477 (discussing cases in which courts have enforced browsewrap agreements).

18. See Robert A. Hillman, "Online Consumer Standard Form Contracting Practices: A Survey and Discussion of Legal Implications," in *Consumer Protection in the Age of the "Information Economy,"* ed. Jane K. Winn (Aldershot, UK: Ashgate Publishing, 2006), 283–312.

19. See, for example, Davidson & Assoc. v. Jung, 422 F.3d 630, 632 (8th Cir. 2005); Capsi v. Microsoft Network LLC, 732 A.2d 528, 529 (N.J. Sup. Ct. App. Div. 1999). See also Lemley, "Terms of Use," 466 (noting that every court to consider the question as of 2006 has held that clickwrap agreements are enforceable).

20. See, for example, Margaret Jane Radin, *Boilerplate: The Fine Print, Vanishing Rights, and the Rule of Law* (Princeton, NJ: Princeton University Press, 2012), 40–41; Kessler, "Contracts of Adhesion," 632.

21. See Florencia Marotta-Wurgler, "What's in a Standard Form Contract? An Empirical Analysis of Software License Agreements," *Journal of Empirical Legal Studies* 4 (2007): 677–713.

22. See, for example, Williams v. Walker-Thomas Furniture Co., 350 F.2d 445 (D.C. Cir. 1965) (refusing to enforce a cross-collateralization agreement entered into by an unsophisticated consumer).

23. See Russell Korobkin, "Bounded Rationality, Standard Form Contracts, and Unconscionability," *University of Chicago Law Review* 70 (2003): 1203–95.

24. See Oren Bar-Gill, *Seduction by Contract: Law, Economics, and Psychology in Consumer Markets* (New York: Oxford University Press, 2013), 19 (arguing that "limited processing ability prevents consumers from accurately aggregating the different price components into a single, total expected price that would serve as the basis for choosing the optimal product"). Below I point out that, even if consumers are completely unaware of cost-shifting terms, price competition will tend to transform any rents earned by corporations through boilerplate into lower prices for consumers. However, if consumers valued the inadvertently contracted-away rights more than the corporation, there would still be an economic loss even if the corporation is earning no rents at the expense of the consumer. This scenario—lost consumer surplus with no rents to the offeror—depends on the assumption that consumers are unable to recognize that they value the lost rights more than the decrease in the price realized by competition between firms employing the same boilerplate. If consumers recognize this problem, then they will demand different contract terms. This may be what we observe in some markets—for example, where products are sold with optional warranties, which push risk back onto offerors that would otherwise be borne by consumers under standard boilerplate terms.

25. See George Akerlof, "The Market for 'Lemons': Quality Uncertainty and the Market Mechanism," *Quarterly Journal of Economics* 84, no. 3 (1970): 488–500.

26. See Bar-Gill, *Seduction by Contract*, 17 ("Sellers offering superior, yet unappreciated products and contracts may try to compete by educating consumers and fighting misperception").

27. See Radin, *Boilerplate*, 26–29.

28. Ibid., xiii–xiv. See Global Travel Mktg. v. Shea, 908 So.2d 392 (Fla. 2005) (the case discussed by Radin).

29. One detailed survey of reports of wild animal attacks, for example, found that only four people had been killed by hyenas in Uganda in the entire twentieth century. See Jonny Löe and Eivin Röskaft, "Large Carnivores and Human Safety: A Review," *AMBIO: A Journal of the Human Environment* 33, no. 6 (August 1, 2004): 284.

30. A. J. Dickman, "Complexities of Conflict: The Importance of Considering Social Factors for Effectively Resolving Human–Wildlife Conflict," *Animal Conservation* 13, no. 5 (2010). See Löe and Röskaft, "Large Carnivores and Human Safety," 284.

31. See Bar-Gill, *Seduction by Contract*, 8 ("Sellers who ignore consumer biases and misperceptions will lose business and forfeit revenue and profits. Over time, the sellers who remain in the market, profitably, will be the ones who have adapted their contracts and prices to respond, in the most optimal way, to the psychology of their customers").

32. See, for example, Radin, *Boilerplate*, 160 (suggesting that rights to trial by jury should be market inalienable). See also Margaret Jane Radin, *Contested Commodities* (Cambridge, MA: Harvard University Press, 1996) (setting forth an extended argument in favor of treating many legal rights as inalienable or as inalienable in market transactions).

33. See Radin, *Boilerplate*, 43 (lauding German law). See John H. Langbein, "The German Advantage in Civil Procedure," *University of Chicago Law Review* 52 (1985): 829 ("In civil litigation German judges sit without juries"); Sophie Stijns and R. Blanpain, *International Encyclopaedia of Laws: Tort Law*, vol. 2 (The Hague: Kluwer Law International, 2002), 121 ("The German Code of Civil Procedures does not provide rules for any kind of class action comparable to the U.S. model"); Behr Volker, "Myth and Reality of Punitive Damages in Germany," *Journal of Law and Commerce* 24 (2005): 198 ("Punitive damages are not available under German law").

34. See Radin, *Boilerplate*, chap. 3; W. David Slawson, "Standard Form Contracts and Democratic Control of Lawmaking Power," *Harvard Law Review* 84, no. 3 (January 1, 1971): 529–66; Kessler, "Contracts of Adhesion."

35. Most famously in the American context, the Declaration of Independence insisted that the social contract position was self-evident: "We hold these truths to be self-evident, that all men are created equal, that they are endowed by their

Creator with certain unalienable Rights, that among these are Life, Liberty, and the pursuit of Happiness—That to secure these rights, Governments are instituted among Men, deriving their just powers from the consent of the governed." See also John Locke, *Two Treatises of Government* (New York: Cambridge University Press, 1988); Thomas Hobbes, *Leviathan: Or, The Matter, Forme, & Power of a Common-Wealth Ecclesiasticall and Civill* (New York: Barnes & Noble Books, 2004).

36. See Jean-Jacques Rousseau, *Rousseau: "The Discourses" and Other Early Political Writings*, ed. Victor Gourevitch (New York: Cambridge University Press, 1997); John Rawls, *A Theory of Justice*, rev. ed. (Cambridge, MA: Belknap Press, 1999); Ronald Dworkin, "The Original Position," in *Reading Rawls: Critical Studies on Rawls' a Theory of Justice*, ed. Norman Daniels (Stanford, CA: Stanford University Press, 1989), 16–52.

37. David Hume, *Hume: Political Essays*, ed. Knud Haakonssen (New York: Cambridge University Press, 1994), 193.

38. See Hanah Metchis Volokh, "A Read-the-Bill Rule for Congress," *Missouri Law Review* 76 (2011): 136–84 (discussing the pervasive legislative practice of voting on bills without reading them).

39. See Eyal Zamir, "Contract Law and Theory—Three Views of the Cathedral," *University of Chicago Law Review* 81 (2014): 2077–123.

40. The trinity of voice, exit, and loyalty as mechanisms for mediating conflicts between individuals and organizations or communities, goes back to the work of Albert Hirschman. See generally Albert O. Hirschman, *Exit, Voice, and Loyalty: Responses to Decline in Firms, Organizations, and States* (Cambridge, MA: Harvard University Press, 1970).

41. See Francis Fukuyama, *Political Order and Political Decay: From the Industrial Revolution to the Globalization of Democracy* (New York: Farrar, Straus and Giroux, 2014), 465.

42. There is, of course, a vast public-choice literature on this subject. See Daniel A. Farber and Philip P. Frickey, *Law and Public Choice: A Critical Introduction* (Chicago: University of Chicago Press, 1991); James Buchanan and Gordon Tullock, *The Calculus of Consent* (Indianapolis: Liberty Fund, 1999); Mancur Olson, *The Logic of Collective Action: Public Goods and the Theory of Groups, Second Printing with New Preface and Appendix*, rev. ed. (Cambridge, MA: Harvard University Press, 1971); Kenneth J. Arrow, *Social Choice and Individual Values*, 1st ed. (New York: John Wiley & Sons, 1951).

43. The question of whether economists could make such decisions in practice was the subject of the so-called socialist calculation debate of the early twentieth century. See Bruce Caldwell, "Hayek and Socialism," *Journal of Economic Literature* 35, no. 4 (December 1, 1997): 1856–90; Allin Cottrell and W. Paul Cockshott, "Calculation, Complexity and Planning: The Socialist Calculation Debate Once Again," *Review of Political Economy* 5, no. 1 (1993): 73–112.

44. See Charles Fried, *Contract as Promise: A Theory of Contractual Obligation* (Cambridge, MA: Harvard University Press, 1981), 21.

45. Several scholars have made the point that critics of boilerplate often romanticize the consent present in ordinary contracts and that the consent involved in boilerplate contracts may not be much different than ordinary consent. See Michelle E. Boardman, "Consent and Sensibility: A Review of Margaret Jane Radin's Book, 'Boilerplate: The Fine Print, Vanishing Rights, and the Rule of Law,'" *Harvard Law Review* 127 (2013): 1967–90; Randy E. Barnett, "Consenting to Form Contracts," *Fordham Law Review* 71 (2002): 627–45. There is merit to these claims, but they do not answer the theoretical question of whether this attenuated consent justifies contractual enforcement. Rather, they simply widen the theoretical issue.

46. The distinction between status and contract is useful even if one does not subscribe to its author's simple story of progression from one to the other. See Sir Henry Sumner Maine, *Ancient Law*, 4th American ed. (New York: Henry Holt, 1906).

47. See generally John Witte Jr., *From Sacrament to Contract: Marriage, Religion, and Law in the Western Tradition*, 2nd ed. (Louisville, KY: Westminster John Knox Press, 2012); Brian Bix, "Bargaining in the Shadow of Love: The Enforcement of Premarital Agreements and How We Think about Marriage," *William & Mary Law Review* 40 (1998): 145–207.

48. See Nathan B. Oman, "A Pragmatic Defense of Contract Law," *Georgetown Law Journal* 98 (2009): 80.

49. Ibid., 80–82.

50. See Timur Kuran, *The Long Divergence: How Islamic Law Held Back the Middle East* (Princeton, NJ: Princeton University Press, 2011), 63–77.

51. Nevada v. Hall, 440 U.S. 410, 415 (1979). The case presented the question of whether Nevada could claim sovereign immunity in California court when Nevada's agent had violated California tort law. The court held that Nevada could not unilaterally limit the power of California's courts in this way.

52. Such compacts are subject to the additional requirement that Congress consent to the agreement. See U.S. Const. art. I, § 10, ¶3 ("No State shall, without the Consent of Congress . . . enter into any Agreement or Compact with another State"). In construing interstate compacts, the Supreme Court has held that ordinary principles of contract law control. See, for example, Tarrant Regional Water District v. Herrmann, 133 S. Ct. 2120, 2129 (2013) ("Interstate compacts are construed as contracts under principles of contract law").

53. See Restatement (Third) of Foreign Relations Law of the United States § 102(3) (1987) ("International agreements create law for the states parties thereto"). The existence of customary international law does not negate this point, as such law cannot be unilaterally created by one state and imposed on another. See *id.* at § 102(2) ("Customary international law results from a general and consistent practice of states followed by them from a sense of legal obligation").

54. For a brief summary of how and why credit cards replaced other forms of consumer finance, see Todd J. Zywicki, "The Economics of Credit Cards," *Chapman Law Review* 3 (2000): 94–99.

55. See Peter Wallenstein, *Cradle of America: A History of Virginia*, 2nd ed. (Lawrence: University Press of Kansas, 2014), 14.

56. Samuel Merrifield Berniss, ed., *The Three Charters of the Virginia Company of London, with Seven Related Documents: 1606–1621* (Williamsburg: Virginia 350th Celebration Corp., 1957), 5.

57. See William Edward Nelson, *The Common Law in Colonial America* (New York: Oxford University Press, 2008), 13–15 (discussing the early legal history of the Virginia Company).

58. It was, of course, imperfect, and the Virginia Company continued to profit by abusing nonconsenting parties, most notably African slaves.

59. It is not logically a necessary condition, of course. We could imagine a world of unilaterally authored legal obligations in which conflicts were resolved by some rule other than a requirement of consent. For example, we could have a rule that the obligations authored by an older person will always control over the obligations authored by a younger person. We could even resolve such conflicts by drawing lots. Without trying to imagine every possible alternative rule and offer a critique, there are two things that can be said in favor of a rule that solves the coordination problem with consent. First, alternative rules based on the identity of the authoring party—for example, the rule authored by a white person always controls over the rule authored by a black person—will tend to reinforce precisely the kinds of social and cultural hierarchies whose undermining makes markets valuable. In other words, alternatives to consent will tend to be inconsistent with the goods associated with markets and commerce—the goods that justify the flexible authoring of legal obligations to begin with. Second, as discussed in the text, consent provides a useful feedback mechanism against predatory or otherwise undesirable transactional structures.

60. See ProCD v. Zeidenberg, 86 F.3d 1447 (7th Cir. 1996) (holding that a consumer is bound to terms contained inside of packaging that cannot be read at the time of purchase).

61. See generally Robert A. Hillman and Jeffrey J. Rachlinski, "Standard Form Contracting in the Electronic Age," *New York University Law Review* 77 (2002): 429–95; Hillman, "Online Consumer Standard Form Contracting Practices."

62. For a thorough discussion of the issue, see Volokh, "A Read-the-Bill Rule for Congress."

63. Because statutes consist of amendments to the U.S. Code or state codes, the actual text of legislation consists of instructions to insert or delete words that are meaningless if read in isolation.

64. As has been observed in debates over statutory interpretation: "All the rest in the legislative history is, at most, a statement of a committee. It's not clear

(or indeed even likely) that the other Members of Congress even read that committee report, much less that they agreed with it. And a floor statement by the manager of the bill? There was nobody on the floor. You know that. It is the last surviving legal fiction in American law that legislative history reflects the purpose of the Congress. It does not." Antonin Scalia and John F. Manning, "A Dialogue on Statutory and Constitutional Interpretation," *George Washington Law Review* 80 (2012): 1612.

65. See Equal Employment Opportunity Commission, *The Legislative History of the Civil Rights Act of 1964* (Washington, DC: U.S. Government Printing Office, 1968), 10 ("The House bill went directly to the floor of the Senate instead of being referred to the Senate Judiciary Committee, which was considered by supporters of the measure to be hostile to it").

66. Alexander Hamilton, John Jay, and James Madison, *The Federalist: A Commentary on the Constitution of the United States*, ed. Robert Scigliano (New York: Modern Library, 2001), No. 62.

67. St. George Tucker and William Blackstone, *Blackstone's Commentaries: With Notes of Reference to the Constitution and Laws, of the Federal Government of the United States, and of the Commonwealth of Virginia* (Union, NJ: Lawbook Exchange, 1996), 1:344.

68. See Field v. Clark, 143 U.S. 649, 672 (1892) ("The signing by the Speaker of the House of Representatives, and by the President of the Senate, in open session, of an enrolled bill, is an official attestation by the two houses of such bill as one that has passed Congress. . . . And when a bill, thus attested, receives [the president's] approval, and is deposited in the public archives, its authentication as a bill that has passed Congress should be deemed complete and unimpeachable").

69. See U.S. Const. amend. I ("Congress shall make no law . . . abridging the freedom of speech, or of the press; or the right of the people peaceably to assemble, and to petition the Government for redress of grievances").

70. See U.S. Const. amend. XV, § 1 ("The right of citizens of the United States to vote shall not be denied or abridged by the United States or by any State on account of race, color, or previous condition of servitude"); U.S. Const. amend. XLX ("The right of citizens of the United States to vote shall not be denied or abridged . . . on account of sex"); U.S. Const. amend. XXIV, § 1 ("The right of citizens of the United States to vote in any primary or other election for President or Vice President, for electors for President or Vice President, or for Senatory or Representative in Congress, shall not be denied or abridged by the United States or any State by reason of failure to pay any poll tax or other tax"); U.S. Const. amend. XXVI, § 1 ("The right of citizens of the United States, who are eighteen years of age or older, to vote shall not be denied or abridged by the United States or by any State on account of age").

71. See Joseph M. Perillo, *Calamari and Perillo on Contracts*, 6th ed., Hornbook Series (St. Paul, MN: Thomson/West, 2009), 342.

72. See, for example, Step-Savers Data Systems, Inc. v. Wyse Technology, 939 F.3d 91 (3d Cir. 1991) (holding that a customer was not bound by terms contained in a box shipped after the contract was formed over the phone).

73. See Principles of the Law of Software Contracts § 2.02(c)(1)-(2) (2009). The reporters justify the safe harbor in this section on the grounds that it guarantees to offerees an opportunity to access terms prior to agreeing to them. See Robert A. Hillman and Maureen A. O'Rourke, "Principles of the Law of Software Contracts: Some Highlights," *Tulane Law Review* 84 (2010): 1529–32.

74. See Omri Ben-Shahar and Carl E. Schneider, *More Than You Wanted to Know: The Failure of Mandated Disclosure* (Princeton, NJ: Princeton University Press, 2014), 50–51 (summarizing evidence that disclosing contract terms is not an effective method of constraining abusive terms). In her extensive study of end-user license agreements, for example, Florencia Marotta-Wurgler found no meaningful difference in the quality of terms in contracts that consumers had the ability to read prior to closing the deal and those included in pay-now-terms-later transactions. See Florencia Marotta-Wurgler, "Are 'Pay, Now Terms Later' Contracts Worse for Buyers? Evidence from Software License Agreements," *Journal of Legal Studies* 38 (2009): 309–43. See also Florencia Marotta-Wurgler, "Will Increased Disclosure Help? Evaluating the Recommendations of the ALI's 'Principles of the Law of Software Contracts,'" *University of Chicago Law Review* 78 (2011): 165–86 (arguing that disclosure requirements are unlikely to have much effect on form contracting).

75. See Alan Schwartz and Louis L. Wilde, "Intervening in Markets on the Basis of Imperfect Information: A Legal and Economic Analysis," *University of Pennsylvania Law Review* 127, no. 3 (January 1, 1979): 630–82; George L. Priest, "A Theory of the Consumer Product Warranty," *Yale Law Journal* 90, no. 6 (May 1, 1981): 1297–352; Howard Beals, Richard Craswell, and Steven Salop, "The Efficient Regulation of Consumer Information," *Journal of Law and Economics* 21 (1981): 491–539; Avery Katz, "Your Terms or Mine? The Duty to Read Fine Print in Contracts," *RAND Journal of Economics* 21 (1990): 518–37; Clayton Gillette, "Pre-Approved Contracts for Internet Commerce," *Houston Law Review* 42 (2005): 975–1013; Douglas G. Baird, "The Boilerplate Puzzle," *Michigan Law Review* 104 (2006): 933–52.

76. Grocery store coupons are a simple example of price discrimination.

77. See Yannis Bakos, Florencia Marotta-Wurgler, and David R. Trossen, "Does Anyone Read the Fine Print? Consumer Attention to Standard-Form Contracts," *Journal of Legal Studies* 43, no. 1 (January 1, 2014): 1–35.

78. Ibid., 3, 8–9. Furthermore, those who did read the terms generally spent mere seconds on the page.

79. See, for example, Eyal Zamir and Yuval Farkash, "Standard Form Contracts: Empirical Studies, Normative Implications, and the Fragmentation of Legal Scholarship," *Jerusalem Review of Legal Studies*, forthcoming, 10–11, http://papers

.ssrn.com/sol3/papers.cfm?abstract_id=2546863 ("However, the fact that virtually no one reads standard forms even in an environment conducive to reading—such as the comfort of one's home or office—indicates that the informed minority essentially does not exist").

80. After a lecture summarizing Marotta-Wurgler's research for a contracts course and confidently informing my first-year students, "There is no one who shops by reading fine print," one of my students contacted me after class and claimed that she obsessively reads the cancellation policies for airline tickets and warranty terms for major appliances because that is what her mother taught her to do.

81. Marotta-Wurgler, "What's in a Standard Form Contract?" 710–12.

82. In a perfectly competitive market, any firm that reaped rents from boilerplate would rapidly have its boilerplate copied by competitors, who would then push down prices, eliminating the rents. Alternatively, some firms may be less efficient than other firms and compensate for that inefficiency by offering "bad" contract terms, which would explain why terms don't affect price. In a competitive market, however, these inefficient firms ought to be competed into bankruptcy. Both stories are consistent with Marotta-Wurgler's empirical results, and her data, because they do not include profits, do not allow us to determine which story is true. What we do know is that the firms don't seem to be operating in a perfectly competitive market.

83. Much of the debate over arbitration assumes that it leads to smaller recoveries for consumers. For purposes of argument, I accept this premise in the analysis above. It's difficult, however, to find broad empirical studies (as opposed to anecdotal evidence) supporting this conclusion. A study conducted by Public Citizen in California purported to find evidence of pervasive bias based on the fact that debt collection actions sent to arbitration were overwhelmingly decided in favor of the creditor. See Public Citizen, "The Arbitration Trap: How Credit Card Companies Ensnare Consumers," September 27, 2007, http://www.citizen.org/documents/ArbitrationTrap.pdf. Critics of the study point out that creditors are overwhelmingly successful in debt collection actions, regardless of forum, and the study made no effort to systematically compare outcomes between arbitration and conventional litigation. See Sarah R. Cole and Kristen M. Blankley, "Empirical Research on Consumer Arbitration: What the Data Reveals," *Penn State Law Review* 113 (2009): 1051–78. Preliminary studies by the Consumer Financial Protection Bureau mandated by the Dodd-Frank Act also failed to produce alarming evidence of anticonsumer bias, although the study did reveal that class-action waivers were common. See Consumer Financial Protection Bureau, "Arbitration Study Preliminary Results," Section 1028(a) Study Results (Washington, DC: Consumer Financial Protection Bureau, December 12, 2013). Theodore Eisenberg, Geoffrey Miller, and Emily Sherwin have found that firms are more likely to include arbitration agreements in contracts with consumers than in contracts with

other corporations. See Theodore Eisenberg, Geoffrey P. Miller, and Emily Sherwin, "Arbitration's Summer Soldiers: An Empirical Study of Arbitration Clauses in Consumer and Nonconsumer Contracts," *University of Michigan Journal of Law Reform* 41 (2008): 871–96. This may indicate that arbitration is being used systematically to the disadvantage of consumers. It may also, however, simply indicate that the benefits of low-cost dispute resolution (arbitration) are higher in relatively common and simple consumer transactions and that the benefits of high-quality dispute resolution (litigation) are higher in relatively rare and complex corporation-to-corporation disputes. Interestingly, Marotta-Wurgler found no evidence that software companies use dispute resolution clauses strategically. Arbitration clauses are rare, as are forum selection clauses. Choice-of-law clauses virtually always designate the law of the state where the company is located, even when that state is quite pro-consumer. See Florencia Marotta-Wurgler, "'Unfair' Dispute Resolution Clauses: Much Ado about Nothing?" in *Boilerplate: The Foundation of Market Contracts*, ed. Omri Ben-Shahar (New York: Cambridge University Press, 2007).

84. Suppose that we refuse to enforce the boilerplate agreement with the consumer. This will likely benefit those consumers who would have disputed the boilerplate but will reduce the revenues of the corporation, which will result in higher prices in a reasonably competitive market for consumers who never have disputes with the corporation. The refusal to enforce the contract, would, therefore also tend to distribute resources from one set of consumers to another set of consumers rather than from corporation to consumers. Alternatively, the corporation may simply refuse to contract with certain classes of consumers, which may result in a net decrease in their wealth.

85. See John C. P. Goldberg and Benjamin Zipursky, "Torts as Wrongs," *Texas Law Review* 88 (2010): 917–86; Benjamin Zipursky, "Civil Recourse, Not Corrective Justice," *Georgetown Law Journal* 91, no. 3 (2003): 695–757. For a skeptical response to Goldberg and Zipursky's approach to torts, see Jane Stapleton, "Evaluating Goldberg and Zipursky's Civil Recourse Theory," *Fordham Law Review* 75 (2007): 1529–62.

86. See Elizabeth Anderson, *Value in Ethics and Economics* (Cambridge, MA: Harvard University Press, 1995), 55–59.

87. The seminal article on this issue is Stewart Macaulay, "Non-Contractual Relations in Business: A Preliminary Study," *American Sociological Review* 28 (1963): 55–67.

88. See Lisa Bernstein, "Merchant Law in a Merchant Court: Rethinking the Code's Search for Immanent Business Norms," *University of Pennsylvania Law Review* 144 (1996): 1765–82.

89. See Bebchuk and Posner, "One-Sided Contracts in Competitive Consumer Markets."

90. See Baird, "The Boilerplate Puzzle," 938–39.

91. 161 A.2d 69 (N.J. 1960) (refusing to enforce a boilerplate contract disclaiming the warranty of merchantability).

92. William C. Whitford, "Strict Products Liability and the Automobile Industry: Much Ado about Nothing," *Wisconsin Law Review* 1968 (1968): 162.

93. It is not a sufficient condition because, as discussed in chapter 5, the heart of contract is the commercial transaction, and in many cases we simply lack good reasons for enforcing otherwise fully informed and consensual undertakings that lack a commercial purpose.

94. The *Restatement (Second)* in this section is influenced by a proposal made by Karl Llwelleyn in his book, *The Common Law Tradition*. Llewellyn wrote:

> The answer, I suggest, is this: Instead of thinking about "assent" to boiler-plate clauses, we can recognize that so far as concerns the specific, there is no assent at all. What has in fact been assented to, specifically, are the few dickered terms, and the broad type of the transactions, and but one thing more. That one thing more is a blanket asset (no specific assent) to any not unreasonable or indecent terms the seller may have on his form, which do not alter or eviscerate the reasonable meaning of the dickered terms. The fine print which has not been read has no business to cut under the reasonable meaning of those dickered terms which constitute the dominant and the only real expression of agreement, but much of it commonly belongs in.

Karl N. Llewellyn, *The Common Law Tradition: Deciding Appeals* (New York: Little, Brown, 1960), 370. See Restatement (Second) of Contracts § 211 rep. note (citing *The Common Law Tradition* and Llewellyn's 1939 *Harvard Law Review* book review).

95. *Id.* at § 211(3).

96. William Shakespeare, *The Merchant of Venice*, in *The Complete Works: The New Pelican Text*, eds. Stephen Orgel and A. R. Braunmuller (New York: Penguin Books, 2002), I.iii.139–46.

97. Dworkin, "The Original Position," 18. Dworkin made this point in the context of a critique of John Rawls's original position specifically and the social contract tradition more generally. His simple and powerful argument is that consent creates more obligations because it actually happens not because it might have happened. As should be clear at this point, I do not believe that consent provides a justification for enforcing contracts. I do, however, agree with Dworkin that if one is going to ground obligations in consent, then actual consent seems rather more ethically weighty than hypothetical consent.

98. See Llewellyn, *The Common Law Tradition*, 370.

99. See Rakoff, "Contracts of Adhesion," 1250–55.

100. See Kuran, *The Long Divergence*; Timur Kuran, "The Economic Roots of

Political Underdevelopment in the Middle East: A Historical Perspective," *Southern Economic Journal* 78, no. 4 (April 1, 2012): 1086–95; Timur Kuran, "Why the Middle East Is Economically Underdeveloped: Historical Mechanisms of Institutional Stagnation," *Journal of Economic Perspectives* 18, no. 3 (July 1, 2004): 71–90; Timur Kuran, "The Islamic Commercial Crisis: Institutional Roots of Economic Underdevelopment in the Middle East," *Journal of Economic History* 63, no. 2 (June 1, 2003): 414–46.

101. *In re Colonial Ford*, 24 B.R. 1014, 1016 (Bankr. D. Utah 1982) (Mabey J.) (quoting *In re Curley Valley Associates*, 14 B.R. 506, 511 (Bankr. D. Utah 1981)) [internal quotation marks omitted]. See also Eric Posner, "A Theory of Contract Law under Conditions of Radical Judicial Error," *Northwestern University Law Review* 94 (2000): 749–74.

102. Barnett, "Consenting to Form Contracts," 636.

103. 105 F.3d 1147 (7th Cir. 1997) (holding that the purchaser of a computer is bound by terms contained in the computer's packaging even though the terms were not readily available until after the purchase was completed).

104. 86 F.3d 1447 (7th Cir. 1996) (upholding the enforceability of a so-called shrinkwrap license in which one is deemed to have accepted terms by opening a package that must be opened to read the terms).

105. Barnett, "Consenting to Form Contracts," 640.

106. Ibid., 638.

107. In fairness to Barnett, there are critics of boilerplate, such as Margaret Radin, who do use language suggesting that the person who clicks "I agree" has not consented to anything. See Radin, *Boilerplate*. For the reasons given by Barnett, I find such arguments unpersuasive. However, such arguments also strike me as peripheral to the critique of boilerplate agreements—a kind of conceptual and rhetorical overreach rather than a serious objection.

108. Randy E. Barnett, "A Consent Theory of Contract," *Columbia Law Review* 86 (1986): 318. The context is Barnett's discussion of doctrines surrounding incapacity, infancy, and intoxication.

109. See David Horton, "Unconscionability Wars," *Northwestern University Law Review* 106 (2012): 387–408.

110. Arthur Allen Leff, "Unconscionability and the Code—The Emperor's New Clause," *University of Pennsylvania Law Review* 115 (1967): 487.

111. See, for example, Pierce v. Catalina Yachts, Inc., 2 P.3d 618, 623 (Alaska 2000) ("Courts are more likely to find unconscionability when a consumer is involved, when there is a disparity in bargaining power, and when the consequential damages clause is on a pre-printed form").

112. See, for example, Gatton v. T-Mobile USA, Inc., 61 Cal. Rptr. 3d 344 (Ct. App. 2007) (finding an arbitration agreement unconscionable even in situations where the consumer admitted to being aware of the clause in the boilerplate and having other alternatives).

113. Furthermore, it is worth noting that such disclosure rules are not costless. As Judge Easterbrook pointed out in *Hill v. Gateway 2000, Inc.*, it would be needlessly costly to require that sellers read lengthy contract terms to buyers in the case of sales over the phone. Nevertheless, in a world of online shopping, I am not convinced that the costs of such disclosure would be high, although there is little evidence to suggest that it serves any useful purpose.

114. Indeed, most antitrust scholars would assume that monopolists will extract rents by charging monopoly prices rather than investing in artfully drafted boilerplate. See Douglas G. Baird, *Reconstructing Contracts* (Cambridge, MA: Harvard University Press, 2013), 134 (arguing that the optimal strategy for a monopolist would be to raise prices rather than extract rents via complex boilerplate).

115. I tend to be skeptical of such claims, but even if one finds them persuasive, it's worth noting that they justify only the transformation of such claims into cash. One might still bargain over such claims in some other medium. As Elizabeth Anderson has put it: "If different principles appear to generate conflicting recommendations, the task for a rational agent is not to weight and aggregate their consequences, but to seek more refined interpretations of their demands so that all of them can be satisfied. This is the traditional task of casuistry, reasoning by analogy, and other commonsense modes of practical reasoning familiar to ordinary life." Anderson, *Value in Ethics and Economics*, 62–63.

116. For example, under Israeli Standard Contracts Law of 1964 and the revision of that law in 1981, certain terms are legislatively designated as unenforceable; courts are given the general power to strike down or alter unfair terms; and contract drafters, government officials, or designated consumer advocates may submit boilerplate to a special regulatory body that will either approve, alter, or disallow the terms. The decisions of this body then apply to all similar contracts for five years. See generally Varda Lusthaus, "Standard Contracts in Israel: New Developments," *Rabels Zeitschrift Für Ausländisches Und Internationales Privatrecht/The Rabel Journal of Comparative and International Private Law* 54, no. 3 (January 1, 1990): 551–78 (summarizing Israeli law). The 1964 Israeli law was modeled in part on sections 1341 and 1342 of the Italian Civil Code, which invalidates certain kinds of one-side contract clauses. See Kenneth Frederick Berg, "The Israeli Standard Contracts Law 1964: Judicial Controls of Standard Form Contracts," *International and Comparative Law Quarterly* 28, no. 4 (October 1, 1979): 561–62 (describing the influence of the Italian Civil Code on the Israel Standard Contract Law). Interestingly, the Italian approach does not confine the invalidation of disfavored provisions to boilerplate agreements, but rather applies the rules to all contracts. See Gino Gorla, "Standard Conditions and Form Contracts in Italian Law," *American Journal of Comparative Law* 11 (1962): 2–3 (providing an English translation and discussion of sections 1341 and 1342 of the Italian Civil Code).

117. Even Randy Barnett, for example, articulates substantive limits on freedom of contract, insisting that certain rights are inalienable and therefore cannot

be the subject of contractual obligations. See Randy E. Barnett, "Contract Remedies and Inalienable Rights," *Social Philosophy and Policy* 4, no. 1 (1986): 179–203.

Chapter Eight

1. Charles Fried's *Contract as Promise*, for example, cabins its discussion of unconscionability by lumping it in with a discussion of duress, treating both doctrines as primarily concerned with the freedom of contracting parties. His book contains no chapter on contracts void on public policy grounds. See Charles Fried, *Contract as Promise: A Theory of Contractual Obligation* (Cambridge, MA: Harvard University Press, 1981), 103–9.

2. See Randy E. Barnett, "Consenting to Form Contracts," *Fordham Law Review* 71 (2002): 627–45; Randy E. Barnett, "A Consent Theory of Contract," *Columbia Law Review* 86 (1986): 318.

3. For example, Grant Gilmore, *The Death of Contract* (Columbus: Ohio State University Press, 1995); Jean Braucher, "Contract versus Contractarianism: The Regulatory Role of Contract Law," *Washington and Lee Law Review* 47 (Fall 1990): 697–739; Duncan Kennedy, "Form and Substance in Private Law Adjudication," *Harvard Law Review* 89 (1976): 1685–1778.

4. See P. S. Atiyah, *The Rise and Fall of Freedom of Contract* (New York: Oxford University Press, 1985); Lawrence M. Friedman, *Contract Law in America: A Social and Economic Case Study*, repr. ed. (New Orleans, LA: Quid Pro Books, 2011).

5. See generally Richard A. Epstein, "Contracts Small and Contract Large: Contract Law through the Lens of Laissez-Faire," in *The Fall and Rise of Freedom of Contract*, ed. F. H Buckley (Durham, NC: Duke University Press, 1999), 25–61.

6. Gilmore, *The Death of Contract*, 103–5.

7. See Anthony T. Kronman, "Paternalism and the Law of Contracts," *Yale Law Journal* 92 (1983): 763–97; Duncan Kennedy, "Distributive and Paternalist Motives in Contract and Tort Law, with Special Reference to Compulsory Terms and Unequal Bargaining Power," *Maryland Law Review* 41 (1982): 563–658.

8. For example, Todd D. Rakoff, "Contracts of Adhesion: An Essay in Reconstruction," *Harvard Law Review* 96 (April 1983): 1173–274; Friedrich Kessler, "Contracts of Adhesion—Some Thoughts about Freedom of Contract," *Columbia Law Review* 43 (1943): 629–42.

9. See Herbert S. Klein, *The Atlantic Slave Trade*, 2nd ed., New Approaches to the Americas (New York: Cambridge University Press, 2010).

10. For numbers on the slave trade, see Marcus Rediker, *The Slave Ship: A Human History* (New York: Viking, 2007), 5.

11. See Nightingale v. Bridges, 89 Eng. Rep. 496 (K.B. 1689) (invalidating the grant of judicial power to the Royal African Company to enforce its own monopoly

against independent slave traders, thus opening up the African slave trade to private entrepreneurs). See William A. Pettigrew, *Freedom's Debt: The Royal African Company and the Politics of the Atlantic Slave Trade, 1672–1752* (Chapel Hill: University of North Carolina Press, 2013); William A. Pettigrew, "Free to Enslave: Politics and the Escalation of Britain's Transatlantic Slave Trade, 1688–1714," *William and Mary Quarterly*, Third Series, 64, no. 1 (January 1, 2007): 3–38.

12. Rediker, *The Slave Ship*, 5.

13. See Klein, *The Atlantic Slave Trade*, 8–9.

14. Fried, *Contract as Promise*, 21.

15. Michael J. Trebilcock, *The Limits of Freedom of Contract* (Cambridge, MA: Harvard University Press, 1993), 145.

16. See Sea Air Support, Inc. v. Herrman, 613 P.2d 413 (Nev. 1980); Sadler v. Eighth Judicial District Court, 614 P.2d 10 (Nev. 1980). For a summary of the common law's treatment of gambling contracts, see Roy Kreitner, *Calculating Promises: The Emergence of Modern American Contract Doctrine* (Stanford, CA: Stanford University Press, 2007), 97–100.

17. See *Sea Air Support, Inc.*, 613 P.2d at 414.

18. I am using the phrase "contracts in restraint of trade" extremely loosely here. Nineteenth-century common law courts developed a fairly complicated set of doctrines that differentiated between cartels, price-fixing contracts, and other attempts by producers to sidestep market competition. See Phillip E. Areeda and Herbert Hovenkamp, *Antitrust Law*, 3rd ed., vol. 1 (New York: Aspen Publishers, 2006), 64–79.

19. It should be noted that there are difficulties in maintaining a price-fixing cartel in the absence of contractual enforcement due to the strong incentive for price fixers to cheat on their co-conspirators. Richard A. Posner, *Economic Analysis of Law*, 8th ed. (New York: Aspen Publishers, 2010), 309–11.

20. For background on the passage of the Sherman Act, see generally Herbert Hovenkamp, *Enterprise and American Law: 1836–1937* (Cambridge, MA: Harvard University Press, 1991), 241–67.

21. See 15 U.S.C. § 1 (2009) ("Every contract, combination in the form of a trust or otherwise, or conspiracy, in restraint of trade or commerce among the several States, or with foreign nations, is declared to be illegal").

22. *Id.*

23. See, for example, United States v. Greenhut, 50 Fed. 469 (D. Mass. 1892); United States v. Patterson, 55 Fed. 605 (D. Mass. 1893).

24. See Michael J. Sandel, *What Money Can't Buy: The Moral Limits of Markets* (New York: Farrar, Straus and Giroux, 2013); Margaret Jane Radin, *Contested Commodities* (Cambridge, MA: Harvard University Press, 1996); Elizabeth Anderson, *Value in Ethics and Economics* (Cambridge, MA: Harvard University Press, 1995).

25. See Anderson, *Value in Ethics and Economics*, 62–63.

26. See Radin, *Contested Commodities*, 88–89 (arguing that pragmatism "denies that rationality or truth consists of linear deductions from an unquestioned foundational reality or truth").

27. See Michele Polo, "Internal Cohesion and Competition among Criminal Organisations," in *The Economics of Organized Crime*, eds. Gianluca Fiorentini and Sam Peltzman (New York: Cambridge University Press, 1995), 87–109.

28. The opposite may also be true, as in Nevada, where regulations support and regulate gambling, while the law of contracts refuses to recognize gambling contracts.

29. Much of the discussion has centered on John Stuart Mill's famous harm principle, which specifies that restrictions on liberty are only justified to prevent harm to others. For a succinct summary of Mill's argument, see David Brink, "Mill's Moral and Political Philosophy," in *The Stanford Encyclopedia of Philosophy,* ed. Edward N. Zalta (Stanford, CA: Metaphysics Research Lab, Fall 2014), http://plato.stanford.edu/archives/fall2014/entries/mill-moral-political/. For a discussion of the philosophical debates over the harm principle, see David Lyons, "Liberty and Harm to Others," *Canadian Journal of Philosophy* 5 (1979): 1–19.

30. Robert Fogel and Stanley L. Engerman famously argued that, contrary to the claims of some historians, slave-dependent agriculture was profitable and slave owners had economic incentives to moderate their treatment of slaves. See generally Robert William Fogel and Stanley L. Engerman, *Time on the Cross: The Economics of American Slavery*, reissue ed. (New York: W. W. Norton, 2013). Without wading into the historiographic controversy over Fogel and Engerman's argument, I note merely that their claim does not speak to the argument about economic efficiency that I make in the text. My claim is not that slavery wasn't profitable but that it is unlikely that it was socially efficient using the criteria of welfare economics. This is because even if cotton plantations were profitable and slave owners had incentives to moderate their treatment of slaves, the slaves themselves suffered disutility not priced in the plantations' profit calculus. This means both that there was substantial misery by slaves who would have to be considered in any Kaldor-Hicks-style assessment and that investment in enslaved agricultural was overincentivized due to negative externalities. The resulting capital misallocation presumably created further inefficiencies in the slave economy. As should be clear from my discussion in chapter 4, the negative moral assessment of slavery does not ultimately depend on judgments of its social efficiency or inefficiency.

31. Navigation Co. v. Windsor, 87 U.S. 64, 68 (1873).

32. In the 1937 case of *Warner Brother's Pictures, Inc. v. Nelson*, [1937] 1 K.B. 209, the Court of King's Bench issued a negative injunction against a movie star who had violated a covenant not to make movies with a rival studio. The Court noted: "The defendant is stated to be a person of intelligence, capacity and means, and no evidence was adduced to show that, if enjoined from doing the specified acts otherwise than for the plaintiffs, she will not be able to employ herself both

usefully and remuneratively in other spheres of activity, though not as remuneratively as in her special line." *Id.* at 219.

33. *Navigation Co.*, 87 U.S. at 68.

34. See Williams v. Walker-Thomas Furniture, Co., 350 F.2d 445 (D.C. Cir. 1965). See Arthur Allen Leff, "Unconscionability and the Code—The Emperor's New Clause," *University of Pennsylvania Law Review* 115 (1967): 485–559.

35. Leff, "Unconscionability and the Code."

36. Indeed, in modern litigation, unconscionability is less often used to provide relief from a harsh and perhaps inconsiderately entered into contract than as a way for courts to police arbitration agreements that they view as undermining efforts to regulate markets. See David Horton, "Unconscionability Wars," *Northwestern University Law Review* 106 (2012): 387–408.

37. Discover Bank v. Superior Court, 113 P.3d 1100 (Cal. 2005).

38. *Id.* at 1110.

39. In *Gatton v. T-Mobile, USA, Inc.*, 152 Cal. App. 4th 571 (2007), for example, the California Court of Appeals found an arbitration agreement unconscionable, even though the consumer conceded to being aware of the clause, the availability of competitors offering different contract terms, and a lower price as a result of the arbitration clause. In such a case, it is difficult to say that procedural unconscionability is present. Rather, the objection seems to be wholly directed toward the substance of the contract.

40. *Id.* at 1105 (quoting *Vasquez v. Superior Court*, 484 P.2d 964 (Cal. 1971)).

41. *Discover Bank* was ultimately preempted by the U.S. Supreme Court in *AT&T Mobility v. Conception*, 563 U.S. 321 (2011), which ruled that California's unconscionability doctrine in *Discover Bank* ran afoul of the Federal Arbitration Act. Furthermore, the California Supreme Court's analysis rests on an optimistic view of the virtues of class-action lawsuits, which are not without their own costs. Indeed, some states, far from invalidating class-action waivers in consumer cases, do not even allow class-action lawsuits in consumer cases or otherwise restrict class-action suits. See, for example, Ala. Code § 8-19-10 (2014) ("A consumer or other person bringing an action under this chapter may not bring an action on behalf of a class; provided, however, that the office of the Attorney General or district attorney shall have the authority to bring action in a representative capacity on behalf of any named person or persons"); Ga. Code Ann. § 10-1-399 (2014) ("Any person who suffers injury or damages . . . may bring an action individually, but not in a representative capacity"); Mont. Code Ann. § 30-13-133(1) (2014) ("A consumer who suffers . . . may bring an individual but not a class action").

42. V. S. Blazer et al., "Intersex (Testicular Oocytes) in Smallmouth Bass from the Potomac River and Selected Nearby Drainages," *Journal of Aquatic Animal Health* 19, no. 4 (2007): 242–53. While I have tried to be largely agnostic about what precisely constitutes harm, a massive question beyond the scope of this book,

as a fly fisherman, I am comfortable in asserting unequivocally that threatening smallmouth bass populations is harmful.

43. See Radin, *Contested Commodities*, 2–3. Elizabeth Anderson offers a variation on this argument. According to Anderson, the danger of commodification comes from treating all forms of human activity as amenable to a single moral rubric. As a moral pluralist, Anderson argues that such a view denies the necessary recognition that some kinds of activities are higher than others. Inappropriate commodification, on this view, involves a kind of desecration. See, for example, Anderson, *Value in Ethics and Economics*, 163–67, 189.

44. For an account of the rise and functioning of futures markets, see Emily Lambert, *The Futures: The Rise of the Speculator and the Origins of the World's Biggest Markets* (New York: Basic Books, 2010). For a discussion of the legal development of futures contracts, see Kreitner, *Calculating Promises*, 105–25.

45. See Radin, *Contested Commodities*, 12–15.

46. As Marx put the point in *Das Capital*:

> Capitalist production, therefore, of itself reproduces the separation between labour-power and the means of labour. It thereby reproduces and perpetuates the condition for exploiting the labourer. It incessantly forces him to sell his labour-power in order to live, and enables the capitalist to purchase labour-power in order that he may enrich himself. It is no longer a mere accident, that capitalist and labourer confront each other in the market as buyer and seller. It is the process itself that incessantly hurls back the labourer on to the market as a vendor of his labour-power, and that incessantly converts his own product into a means by which another man can purchase him. In reality, the labourer belongs to capital before he has sold himself to capital. His economic bondage is both brought about and concealed by the periodic sale of himself, by his change of masters, and by the oscillations in the market-price of labour-power.

Karl Marx, *Capital: A Critique of Political Economy*, ed. Friedrich Engels (New York: Cosimo Classics, 2013), 632–33.

47. For example, Marx's argument seems to have rested on David Ricardo's theory of wages. In 1817, Ricardo argued that "the natural price of labour is that price which is necessary to enable the labourers, one with another, to subsist and to perpetuate their race, without either increase or diminution." David Ricardo, *The Principles of Political Economy and Taxation* (Mineola, NY: Dover, 2004), 52. In Marx's vision, the economic desperation of the workers gave the capitalist virtually unlimited control over the proletariat. Ricardo's theory of wages, however, proved to be incorrect. Over the course of the nineteenth century, wages and standards of living for industrial workers in Britain actually rose as industrialization proceeded.

See Peter H. Lindert and Jeffery G. Williamson, "English Workers' Living Standard during the Industrial Revolution: A New Look," *Economic History Review* 36 (1983): 1–25; Gregory Clark, "The Condition of the Working Class in England, 1209–2004," *Journal of Political Economy* 113 (2005): 1307–40.

48. See also David C. Rose, *The Moral Foundation of Economic Behavior* (New York: Oxford University Press, 2011), 34–36.

49. See Radin, *Contested Commodities*, 102–4.

50. I do not mean to suggest that her argument falls into the slippery-slope fallacy. Some slopes are in fact slippery, and the probability that doing A, which is unobjectionable, will lead to B, which is objectionable, can be a perfectly legitimate argument. See Eugene Volokh, "The Mechanisms of the Slippery Slope," *Harvard Law Review* 116 (2003): 1026–137.

51. See Radin, *Contested Commodities*, 138–39.

52. The watershed case enforcing a surrogacy contract was *Johnson v. Calvert*, 851 P.2d 776 (Cal. 1993). Under current law, some states prohibit the enforcement of surrogacy contracts, some of them going so far as to make such contracts a criminal offense. See, for example, Ariz. Rev. Stat. Ann. § 25-218(B) (2007) *declared partially unconstitutional in* Soos v. Superior Court, 897 P.2d 1356 (Ariz. Ct. App. 1994) *rev. denied* (July 11, 1995) (withholding enforcement of any surrogacy contracts); D.C. Code Ann. § 16-402 (Lexis Nexis 1997) (specifying civil and criminal punishments for those involved in surrogacy agreements). Other states, however, will enforce commercial surrogacy agreements, subject to various limitations. See, for example, Fla. Stat. Ann. § 742.15(2) (West 2005); Utah Code Ann. § 78B-15-801 *et seq.* (2008); Tex. Fam. Code Ann. § 160.751 *et seq.* (Vernon 2008). Also, in many states there is no clear law on the issue. See Sonia Bychkov Green, "Interstate Intercourse: How Modern Assisted Reproductive Technologies Challenge the Traditional Realm of Conflicts of Law," *Wisconsin Journal of Law, Gender and Society* 24, no. 1 (Spring 2009): 58–73 (providing a brief summary on the issue in each of the 50 states and the District of Columbia); see also Martha A. Field, "Compensated Surrogacy," *Washington Law Review* 89 (2014): 1160–67 (summarizing various approaches taken under U.S. law).

53. The literature on surrogacy contracts is vast, and my goal here is not to offer a meaningful contribution to it other than pointing out that twenty years after Radin made her initial arguments, we may now have enough experience to judge based on empirical observation. One extensive review of empirical studies on surrogate mothers concluded that "the empirical data consistently offers little support for the widely expressed concerns about contractual parenting being emotionally damaging or exploitive for surrogate mothers, children or intended/social parents." Karen Busby and Delaney Vun, "Revisiting the Handmaid's Tale: Feminist Theory Meets Empirical Research on Surrogate Mothers," *Canadian Journal of Family Law* 26 (2010): 22 (internal quotation marks omitted); but see Field, "Compensated Surrogacy," 1170–71 (collecting anecdotes in support of the claim

that surrogacy contracts create "an attitude that if you have money you can buy anything, including the perfect baby and a birthmother to produce it for you. You can achieve these priceless contributions to your life, while avoiding responsibility if things go wrong").

54. Charles de Secondat Montesquieu, *The Spirit of the Laws*, eds. Anne Myers Cohler, Basia Carolyn Miller, and Harold Samuel Stone, Cambridge Texts in the History of Political Thought (Cambridge: Cambridge University Press, 1989), 338.

55. Ibid., 339.

56. The most famous example of this phenomenon was discovered by Richard Titmus, who argued that the market for blood in the United States tended to crowd out donations. See Richard M. Titmus, *The Gift Relationship: From Human Blood to Social Policy*, expanded ed. (New York: New Press, 1997).

57. For example, hospitality norms are often highly developed in societies that rely on feuding norms to limit predation and conflict. Nathan B. Oman, "Consent to Retaliation: A Civil Recourse Theory of Contractual Liability," *Iowa Law Review* 96 (2011): 545.

58. See King v. Young, Berkman, Berman & Karpf, P.A., 709 So. 2d 572 (Fla. 1998) (refusing to enforce a contract promising to pay a bonus to an attorney for successfully procuring a divorce), Rogers v. Webb, 558 N.W.2d 155 (Iowa 1997) (refusing to enforce a contract promising to pay a contingency fee to a nonlawyer for aiding in a successful divorce suit).

59. See Capazzoli v. Holzwasser, 490 N.E.2d 420 (Mass. 1986); Hoffman v. Boyd, 698 So.2d 346 (Fla. Dist. Ct. App. 1997). See also Restatement (Second) of Contracts § 190(2) (1981) ("A promise that tends to unreasonably to encourage divorce or separation is unenforceable on the grounds of public policy").

60. See Reynolds v. Reynolds, 230 S.E.2d 842 (Ga. 1976).

61. Compare Restatement Contracts § 587 (1932) ("A bargain between married persons or persons contemplating marriage to change the essential incidents of marriage is illegal").

62. Posner v. Posner, 233 S.2d 381, 382 (Fla. 1970) (citing Gallemore v. Gallemore, 94 Fla. 516 (1927) and Allen v. Allen, 111 Fla. 733 (1933)).

63. *Id.*

64. See Uniform Premarital and Marital Agreements Act § 9.

65. Uniform Premarital and Marital Agreements Act § 9(a)(2).

66. Uniform Premarital and Marital Agreements Act §§ 9(a)(4), 9(c).

67. Anderson, *Value in Ethics and Economics*, 180.

68. See, for example, *In re* Marriage of Shaban, 105 Cal. Rptr. 2d 863, 865-66 (Cal. Ct. App. 2001); *In re* Marriage of Dajani, 251 Cal. Rptr. 871, 871-72 (Cal. Ct. App. 1988); Akileh v. Elchahal, 666 So. 2d 246, 247-48 (Fla. Dist. Ct. App. 1996); Aleem v. Aleem, 947 A.2d 489, 494 (Md. 2008); Aleem v. Aleem, 931 A.2d 1123, 1126, 1129 (Md. Ct. Spec. App. 2007); Chaudry v. Chaudry, 388 A.2d 1000, 1003, 1006 (N.J. Super. Ct. App. Div. 1978); Odatalla v. Odatalla, 810 A.2d 93, 95, 98

(N.J. Super. Ct. Ch. Div. 2002); Habibi-Fahnrich v. Fahnrich, No. 46186/93, 1995 WL 507388, at *1 (N.Y. Sup. Ct. Jul. 10, 1995); Aziz v. Aziz, 488 N.Y.S.2d 123, 123-24 (N.Y. Sup. Ct. 1985); Zawahiri v. Alwattar, No. 07AP-925, 2008 WL 2698679, at *1 (Ohio Ct. App. Jul. 10, 2008); Mir v. Birjandi, No. 2006 CA 63, 2007 WL 4170868, at *1 (Ohio Ct. App. Nov. 21, 2007); Ahmad v. Ahmad, No. L-00-1391, 2001 WL 1518116, at *4 (Ohio Ct. App. 2001); Ahmed v. Ahmed, 261 S.W.3d 190, 193 (Tex. Ct. App. 2008).

69. See Nathan B. Oman, "How to Judge Sharia Contracts: A Guide to Islamic Marriage Agreements in American Courts," *Utah Law Review* 2011 (2011): 287–334; Nathan B. Oman, "Bargaining in the Shadow of God's Law: Islamic Mahr Contracts and the Perils of Legal Specialization," *Wake Forest Law Review* 45 (2010): 579–606.

70. See Anderson, *Value in Ethics and Economics*, 163–67.

71. See Radin, *Contested Commodities*, 57–60. See also Margaret Jane Radin, "Property and Personhood," *Stanford Law Review* 34 (1982): 957–1015.

72. The classic book on the scandal, based in part on interviews with the participants, is Eliot Asinof, *Eight Men Out: The Black Sox and the 1919 World Series* (Evanston, IL: Holtzman Press, 1963). More recent studies have focused on the unsuccessful attempt to cover up the scandal and its wider cultural meaning. See Gene Carney, *Burying the Black Sox: How Baseball's Cover-Up of the 1919 World Series Fix Almost Succeeded* (Washington, DC: Potomac Books, 2006); Daniel A. Nathan, *Saying It's So: A Cultural History of the Black Sox Scandal* (Urbana: University of Illinois Press, 2003).

73. See Harold Seymour, *Baseball: The Early Years* (New York: Oxford University Press, 1960), 104–16 (providing an account of the origins of the Reserve Clause in the late 1870s and its subsequent history).

74. See Flood v. Kuhn, 407 U.S. 258 (1972) (upholding the enforcement of the Reserve Clause against a challenge on antitrust grounds); Federal Baseball Club v. National League, 259 U.S. 200 (1922) (holding that professional baseball was not subject to federal antitrust laws). But see 15 U.S.C. § 26b (1998) (setting forth the Curt Flood Act of 1998, which removes baseball's exemption from antitrust laws in cases involving collective bargaining agreements). See generally Thomas J. Ostertag, "Baseball's Antitrust Exemption: Its History and Continuing Importance," *Virginia Sports and Entertainment Law Journal* 4 (2004): 54–67.

75. Sandel, *What Money Can't Buy*, 94.

76. Ibid., 95.

77. An engagement ring is, of course, a store of wealth, but no enraptured fiancé loves her engagement ring because she plans on selling it for cash.

78. See generally Joshua Ronen, "Corporate Audits and How to Fix Them," *Journal of Economic Perspectives* 24, no. 2 (Spring 2010): 189–210.

79. In the case of bond rating agencies, the issue is complicated by the relationship between the agencies and various regulatory regimes. Much of the value of

an investment-grade bond rating does not come from any information that such a rating purportedly discloses to the market. Rather, the value comes from the fact that certain heavily regulated investors—such as pension funds—are required to hold investment-grade securities. See Frank Partnoy, "The Siskel and Ebert of Financial Markets? Two Thumbs Down for the Credit Rating Agencies," *Washington University Law Quarterly* 77 (1999): 666 ("Credit ratings are valuable, not because they contain valuable information, but because they grant issuers 'regulatory licenses.' In simple terms, a good rating entitles the issuer (and the investors in a particular issue) to certain advantages related to regulation"). A similar but less powerful dynamic is at work with accounting firms, in that the Securities and Exchange Commission requires all publicly traded companies to publish independently audited financial statements. See Ronen, "Corporate Audits and How to Fix Them," 190. However, unlike investment-grade bond ratings, these reports do not give companies access to an otherwise restricted pool of investors.

80. As articulated by *The Economist*, the concern can be stated thus: "An audit is supposed to be a cold-eyed outsider's look at a company's finances. For an auditor to provide its client even with tax advice or reviews of internal controls (which are both permitted under American law) involves a closeness that makes some observers nervous. If there really is synergy between providing these services and an audit, there is cause for concern about the auditor's independence." "A Conflict of Interest?" *The Economist*, October 14, 2010, http://www.economist.com/node/17257817.

81. In the final year before its collapse, Enron paid Arthur Andersen more than $50 million in auditing and consulting fees. After the collapse of the Texas-based energy company amid evidence of massive fraud, the Securities and Exchange Commission began an investigation of Arthur Andersen, which resulted in massive shredding of presumably incriminating documents by the accounting firm. See Ronen, "Corporate Audits and How to Fix Them," 191.

82. Arthur Andersen was criminally convicted of fraud in association with its Enron audits in June 2002, although the conviction was subsequently overturned on appeal. See Arthur Andersen LLP v. United States, 544 U.S. 696 (2005).

83. To be clear, this is an analogy. I am obviously not claiming that new cars lose value when they are sold because they are being allocated by a market rather than some other mechanism. I am only making the point that, just because selling new cars destroys part of their value, we don't refuse to enforce sales contracts or prohibit selling new cars.

84. This hasn't always stopped people from trying. Consider the case of *Roth v. Patino*, 185 Misc. 235 (N.Y. Sup. Ct. 1945), in which a wealthy eighty-year-old man promised a twenty-year-old woman $1,000 if, among other things, she would "consider and act towards him as if he were her father." *Id.* at 236. The contract was not enforced, on the grounds that it was an oral agreement falling within the statute of frauds. Alternatively, the court suggested that the contract, which required the

young woman "to devote all or substantially all her time to the defendant; to account to him for all her waking moments; to be at his beck, call and direct should he desire," as "inconsistent with and destructive of the plaintiff's marriage." *Id.* One might also point out that it isn't possible to purchase filial piety.

85. Compare George Akerlof, "The Market for 'Lemons': Quality Uncertainty and the Market Mechanism," *Quarterly Journal of Economics* 84, no. 3 (1970): 488–500.

Conclusion

1. William Shakespeare, *The Merchant of Venice*, in *The Complete Works: The New Pelican Text*, eds. Stephen Orgel and A. R. Braunmuller (New York: Penguin Books, 2002), III.iii.24–32.

Bibliography

Acemoglu, Daron, and James A. Robinson. *Why Nations Fail: The Origins of Power, Prosperity, and Poverty*. London: Profile Books, 2012.

Ackerman, Bruce A. *Social Justice in the Liberal State*. New Haven, CT: Yale University Press, 1980.

Aeschylus. *The Oresteia*. Translated by Robert Fangles. New York: Penguin Books, 1984.

"Agent Infiltrated Terror Cell, U.S. Says." *CNN.com*, August 11, 2006. http://www.cnn.com/2006/US/08/10/us.security/index.html.

Akerlof, George. "The Market for 'Lemons': Quality Uncertainty and the Market Mechanism." *Quarterly Journal of Economics* 84, no. 3 (1970): 488–500.

Anderson, Elizabeth. *Value in Ethics and Economics*. Cambridge, MA: Harvard University Press, 1995.

Andrade, Luis F., Jose M. Barra, and Heinz-Peter Elstrodt. "All in the Familia." *McKinsey Quarterly* 2001 Special Edition, no. 4 (2001): 81–89.

Angell, LC. "Report: Terrorists Planned to Use iPod as Detonator." *iLounge.com*, August 10, 2006. http://www.ilounge.com/index.php/news/comments/report-terrorists-planned-to-use-ipod-as-detonator/.

Applebaum, Anne. *Gulag: A History of the Soviet Camps*. London: Allen Lane, 2003.

Arberry, A. J., trans. *The Koran Interpreted*. New York: Simon & Schuster, 1996.

Areeda, Phillip E., and Herbert Hovenkamp. *Antitrust Law*. 3rd ed. Vol. 1. 14 vols. New York: Aspen Publishers, 2006.

Ariely, Dan. *Predictably Irrational: The Hidden Forces That Shape Our Decisions*. New York: Harper, 2008.

Aristotle. *Nicomachean Ethics*. Translated by F. H. Peters. New York: Barnes & Noble, 2004.

Armitage, Simon, trans. *Sir Gawain and the Green Knight*. New York: W. W. Norton, 2013.

Arrow, Kenneth J. *Social Choice and Individual Values*. 1st ed. New York: John Wiley & Sons, 1951.

Arrow, Kenneth J., and Gerard Debreu. "Existence of an Equilibrium for a Competitive Economy." *Econometrica* 22, no. 3 (1954): 265–90.

Asinof, Eliot. *Eight Men Out: The Black Sox and the 1919 World Series*. Evanston, IL: Holtzman Press, 1963.

Atiyah, P. S. *Essays on Contract*. Repr., with a new chapter. Oxford: Clarendon Press; New York: Oxford University Press, 1990.

———. *Promises, Morals, and Law*. Oxford: Clarendon Press, 1982.

———. *The Rise and Fall of Freedom of Contract*. New York: Oxford University Press, 1985.

Audi, Robert. *Religious Commitment and Secular Reason*. New York: Cambridge University Press, 2000.

Axelrod, Robert. *The Evolution of Cooperation*. Rev. ed. New York: Basic Books, 2006.

Baird, Douglas G. "The Boilerplate Puzzle." *Michigan Law Review* 104 (2006): 933–52.

———. *Reconstructing Contracts*. Cambridge, MA: Harvard University Press, 2013.

Baker, J. H. *An Introduction to English Legal History*. 4th ed. London: Butterworths LexisNexis, 2011.

Bakos, Yannis, Florencia Marotta-Wurgler, and David R. Trossen. "Does Anyone Read the Fine Print? Consumer Attention to Standard-Form Contracts." *Journal of Legal Studies* 43, no. 1 (January 1, 2014): 1–35.

Banfield, Edward C. *The Moral Basis of a Backward Society*. Glencoe, IL: Free Press, 1958.

Bar-Gill, Oren. *Seduction by Contract: Law, Economics, and Psychology in Consumer Markets*. New York: Oxford University Press, 2013.

Barnett, Randy E. "A Consent Theory of Contract." *Columbia Law Review* 86 (1986): 269–321.

———. "Consenting to Form Contracts." *Fordham Law Review* 71 (2002): 627–45.

———. "Contract Remedies and Inalienable Rights." *Social Philosophy and Policy* 4, no. 1 (1986): 179–203.

———. "Some Problems with Contract as Promise." *Cornell Law Review* 77 (1991): 1022–33.

Barnett, Randy E., and Mary E. Becker. "Beyond Reliance: Promissory Estoppel, Contract Formalities, and Misrepresentation." *Hofstra Law Review* 15 (1987): 443–97.

"Barrat." *Oxford English Dictionary*. New York: Oxford University Press, 1989.

"Barter." *Oxford English Dictionary*. New York: Oxford University Press, 1989.

Basu, Priya. *Improving Access to Finance for India's Rural Poor*. Washington, DC: World Bank, 2006.

Bates, Robert H. *Prosperity and Violence: The Political Economy of Development*. New ed. New York: W. W. Norton, 2001.

Beals, Howard, Richard Craswell, and Steven Salop. "The Efficient Regulation of Consumer Information." *Journal of Law and Economics* 21 (1981): 491–539.

Bebchuk, Lucian A., and Richard A. Posner. "One-Sided Contracts in Competitive Consumer Markets." In *Boilerplate: The Foundation of Market Contracts*, edited by Omri Ben-Shahar, 3–11. New York: Cambridge University Press, 2007.

Ben-Shahar, Omri, and Carl E. Schneider. *More Than You Wanted to Know: The Failure of Mandated Disclosure*. Princeton, NJ: Princeton University Press, 2014.

Benson, Peter. "Contract." In *A Companion to Philosophy of Law and Legal Theory*, edited by Dennis Patterson, 24–56. Cambridge, MA: Wiley-Blackwell, 1996.

———. "The Unity of Contract Law." In *The Theory of Contract Law: New Essays*, edited by Peter Beson, 118–205. New York: Cambridge University Press, 2006.

Bentham, Jeremy. *An Introduction to the Principals of Morals and Legislation*. New York: Oxford University Press, 1996.

———. "Last Epigrams and Sayings." In *A Bentham Reader*, edited by Mary Peter Mack, 359–363. New York: Pegasus, 1969.

Berg, Kenneth Frederick. "The Israeli Standard Contracts Law 1964: Judicial Controls of Standard Form Contracts." *International and Comparative Law Quarterly* 28, no. 4 (October 1, 1979): 560–74.

Berkowitz, Peter. *Virtue and the Making of Modern Liberalism*. Princeton, NJ: Princeton University Press, 1999.

Berniss, Samuel Merrifield, ed. *The Three Charters of the Virginia Company of London, with Seven Related Documents: 1606–1621*. Williamsburg: Virginia 350th Celebration Corp., 1957.

Bernstein, Lisa. "Merchant Law in a Merchant Court: Rethinking the Code's Search for Immanent Business Norms." *University of Pennsylvania Law Review* 144 (1996): 1765–1821.

Bernstein, William J. *A Splendid Exchange: How Trade Shaped the World*. New York: Atlantic Monthly Press, 2008.

Bird, Antonia, dir. *Priest*. Miramax Films, 1994.

Birks, Peter. *Unjust Enrichment*. New York: Oxford University Press, 2005.

Bix, Brian. "Bargaining in the Shadow of Love: The Enforcement of Premarital Agreements and How We Think About Marriage." *William & Mary Law Review* 40 (1998): 145–207.

———. *Contract Law: Rules, Theory, and Context*. New York: Cambridge University Press, 2012.

Blazer, V. S., L. R. Iwanowiz, D. D. Iwanowicz, D. R. Smith, J. A. Young, J. D. Hendrick, S. W. Foster, and S. J. Reeser. "Intersex (Testicular Oocytes) in Smallmouth Bass from the Potomac River and Selected Nearby Drainages." *Journal of Aquatic Animal Health* 19, no. 4 (2007): 242–53.

Bloxham, Donald. *The Final Solution: A Genocide*. New York: Oxford University Press, 2009.

Boardman, Michelle E. "Consent and Sensibility: A Review of Margaret Jane Radin's Book, 'Boilerplate: The Fine Print, Vanishing Rights, and the Rule of Law.'" *Harvard Law Review* 127 (2013): 1967–90.

Botterweck, G. Johannes, Helmer Ringgren, and Heinz-Josef Fabry, eds. *Theological Dictionary of the Old Testament*. Vol. 7. 7 vols. Grand Rapids, MI: Eerdmans, 1995.

Bradford, David F., Rebecca Schlieckert, and Stephen H. Shore. "The Environmental Kuznets Curve: Exploring a Fresh Specification." NBER Working Paper 8001. National Bureau of Economic Research, Cambridge, MA, November 2000.

Braucher, Jean. "Contract versus Contractarianism: The Regulatory Role of Contract Law." *Washington and Lee Law Review* 47 (Fall 1990): 697–739.

Breen, T. H. *The Marketplace of Revolution: How Consumer Politics Shaped American Independence*. New York: Oxford University Press, 2004.

Bridgeman, Curtis. "Allegheny College Revisited: Cardozo, Consideration, and Formalism in Context." *University of California, Davis Law Review* 39 (2005): 149–87.

Brink, David. "Mill's Moral and Political Philosophy." In *The Stanford Encyclopedia of Philosophy*, edited by Edward N. Zalta. Stanford, CA: Metaphysics Research Lab, Fall 2014. http://plato.stanford.edu/archives/fall2014/entries/mill-moral-political/.

Buchanan, Allen E. *Ethics, Efficiency, and the Market*. Totowa, NJ: Rowman & Allanheld, 1985.

Buchanan, James, and Gordon Tullock. *The Calculus of Consent*. Indianapolis: Liberty Fund, 1999.

Buchanan, James M., and Viktor J. Vanberg. "The Market as a Creative Process." In *The Philosophy of Economics: An Anthology*, edited by Daniel M. Hausman, 3rd ed. New York: Cambridge University Press, 2008.

Burke, Edmund. *Reflections on the Revolution in France*. Edited by J. C. D. Clark. Stanford, CA: Stanford University Press, 2001.

Busby, Karen, and Delaney Vun. "Revisiting the Handmaid's Tale: Feminist Theory Meets Empirical Research on Surrogate Mothers." *Canadian Journal of Family Law* 26 (2010): 13–93.

Caldwell, Bruce. "Hayek and Socialism." *Journal of Economic Literature* 35, no. 4 (December 1, 1997): 1856–90.

Cantoni, Davide. "The Economic Effects of the Protestant Reformation: Testing the Weber Hypothesis in the German Lands." *Barcelona GSE*, Working Paper 524. Barcelona Graduate School of Economics, Barcelona, 2010.

Carlyle, Thomas. *Chartism*. 2nd ed. London: Chapman and Hall, Strand, 1891.

Carney, Gene. *Burying the Black Sox: How Baseball's Cover-up of the 1919 World Series Fix Almost Succeeded*. Washington, DC: Potomac Books, 2006.

Carter, Stephen L. *The Culture of Disbelief: How American Law and Politics Trivialize Religious Devotion*. New York: Anchor Books, 1994.

Chaudhuri, Shubham, and Alexander S. P. Plaff. "Household Income, Fuel Choice, and Indoor Air Quality: Microfoundations of an Environmental Kuznets Curve." Columbia University Economics Department Working Paper. Columbia University, New York, 1998.

Chua, Amy. *World on Fire: How Exporting Free Market Democracy Breeds Ethnic Hatred and Global Instability*. New York: Anchor Books, 2004.

Clark, Gregory. "The Condition of the Working Class in England, 1209–2004." *Journal of Political Economy* 113 (2005): 1307–40.

Coase, Ronald. "The Problem of Social Cost." *Journal of Law and Economics* 3 (1960): 1–44.

Coleman, Jules L. *Markets, Morals and the Law*. New York: Oxford University Press, 1988.

———. *Risks and Wrongs*. New York: Oxford University Press, 1992.

Cole, Sarah R., and Kristen M. Blankley. "Empirical Research on Consumer Arbitration: What the Data Reveals." *Penn State Law Review* 113 (2009): 1051–78.

"A Conflict of Interest?" *The Economist*, October 14, 2010. http://www.economist.com/node/17257817.

Consumer Financial Protection Bureau. "Arbitration Study Preliminary Results." Section 1028(a) Study Results. Washington, DC: Consumer Financial Protection Bureau, December 12, 2013.

Cooter, Robert. "Unity in Tort, Contract, and Property: The Model of Precaution." *California Law Review* 73 (1985): 1–51.

Cooter, Robert, and Ariel Porat. "Anti-Insurance." *Journal of Legal Studies* 31 (2002): 203.

Cooter, Robert, and Thomas Ulen. *Law and Economics*. 6th ed. Boston: Pearson/Addison Wesley, 2012.

Coppola, Francis Ford, dir. *The Godfather*. Paramount Pictures, 1972.

Cottrell, Allin, and W. Paul Cockshott. "Calculation, Complexity and Planning: The Socialist Calculation Debate Once Again." *Review of Political Economy* 5, no. 1 (1993): 73–112.

Craswell, Richard. "Contract Law, Default Rules, and the Philosophy of Promising," *Michigan Law Review* 89 (1989): 489–529.

———. "Contract Remedies, Renegotiation, and the Theory of Efficient Breach." *Southern California Law Review* 61 (1988): 629–70.

Crawford, Darryl. "Chinese Capitalism: Cultures, the Southeast Asian Region and Economic Globalisation." *Third World Quarterly* 21, no. 1 (2000): 69–86.

Dasgupta, Susmita, Benoit Laplante, Hua Wang, and David Wheeler. "Confronting the Environmental Kuznets Curve." *Journal of Economic Perspectives* 16, no. 1 (Winter 2002): 147–68.

Davidson, Robert. *Genesis 12–50*. Cambridge: Cambridge University Press, 1979.

Defoe, Daniel. *Robinson Crusoe*. Edited by John Richetti. London: Penguin Classics, 2003.

Delacroix, Jacques, and François Nielsen. "The Beloved Myth: Protestantism and the Rise of Industrial Capitalism in Nineteenth-Century Europe." *Social Forces* 80, no. 2 (December 1, 2001): 509–53.

Dellinger, Myanna. "J. Greeley McGowin, 80 Years Ago." *ContractsProf Blog*, September 1, 2005. http://lawprofessors.typepad.com/contractsprof_blog/2005/09/j_greeley_mcgow.html.

De Soto, Hernando. *The Mystery of Capital: Why Capitalism Triumphs in the West and Fails Everywhere Else*. Repr. ed. New York: Basic Books, 2003.

Diamond, Jared. *Guns, Germs, and Steel*. New York: W. W. Norton, 1997.

Dickens, Charles. *A Christmas Carol and Other Christmas Books*. Edited by Robert Douglas-Fairhurst. New York: Oxford University Press, 2006.

Dickman, A. J. "Complexities of Conflict: The Importance of Considering Social Factors for Effectively Resolving Human–Wildlife Conflict." *Animal Conservation* 13, no. 5 (2010): 458–66.

Dixit, Avinash. *Lawlessness and Economics: Alternative Modes of Governance*. Princeton, NJ: Princeton University Press, 2004.

Doepke, Matthias, Michèle Tertilt, and Alessandra Voena. "The Economics and Politics of Women's Rights." SSRN Scholarly Paper. Rochester, NY: Social Science Research Network, December 1, 2011. http://papers.ssrn.com/abstract=1973883.

Donald, David Herbert. *Charles Sumner*. New York: Da Capo Press, 1996.

Dougherty, Frank. "Buildup Is on for Sears Blast." *Philly.com*, October 14, 1994. http://articles.philly.com/1994-10-14/news/25875038_1_plunger-implosion-roosevelt-boulevard.

Drelichman, Mauricio, and Hans-Joachim Voth. *Lending to the Borrower from Hell: Debt, Taxes, and Default in the Age of Philip II*. Princeton, NJ: Princeton University Press, 2014.

Dunn, Richard S. *Sugar and Slaves: The Rise of the Planter Class in the English West Indies, 1624–1713*. Chapel Hill: University of North Carolina Press, 1972.

Dworkin, Ronald. *A Matter of Principle*. Cambridge, MA: Harvard University Press, 1985.

———. "The Original Position." In *Reading Rawls: Critical Studies on Rawls' A Theory of Justice*, edited by Norman Daniels, 16–52. Stanford, CA: Stanford University Press, 1989.

———. "Why Efficiency?" *Hofstra Law Review* 8 (1979): 563–90.

Easterly, William. *The White Man's Burden: Why the West's Efforts to Aid the Rest Have Done So Much Ill and So Little Good*. New York: Penguin Press, 2006.

Eberhard, Mary Jane West. "The Evolution of Social Behavior by Kin Selection." *Quarterly Review of Biology* 50, no. 1 (March 1, 1975): 1–33.

Edlin, Aaron S. "Cadillac Contracts and Up-front Payments: Efficient Investment under Expectation Damages." *Journal of Law, Economics and Organization* 12 (1996): 98–118.

Edlin, Aaron S., and Stefan Reichelstein. "Holdups, Standard Breach Remedies, and Optimal Investment." *American Economic Review* 86, no. 3 (June 1, 1996): 478–501.

Eisenberg, Melvin A. "Actual and Virtual Specific Performance, the Theory of Efficient Breach, and the Indifference Principle in Contract Law." *California Law Review* 93 (2005): 975–1050.

———. "The Limits of Cognition and the Limits of Contract." *Stanford Law Review* 47 (1995): 211–59.

Eisenberg, Theodore, Geoffrey P. Miller, and Emily Sherwin. "Arbitration's Summer Soldiers: An Empirical Study of Arbitration Clauses in Consumer and Nonconsumer Contracts." *University of Michigan Journal of Law Reform* 41 (2008): 871–96.

Elliott, Binns L. *The Book of the Prophet Jeremiah: With Introduction and Notes.* Westminister Commentaries. London: Methuen, 1919.

Ephron, Nora, dir. *You've Got Mail.* Warner Brothers, 1998.

Epstein, Richard A. "Contracts Small and Contract Large: Contract Law through the Lens of Laissez-faire." In *The Fall and Rise of Freedom of Contract*, edited by F. H Buckley, 25–61. Durham, NC: Duke University Press, 1999.

———. *Forbidden Grounds: The Case against Employment Discrimination Laws.* Cambridge, MA: Harvard University Press, 1995.

———. *Takings: Private Property and the Power of Eminent Domain.* Cambridge, MA: Harvard University Press, 1985.

Equal Employment Opportunity Commission. *The Legislative History of the Civil Rights Act of 1964.* Washington, DC: U.S. Government Printing Office, 1968.

"Ethiopia." World Bank, Washington, DC, n.d. http://data.worldbank.org/country/ethiopia.

Falk, Ze'ev W. *Hebrew Law in Biblical Times: An Introduction.* 2nd ed. Provo, UT: Brigham Young University Press, 2001.

Farber, Daniel A., and Philip P. Frickey. *Law and Public Choice: A Critical Introduction.* Chicago: University of Chicago Press, 1991.

Farber, Daniel A., and John H. Matheson. "Beyond Promissory Estoppel: Contract Law and the 'Invisible Handshake.'" *University of Chicago Law Review* 52 (1985): 903–47.

Farnsworth, E. Allan. *Farnsworth on Contracts.* 3rd ed. Vol. 1. 3 vols. New York: Wolters Kluwer Law & Business, 2004.

———. *Farnsworth on Contracts.* 3rd ed. Vol. 3. 3 vols. Boston: Wolters Kluwer, 2004.

Fay, C. R. *Adam Smith and the Scotland of His Day.* New York: Cambridge University Press, 1956.

Fensham, F. Charles. "Malediction and Benediction in Ancient Near Eastern Vassal-Treaties and the Old Testament." *Zeitschrift fur Alttestamentliche Wissenschaft*, 74 (1962): 1–9.

Ferguson, Niall. *The Cash Nexus: Money and Power in the Modern World, 1700–2000*. New York: Basic Books, 2001.

———. *Civilization: The West and the Rest*. 1st ed. New York: Penguin Press, 2011.

Field, Hugh J., and Erick De Clercq. "Anti-Viral Drugs: A Short History of Their Discovery and Development." *Microbiology Today* 31 (2004): 58–61.

Field, Martha A. "Compensated Surrogacy." *Washington Law Review* 89 (2014): 1155–84.

Fischoff, Ephraim. "The Protestant Ethic and the Spirit of Capitalism: The History of a Controversy." *Social Research* 11, no. 1 (February 1, 1944): 53–77.

Fogel, Robert William, and Stanley L. Engerman. *Time on the Cross: The Economics of American Slavery*. Reissue ed. New York: W. W. Norton, 2013.

Foundation for AIDS Research. "World-Wide Statistics." New York: amfAR, July 2015. http://www.amfar.org/about-hiv-and-aids/facts-and-stats/statistics--worldwide/.

Freeman, Joanne B. *Affairs of Honor: National Politics in the New Republic*. New Haven, CT: Yale Nota Bene, 2002.

Fried, Charles. *Contract as Promise: A Theory of Contractual Obligation*. Cambridge, MA: Harvard University Press, 1981.

Friedman, Benjamin M. *The Moral Consequences of Economic Growth*. New York: Knopf, 2005.

Friedman, Lawrence M. *Contract Law in America: A Social and Economic Case Study*. Repr. ed. New Orleans, LA: Quid Pro Books, 2011.

Friedman, Milton. "The Social Responsibility of Business Is to Pursue Profits." *New York Times Magazine*, September 13, 1970.

Frost, Robert, "Mending Wall." In *The Poetry of Robert Frost*, edited by Edward Connery Lathem, 33–34. New York: Holt, Rinehart & Winston, 1969.

Fukuyama, Francis. *The Origins of Political Order: From Prehuman Times to the French Revolution*. New York: Farrar, Straus and Giroux, 2011.

———. *Political Order and Political Decay: From the Industrial Revolution to the Globalization of Democracy*. New York: Farrar, Straus and Giroux, 2014.

———. *Trust: The Social Virtues and the Creation of Prosperity*. 1st ed. New York: Free Press, 1996.

Fuller, L. L., and William R. Perdue. "The Reliance Interest in Contract Damages, Pt. 1." *Yale Law Journal* 46 (1936): 52–96.

———. "The Reliance Interest in Contract Damages, Pt. 2." *Yale Law Journal* 46 (1936): 373–420.

Fuller, Lon L. *The Morality of Law*. Rev. ed. New Haven, CT: Yale University Press, 1969.

Gardner, George K. "An Inquiry into the Principles of the Law of Contracts." *Harvard Law Review* 46 (1932): 1–43.

George, Robert P. *In Defense of Natural Law*. Oxford: Clarendon Press, 1993.

Gillette, Clayton. “Pre-Approved Contracts for Internet Commerce.” *Houston Law Review* 42 (2005): 975–1013.

Gilmore, Grant. *The Death of Contract*. Columbus: Ohio State University Press, 1995.

Glickman, Lawrence B. “Chick-fil-A Day a Reminder That Boycotts Often Backfire.” *Bloomberg*, August 3, 2012. http://www.bloomberg.com/news/2012-08-03/chick-fil-a-day-a-reminder-that-boycotts-often-backfire.html.

Goetz, Charles J., and Robert E. Scott. “Enforcing Promises: An Examination of the Basis of Contract.” *Yale Law Journal* 89, no. 7 (1980): 1261–1322.

———. “The Mitigation Principle: Toward a General Theory of Contractual Obligation.” *Virginia Law Review* 69 (1983): 967–1024.

Gold, Andrew. “A Property Theory of Contract.” *Northwestern University Law Review* 103 (2009): 1–62.

Goldberg, John C. P. “The Constitutional Status of Tort Law: Due Process and the Right to a Law for the Redress of Wrongs.” *Yale Law Journal* 115 (2005): 524–627.

Goldberg, John C. P., and Benjamin Zipursky. “Torts as Wrongs.” *Texas Law Review* 88 (2010): 917–86.

Goldberg, Victor P. “Bloomer Girl Revisited or How to Frame an Unmade Picture.” *Wisconsin Law Review* 1998 (1998): 1051–84.

Gordley, James. “Contract.” In *The Oxford Handbook of Legal Studies*, edited by Peter Cane and Mark Tushnet. New York: Oxford University Press, 2003.

———. *The Philosophical Origins of Modern Contract Doctrine*. New York: Oxford University Press, 1993.

Gorla, Gino. “Standard Conditions and Form Contracts in Italian Law.” *American Journal of Comparative Law* 11 (1962): 1–20.

Graeber, David. *Debt: The First 5,000 Years*. London: Melville House, 2012.

Green, Sonia Bychkov. “Interstate Intercourse: How Modern Assisted Reproductive Technologies Challenge the Traditional Realm of Conflicts of Law.” *Wisconsin Journal of Law, Gender and Society* 24, no. 1 (Spring 2009): 25–115.

Grindley, Lucas. “Angry Alderman Again Threatens to Stop Chick-fil-A from Expanding to Chicago Neighborhood.” *Advocate.com*, September 23, 2012. http://www.advocate.com/business/2012/09/23/angry-alderman-again-threatens-stop-chick-fil-expanding-chicago-neighborhood.

Grossman, Gene M., and Alan B. Krueger. “Economic Growth and the Environment.” *Quarterly Journal of Economics* 110, no. 2 (May 1995): 353–77.

Haidt, Jonathan. *The Righteous Mind: Why Good People Are Divided by Politics and Religion*. 1st ed. New York: Pantheon, 2012.

Hamilton, Alexander, John Jay, and James Madison. *The Federalist: A Commentary on the Constitution of the United States*. Edited by Robert Scigliano. New York: Modern Library, 2001.

Hansen, Randall. *Fire and Fury: The Allied Bombing of Germany 1942–1945*. New York: Doubleday, 2008.

Hardy, M. L. J. *Blood Feuds and the Payment of Blood Money in the Middle East.* Beirut: Catholic Press, 1963.

Hargrove, Dan L. "Soldiers of *Qui Tam* Fortune: Do Military Service Members Have Standing to File *Qui Tam* Actions under the False Claims Act?" *Public Contract Law Journal* 34, no. 1 (Fall 2004): 45–97.

Hart, H. L. A. "American Jurisprudence through English Eyes: The Nightmare and the Noble Dream." *Georgia Law Review* 11 (1977): 969–90.

Harwell Wells, C. A. "The End of the Affair? Anti-Dueling Laws and Social Norms in Antebellum America." *Vanderbilt Law Review* 54 (2001): 1805–47.

Hausman, Daniel M, and Michael S. McPherson. *Economic Analysis, Moral Philosophy and Public Policy*. Cambridge: Cambridge University Press, 2006.

Hayek, F. A. "The Use of Knowledge in Society." *American Economic Review* 35, no. 4 (1945): 519–30.

Henrich, Joseph. "Does Culture Matter in Economic Behavior? Ultimatum Game Bargaining among the Machiguenga of the Peruvian Amazon." *American Economic Review* 90, no. 4 (2000): 973–79.

Henrich, Joseph, Robert Boyd, Samuel Bowles, Colin Camerer, Ernst Fehr, Herbert Gintis, and Richard McElreath. "In Search of Homo Economicus: Behavioral Experiments in 15 Small-Scale Societies." *American Economic Review* 91, no. 2 (2001): 73–78.

Henrich, Joseph, Robert Boyd, Colin Camerer, Ernst Fehr, Richard McElreath, M. Alvard, J. Ensminger, et al. " 'Economic Man' in Cross-Cultural Perspective: Behavioral Experiments in 15 Small-Scale Societies." *Behavioral and Brain Science* 28, no. 6 (2005): 795–815.

Herget, James E. *American Jurisprudence, 1870–1970: A History*. Houston: Rice University Press, 1990.

Herodotus. *The Histories*. Translated by C. C. Macaulay. New York: Barnes & Noble Classics, 2004.

Hillman, Robert A. "Contract Lore." *Journal of Corporation Law* 27 (2002): 505–18.

———. "Limits of Behavioral Decision Theory in Legal Analysis: The Case of Liquidated Damages." *Cornell Law Review* 85, no. 3 (March 2000): 717–38.

———. "Online Consumer Standard Form Contracting Practices: A Survey and Discussion of Legal Implications." In *Consumer Protection in the Age of the "Information Economy,"* edited by Jane K. Winn, 283–312. Aldershot, UK: Ashgate Publishing, 2006.

Hillman, Robert A., and Maureen A. O'Rourke. "Principles of the Law of Software Contracts: Some Highlights." *Tulane Law Review* 84 (2010): 1519–39.

Hillman, Robert A., and Jeffrey J. Rachlinski. "Standard Form Contracting in the Electronic Age." *New York University Law Review* 77 (2002): 429–95.

Hilton, F. G. Hank, and Arik Levinson. "Factoring Environmental Kuznets Curve: Evidence from Automotive Lead Emissions." *Journal of Environmental Economics and Management* 35 (1998): 126–41.

Hirschman, Albert O. *Exit, Voice, and Loyalty: Responses to Decline in Firms, Organizations, and States*. Cambridge, MA: Harvard University Press, 1970.

———. *The Passions and the Interests: Political Arguments for Capitalism before Its Triumph*. Princeton, NJ: Princeton University Press, 1977.

Hobbes, Thomas. *Hobbes: Leviathan: Revised Student Edition*. Edited by Richard Tuck. New York: Cambridge University Press, 1996.

Hobson, J. A. *Imperialism: A Study*. New York: Cosimo Classics, 2005.

Hodgson, Marshall G. S. *The Venture of Islam, Volume 1: The Classical Age of Islam*. Chicago: University of Chicago Press, 1974.

Holmes, Oliver Wendell. *The Common Law*. Edited by Mark DeWolfe Howe. Boston: Little, Brown, 1993.

Homer. *The Iliad*. Repr. ed. New York: Penguin Books, 1991.

Horton, David. "Unconscionability Wars." *Northwestern University Law Review* 106 (2012): 387–408.

Hovenkamp, Herbert. *Enterprise and American Law: 1836–1937*. Cambridge, MA: Harvard University Press, 1991.

———. "Rationality in Law and Economics." *George Washington Law Review* 60, no. 2 (January 1992): 293–338.

Hume, David. *Hume: Political Essays*. Edited by Knud Haakonssen. New York: Cambridge University Press, 1994.

Hyde, Dominic. "Sorites Paradox." In *The Stanford Encyclopedia of Philosophy, edited by Edward N. Zalta*. Stanford, CA: Metaphysics Research Lab, Winter 2011. http://plato.stanford.edu/archives/win2011/entries/sorites-paradox/.

Ibbetson, David. *A Historical Introduction to the Law of Obligations*. New York: Oxford University Press, 1999.

Isaacs, Nathan. "The Standardizing of Contracts." *Yale Law Journal* 27 (1917): 34–48.

Johnson, M. Alex. "Southern Baptists End 8-Year Disney Boycott." *Msnbc.com*, June 22, 2005.

Jonaitis, Aldona, ed. *Chiefly Feasts: The Enduring Kwakiutl Potlatch*. Seattle: University of Washington Press, 1991.

Jones, David. *The Bankers of Puteoli: Finance, Trade and Industry in the Roman World*. Stroud, UK: Tempus, 2006.

Kahn, Matthew E. "A Household Level Environmental Kuznets Curve." *Economics Letters* 59, no. 2 (1998): 269–73.

Kaplow, Louis, and Steven Shavell. *Fairness versus Welfare*. Cambridge, MA: Harvard University Press, 2002.

Karavenic, Ivor, and Fred H. Smith. "The Middle/Upper Paleolithic Interface and the Relationship of Neanderthals and Early Modern Humans in the Hrvatsko Zagorje, Croatia." *Journal of Human Evolution* 34 (1998): 223–48.

Karlfeldt, Erik Axel. "Award Ceremony Speech." Presentation speech presented at the Nobel Prize in Literature 1930, December 10, 1930. http://www.nobelprize.org/nobel_prizes/literature/laureates/1930/press.html.

Katz, Avery. "Your Terms or Mine? The Duty to Read Fine Print in Contracts." *RAND Journal of Economics* 21 (1990): 518–37.

Kelly, Michael B. "The Phantom Reliance Interest in Contract Damages." *Wisconsin Law Review* 1992 (1992): 1755–1846.

Kennedy, David M. *Freedom from Fear: The American People in Depression and War 1929–1945*. New York: Oxford University Press, 1999.

Kennedy, Duncan. "Distributive and Paternalist Motives in Contract and Tort Law, with Special Reference to Compulsory Terms and Unequal Bargaining Power." *Maryland Law Review* 41 (1982): 563–658.

———. "Form and Substance in Private Law Adjudication." *Harvard Law Review* 89 (1976): 1685–1778.

———. "The Stages of the Decline of the Public/Private Distinction." *University of Pennsylvania Law Review* 130 (1982): 1349–57.

Kennedy, Randall. "Martin Luther King's Constitution: A Legal History of the Montgomery Bus Boycott." *Yale Law Journal* 98 (1989): 999–1067.

Kessler, Friedrich. "Contracts of Adhesion—Some Thoughts about Freedom of Contract." *Columbia Law Review* 43 (1943): 629–42.

Keynes, John Maynard. *The General Theory of Employment, Interest, and Money*. New York: Harcourt Brace, 1935.

Kimel, Dori. *From Promise to Contract: Towards a Liberal Theory of Contract*. Portland, OR: Hart, 2005.

Kim, Nancy S. *Wrap Contracts: Foundations and Ramifications*. New York: Oxford University Press, 2013.

King, Martin Luther, Jr. "I Have a Dream," August 23, 1963. The Avalon Project, Yale Law School. http://avalon.law.yale.edu/20th_century/mlk01.asp.

Klein, Herbert S. *The Atlantic Slave Trade*. 2nd ed. New Approaches to the Americas. New York: Cambridge University Press, 2010.

Kornhauser, Lewis A. "Reliance, Reputation, and Breach of Contract." *Journal of Law and Economics* 26, no. 3 (October 1, 1983): 691–706.

Korobkin, Russell. "Behavioral Economics, Contract Formation, and Contract Law." In *Behavioral Law and Economics*, edited by Cass R. Sunstein, 116–43. New York: Cambridge University Press, 2000.

———. "Bounded Rationality, Standard Form Contracts, and Unconscionability." *University of Chicago Law Review* 70 (2003): 1203–95.

Kraus, Jody S. "Legal Theory and Contract Law: Groundwork for the Reconciliation of Autonomy and Efficiency." *Social, Political, and Legal Philosophy* 1 (2002): 385–446.

———. "Philosophy of Contract Law." In *The Oxford Handbook of Jurisprudence and Philosophy of Law*, edited by Jules L. Coleman and Scott J. Shapiro, 815–67. New York: Oxford University Press, 2002.

———. "Reconciling Autonomy and Efficiency in Contract Law: The Vertical Integration Strategy." *Noûs* 35 (January 1, 2001): 420–41.

Kreitner, Roy. *Calculating Promises: The Emergence of Modern American Contract Doctrine*. Stanford, CA: Stanford University Press, 2007.

———. "Multiple Markets and the Justification of Contract." *Iowa Law Review Bulletin* 98 (2013): 20–27.

Kronman, Anthony T. "Paternalism and the Law of Contracts." *Yale Law Journal* 92 (1983): 763–97.

Kuran, Timur. "The Economic Roots of Political Underdevelopment in the Middle East: A Historical Perspective." *Southern Economic Journal* 78, no. 4 (April 1, 2012): 1086–95.

———. "The Islamic Commercial Crisis: Institutional Roots of Economic Underdevelopment in the Middle East." *Journal of Economic History* 63, no. 2 (June 1, 2003): 414–46.

———. *The Long Divergence: How Islamic Law Held Back the Middle East*. Princeton, NJ: Princeton University Press, 2011.

———. "Why the Middle East Is Economically Underdeveloped: Historical Mechanisms of Institutional Stagnation." *Journal of Economic Perspectives* 18, no. 3 (July 1, 2004): 71–90.

Kuznets, Simon. "Economic Growth and Income Inequality." *American Economic Review* 45, no. 1 (March 1, 1955): 1–28.

LaCroix, Alison L. "To Gain the Whole World and Lose His Own Soul: Nineteenth-Century American Dueling as Public Law and Private Code." *Hofstra Law Review* 33 (2004): 501–69.

Lambert, Emily. *The Futures: The Rise of the Speculator and the Origins of the World's Biggest Markets*. New York: Basic Books, 2010.

Landes, David S. *The Wealth and Poverty of Nations: Why Some Are So Rich and Some So Poor*. New York: W. W. Norton, 1999.

Langbein, John H. "The German Advantage in Civil Procedure." *University of Chicago Law Review* 52 (1985): 823–66.

Laycock, Douglas. *Modern American Remedies: Cases and Materials*. 4th ed. New York: Aspen Publishers, 2010.

Leeson, Peter T. "Ordeals." *Journal of Law and Economics* 55, no. 3 (August 1, 2012): 691–714.

Lefebve, Lous. "Food Exchange Strategies in an Infant Chimpanzee." *Journal of Human Evolution* 11, no. 3 (1982): 195–204.

Leff, Arthur Allen. "Unconscionability and the Code—The Emperor's New Clause." *University of Pennsylvania Law Review* 115 (1967): 485–559.

Lemley, Mark A. "Terms of Use." *Minnesota Law Review* 91 (2006): 459–83.

Levinson, Arik. "The Ups and Downs of the Environmental Kuznets Curve." Orlando, FL: UCF/Centre Conference on the Environment, 2000.

Lewis, Bernard. *Semites and Anti-Semites: An Inquiry into Conflict and Prejudice*. New York: W. W. Norton, 1999.

Lewis, Sinclair. *Babbitt*. New York: Harcourt Brace, 1922.

Lincoln, Abraham. "Second Inaugural Address." March 4, 1865. The Avalon Project, Yale Law School. http://avalon.law.yale.edu/19th_century/lincoln2.asp.

Lindert, Peter H., and Jeffery G. Williamson. "English Workers' Living Standard During the Industrial Revolution: A New Look." *Economic History Review* 36 (1983): 1–25.

Lindholm, Charles. *Generosity and Jealousy: The Swat Pukhtun of Northern Pakistan*. New York: Columbia University Press, 1982.

Llewellyn, Karl N. "Book Review." *Harvard Law Review* 52 (1939): 700–705.

———. *The Common Law Tradition: Deciding Appeals*. New York: Little, Brown, 1960.

———. "What Price Contract? An Essay in Perspective." *Yale Law Journal* 40 (1931): 704–51.

Locke, John. *Two Treaties of Government*. Edited by Peter Laslett. New York: Cambridge University Press, 1989.

Löe, Jonny, and Eivin Röskaft. "Large Carnivores and Human Safety: A Review." *AMBIO: A Journal of the Human Environment* 33, no. 6 (August 1, 2004): 283–88.

Lowry, Todd S. "Lord Mansfield and the Law Merchant: Law and Economics in the Eighteenth Century." *Journal of Economic Issues* 7, no. 4 (1973): 605–22.

Lusthaus, Varda. "Standard Contracts in Israel: New Developments." *Rabels Zeitschrift Für Ausländisches Und Internationales Privatrecht/The Rabel Journal of Comparative and International Private Law* 54, no. 3 (January 1, 1990): 551–78.

Lyons, David. "Liberty and Harm to Others." *Canadian Journal of Philosophy* 5 (1979): 1–19.

Macaulay, Stewart. "Non-Contractual Relations in Business: A Preliminary Study." *American Sociological Review* 28 (1963): 55–67.

MacCulloch, Diarmaid. *The Reformation: A History*. New York: Viking, 2004.

Macedo, Stephen. *Liberal Virtues: Citizenship, Virtue, and Community in Liberal Constitutionalism*. New York: Oxford University Press, 1990.

Machovec, Frank. *Perfect Competition and the Transformation of Economics*. New York: Routledge, 1995.

MacKinnon, Catharine A. *Only Words*. Cambridge, MA: Harvard University Press, 1993.

MacNeil, Ian. *The Relational Theory of Contract: Selected Works of Ian MacNeil*. Edited by David Campbell. London: Sweet & Maxwell, 2001.

Maddison, Angus. *Contours of the World Economy 1–2030 A.D.: Essays in Macro-Economic History*. New York: Oxford University Press, 2007.

———. *Monitoring the World Economy, 1820–1992*. Washington, DC: Development Centre of the Organisation for Economic Co-operation and Development, 1995.

"The Magic of Diasporas: Immigrant Networks Are a Rare Bright Spark in the World Economy. Rich Countries Should Welcome Them." *The Economist*, November 19, 2011. http://www.economist.com/node/21538742.

Maine, Sir Henry Sumner. *Ancient Law*. 4th American ed. New York: Henry Holt, 1906.

Markovits, Daniel. "Contract and Collaboration." *Yale Law Journal* 113 (2004): 1417–1518.

———. "Making and Keeping Contracts." *Virginia Law Review* 92 (2006): 1325–74.

———. "Promise as an Arm's-Length Relation." In *Promises and Agreements: Philosophical Essays*, edited by Hanoch Sheinman, 295–326. New York: Oxford University Press, 2011.

Marlowe, Christopher. *Doctor Faustus and Other Plays*. Edited by David Bevington and Eric Rasmussen. New York: Oxford University Press, 2008.

Marotta-Wurgler, Florencia. "Are 'Pay, Now Terms Later' Contracts Worse for Buyers? Evidence from Software License Agreements." *Journal of Legal Studies* 38 (2009): 309–43.

———. "'Unfair' Dispute Resolution Clauses: Much Ado About Nothing?" In *Boilerplate: The Foundation of Market Contracts*, edited by Omri Ben-Shahar, 45–65. New York: Cambridge University Press, 2007.

———. "What's in a Standard Form Contract? An Empirical Analysis of Software License Agreements." *Journal of Empirical Legal Studies* 4 (2007): 677–713.

———. "Will Increased Disclosure Help? Evaluating the Recommendations of the ALI's 'Principles of the Law of Software Contracts.'" *University of Chicago Law Review* 78 (2011): 165–86.

Marx, Karl. *Capital: A Critique of Political Economy*. Edited by Friedrich Engels. New York: Cosimo Classics, 2013.

Masugi, Ken. "Race, the Rule of Law, and the Merchant of Venice: From Slavery to Citizenship." *Notre Dame Journal of Law, Ethics and Public Policy* 11 (1997): 197–224.

Mattei, Ugo. "The Comparative Law and Economics of Penalty Clauses in Contracts." *American Journal of Comparative Law* 43 (1995): 427–44.

Mayer, David N. *Liberty of Contract: Rediscovering a Lost Constitutional Right*. Washington, DC: Cato Institute, 2011.

McBrearty, Sally, and Alison S. Brooks. "The Revolution That Wasn't: A New Interpretation of the Origin of Modern Human Behavior." *Journal of Human Evolution* 39 (2000): 453–563.

McCloskey, Deirdre N. *Bourgeois Dignity: Why Economics Can't Explain the Modern World*. Chicago: University of Chicago Press, 2010.

McPherson, Edward. *The Political History of the United States of America during the Period of Reconstruction*. 2nd ed. Washington, DC: Solomons & Chapman, 1875.

Meador, Patricia, and Elizabeth S. Warren. "False Claims Act: A Civil War Relic Evolves into a Modern Weapon." *Tennessee Law Review* 65, no. 2 (Winter 1998): 455–83.

Medina, Barak, and Eyal Zamir. *Law, Economics, and Morality*. New York: Oxford University Press, 2010.

Miguel, Edward. "Poverty and Witch Killing." *Review of Economic Studies* 72, no. 4 (2005): 1153–72.

Miller, William. *Bloodtaking and Peacemaking*. Chicago: University of Chicago Press, 1990.

———. *Eye for an Eye*. New York: Cambridge University Press, 2005.

Mill, John Stuart. *On Liberty*. Mineola, NY: Dover Publications, 2002.

Montesquieu, Charles de Secondat. *The Spirit of the Laws*. Edited by Anne Myers Cohler, Basia Carolyn Miller, and Harold Samuel Stone. Cambridge Texts in the History of Political Thought. Cambridge: Cambridge University Press, 1989.

Morgan, Edmund. *The Stamp Act Crisis: Prologue to Revolution*. Chapel Hill: University of North Carolina Press, 1953.

Mulhall, Stephen, and Adam Swift. *Liberals and Communitarians*. Cambridge, MA: Blackwell, 1992.

Nathan, Daniel A. *Saying It's So: A Cultural History of the Black Sox Scandal*. Urbana: University of Illinois Press, 2003.

Nelson, William Edward. *The Common Law in Colonial America*. New York: Oxford University Press, 2008.

Nicholas, Barry. *An Introduction to Roman Law*. Oxford: Clarendon Press, 1962.

Noonan, John Thomas. *The Scholastic Analysis of Usury*. Cambridge, MA: Harvard University Press, 1957.

North, Douglass C. *Understanding the Process of Economic Change. Princeton Economic History of the Western World.* Princeton, NJ: Princeton University Press, 2005.

North, Douglass C., John Joseph Wallis, and Barry R. Weingast. *Violence and Social Orders: A Conceptual Framework for Interpreting Recorded Human History*. New York: Cambridge University Press, 2009.

Nozick, Robert. "Coercion." In *Socratic Puzzles*, 15–44. Cambridge, MA: Harvard University Press, 1997.

Nussbaum, Martha Craven. *Liberty of Conscience: In Defense of America's Tradition of Religious Equality*. Princeton, NJ: Basic Books, 2008.

Obama, Barack. "A New Era of Service: Speech at the University of Colorado, Colorado Springs." *Rocky Mountain News*, July 2, 2008.

O'Connor, Timothy. "Free Will." In *The Stanford Encyclopedia of Philosophy*, edited by Edward N. Zalta. Stanford, CA: Metaphysics Research Lab, Fall 2014. http://plato.stanford.edu/archives/fall2014/entries/freewill/.

Olson, Mancur. *The Logic of Collective Action: Public Goods and the Theory of Groups*. Cambridge, MA: Harvard University Press, 1971.

Oman, Nathan B. "Bargaining in the Shadow of God's Law: Islamic Mahr Contracts and the Perils of Legal Specialization." *Wake Forest Law Review* 45 (2010): 579–606.

———. "Consent to Retaliation: A Civil Recourse Theory of Contractual Liability." *Iowa Law Review* 96 (2011): 529–79.

———. "Corporations and Autonomy Theories of Contract: A Critique of the *New Lex Mercatoria*." *Denver University Law Review* 83, no. 1 (2005): 101–45.

———. "The Failure of Economic Interpretations of the Law of Contract Damages." *Washington and Lee Law Review* 64 (2007): 829–75.

———. "The Honor of Private Law." *Fordham Law Review* 80 (2011): 31–71.

———. "How to Judge Sharia Contracts: A Guide to Islamic Marriage Agreements in American Courts." *Utah Law Review* 2011 (2011): 287–334.

———. "Markets as a Moral Foundation for Contract Law." *Iowa Law Review* 98 (2012): 183–230.

———. "A Pragmatic Defense of Contract Law." *Georgetown Law Journal* 98 (2009): 77–116.

———. "Promise and Private Law." *Suffolk University Law Review* 45 (2012): 935–60.

———. "Unity and Pluralism in Contract Law." *Michigan Law Review* 103 (2005): 1483–1506.

———. "Why There Is No Duty to Pay Damages: Powers, Duties, and Private Law." *Florida State Law Review* 39 (2011): 137–161.

Osborne, D. K. "Cartel Problems." *American Economic Review* 66, no. 5 (December 1, 1976): 835–44.

Oster, Emily. "Witchcraft, Weather and Economic Growth in Renaissance Italy." *Journal of Economic Perspectives* 18, no. 1 (2004): 215–28.

Ostertag, Thomas J. "Baseball's Antitrust Exemption: Its History and Continuing Importance." *Virginia Sports and Entertainment Law Journal* 4 (2004): 54–67.

O'Sullivan, Janet. "In Defense of Foakes v. Beer." *Cambridge Law Journal* 55, no. 2 (1996): 219–28.

Partnoy, Frank. "The Siskel and Ebert of Financial Markets? Two Thumbs Down for the Credit Rating Agencies." *Washington University Law Quarterly* 77 (1999): 619–712.

Pennock, J. Roland, and John W. Chapman, eds. *Coercion*. Nomos 14. Chicago: Aldine-Atherton, 1972.

Perillo, Joseph M. *Calamari and Perillo on Contracts*. 6th ed. Hornbook Series. St. Paul, MN: Thomson/West, 2009.

Pettigrew, William A. *Freedom's Debt: The Royal African Company and the Politics of the Atlantic Slave Trade, 1672–1752*. Chapel Hill: University of North Carolina Press, 2013.

———. "Free to Enslave: Politics and the Escalation of Britain's Transatlantic Slave Trade, 1688–1714." *William and Mary Quarterly*, Third Series, 64, no. 1 (January 1, 2007): 3–38.

"Photo Journal: Ethiopian Wood Collector." *BBC News*, n.d. http://news.bbc.co.uk/2/shared/spl/hi/picture_gallery/04/africa_ethiopian_wood_collector/html/1.stm.

Pigou, Arthur Cecil. *The Economics of Welfare*. Palgrave Classics in Economics. New York: Palgrave Macmillan, 2013.

Plato. *The Republic of Plato*. Translated by Allan David Bloom. 2nd ed. New York: Basic Books, 1991.

Plutarch. "Crassus." In *Plutarch's Lives*. Edited by Arthur Hugh Clough. Translated by John Dryden and James Atlas. Vol. 1. New York: Modern Library, 2001.

Polinsky, A. Mitchell. *Introduction to Law and Economics*. 2nd ed. Boston: Little, Brown Law and Business, 1989.

Polinsky, A. Mitchell, and Yeon-Koo Che. "Decoupling Liability: Optimal Incentives for Care and Litigation." *RAND Journal of Economics* 22, no. 4 (December 1, 1991): 562–70. doi:10.2307/2600989.

Pollock, Frederick, and Frederic William Maitland. *The History of English Law: Before the Time of Edward I*. 2nd ed. Cambridge University Press, 1968.

Polo, Michele. "Internal Cohesion and Competition among Criminal Organisations." In *The Economics of Organized Crime*, edited by Gianluca Fiorentini and Sam Peltzman, 87–109. New York: Cambridge University Press, 1995.

Posner, Eric A. "Altruism, Status, and Trust in the Law of Gifts and Gratuitous Promises." *Wisconsin Law Review* 1997 (1997): 567–600.

———. "A Theory of Contract Law under Conditions of Radical Judicial Error." *Northwestern University Law Review* 94 (2000): 749–74.

Posner, Richard A. *Economic Analysis of Law*. 8th ed. New York: Aspen Publishers, 2010.

———. *The Economics of Justice*. Cambridge, MA: Harvard University Press, 1981.

———. "The Problematics of Moral and Legal Theory." *Harvard Law Review* 111 (1998): 1637–1717.

———. "Utilitarianism, Economics, and Legal Theory." *Journal of Legal Studies* 8 (1979): 103–40.

———. *Economic Analysis of Law*. 1st ed. Boston: Little, Brown, 1972.Pratt, Michael. "Contract, Not Promise." *Florida State Law Review* 35 (2008): 801–16.

Priest, George L. "A Theory of the Consumer Product Warranty." *Yale Law Journal* 90, no. 6 (May 1, 1981): 1297–1352.

Public Citizen. "The Arbitration Trap: How Credit Card Companies Ensnare Consumers," September 27, 2007. http://www.citizen.org/documents/ArbitrationTrap.pdf.

Putnam, Robert D, Robert Leonardi, and Raffaella Nanetti. *Making Democracy Work: Civic Traditions in Modern Italy*. Princeton, NJ: Princeton University Press, 1993.

Radin, Margaret Jane. *Boilerplate: The Fine Print, Vanishing Rights, and the Rule of Law*. Princeton, NJ: Princeton University Press, 2012.

———. *Contested Commodities*. Cambridge, MA: Harvard University Press, 1996.

———. "Property and Personhood." *Stanford Law Review* 34 (1982): 957–1015.

Rafique, Shaheel. "Implications of Information Credit for Policy Development in India for Building Inclusive Financial Sectors." *Asia-Pacific Development Journal* 13, no. 1 (2006): 101–27.

Rakoff, Todd D. "Contracts of Adhesion: An Essay in Reconstruction." *Harvard Law Review* 96 (April 1983): 1173–1274.

Rawls, John. "The Idea of Public Reason Revisited." *University of Chicago Law Review* 64 (1997): 765–807.

———. *Political Liberalism*. New York: Columbia University Press, 1993.

———. *A Theory of Justice*. Rev. ed. Cambridge, MA: Belknap Press, 1999.

———. "Two Concepts of Rules." *Philosophical Review* 64, no. 1 (January 1, 1955): 3–32.

Raz, Joseph. "Promises in Morality and Law." *Harvard Law Review* 95 (1982): 916–38.

Rediker, Marcus. *The Slave Ship: A Human History*. New York: Viking, 2007.

Ricardo, David. *The Principles of Political Economy and Taxation*. Mineola, NY: Dover Publications, 2004.

Ridout, Travis N., and Kathleen Searles. "It's My Campaign I'll Cry If I Want To: How and When Campaigns Use Emotional Appeals." *Political Psychology* 32, no. 3 (2011): 439–58.

Rogerson, William P. "Efficient Reliance and Damage Measures for Breach of Contract." *RAND Journal of Economics* 15, no. 1 (April 1, 1984): 39–53.

Ronen, Joshua. "Corporate Audits and How to Fix Them." *Journal of Economic Perspectives* 24, no. 2 (Spring 2010): 189–210.

Rose, David C. *The Moral Foundation of Economic Behavior*. New York: Oxford University Press, 2011.

Rosenberg, Nathan, and L. E. Birdzell. *How the West Grew Rich*. New York: Basic Books, 1987.

Rousseau, Jean-Jacques. *Rousseau: "The Discourses" and Other Early Political Writings*. Edited by Victor Gourevitch. New York: Cambridge University Press, 1997.

R. S. G. "Risk of Loss in Commercial Transactions: Efficiency Thrown into the Breach." *Virginia Law Review* 65, no. 3 (April 1979): 557–72.

Sachs, Jeffrey D. *The End of Poverty: Economic Possibilities for Our Time*. London: Allen Lane, 2005.

Sacks, David Harris. "The Promise and the Contract in Early Modern England: Slade's Case in Perspective." In *Rhetoric and Law in Early Modern Europe*, edited by Victoria Ann Kahn and Lorna Hutson, 28–53. New Haven, CT: Yale University Press, 2001.

Samuels, Elizabeth. "Stories Out of School: Teaching the Case of Brown v. Voss." *Cardozo Law Review* 16 (1995): 1445–1510.

Sandel, Michael J. *What Money Can't Buy: The Moral Limits of Markets*. New York: Farrar, Straus and Giroux, 2013.

Satz, Debra. *Why Some Things Should Not Be for Sale: The Moral Limits of Markets*. New York: Oxford University Press, 2010.

Scalia, Antonin, and John F. Manning. "A Dialogue on Statutory and Constitutional Interpretation." *George Washington Law Review* 80 (2012): 1610–19.

Schwartz, Alan. "Contracting about Bankruptcy." *Journal of Law, Economics, and Organization* 13 (1997): 127–46.

Schwartz, Alan, and Robert E. Scott. "Contract Theory and the Limits of Contract Law." *Yale Law Journal* 113 (2003): 541–619.

Schwartz, Alan, and Louis L. Wilde. "Intervening in Markets on the Basis of Imperfect Information: A Legal and Economic Analysis." *University of Pennsylvania Law Review* 127, no. 3 (January 1, 1979): 630–82.

Scitovsky, Tibor. "A Note on Welfare Propositions in Economics." *Review of Economic Studies* 9 (1941): 77–81.

Sen, Amartya. "The Impossibility of a Paretian Liberal." In *Choice, Welfare, and Measurement*. 285–90. Cambridge, MA: MIT Press, 1982.

———. "Interpersonal Comparisons of Welfare." In *Choice, Welfare, and Measurement*, 264–81. Cambridge, MA: MIT Press, 1982.

Seymour, Harold. *Baseball: The Early Years*. New York: Oxford University Press, 1960.

Shakespeare, William. *The Merchant of Venice*. In *The Complete Works: The New Pelican Text*, edited by Stephen Orgel and A. R. Braunmuller. New York: Penguin Books, 2002.

———. *The Merchant of Venice, A Longman Cultural Edition*. Edited by Lawrence Danson. New York: Longman, 2004.

Shapiro, Fred, and Michelle Pearse. "The Most-Cited Law Review Articles of All Time." *Michigan Law Review* 110 (2012): 1483–1520.

Shavell, Steven. "Damage Measures for Breach of Contract." *Bell Journal of Economics* 11, no. 2 (October 1, 1980): 466–90.

———. "The Design of Contracts and Remedies for Breach." *Quarterly Journal of Economics* 99, no. 1 (February 1, 1984): 121–48.

Shell, G. Richard. "Trade Legalism and International Relations Theory: An Analysis of the World Trade Organization." *Duke Law Journal* 44 (1995): 829–927.

Shermer, Michael. *The Mind of the Market: Compassionate Apes, Competitive Humans, and Other Tales from Evolutionary Economics*. New York: Times Books, 2007.

Shiffrin, Seana Valentine. "The Divergence of Contract and Promise." *Harvard Law Review* 120 (2007): 708–53.

Shlaes, Amity. *The Forgotten Man: A New History of the Great Depression*. New York: Harper Perennial, 2008.

Sills, Joanne. "She'll Have a Blast: Woman, 28, Wins Sears Implosion Contest; $2,190 Raised for Hero Scholarship Fund." *Philly.com, October 27, 1994*. http://

articles.philly.com/1994-10-27/news/25871056_1_sears-building-roosevelt-boulevard-contest.

Simpson, A. W. Brian. *History of the Common Law of Contract: The Rise of the Action of Assumpsit*. Oxford: Clarendon Press, 1975.

———. "The Place of Slade's Case in the History of Contract." In *Law, Liberty, and Parliament*, by Allen D. Boyer, 70–85. Indianapolis: Liberty Fund, 2004.

Singer, Joseph. "No Right to Exclude: Public Accommodations and Private Property." *Northwestern University Law Review* 90 (1996): 1283–1497.

Sitton, Lea. "An Explosive Finale for Giant Sears: A Landmark Will Go as It Came: In Record-Setting Fashion." *Philly.com*, October 24, 1994. http://articles.philly.com/1994-10-24/news/25874324_1_sears-implosion-explosives.

Slawson, W. David. "Standard Form Contracts and Democratic Control of Lawmaking Power." *Harvard Law Review* 84, no. 3 (January 1, 1971): 529–66.

Smart, J. J. C., and Bernard Williams. *Utilitarianism: For and Against*. Cambridge: Cambridge University Press, 1973.

Smith, Adam. *The Wealth of Nations*. Edited by C. J. Bullock. New York: Barnes & Noble, 2004.

Smith, Joseph, Jr., trans. *The Book of Mormon*. Salt Lake City, UT: The Church of Jesus Christ of Latter-day Saints, 1981.

Smith, Stephen A. *Contract Theory*. Clarendon Law Series. New York: Oxford University Press, 2004.

Smith, Steven D. *The Disenchantment of Secular Discourse*. Cambridge, MA: Harvard University Press, 2010.

"Southern Baptists Vote for Disney Boycott." *CNN.com*, June 18, 1997.

Stapleton, Jane. "Evaluating Goldberg and Zipursky's Civil Recourse Theory." *Fordham Law Review* 75 (2007): 1529–62.

Stasavage, David. "Cities, Constitutions, and Sovereign Borrowing in Europe, 1274–1785." *International Organization* 61, no. 3 (2007): 489–525.

Sterk, Stewart E. "Neighbors in American Land Law." *Columbia Law Review* 87 (1987): 55–104.

Stewart, Frank Henderson. *Honor*. 1st ed. Chicago: University of Chicago Press, 1994.

Stijns, Sophie, and R. Blanpain. *International Encyclopaedia of Laws: Tort Law*. Vol. 2. The Hague: Kluwer Law International, 2002.

Stoebuck, William B., and Dale A. Whitman. *The Law of Property*. 3rd ed. St. Paul, MN: West, 2000.

Stone, Oliver, dir. *Wall Street*. Twentieth Century Fox, 1987.

Stout, Martha. "The Ice People." *Psychology Today* 38 (2005): 72–74.

Strauss, Barry S. *The Spartacus War*. New York: Simon & Schuster, 2009.

Strawson, Peter F. "Freedom and Resentment." *Proceedings of the British Academy* 48 (1962): 1–25.

Strossen, Nadine. *Defending Pornography: Free Speech, Sex, and the Fight for Women's Rights*. New York: Scribner, 1995.

Sunstein, Cass R., ed. *Behavioral Law and Economics*. New York: Cambridge University Press, 2000.

———. *The Cost-Benefit State: The Future of Regulatory Protection*. Chicago: American Bar Association, 2003.

———. *Free Markets and Social Justice*. New York: Oxford University Press, 1997.

———. *Going to Extremes: How Like Minds Unite and Divide*. New York: Oxford University Press, 2009.

Sutcliffe, Adam. "Jewish History in an Age of Atlanticism." In *Atlantic Diasporas: Jews, Conversos, and Crypto-Jews in the Age of Mercantilism, 1500–1800*, edited by Richard L. Kagan and Philip D. Morgan, 18–30. Baltimore: Johns Hopkins University Press, 2009.

Tawney, R. H. *Religion and the Rise of Capitalism*. New York: Harcourt Brace, 1926.

Temin, Peter. *The Roman Market Economy*. Princeton, NJ: Princeton University Press, 2013.

"Terrorist Plot Said to Have Involved Apple iPod as Detonator." *Macdailynews.com*, August 10, 2006. http://macdailynews.com/2006/08/10/terrorist_plot_said_to_have_involved_apple_ipod_as_detonator/.

Thready, Deborah I. "A Fish Story: Alaska Packers' Association v. Domenico." *Utah Law Review* 2000 (2000): 185–221.

Titmus, Richard M. *The Gift Relationship: From Human Blood to Social Policy*. Expanded ed. New York: New Press, 1997.

Tocqueville, Alexis de. *Democracy in America*. Edited by Isaac Kramnick. Translated by Gerald Bevan. New York: Penguin Books, 2002.

Tolstoy, Leo. *Anna Karenina*. Translated by Richard Pevear and Larissa Volokhonsky. New York: Penguin Classics, 2004.

Trebilcock, Michael J. *The Limits of Freedom of Contract*. Cambridge, MA: Harvard University Press, 1993.

Tucker, St. George, and William Blackstone. *Blackstone's Commentaries: With Notes of Reference to the Constitution and Laws, of the Federal Government of the United States, and of the Commonwealth of Virginia*. 5 vols. Union, NJ: Lawbook Exchange, 1996.

Ṭufail, Abu Bakr Muḥammed bin. *Journey of the Soul: The Story of Hai bin Yaqz'ān*. Translated by Riad Kocache. London: Octagon Press, 1982.

Unger, Roberto Mangabeira. "The Critical Legal Studies Movement." *Harvard Law Review* 96 (1983): 561–675.

United States Census Bureau. "Household Income." *2012 Statistical Abstract of the United States*. Washington, DC: U.S. Census Bureau, 2012. https://www.census.gov/library/publications/2011/compendia/statab/131ed/income-expenditures-poverty-wealth.html.

Vawter, Bruce. *On Genesis: A New Reading*. 1st ed. Garden City, NY: Doubleday, 1977.

Volker, Behr. "Myth and Reality of Punitive Damages in Germany." *Journal of Law and Commerce* 24 (2005): 197–224.

Volokh, Eugene. "The Mechanisms of the Slippery Slope." *Harvard Law Review* 116 (2003): 1026–137.

Volokh, Hanah Metchis. "A Read-the-Bill Rule for Congress." *Missouri Law Review* 76 (2011): 136–84.

Waldron, Jeremy. *The Dignity of Legislation*. New York: Cambridge University Press, 1999.

Wallenstein, Peter. *Cradle of America: A History of Virginia*. 2nd ed. Lawrence: University Press of Kansas, 2014.

Wallis, John Joseph, and Douglas C. North. "Measuring the Transaction Sector in the American Economy, 1870–1970." In *Long-Term Factors in American Economic Growth*, edited by Stanley L. Engerman and Robert E. Gallman, 95–162. Chicago: University of Chicago Press, 1992.

Wang, Pingo, Alok K. Bohara, Robert P. Berrens, and Kishore Gawande. "A Risk-Based Environmental Kuznets Curve for US Hazardous Waste Sites." *Applied Economics Letters* 5, no. 12 (1998): 761–63.

Weber, Max. *The Protestant Ethic and the Spirit of Capitalism*. Edited by Richard Swedberg. New York: W. W. Norton, 2009.

Weg, Eython, and Vernon Smith. "On the Failure to Induce Meager Offers in Ultimatum Games." *Journal of Economic Psychology* 14, no. 1 (2003): 17–18.

Weinstein, Joshua I. "The Market in Plato's Republic." *Classical Philology* 104, no. 4 (October 2009): 439–58.

Welsh, Teresa. "Should Cities Boycott Chick-fil-A over Gay Marriage?" *U.S. News & World Report*, July 27, 2012. http://www.usnews.com/opinion/articles/2012/07/27/should-cities-boycott-anti-gay-marriage-chick-fil-a.

White, James J., and Robert S. Summers. *Uniform Commercial Code*. 5th ed. St. Paul, MN: West Group, 2000.

Whitford, William C. "Strict Products Liability and the Automobile Industry: Much Ado about Nothing." *Wisconsin Law Review* 1968 (1968): 83–171.

Wilkinson-Ryan, Tess, and Jonathan Baron. "Moral Judgment and Moral Heuristics in Breach of Contract." *Journal of Empirical Legal Studies* 6 (2009): 405–23.

Williams, George Huntston. *The Radical Reformation*. Philadelphia: Westminster Press, 1962.

Williamson, Oliver E. "Transaction-Cost Economics: The Governance of Contractual Relations." *Journal of Law and Economics* 22, no. 2 (October 1979): 233–61.

Willson, Michael Jay. "A View of Justice in Shakespeare's *The Merchant of Venice* and *Measure for Measure*." *Notre Dame Law Review* 70 (1995): 695–726.

Witte, Jr., John. *From Sacrament to Contract: Marriage, Religion, and Law in the Western Tradition*. 2nd ed. Louisville, KY: Westminster John Knox Press, 2012.

W. M. R. "Negligence-Innkeepers-Liability for Loss of or Injury to Goods of Guest." *Texas Law Review* 6 (1928): 545–46.

World Health Organization. "Media Centre: HIV/AIDS." November 2015. http://www.who.int/mediacentre/factsheets/fs360/en/.

World Health Organization. "Media Centre: Malaria." *October 2015*. http://www.who.int/mediacentre/factsheets/fs094/en/.

Wrigley, E. Anthony. "Reflections on the History of the Family." *Daedalus* 106, no. 2 (Spring 1977): 71–85.

Wyatt-Brown, Bertram. *Southern Honor: Ethics and Behavior in the Old South*. New York: Oxford University Press, 1982.

Yamagishi, Toshio. *Trust: The Evolutionary Game of Mind and Society (The Science of the Mind)*. Tokyo: Springer, 2011.

Yoshino, Kenji. "The Lawyer of Belmont." *Yale Journal of Law and the Humanities* 9 (1997): 183–216.

Yunus, Muhammad. *Banker to the Poor: Micro-Lending and the Battle against World Poverty*. New York: Public Affairs, 2008.

Zamir, Eyal. "Contract Law and Theory—Three Views of the Cathedral." *University of Chicago Law Review* 81 (2014): 2077–123.

Zamir, Eyal, and Yuval Farkash. "Standard Form Contracts: Empirical Studies, Normative Implications, and the Fragmentation of Legal Scholarship." *Jerusalem Review of Legal Studies*, forthcoming. http://papers.ssrn.com/sol3/papers.cfm?abstract_id=2546863.

Zipursky, Benjamin. "Civil Recourse, Not Corrective Justice." *Georgetown Law Journal* 91 (2003): 695–756.

Zywicki, Todd J. "The Economics of Credit Cards." *Chapman Law Review* 3 (2000): 79–172.

Table of Authorities

Cases

Ahmad v. Ahmad, No. L-00-1391, 2001 WL 1518116 (Ohio Ct. App. 2001)
Ahmed v. Ahmed, 261 S.W.3d 190 (Tex. Ct. App. 2008)
Akileh v. Elchahal, 666 So. 2d 246 (Fla. Dist. Ct. App. 1996)
Alaska Packers Association v. Domenico, 117 F. 99 (9th Cir. 1902)
Aleem v. Aleem, 931 A.2d 1123 (Md. Ct. Spec. App. 2007)
Aleem v. Aleem, 947 A.2d 489 (Md. 2008)
Allegheny College v. National Chautauqua County Bank, 159 N.E. 173 (N.Y. 1927)
Allen v. Allen, 111 Fla. 733 (1933)
Arthur Andersen LLP v. United States, 544 U.S. 696 (2005)
AT&T Mobility v. Conception, 563 U.S. 321 (2011)
Aziz v. Aziz, 488 N.Y.S.2d 123 (N.Y. Sup. Ct. 1985)
Balfour v. Balfour [1919] 2 K.B. 571, 578, 579-80
Ballard v. Parkstone Energy, LLC, 522 F. Supp. 2d 695 (S.D.N.Y. 2007)
Batsakis v. Demotsis, 226 S.W.2d 673 (Tex. Ct. App. 1949)
Be In, Inc. v. Google Inc., 2013 WL 5568706 (N.D. Cal. 2013)
Brown v. Voss, 715 P.2d 514 (Wash. 1986)
Capazzoli v. Holzwasser, 490 N.E.2d 420 (Mass. 1986)
Capsi v. Microsoft Network LLC, 732 A.2d 528 (N.J. Sup. Ct. App. Div. 1999)
Chaudry v. Chaudry, 388 A.2d 1000 (N.J. Super. Ct. App. Div. 1978)
Cotnam v. Wisdom, 104 S.W. 164 (Ark. 1907)
Davidson & Assoc. v. Jung, 422 F.3d 630 (8th Cir. 2005)
Discover Bank v. Superior Court, 113 P.3d 1100 (Cal. 2005)
Drennan v. Star Paving Co., 333 P.2d 757 (Cal. 1958)
Federal Baseball Club v. National League, 259 U.S. 200 (1922)
Feinberg v. Pfeiffer Co., 322 S.W.2d 163 (Mo. Ct. App. 1959)

Field v. Clark, 143 U.S. 649, 672 (1892)

Flood v. Kuhn, 407 U.S. 258 (1972)

Foakes v. Beer, (1884) 9 App. Cas. 605 (H.L.)

Gallemore v. Gallemore, 94 Fla. 516 (1927)

Gatton v. T-Mobile, USA, Inc., 152 Cal. App. 4th 571 (2007)

Gayle v. Browder, 352 U.S. 903 (1956)

Global Travel Mktg. v. Shea, 908 So. 2d 392 (Fla. 2005)

Griswold v. Connecticut, 381 U.S. 479 (1965)

Habibi-Fahnrich v. Fahnrich, No. 46186/93, 1995 WL 507388 (N.Y. Sup. Ct. Jul. 10, 1995)

Hadley v. Baxendale, 156 Eng. Rep. 145 (Ex. 1854)

Hamer v. Sidway, 27 N.E. 256 (N.Y. 1891)

Hamilton Cnty. Assessor v. SPD Realty, LLC, 9 N.E.3d 773 (Ind. T.C. 2014)

Harrington v. Taylor, 36 S.E.2d 227 (N.C. 1946)

Harris v. Watson, (1791) Peake 102

Henningsen v. Bloomfield Motors, Inc., 161 A.2d 69 (N.J. 1960)

Hill v. Gateway 2000, Inc., 105 F.3d 1147 (7th Cir. 1997)

Hoffman v. Boyd, 698 So. 2d 346 (Fla. Dist. Ct. App. 1997)

In re Colonial Ford, 24 B.R. 1014 (Bankr. D. Utah 1982)

In re Estate of Lipsky, 256 N.Y.S.2d 429 (Sur. Ct. 1965)

In re Marriage of Dajani, 251 Cal. Rptr. 871 (Cal. Ct. App. 1988)

In re Marriage of Shaban, 105 Cal. Rptr. 2d 863 (Cal. Ct. App. 2001)

In re Zappos.com Inc. Customer Data Security Breach Litigation, 893 F.Supp.2d 1058 (D. Nev. 2012)

James B. Beam Distilling Co. v. Georgia, 501 U.S. 529 (1991)

James Baird Co. v. Gimbel Bros., Inc., 64 F.2d 344 (2d Cir. 1933)

Jewish Federation of Cent. New Jersey v. Barondess, 560 A.2d 1353 (N.J. Super. Ct. 1989)

Johnson v. Calvert, 851 P.2d 776 (Cal. 1993)

King v. Duluth, Missabe & Northern Railway Co., 63 N.W. 1105 (Minn. 1895)

King v. Young, Berkman, Berman & Karpf, P.A., 709 So. 2d 572 (Fla. 1998)

Lake River Corp. v. Carborundum Co., 769 F.2d 1284 (7th Cir. 1985)

Lawrence v. Texas, 539 U.S. 558 (2003)

Lock v. Encompass Ins. Co., No. 07-CV-14257, 2009 WL 804151 (E.D. Mich. Mar. 25, 2009)

Lynch v. CIBY 2000, No. CV 97-9022, 1998 U.S. Dist. LEXIS 23496 (C.D. Cal. Aug. 13, 1998)

Mahalsky v. Salem Tool Co., 461 F.2d 581, 584 (6th Cir. 1972)

Mahoney v. Delaware McDonald's Corp., 770 F.2d 123 (8th Cir. 1985)

Mir v. Birjandi, No. 2006 CA 63, 2007 WL 4170868 (Ohio Ct. App. Nov. 21, 2007)
Morrow v. First Nat'l Bank of Hot Springs, 550 S.W.2d 429 (Ark. 1977)
Navigation Co. v. Windsor, 87 U.S. 64, 68 (1873)
Nevada v. Hall, 440 U.S. 410 (1979)
New York v. Ferber, 458 U.S. 747 (1982)
Nguyen v. Barnes & Noble, Inc., 763 F.3d 1171 (9th Cir. 2014)
Nightingale v. Bridges, (1689) 89 Eng. Rep. 496 (K.B.)
Odatalla v. Odatalla, 810 A.2d 93 (N.J. Super. Ct. Ch. Div. 2002)
OneBeacon Ins. Co. v. Parker, Kern, Nard & Wenzel, No. 1:09-cv-00257 AWI GSA, 2009 WL 2914203 (E.D. Cal. Sept. 9, 2009)
Peavey Elecs. Corp. v. Baan U.S.A., Inc., 10 So. 3d 945 (Miss. Ct. App. 2009)
Pierce v. Catalina Yachts, Inc., 2 P.3d 618 (Alaska 2000)
Pillans v. Van Mierop, (1765) 97 Eng. Rep. 1035 (K.B.)
Pinnel's Case (1602) 5 Co. Rep. 117a
Pitts v. McGraw-Edison Co., 329 F.2d 412 (6th Cir. 1964)
Planned Parenthood of Southeastern Pennsylvania v. Casey, 505 U.S. 833 (1992)
Posner v. Posner, 233 So. 2d 381 (Fla. 1970)
ProCD v. Zeidenberg, 86 F.3d 1447 (7th Cir. 1996)
Register.com, Inc. v. Verio, Inc., 356 F.3d 393 (2d Cir. 2004)
Renaud v. Simmons, 254 S.W.2d 418 (Tex. Civ. App. 1952)
Reynolds v. Reynolds, 230 S.E.2d 842 (Ga. 1976)
Richmond Am. Homes of Colo., Inc. v. United States, 80 Fed. Cl. 656 (2008)
Ricketts v. Scothorn, 77 N.W. 365 (Neb. 1898)
Rockingham County v. Luten Bridge Co., 35 F.2d. 301 (4th Cir. 1929)
Rogers v. Webb, 558 N.W.2d 155 (Iowa 1997)
Rose & Frank Co. v. J. R. Crompton & Bros., [1925] A.C. 445 (H.L.)
Roth v. Patino, 185 Misc. 235 (N.Y. Sup. Ct. 1945)
Sable Commc'ns of California, Inc. v. F.C.C., 492 U.S. 115 (1989)
Sadler v. Eighth Judicial District Court, 614 P.2d 10 (Nev. 1980)
Salsbury v. Northwestern Bell Tel. Co., 221 N.W.2d 609 (Iowa 1974)
Schwartzreich v. Bauman-Basch, 131 N.E. 887 (N.Y. 1921)
Schwinder v. Austin Bank of Chicago, 809 N.E.2d 180 (Ill. App. Ct. 2004)
Sea Air Support, Inc. v. Herrman, 613 P.2d 413 (Nev. 1980)
Slade's Case, (1602) 76 Eng. Rep. 1072 (K.B.)
Soos v. Superior Court, 897 P.2d 1356 (Ariz. Ct. App. 1994)
Southwest Airlines Co. v. BoardFirst, LLC, 2007 WL 4823761 (N.D. Tex. 2007)
Specht v. Netscape Communications Corp., 306 F.3d 17 (2d Cir. 2002)
Step-Savers Data Systems, Inc. v. Wyse Technology, 939 F.3d 91 (3d Cir. 1991)
Stilk v. Myrick, (1809) 170 Eng. Rep. 1168 (K.B.)

Tarrant Regional Water District v. Herrmann, 133 S. Ct. 2120 (2013)
Ticketmaster Corp. v. Tickets.com, Inc., 2003 WL 21406289 (C.D. Cal. 2003)
Torres-Rosario v. United States, Civil No. 07-1282, 2010 WL 174884 (D.P.R. Jan. 13, 2010)
United States v. Greenhut, 50 Fed. 469 (D. Mass. 1892)
United States v. Ogle, 613 F.2d 233 (10th Cir. 1979)
United States v. Patterson, 55 Fed. 605 (D. Mass. 1893)
United States v. Stump Home Specialties Mfg., 905 F.2d 1117 (7th Cir. 1990)
Van Tassell v. United Marketing Group, LLC, 795 F.Supp.2d 770 (N.D. Ill. 2011)
Warner Brother's Pictures, Inc. v. Nelson, [1937] 1 K.B. 209
Webb v. McGowin, 168 So. 196 (Ala. App. 1936)
Welch v. Metro-Goldwyn-Mayer Film Co., 254 Cal. Rptr. 645 (Ct. App. 1988)
Whitney v. California, 274 U.S. 357 (1927)
Williams v. Walker-Thomas Furniture Co., 350 F.2d 445 (D.C. Cir. 1965)
Zawahiri v. Alwattar, No. 07AP-925, 2008 WL 2698679 (Ohio Ct. App. Jul. 10, 2008)

Other Authorities

15 U.S.C. § 1 (2009)
15 U.S.C. § 26b (1998)
Ala. Code § 8-19-10 (2014)
Ariz. Rev. Stat. Ann. § 25-218(B) (2007)
Comprehensive Anti-Apartheid Act of 1986, Pub. L. No. 99-440, 100 Stat. 1086 (effective Oct. 2, 1986)
D.C. Code Ann. § 16-402 (Lexis Nexis 1997)
Fla. Stat. Ann. § 742.15(2) (West 2005)
Ga. Code Ann. § 10-1-399 (2014)
Mont. Code Ann. § 30-13-133(1) (2014)
Principles of the Law of Software Contracts § 2.02(c)(1)-(2) (2009)
Restatement (Second) of Contracts § 1 (1981)
Restatement (Second) of Contracts § 21 (1981)
Restatement (Second) of Contracts § 71(1) (1981)
Restatement (Second) of Contracts § 87(1)(a) (1981)
Restatement (Second) of Contracts § 87(1)(a) cmt. c (1981)
Restatement (Second) of Contracts § 89(a) (1981)
Restatement (Second) of Contracts § 90 cmt. b. (1981)
Restatement (Second) Contracts § 90(1) (1981)

Restatement (Second) Contracts § 90(2) (1981)
Restatement (Second) of Contracts § 162 (1981)
Restatement (Second) of Contracts § 190(2) (1981)
Restatement (Second) of Contracts § 208 (1981)
Restatement (Second) of Contracts § 211 rep. note (1981)
Restatement (Second) of Contracts § 211(3). rep. ncte (1981)
Restatement (Second) of Contracts § 344 (1981)
Restatement (Second) of Contracts § 347 (1981)
Restatement (Second) of Contracts § 349 (1981)
Restatement (Second) of Contracts § 350 (1981)
Restatement (Second) of Contracts § 352 (1981)
Restatement (Second) of Contracts § 356 (1981)
Restatement (Second) of Contracts § 365 cmt. a (1981)
Restatement (Third) of Foreign Relations Law of the United States § 102(2) (1987)
Restatement (Third) of Foreign Relations Law of the United States § 102(3) (1987)
Restatement Contracts § 587 (1932)
Tex. Fam. Code Ann. § 160.751 *et seq.* (Vernon 2008)
UCC § 2-209(1)
UCC § 2-305
UCC § 2-509(1)
UCC § 2-509(2)
UCC § 2-509(3)
UCC § 2-509(4)
UCC § 307-08
Uniform Premarital and Marital Agreements Act § 9
Uniform Premarital and Marital Agreements Act § 9(a)(2)
Uniform Premarital and Marital Agreements Act § 9(a)(4)
Uniform Premarital and Marital Agreements Act § 9(c)
United Nations Convention on Contracts for the International Sale of Goods (CISG), 19 I.L.M. 668, Arts. 14–24 (1980)
U.S. Const. amend. I
U.S. Const. amend. XV, § 1
U.S. Const. amend. XXIV, § 1
U.S. Const. amend. XXVI, § 1
U.S. Const. art. I, § 10
Utah Code Ann. § 78B-15-801 *et seq.* (2008)

Index